Party Coalitions
in the 1980s

PARTY COALITIONS
IN THE 1980s

Seymour Martin Lipset, *Editor*
John B. Anderson
David S. Broder
Walter Dean Burnham
Patrick H. Caddell
Jerome M. Clubb
E. J. Dionne, Jr.
Alan M. Fisher
Michael Harrington
S. I. Hayakawa
Richard Jensen
Paul Kleppner
Everett Carll Ladd
Arthur H. Miller
Howard Phillips
Norman Podhoretz
Nelson W. Polsby
Richard M. Scammon
William Schneider
Martin P. Wattenberg
Richard B. Wirthlin

Institute for Contemporary Studies
San Francisco, California

324.0973
P275 L7

Inquiries, book orders, and catalog requests should be addressed to the Institute for Contemporary Studies, Suite 811, 260 California Street, San Francisco, California 94111—415–398–3010.

Library of Congress Catalog No. 81–83095.

Library of Congress Cataloging in Publication Data
Main entry under title:

Party coalitions in the 1980s.

    Bibliography: p.
    Includes index.
    1. Political parties—United States—Addresses, essays, lectures. 2. Party affiliation—United States—Addresses, essays, lectures. 3. United States—Politics and government—1981- —Addresses, essays, lectures. I. Lipset, Seymour Martin. II. Anderson, John Bayard, 1922- . III. Institute for Contemporary Studies.
JK2261.P313   324'.0973   81–83095
ISBN 0–917616–45–6   AACR2
ISBN 0–917616–43–X (pbk.)

CONTENTS

III

Contemporary Politics

IV

The 1980 Campaign

V

Realignment in the 1980 Election

VI

The Future of American Politics

VII

Conclusion

CONTRIBUTORS

JOHN B. ANDERSON
Former congressman (R—Illinois) and independent presidential candidate

DAVID S. BRODER
Associate editor, Washington Post

WALTER DEAN BURNHAM
Professor of political science,
Massachusetts Institute of Technology

PATRICK H. CADDELL
President, Cambridge Survey Research and
Caddell Associates

JEROME M. CLUBB
Executive director, Inter-university Consortium for
Political and Social Research; professor of history,
University of Michigan

E. J. DIONNE, JR.
Political reporter, New York Times

ALAN M. FISHER
Assistant professor of political science,
California State University, Dominguez Hills

MICHAEL HARRINGTON
National chair, Democratic Socialist Organizing Committee;
professor of political science, Queens College

S. I. HAYAKAWA
U.S. senator (R—California)

RICHARD JENSEN
Director, Family and Community History Center, Newberry Library;
professor of history, University of Illinois, Chicago

PAUL KLEPPNER
Professor of history and political science,
Northern Illinois University, De Kalb

EVERETT CARLL LADD
Professor of political science; director, Institute for
Social Inquiry, University of Connecticut; executive director,
Roper Center for Public Opinion Research

SEYMOUR MARTIN LIPSET
Professor of political science and sociology; senior fellow,
Hoover Institution on War, Revolution and Peace,
Stanford University

ARTHUR H. MILLER
Associate professor of political science;
senior study director, Center for Political Studies,
University of Michigan

HOWARD PHILLIPS
National director, The Conservative Caucus, Inc.

NORMAN PODHORETZ
Editor, Commentary

NELSON W. POLSBY
Professor of political science,
University of California, Berkeley

RICHARD M. SCAMMON
Director, Elections Research Center;
editor, America Votes

WILLIAM SCHNEIDER
Senior research fellow, Hoover Institution on
War, Revolution and Peace, Stanford University

MARTIN P. WATTENBERG
Doctoral candidate, University of Michigan

RICHARD B. WIRTHLIN
President, Decima Research and Decision/Making/Information

PREFACE

Toward the end of the 1970s major changes seemed to be working in the American political system. Even more important, curiosity was high whether a long-awaited "critical election" would follow the pattern set by the elections of 1860, 1896, and 1932, and would effect a fundamental realignment in U.S. coalition politics. In response to these questions, the institute published *Emerging Coalitions in American Politics* in the spring of 1978, edited by Seymour Martin Lipset. In that book, twenty-two political scientists and others experienced in government and politics grappled with what seemed to be a fluid situation, and many drew up scenarios on how, and under what circumstances, each of the two major parties might design a strategy for building a majority political coalition.

The 1980 election made a sequel to that book inevitable. Ronald Reagan's overwhelming (and, to many, surprising) electoral victory raised the question of whether it would prove to be "critical"—that is, fundamentally realigning. For this new volume, Professor Lipset used certain chapters from the older book without revision, particularly those covering electoral history. Others—those by Broder, Polsby, Clubb, Schneider, and Ladd—were updated, and a number of new articles were added, including major chapters by Patrick Caddell and Richard Wirthlin, the respective pollsters of Jimmy Carter and Ronald Reagan.

The purpose of this study is not solely to look back at the 1980 election, though there is much of that. It is also to look ahead as the Reagan administration moves into its presidential term, and to examine options and prospects—where the future may lead—toward the 1982 midterm elections and beyond. Since politics is the science of influencing governmental policy while, at the same time, being influenced by it, the chapters in this new book should give readers insights and perspectives from which they may observe the current unfolding presidential administration.

A. Lawrence Chickering
Executive Director
Institute for Contemporary Studies

San Francisco, California
November 1981

FOREWORD

This book is both an updating of the volume published by the Institute for Contemporary Studies in 1978, *Emerging Coalitions in American Politics*, and a new work. The earlier book was an attempt to interpret the coalition character of the American party system in its historical and contemporary context. The historical chapters apart, much of the analysis reflected the special conditions of the post-Watergate Carter era. A number of the essays examined the prospects for political realignment and the formation of new coalitions in a period of centrist leadership. The post-World War II presidents, from Dwight Eisenhower on, generally sought to stay close to the ideological center, with the exception of Lyndon Johnson's first two years in office. Even the highly controversial Richard Nixon pursued Keynesian policies in his domestic program, as well as détente abroad. As I point out in chapter 2, it would be difficult to demonstrate which party was more liberal or conservative from its record in office.

Yet, at the same time, sharply ideological factions were gaining strength in each major party. New Politics social liberals, identified with Robert and Edward Kennedy and George McGovern, were becoming increasingly influential among the Democrats, while a conservative *laissez-faire* faction, led by Ronald Reagan, was growing within the Republican ranks. The moderate center, however, was still able to name the nominees of both parties in 1976.

This book appears in the first year of the Reagan administration. The new president, as many have noted, is the first postwar Republican occupant of the White House to attempt to reverse the big-government welfare-state policies introduced by Franklin Roosevelt and pursued to a greater or lesser extent by his pre-Reagan successors. The nomination and election of a strongly ideological conservative poses a question — does his victory represent a movement or a blip in American political history? Are we at the start of a new era?

It is still too early to come up with any definitive interpretation of the long-term meaning of the 1980 turnover. Ideological politics of a quite divergent sort are powerful in both parties. Reagan's nomination, of course, represented a victory for the GOP Right. And in the Democratic party, the New Politics challenger, Edward Kennedy, led the incumbent president, Jimmy Carter, in the opinion polls for a number of months. His candidacy was blocked in large part because of the revival of the character issue — his behavior at Chappaquiddick — and, just as importantly, by the effect of the Iranian hostage issue in reviving support for the president. Among Republican moderates and New Politics Democrats, dissatisfaction with their parties' nominees led to a brief upsurge of support for the independent third candidacy of a socially liberal, moderate Republican, John Anderson.

Clearly, the American electorate was sharply divided in 1980. The two-party system revealed its growing inability to mediate the large number of economic and social issues. This difficulty, caused by the spread from the 1960s on of single-issue protest groups on the Left and Right, has contributed to the steady decline in the proportion of those voting and to the increase in those describing themselves as independents rather than as Democrats or Republicans. The confusion among the electorate, however, did not prevent a decisive outcome to the 1980 contest, as increasing economic difficulties led to a sharp rejection of the incumbent party. But since the election turned on a vote against a "failed" ad-

ministration rather than a positive choice between alternative orientations, it is impossible to say that a realignment—
the creation of a new long-term Republican majority—has
occurred. The party system and the allegiance of the principal social groupings are still in flux. Whether realignment
develops depends on what happens between now and 1984. It
is worth recalling that the realignment of the 1930s did not
occur in 1932, but took shape in the elections of 1934
and 1936.

Many of the essays in this book discuss the future
prospects of the party system and are based to a large extent
on interpretations of the politics of the 1970s and of the 1980
election. Except for the historical chapters, these articles are
major revisions of chapters in *Emerging Coalitions* or are
new. Twelve of the twenty-one authors were not represented
in the earlier volume, so this is largely a new rather than a
revised work.

In selecting authors for the various chapters, I sought
people who could contribute objective analyses of developments among the voters and parties, and the result has produced inevitable disagreement. The pollsters for the presidential candidates, Patrick Caddell and Richard Wirthlin,
clearly differ in their perceptions of what happened during
the election year, and some of the academics who analyze the
1980 election empirically diverge occasionally on certain
points of fact. Such disagreements stem inevitably from
differences in the findings of various survey research
organizations who report the attitudes or voting behavior of
subgroups in the population, or from polls taken at different
times in which the wording of questions may have varied. On
the whole, however, while interpretations may differ, the
substantive reports are in harmony with each other.

Section VI, "The Future of American Politics," attempts
something fundamentally different. In that section, we
deliberately departed from emphasis on objective analysis
and asked six political intellectuals, representing clearly

defined places on the political and ideological spectra, to write short statements analyzing recent events and trends in terms of their value preferences. Their disagreements are open and explicit.

I am deeply appreciative to the authors of these articles for taking on their assignments and delivering them so promptly. I would especially like to express my gratitude to A. Lawrence Chickering and David B. Givens of the Institute for Contemporary Studies for editorial assistance far beyond the call of duty. Finally, I would like to thank my friend, H. Monroe Browne, who has just retired as president of the institute, for his continued intellectual encouragement. Although a strong political activist, he understood that scholarly work cannot and should not reflect the ideological or partisan interests of the sponsors, that the freedom to look for the truth inevitably involves support for views that run counter to the beliefs of any individual or political tendency.

Seymour Martin Lipset

Stanford, California
November 1981

I

Background and Issues

1

DAVID S. BRODER

Introduction

The cyclical history of political realignments. Constructing majorities. Mass communications, mobility, and political allegiances. Decomposition of parties and coalitions. The postwar voter and the 1980 elections. The reappearance of party politics.

The election of 1980 did more than break the Democrats' control of the White House and Congress. It also shattered some important assumptions about the character of our voting coalitions and the condition of our political parties. It opened some possibilities for the remainder of the century that had not been there before.

At quite another level, it required a fresh look at the topic the Institute for Contemporary Studies and many of these same authors addressed in the book *Emerging Coalitions in American Politics* in the spring of 1978. In the introduction to

that earlier volume, I reviewed the cyclical history of past political realignments and the regularity with which they
seemed to occur.

The first party system took shape with the election of
Thomas Jefferson as president in 1800, ending the
Federalists' unchallenged control of the early years of the republic. In 1828 the election of Andrew Jackson signaled the
victory of the frontier over the Tidewater landed and commercial aristocracy and brought about a second party
system. In 1860 the election of Abraham Lincoln brought the
new Republican party to power and precipitated the out-
break of the Civil War. In 1896 Republican William
McKinley won a landmark victory for industrialism over the
agrarian-populist forces which had gained dominance in the
Democratic party with the nomination of William Jennings
Bryan. And in 1932 the election of Franklin D. Roosevelt
brought to power the New Deal coalition and signaled the advent of the welfare state.

The steady rhythm of that change had made many observers suggest that the United States was overdue for another
critical election and the emergence of a sixth great party
system—one with a clear mandate and a prospect of forging
a stable governing coalition. But the prospects did not appear
bright.

In the years since America emerged victorious from World
War II with a vastly expanded economy, new international
responsibilities, a markedly more educated and mobile
population, and a new system of internal communication
keyed to the television tube, it also appeared to have
developed a new form of politics.

THE POLITICS OF COALITION-BUILDING

That politics was independent, individualistic, personality-
oriented, and essentially anti-party. The statement, "I vote

for the person, not the party," became part of the new voters' creed. It was a time of divided government. For fourteen of the twenty-four years between 1952 and 1976, Democrats controlled Congress while Republican presidents occupied the White House. Jimmy Carter, who restored the Democrats to power in 1976, began his campaign at Roosevelt's vacation home in Warm Springs, Georgia. But he was accurately described by Tom Wicker of the *New York Times* not as Roosevelt's heir, but as "the most conservative Democratic president since Grover Cleveland."

He was an embodiment of the individualistic, entrepreneurial politics of his time—a self-starter who captured the Democratic nomination as "Jimmy Who," and who never paused in his pursuit of power to build the alliances within his own party coalition that might have enabled him to govern. By the time the earlier edition of this book appeared, fifteen months into Carter's presidency, it was appropriate to say that the United States had "reached the point where it is possible to talk accurately about an opposition Congress of the same party as the president."

The roots of that situation lay far deeper than the personality and political problems of President Carter. The philosophical and practical tensions were built into a society whose bedrock ideals include both the dignity of the individual and the rule of the majority. In such a society, it was close to inevitable that the politics would rest on the ability to build coalitions.

While a variety of philosophical rationalizations may be—and have been—invented to reconcile the opposing impulses of individualism and majoritarianism, only one practical device has been found for rendering them compatible in a diverse, continent-sized republic like the United States of America.

That device is coalition-building, the process of constructing majorities from the broad sentiments and interests that can be found to bridge the narrower needs and hopes of separate individuals and communities.

The Founding Fathers understood that this sort of politics was built into their design of a Constitution, and yet they were uneasy with it. They were acutely concerned that such coalitions could too easily become conspiracies of a particular sort; that majorities would be formed to seize the property or limit the liberties of the wealthier or more opinionated few. Their hope was that, in a federal republic of large scale and great diversity, this danger would be—if not entirely removed—at least substantially diminished. As Madison or Hamilton wrote in *Federalist 51*, "In the extended Republic of the United States, and among the great variety of interests, parties and sects which it embraces, a coalition of a majority of the whole society could seldom take place on any other principles than those of justice or the general good."

The founders were less concerned about the question whether, in such a society, a coalition of the majority could take place at all. Their America was, of course, a smaller, less-complex society than our own, and one with a far more restricted electorate. Yet even in that society it was by no means certain that effective coalition-building devices would be found, for there were sharp rivalries and suspicions between the large states and the small, the North and the South, the frontier and the seacoast.

And yet, as we have seen, the process of coalition-building began in the first decade of the republic, and it took the form of the creation of political parties. The Federalists and the Republican-Democrats went their separate ways, dividing on issues of foreign policy, commerce, and the role of the national government in the federal system. And for the next hundred and fifty years, our history was shaped by the shifting coalitions of the political parties.

The history of that century and a half was testament to both the flexibility of the party coalitions and the essential function they played in the working of our democracy. And yet for the last thirty years the forces that were splintering the party coalitions seemed far more evident than the forces that would keep them alive.

Television was one of those disintegrative forces. It is a highly personalized medium which takes politicians one at a time, subjects them to extraordinarily intimate scrutiny, and then either rejects them or moves them up to superstar status. The political parties as such had little visibility on television, and television—in at least one respect—seemed overtly anti-party. From 1952, when television "took over" the halls where the major parties met to conduct their business every four years through 1980, neither party took more than one ballot to nominate its presidential candidate.

There was no evidence that the parties had developed greater efficiency or internal agreement; on the contrary, the picture emerging on television was often one of intra-party antagonists bitterly complaining about their differences with the dominant faction. But instead of the convention being used as a device for patiently negotiating the solutions to those coalitional problems, it was compressed to meet the "show business standards" of a fast-moving television show.

In a broader sense, technology also appeared to atomize our politics. Scientific public-opinion polling enabled individual candidates to test the electorate's attitudes and to shape their individual appeals accordingly. Mass communications—electronically selected mailing lists, telephone banks, and mass-media advertising—allowed the individual candidate to bypass intermediate organizations and carry his message directly to the individual voter. All of this cost large amounts of money. And the candidates became adept at securing those funds from their own supporters.

But beyond these surface changes, there were deeper roots to the decomposition of coalition politics and the political parties. The mobility—both geographical and social—of postwar Americans tended to make associative politics harder to sustain. When the extended family of three generations was gathered in one place over a long period of years, traditional political allegiances—like other forms of group identity—were easily reinforced. But the American family contracted and seemed to be always on the move, so inherited or environmental preferences lost force.

The great advance in public education in the past generation also played a part in loosening political ties. The better-educated voters rejected the notion that they could do no more than make a single mark on the ballot, voting straight-ticket Republican or Democratic. They believed they were wiser than their parents who voted in that fashion, and that they were capable of making discriminating judgments on the individual worth of the candidates whose flickering images they had seen on their living-room screens. So they went down the ballot, picking one from Column A and one from Column B, as if they were in a Chinese restaurant. They did not ask themselves whether the resulting mixture was politically digestible, whether it had the elements of a coalition capable of governing. Quite often, it did not.

The affluence of the United States also entered the picture, expanding the variety of choice not only of candidates but of issues. The fewer people in a society who worry about their own economic survival, the more who are available for recruitment to causes which are more marginal—not to say esoteric—in their appeal. Postwar America became the homeland of movements. Many of those movements are hardly to be scorned: civil rights, peace in Vietnam, environmental protection, consumer rights, women's rights, even the rights of the unborn have all been championed. But the characteristic of the movements, as distinguished from coalitions or parties, is their dedication to a single cause or to a closely related set of goals. They are, almost by definition, exclusive and exclusionary; their impact on politics, therefore, is to fractionate, not to coalesce.

Finally, postwar Americans developed such a powerful sense of our unique values and sensibilities that we were no longer sure anybody could represent us in all our splendor. The notion of a republic rests on the legitimacy of the con-

cept of representation. But that notion was challenged, particularly in the Democratic party, by the opposing principle
of participation, and from 1968 to 1980 the Democrats conducted unceasing experiments in devising new opportunities
for participation. There was a quantum jump in the number
of presidential primaries, and the effect was to reduce the influence of "insiders" in the nominating process of both parties, thereby further facilitating the success of self-centered
candidates with little proven ability to enlist others in the
process of coalition-building.

THE 1980 ELECTION

It was in this atomized, fractionated, unstable, and frustrat-
ing politics that the election of 1980 took place—and
seemingly transformed the scene. Everything we have said
suggests skepticism about the likelihood of a single election
or a single figure—Ronald Reagan—reversing the disintegrative trends in our politics. But there is no doubt that
1980 forces a reassessment of our political and institutional scene.

It was an explosion of major dimensions. Reagan received
an absolute majority of the popular votes in a three-way race
with Carter and Independent John B. Anderson, who drew
off small amounts of support from both parties and gained 7
percent of the total. He defeated the incumbent president of
the United States by a 10–1 margin in electoral votes, making Carter the first elected president of this century since
Herbert Hoover to fail to be reelected.

At the same time, the Republicans captured the majority
in the U.S. Senate for the first time in twenty-six years. And
at the same time, they reduced the Democratic majority in
the House of Representatives by more than half.

The major factors in the upheaval were not hard to dis-
cern. Mr. Carter had, to put it as politely as possible, a rather

light hold on the loyalties and affections of important constituencies within his own party and had to survive a strong
challenge for renomination from Senator Edward M.
Kennedy. Inflation had reduced real living standards for most
American families below the 1976 level. The captivity of
fifty-two American hostages in Iran for a year seemed to
symbolize the ineffectuality of American power and policy in
the world. And a politically active group of church people,
upset about public policy on abortions, prayer in school, and
other issues, mobilized on behalf of the conservative candidate as well.

But changing presidents is not that unusual. Party control
of the White House switched four times just between 1960
and 1980. What was unusual about the recent election was
the reappearance of a party vote.

The dimensions of that change are a matter of interpretation, and varying analyses are offered in the final chapters of
this book. What is not in doubt is the fact that the victorious
Republican party had been behaving in a most uncharac-
teristic manner for an American political party in the years
leading up to its win.

When Bill Brock of Tennessee became Republican chairman in 1977, he said it was his goal to rebuild the party, not
from the top down—not from the presidency down—as had
been tried so often before, but from the ground up. It was a
decision received with welcome by Republican workers who
had seen President Richard Nixon convert the GOP machinery to his exclusive personal use in his 1972 reelection campaign and then take the party down to ruin by his abuse of
power in the Watergate scandal.

Brock inherited a broad fund-raising base and further expanded it. Along with the separate but coordinated financial
arms of the House and Senate campaign committees, the Republican National Committee raised an unprecedented $111
million for the 1980 campaigns. For the first time in many

years, the largest single contribution almost every Republican candidate received came from—the Republican party.

Brock used much of the money to rebuild the party's organizational base in local communities and the key states. And he did one other thing. For the first time since the television age, he put a political party on television with a year-long program of institutional advertising, modeled on that of the British Conservative party in the year before the Thatcher government's victory in the spring election of 1979. It was financed to the extent of $9 million.

How much these efforts contributed to the 1980 victory cannot be proved, but the themes of the Reagan campaign echoed those of the Republican ads. Reagan, unlike most other recent Republican nominees and presidents, worked hard for the election of others on the ticket. In a symbolic ceremony, he and his running mate, George Bush, appeared on the steps of the Capitol as the campaign began and, with Republican members of Congress and GOP congressional candidates, signed a pledge of the program they would enact if they came to power. It was as close to a parliamentary party's "manifesto" as anything seen in decades in American politics.

VOTER VOLATILITY IN THE UNITED STATES

In the first months of his presidency there continued to be evidence that 1980's election may have been a landmark political event. The Republicans showed remarkable party cohesion in the early tests on Reagan's budget, holding every GOP senator and representative in line and attracting sixty-three conservative Democrats in the House to establish their de facto policy control of that body.

At the same time, there were indicators of deep-lying movements in the voting populace. A series of polls taken in the first half of 1981 showed that, while Reagan's personal popularity was a bit below other presidents' in their "honeymoon periods," more and more people were starting to identify with the president's party. Two polls taken in May of 1981 showed the Republicans virtually tied with the Democrats in public support—erasing what had been a 3-to-2 deficit for much of the last half century.

One must view such developments with extreme caution, given what we know about the emotional volatility and the structural fragility of American politics. The effects of the Reagan policies were untested in the real world of economics and foreign policy. The efforts to fulfill the hopes of the social-issue conservatives were almost bound to be divisive.

The evidence of coalitional shifts was equivocal at best — as several of our authors point out. The expansion of the electorate that characterized past critical elections simply did not occur in 1980, and the chances of Republicans' gaining seats in Congress in 1982, as the Democrats did in 1934 by way of certifying the historic import of FDR's election — those chances are conjectural.

The reaction of the Democrats to this challenge to their long dominance is uncertain. It was significant that, five months after Reagan took office, the Democratic National Committee took a major step away from the participatory politics of the 1968–1980 period. It revised the convention resolution on the midterm party conference of 1982 to provide that the delegates would consist of elected Democratic officials, members of the national committee, and others selected by state party committees, rather than delegates who were elected at the grass roots. But the ability of the Democrats to match the organizational and financial efforts the Republicans mounted after their 1976 defeat remained very much in doubt.

So did the prospects for the independent, nonparty politics of Anderson and his followers. The former Illinois congressman showed, as George Wallace had before, that ballot-access was not a serious barrier to independent candidacies for the highest office. He also established the principle of federal reimbursement of expenses for independent campaigns, and gained access to one of the two major presidential debates of the fall campaign. All this provides incentives for future independent candidacies outside the two-party system.

This is also food for debate for our authors. The political world looks different now than it did when they came together between the covers of the predecessor volume in 1978. And the chances are that it will look equally different three years from now.

2

SEYMOUR MARTIN LIPSET

Party Coalitions and the 1980 Election

The popular appeal of the Democrats. Republican strategy. Postindustrial and postmaterialist politics. New Politics and class voting. Factional conflict in the GOP. Candidates and pollsters in 1980. Pro-Republican realignments. Social issues and economics. Ideology and the Reagan administration. Taxes and expenditures; regulation and deregulation. Political trends, the two parties, and the changing public.

The 1980 election is the third presidential election out of the last four won by the Republican nominee. In 1976 Jerry Ford—running with the handicap of being the appointed successor of the Watergate villain Richard Nixon, whom he had pardoned, troubled by economic reverses for most of his two-year term, and having performed badly in the television debates—lost to a new face, the populist yet moderate Jimmy Carter, by only 2 percent (50 to 48). More to the point, Ford carried both the Midwest and West, and basically lost the election because Jimmy Carter captured his home region by 54 to 45 percent, the first time a Democrat had done so since Lyndon Johnson in 1964. Carter did this by sharply increasing his vote among his fellow white Southern Baptists far above that received by Democratic presidential nominees in previous postwar elections. Without Carter's religious/regional appeal, it is probable that Ford would have won the election.

Seemingly, therefore, we have been a Republican country on the presidential level for well over a decade. Looking back further to the presidential elections of 1960 and 1964, it should be noted that the former witnessed an extremely narrow triumph for the very moderate John F. Kennedy, 49.7 percent to 49.5 percent. And as in 1976, the result can be credited to the adverse effects of a weak economy for the candidate of the incumbent party, as well as a bad performance by his opponent in the televised debates. The only solid Democratic victory since 1948 occurred in 1964, when the election was perceived as a contest between a moderate, experienced, heir of Kennedy, Lyndon Johnson, and an ultra-Right, hawkish extremist, Barry Goldwater.

CONTINUED DEMOCRATIC DOMINANCE

These results suggest that the New Deal era really ended in 1952 with Dwight Eisenhower's election. Yet, as is obvious from other well known facts, the GOP has not dominated the electorate or public offices. In spite of the fact that in the opinion polls self-defined conservatives have been more numerous than those describing themselves as liberals, Democrats, as Wattenberg and Miller note in chapter 14, have consistently led Republicans by a wide margin among party identifiers and in party registration. In the 1980 GOP presidential landslide year, 44 percent of those surveyed still told Gallup, in the final month before the election, that they were Democrats—down 4 points from 1976; the Republicans moved up slightly, from 23 percent in 1976 to 26 percent in 1980. As the defeated party, the advantage of the Democrats declined slightly in the first half-year of the Reagan term, but they still led the GOP in party identifiers by 42 percent to 28 percent. The Roper Organization also reported the same trend, with Democrats dropping from 48 percent in 1980 to 43 percent in midyear 1981 and Republicans increasing from 23 to 25 percent.

It may be argued that party identification does not mean much—particularly in the current era, when the proportion voting a straight party ticket has declined sharply. Party identification, for many, is simply a traditional label, influenced by family, regional, ethnoreligious, or other group affiliations such as union membership. And the Democrats, particularly since the 1930s, became linked with almost every major identity group except middle-class, non-Southern, white, Anglo-Saxon Protestants.

More important than partisan identification is the fact that most people have voted for Democrats on the courthouse, mayoralty, state legislative, gubernatorial, and congressional levels in the same elections in which they were electing the GOP presidential candidates. For fourteen of the sixteen postwar years up to 1977 in which Republicans held the presidency, the Democrats controlled both houses of Congress. The Republicans made a remarkable comeback in the Senate in 1980, winning 22 of the 36 contested seats, capturing control of the Senate for the first time since 1954, and securing 7 of the 13 contested governorships. But, at the same time, the Democrats retained control of the House of

Representatives by 243 to 192, down from 273 to 159. The Democrats also continue to be dominant on the statehouse level; they have legislative majorities in twenty-eight states, compared to thirteen for Republicans, and seven where party control is divided.

Why do the Democrats maintain so much popular strength, given the shift to the Republicans in national and statewide elections? One answer is inertia and tradition; people do not easily change long-term party identifications, often formed in their youth, though they may reject their party's candidates. Such behavior has been characteristic for most conservative white Southerners, but it is also typical of many Catholics, Jews, trade unionists, and intellectuals, groups which do not see themselves at home in a middle-class, WASP, business-oriented, Republican party.

Jeane Kirkpatrick (1979*b*, p. 33), United Nations ambassador and member of the Reagan cabinet, noted, in explaining why she has remained a Democrat:

Party identification is a real identification. One's party—and the people, symbols, beliefs it comprises—are actually incorporated into the self, so that one is not only part of one's party, but more crucially, one's party is part of one's self. . . . Changing parties is thus like denying part of one's self and one's heritage.

A second factor constraining the relationship between traditional Democrats and the Republican Party is style. . . . Republicans, we say to one another, remind us of corporate board rooms and country clubs. Frequently, they look as if they have "more" money and sound as if they thought every one did. Generally, they seem more formal, more buttoned up—the kind of people who call a man named James, James.

The variation in party voting on different levels of government, as Everett Ladd points out in chapter 7, would also appear to be related to varying degrees of awareness of candidates and what they stand for. Most voters have some knowledge of those who are running for national or statewide offices, because such candidates command atten-

tion in the media. But in most metropolitan areas the activities of congresspeople and state legislators and their opponents are rarely reported in the press or on television. Incumbents, therefore, have a considerable advantage,
through the combination of greater name recognition and
the apparent absence of well-publicized issues separating the
candidates. To these assets should be added the ability of
local representatives to provide ombudsman and other services for their constituents. As a result, a considerable proportion of voters in a particular district feel obligated to—or
think they can rely on—their local representative in Congress or the legislature and vote for him or her, whether a
Left-wing Democrat or Right-wing Republican, in preference
to less well known rivals (Parker and Davidson 1979). As
Tom Mann (1981, p. 41) notes: "About three-fourths of all
House incumbents now win with at least 60 percent of the
major party vote, an increase over the past two decades of
ten to fifteen percentage points." On the other hand, senators are much more vulnerable to defeat, since, as different
studies have demonstrated, "House challengers are considerably less visible to the electorate than Senate
challengers. . . . [And] citizens are more likely to express
negative feelings toward Senate than House incumbents"
(Kuklinski and West 1981, p. 438). Senators are also less
likely than representatives to benefit from constituents'
gratitude for personal services.

THE REPUBLICAN TREND

Continued legislative control by the dominant party,
however, is not an invariant rule. David Broder notes in
chapter 1 that Bill Brock, chairman of the Republican National Committee from 1977 to 1980, deserves great credit
from his party for the GOP gains in congressional elections

during that period. He followed a campaign strategy that emphasized the policy responsibility of Congress, and raised a $9 million fund used largely for television advertising that linked the Democratic control of Congress with economic misfortunes and asked viewers to "Vote Republican. For a Change." Although the GOP did not carry the House in 1980, it did pick up 33 seats, the greatest gain by either party since 1966 (when, in an off-year election, the Republicans recovered from the 1964 Johnson landslide that had swept in the largest Democratic congressional majority in modern times).

The Republican congressional vote has been steadily moving up since the mid-1970s. It climbed from 40.4 percent in 1974 to 42.2 percent in 1976, 45.1 percent in 1978, and 48.7 percent in 1980. The narrow division in the popular vote in the last election did not translate into an equivalent partisan distribution of seats, because many Republican ballots were cast in Midwestern and Rocky Mountain areas where GOP candidates were elected by large majorities, and the Democrats continued to benefit from the congressional district boundaries that had been drawn by Democratically controlled state legislatures in 1970. This anomaly, however, may be partially remedied by changes in party advantages stemming from the forthcoming redistribution of 1982. The more conservative Sun Belt regions will pick up 17 congressional seats at the expense of largely Northern Democratic areas. Two experts on congressional elections, Tom Mann and Norman Ornstein (1981b, pp. 49–50), estimate the resultant redistricting gains for the Republicans at 5 to 10 seats. And within the states, it should be noted that thirty House districts, all located east of the Mississippi, "lost from 10 to 50 percent of their population between 1970 and 1980 . . . and every single one of those thirty seats is now held by a Democrat" (Reeves 1981, p. 43). Conversely, of the 30 seats which have increased most in the last decade, 18 are currently held by Republicans. More generally, "any change which shuffles voters out of or into districts damages incumbents.... Since the Democrats have more incumbents ... the process of redistricting *per se* hurts them" (Mann and Ornstein 1981*b*, p. 50). The Republicans, who increased their senatorial vote by 5.5 percent between 1974 and 1980, may gain further in that house in 1982, when 12 Republicans, 20 Democrats, and 1 Independent are up for reelection.

The decline in Democratic strength is also evident in the state legislatures. The number of states in which the Democrats have controlled both houses fell from thirty-seven in 1974 to twenty-eight in 1980. This drop-off involves a loss of 608 legislative seats.

This review of the electoral trends and results of the 1980 elections suggests that the country has witnessed a gradual but steady drift away from the one-and-a-half party system born in the Depression/New Deal era. Historians may record that this period began with Richard Nixon's landslide victory in 1972, only temporarily halted and deflected, through chance, by the Watergate scandal.

To account for this long-term Republican trend, we must turn to important economic and demographic developments. The period since World War II has been largely one of a sustained high level of economic growth (the last few years forming a prominent exception), with high rates of employment and new job creation, an increase in the number of private entrepreneurs, and a considerable expansion of higher-status jobs. These factors have helped to create a climate of optimism. A great majority of the people surveyed tell pollsters and social scientists that their socioeconomic situation, compared with that of their parents, has improved, and that they expect their children to do even better than themselves. (This personal optimism turned a bit sour during the end of decade-long stagflation.) The shift in the age structure, fewer young people coming of age, more older ones living longer, is a demographic pattern that social scientists have identified through comparative historical analysis as making for greater conservatism (Moller 1968; Lipset 1976, pp. xxxiii–xxxvi). The regional population shifts already noted are from the less affluent, more economically stagnant, Democratic regions to the economically expanding, socially mobile, more conservative areas.

Trade unions, which have been a major support base of the Democrats for campaign activists, financial contributions, and vote support, have dropped in membership from close to one-third of the employed nonagricultural labor force in 1960 to about 21 percent today. And unions have lost over half of the National Labor Relations Board labor representation elections in the last three years, a far higher ratio than that of two decades ago.

POSTINDUSTRIAL DEVELOPMENTS

As important as these structural changes has been the occurrence in the United States and other parts of the developed world of a new type of "cultural" politics that has served to reduce the correlations between socioeconomic class and voting behavior. This development has been linked to the emergence of what some have called the "postindustrial" society (Bell 1973; Touraine 1971).

These economically advanced areas are postindustrial because the trends defining industrial society—increasing involvement of the labor force in the industrial productive apparatus, the growth of factories, large farms, etc.—have ended. Tertiary service occupations rather than production jobs are growing rapidly. The proportion (and, in some countries, the absolute number) of manual workers is declining. The occupations that are expanding are white collar, technical, professional, scientific, and service oriented. The class structure now resembles a diamond bulging at the middle much more than a pyramid. High levels of education are needed for such economies and the number of students has increased many times. Education, science, and intellectual activities have become more important.

The emerging strata of postindustrialism—whose roots are in the university and in the scientific and intellectual worlds, and who are heavily represented in the public sectors and the professions—have developed their own values. According to Ronald Inglehart (1977), these "post-materialist" values (labeled "post-bourgeois" in his original formulation) are related to "self-actualization" needs (aesthetic, intellectual, a sense of belonging, of being held in esteem). These values manifest themselves in a desire for a less impersonal, more environmentally conscious, more cultured society, a freer personal life, and the democratization of politics, work, and community life. Such concerns run counter to those that dominate the traditional classes of industrial society, which are preoccupied more with satisfying material needs, i.e., with sustenance and safety. For people with the latter objectives, the most salient concerns are a high standard of living, a stable economy, economic growth, an enduring family life, crime fighting, and maintenance of order.

Regardless of what we call this change in orientation, it has profoundly affected the political arena. The basic political division of industrial society was materialistic, a struggle over the distribution of wealth and income. But postindustrial politics is increasingly concerned with *noneconomic* or *social issues*—a clean environment, a better culture, equal status for women and minorities, the quality of education, peaceful international relations, greater democratization, and a more permissive morality, particularly as affecting familial and sexual issues.

These concerns have produced new bases for political cleavage which vary from those of industrial society and have given rise to a variety of "single issue" protest movements. Since the existing political parties have found it

difficult to link positions on the new issues to their traditional socioeconomic bases of support, party loyalties and
even rates of voting participation have declined in a number
of countries, including the United States. In effect,
crosspressures deriving from differential commitments to
economic and social values have reduced the saliency of
loyalty to parties, tied largely to the structural sources of
cleavage—class, ethnicity, religion, region.

The reform elements concerned with postmaterialist or
social issues largely derive their strength, not from the
workers and the less privileged, the social base of the Left in
industrial society, but from affluent segments of the well
educated—students, academics, journalists, professionals,
and civil servants. The New Left, the New Politics, receive
their support from such strata. Most workers, on the other
hand, remain concerned with material questions. Less educated, less cosmopolitan, less affluent, less secure, they are
also more traditional and discernibly more conservative in
their social views.

Thus, there are now two Lefts—the materialist and the
postmaterialist—which are rooted in different classes. Conflicts of interest have emerged between them with respect to
the consequences of policies that affect economic growth.
The materialist Left wants an ever-growing pie so the less
privileged can have more, while the postmaterialists are
more interested in maintaining the quality of life they
already enjoy. As political scientist Willard Johnson (1973,
p. 174) argues, the postmaterialist Left "is guilty of debating
the issues in terms of values that, for all their humaneness,
ignore the concerns of the poor. . . . No doubt their concerns
feed on a genuine consideration for the quality of life, but
they seem to me mistaken about the contribution material
goods can make to it." Or, as the late Anthony Crosland
(1974, pp. 77–78), cabinet member in various British Labour
governments, contended, those who seek to limit growth to
protect the environment are "kindly and dedicated people.

But they are affluent, and fundamentally, though of course not consciously, they want to kick the ladder down behind them."

Both Lefts are often in the same party (Democratic, Social Democratic, even Communist, as in Italy), but they have different views and interests. The New Politics intelligentsia does not like trade unions, which, like business, it considers "materialistic" rather than "public interested." Some workers move Right as a result, to more conservative groupings which espouse growth and a competitive, mobile society, and which retain beliefs in traditional social values. The Left, however, picks up support from the growing ranks of the intelligentsia. Thus, as mentioned earlier, the correlations between *class* and *party* voting have been reduced.

THE NEW POLITICS

In the United States, a critical intelligentsia, based on the new middle class, emerged as early as the 1950s with the formation of the "reform" movement within the Democratic party, and constituted the beginning of what was subsequently labeled the "New Politics." "The appearance of significant numbers of college-educated, socially mobile, issue-oriented voters in urban and suburban reform clubs was noted by political observers in New York, California, Wisconsin, Missouri and elsewhere" (Kirkpatrick 1979*a*, p. 43).

The 1960s witnessed the full flowering of the New Politics in the form of opposition to the Vietnam War, struggles for civil rights, for women's liberation and gay liberation, and for environmentalism, as well as the emergence of new lifestyles. Jeane Kirkpatrick (1979*a*, pp. 44–45) emphasizes

[the way] the involvement of basic cultural symbols in the political arena has become a regular feature of our politics. As *avant garde* culture spread through rising college enrollments, the electronic media, and mass-circulation magazines, anti-bourgeois attitudes . . . became the bases of the anti-establishment politics of

the 1960s. . . . It is now clear that the assault on the traditional culture was mounted by young and not-so-young representatives of the relatively privileged classes, while the basic institutions of the society were defended by less-prosperous, less-educated, lower-status citizens.

The conflict between the New Politics Left and the traditional working class—based Left has occurred largely within the Democratic party. Its defeats in the presidential elections of 1968 and 1972 can be attributed in part to the split between the Old Left and New Left. Election surveys indicate that the correlations between class position and party vote in the United States fell in 1952 and 1956, rose in 1960 and 1964, declined to an almost negligible level in 1968 and 1972, increased in 1976, and fell off again in 1980 (Lipset 1981, p. 505). Since 1952 the Democrats have won every election in which class voting has increased, while Republican victories are associated with declines in the correlation. In 1952 and 1956 the defeated Democratic candidate for president was Adlai Stevenson, who has often been called the initiator of the New Politics phenomenon in America. He consciously sought to avoid the New Deal issues, linked to economic and class conflicts, and he emphasized cultural and social concerns.

Class voting moved up somewhat in 1960, largely reflecting John F. Kennedy's special appeal to less privileged, Catholic, ethnic voters. It rose dramatically in 1964, when Senator Barry Goldwater, the Republican nominee, advocated repeal of many welfare state and pro—trade union policies, while Lyndon Johnson emphasized extension of the New Deal type of reform measures. In 1968 New Dealer Hubert Humphrey was the Democratic candidate for the presidency, but he lost votes both to the Left and the Right because of the saliency of noneconomic issues. Many blue-collar voters supported George Wallace, reacting against Humphrey's stand on civil rights, while the New Politics Left, whose supporters had voted for Eugene McCarthy or Bobby Kennedy in the primaries, refused to back Humphrey because of his lack of commitment to ending the war in Vietnam and his links to the Old Politics.

These factors continued to affect electoral behavior in the ensuing decade. In 1972 the New Politics Left won the Democratic party nomination for its candidate George McGovern, but it was defeated soundly in the general election. McGovern was the first Democratic presidential nominee since the 1920s not to receive the support of the labor movement (AFL/CIO), as many blue-collar voters deserted the Democrats to vote for Richard Nixon, who campaigned for traditional values and law and order. The split between the two Lefts in the Democratic party can be seen in the epithet the Humphrey trade union—based wing of the party circulated, depicting McGovern as the candidate of "Amnesty, Abortion, and Acid." Four years later, however, the Democrats were able to win back the White House when *both* parties nominated candidates who were identified as social conservatives. Thus, many workers and Southern whites who had voted previously for Nixon or Wallace returned to the Democratic line to support Jimmy Carter.

The Democratic nomination contest in 1980 was, in some part, a fight between Jimmy Carter, viewed as socially conservative, and a New Politics challenger, Edward Kennedy, who also sought to appeal to workers and minorities on economic issues. The opinion surveys, however, reported a strong relationship between socioeconomic status and candidate preference, with the less privileged and the older voters supporting the incumbent—and the more affluent, better educated, and younger people backing his opponent.

THE REPUBLICAN FACTIONS

The Republicans have also experienced factional conflict during these years, largely between representatives of the party linked to the big business, professional, and executive strata concentrated in metropolitan areas who accept the Keynesian, welfare state orientation introduced by the New Deal, and the more *laissez-faire*, libertarian elements supported disproportionately by the independent business sector and the *nouveaux riches* of the economically expanding Sun Belt. The division also extends to the differences between the more secular, cosmopolitan, social liberals and the more fundamentalist social conservatives. The two principal tendencies have varied in their foreign policy outlook as well—the moderates favor efforts to come to terms with the Soviet Union (détente), while their opponents support a more nationalist, hard line, anti-Communist policy. The Taft-Eisenhower, Goldwater-Rockefeller, Reagan-Ford, and Reagan-Bush contests reflected these divisions. Nixon successfully bridged those differences, in part because of his strong anti-Communist image, although on domestic issues he followed the policies of the centrist, Keynesian sector linked to big business. (In 1980 the candidate of the corporate boardrooms and the strongest supporter within the GOP of the Keynesian, big government policies, John Connally, failed miserably in the presidential primaries in spite of having the largest campaign chest.)

Until 1980 it was generally accepted that presidential candidates representing the moderate wing of the GOP did better in elections than those coming from the seemingly more dogmatic *laissez-faire* one, since the latter alienated the large sector of the electorate that benefited most from federally financed entitlements introduced by the New Deal. This generalization broke down with the growing concern about the contribution of big government to runaway inflation and the growth of backlash social conservatism, a reaction against postmaterialist cultural changes—widespread use of drugs, permissive sexual morality, tension in race relations. These developments led both to secessions from the Democratic party and to increased support for the Republican Right that emphasized traditional verities.

THE 1980 ELECTION

The postmaterialists found both major party nominees, Reagan and Carter, objectionable. For much of the 1980 campaign, they supported an independent alternative, John Anderson, whose campaign stressed an enlightened social liberalism. In a full-page advertisement in the *New York Times* of 27 June 1980 (p. 22E), the Anderson campaign organization called for support because of their candidate's record on five issues: protecting the environment, extending civil rights, passing the Equal Rights Amendment, federally funding abortions for the poor, and reducing excessive government regulations. The opinion polls reported that Anderson's strength (around 22 percent at its height in July but down to 7 percent in the November election) consisted largely of more well-to-do people, college graduates, professionals, Jews, and self-identified liberals. His 300-page "platform" statement issued in August was relatively conservative on economic issues and very liberal on social and foreign policy questions. Survey data also indicated that Anderson's followers were much more socially liberal than Carter's supporters. The trade unions, on the other hand, were strongly opposed to Anderson and endorsed the Democratic nominee, whose strength came disproportionately from the older, less educated, poorer, and working class sections of the population.

In the 1980 presidential election itself, class factors once again became less important, while Anderson's support dropped off rapidly, following a pattern typical of third-party candidacies in the United States. Differences in party orientation toward social issues were more important than in 1976. The Republicans explicitly rejected many of the social programs of the New Politics—the Equal Rights Amendment, government financing of abortions for poor women, and measures such as busing designed to foster racial integration. Although Jimmy Carter tried to avoid being identified with the social policies advocated by the New Politics wing of his party, he could not openly repudiate them and hope to retain its support. Hence, social issues played a somewhat greater role in the outcome of the 1980 election than they had four years earlier. It should be noted, however, that evidence drawn from an examination of congressional election results and opinion surveys does not sustain the frequently voiced belief that the Moral Majority and kindred groups that emphasized these issues had much effect on the outcomes (Lipset and Raab 1981). As Wattenberg and Miller emphasize in chapter 14, the social issues were not salient to most voters.

Economic issues, however, clearly predominated in the 1980 presidential election, just as they had in 1976. The difference was that in 1980 the economic issues worked to the advantage of the Republicans, who were now the "out" party as the Democrats had been four years earlier. The electoral outcome was basically an across-the-board rejection of the Carter administration's failure to manage the economy. More generally, there has been a collapse in the logic of Keynesian economics—a collapse of the perception that it is possible to have ever-increasing spending and a healthy economy, i.e., low inflation and high growth. In the wake of this collapse, Americans have come increasingly to regard the government as the enemy of economic progress, a perception that works to the disadvantage of the Democrats.

The social issue shows up mostly in the *changes* in the Republican vote from 1976 to 1980. As Schneider and Wirthlin point out in this volume (chapters 9 and 10), Reagan's gains over Ford were greatest among labor-union families, manual workers, Southerners, Jews, Catholics, and older voters—in other words, the core "Old Left" constituencies of the New Deal Democratic party. Of the 4.8 million votes that Reagan gained over Ford's 1976 total, 2.4 million, or half of them, were cast in the eleven Southern states, which comprise less than one-quarter of the national electorate (Schneider 1981). Patrick Caddell has emphasized that Democratic congressional candidates tended to hold on to liberal suburban districts outside the South, which had begun to go Democratic as recently as 1974. Their congressional losses were concentrated in the oldest and most Democratic strongholds—in the South and in white, working class districts in the North. In other words, the Democrats had the most trouble holding their more socially conservative supporters against the Reagan onslaught.

REALIGNMENTS

Looking back at the shifts in voting patterns up to and including 1980, it would appear that major realignments have occurred, the bulk of which have contributed to Republican strength. As noted, those groups most disturbed by activist measures to foster equal rights for blacks, particularly native white Southerners, have been moving away from the Democrats since 1948, through backing either third-party candidates such as Strom Thurmond and George Wallace, or GOP nominees. In 1980, not only did Reagan win almost all of the Southern electoral votes, but the Republicans, as Richard Scammon notes, now hold 11 of the 22 senatorial seats in the once Confederate states. The Republicans have become the dominant party in the economically expanding Sun Belt and Mountain regions (see chapter 14). They have picked up support among the less privileged and the trade unionists. Conversely, however, the GOP is much weaker than in the New Deal era among college students and the well educated professional strata, who increasingly constitute the mass base of New Politics Democrats.

There was a continued decline among traditional sources of Democratic party support in the spring of 1981. Basing their analysis on those who stated they identify with a party or are leaning towards one, Adam Clymer and Kathleen Frankovic (1981, p. 45) report that the April *New York Times/CBS News* poll found:

The lowest income group—Democrats outright by a five-to-two margin in 1980—is now only four-to-three Democratic. Among persons from union households, a three-to-one Democratic edge has slipped to two-to-one, and their votes in 1980 dismayed Democrats—Carter got 47 percent of the union household vote to Reagan's 44. Among Catholics, a 44–18 Democratic margin has now slipped to 36–20.

CURRENT ISSUES

The Republicans have, in effect, built an electorally viable, though unstable, coalition of affluent economic conservatives and less educated, more religious, social conservatives. Inflation, the main economic problem of recent times, fosters acceptance of a conservative solution—cutbacks in government spending and activity—even by the relatively underprivileged. The Democrats, on the other hand, have found it increasingly difficult to hold together a coalition of socially liberal and peace oriented, New Politics intelligentsia, blacks, feminists, and trade-union leaders who are generally hard-liners on foreign policy, and economically liberal, but socially conservative, working class whites.

The shift toward the Republicans has also been enhanced by growing international tensions and evidence of a Soviet military buildup. As a result, the pacific and isolationist attitudes that dominated the public mood during the late 1960s and early 1970s, a reaction to the Vietnam War fiasco, have declined greatly. Opinion polls have revealed a steady growth in support for a strong anti-Communist defense and foreign policy posture, an orientation that has worked more to the advantage of Republican than Democratic candidates.

Yet the picture is not completely one-sided. As the surveys and attitude studies of recent years have indicated, significant majorities of Americans, including many Republicans, have come to accept social-welfare/regulatory/economic-planning activities as proper roles for the state (Lipset and Schneider 1981). This is true even though many with such views regard government as a wasteful, inefficient institution, misusing its overly high tax revenues, doing an inadequate job of regulation, and contributing through various policies to inflation and unemployment. The Republicans have gained, not because a majority rejects the welfare/regulatory state, but because many share the impression that the incumbent Democrats did a bad and wasteful job in administering these policies, that another set of politicians may do better—particularly, as of 1980, with respect to economic conditions and, to a lesser extent, to America's international position.

If the opinion polls are to be believed, the evidence is that the public favors a more efficient, less wasteful, lower cost version of the welfare state—i.e., reformed, but not abolished. Most citizens even support an expansion of the state's role in paying for health care. Although the majority is aware that many regulations have serious negative consequences and prefer that these be reformed, it still favors governmental efforts to restrict pollution, protect the environment, and safeguard consumers and workers. The public would like to maintain an excellent educational system, up to and including universities. It supports special help to those in need—the poor, the unemployed, the aged, the handicapped, the inadequately trained, the minorities—but it would deny aid to "welfare chiselers" or to jobless people who refuse to take available jobs, categories which it considers populous.

Most important, the public credits government with the ability to both cause and eliminate inflation and unemployment. The high rate of both—the misery index—in 1979–1980 was almost certainly Ronald Reagan's greatest political asset. If these rates should still be high in 1982, the Republicans could suffer serious electoral reverses. In any case, the GOP will enter that election with the knowledge that the president's party usually loses support in off-year elections as the electorate votes its frustrations, sending the president a message in the knowledge that he will still be in office even if his party loses seats in Congress. (In Britain, Margaret Thatcher, who has four to five years between parliamentary elections, has lost heavily in public support, according to the polls; the Tories are blamed for continued high inflation and unemployment.)

As noted, reactions to the so-called social issues, busing for school integration, affirmative-action quota programs, government-financed abortion, law-and-order concerns, religion in the schools, pornography, have also been credited with the Republican and conservative revival. Support for conservative social positions is correlated with low education and low socioeconomic status and with fundamentalist religious affiliation. Because of their class position, many who are socially conservative also tend to be economically liberal, often Democratic in their past voting behavior. If only a few percent shifted their vote from Democratic to Republican in 1980 because of the social issues, this may have been enough to change election results, particularly in close congressional contests.

The Republicans now face a serious dilemma, however, as they are called on to take action on the social issues by well-organized groups of bullet or single-issue voters. If they do so, as Richard Wirthlin has noted in postelection discussions, they risk antagonizing the disproportionately well educated, socially liberal majority, many of whom are economic conservatives or moderates. The Republican leadership is clearly aware of this problem. National Committee Chairman Richard Richards has frequently criticized the activities of the National Conservative Political Action Committee (NCPAC) and similar groups (Furgurson 1981). The founding father of the Republican and conservative revival, Barry Goldwater, has also strongly criticized Richard Viguerie, the Moral Majority, and the Right to Life group for their focus on single issues. He emphasized that "instead of helping the conservative movement . . . these groups may turn the tide the other way by organizing to get one thing through Congress." He also deprecated the belief that position on social issues is a measure of conservatism, stating, "I don't believe abortion or busing are conservative or liberal," and indicated that he now favors the continuation of the federal Voting Rights Law (Hunt 1981, p. 12). The CBS News Election and Survey Unit (1981b, p. 2) in June 1981 interviewed 159 of the 168 members of the Republican National Committee and found them sharply divided about the role of the Moral Majority. A plurality, 34 percent, wanted to see it "less active" than at present. Only 11 percent favored greater activity, while 19 percent said it should be as active as now.

Spokespeople for Ronald Reagan share these concerns, and have indicated that he will try to stay aloof from congressional struggles on these matters. Presidential aide Powell Moore commented in August: "The White House is not going to get far out on the social issues." White House chief lobbyist Max Friedersdorf "said he does not expect the coalition . . . that passed the budget tax cuts to hold together on social issues," and that it would be difficult, therefore, to lobby for them (Glaser 1981, p. A-16).

Republicans also face an even more important problem in economic policy. As noted frequently in this volume, the 1980 opinion surveys suggest that Reagan's best set of issues involved the economy. His question, "Are you personally better or worse off than four years ago?" had a profound effect on millions of Americans who had seen their real income decline or their jobs disappear. What overwhelmed Jimmy Carter was the widespread belief that he had mismanaged the economy (Ladd 1981, pp. 12–13). Reagan and the Republicans must expect to be judged by the same criteria. They will be pressed to improve the economy, even if it involves following policies which contradict their basic ideology.

IDEOLOGY AND GOVERNMENT POLICY

Conservatives in other countries have faced the same problem. At the 1980 international meeting of the conservative Mount Pelerin Society, a number of papers dealt with the question: "Does the election of conservative governments make a difference?" The answer given generally was "No." These papers pointed to the fact that conservative governments in nations as various as Israel, France, Sweden, and Britain have retained or even extended welfare and government interventionist policies, in violation of their electoral programs. The Swedish bourgeois government, for example, nationalized various bankrupt industries to prevent unemployment.

These conclusions apply to the United States as well. An analysis by Thomas Moore (1981a) of the Hoover Institution comparing policy performance during the sixteen postwar Democratic presidential years (Truman, Kennedy, Johnson, and Carter) with sixteen Republican years (Eisenhower, Nixon, and Ford) found that spending in real dollars (controlling for inflation) for non–defense-related items increased 88 percent under the Democrats and 141 percent under the Republicans. Conversely, spending for defense and international affairs declined 34 percent under the Republicans, while it increased 212 percent under the Democrats. Even after excluding the years of the Korean and Vietnam wars, Moore found that defense expenditures went up 10 percent when Democrats occupied the White House and declined by 9 percent in Republican years. "Budget deficits were equally large under the two parties" (Moore 1981*a*, p. 4).

Seeking to evaluate the record of the different post—World War II presidential incumbencies with respect to government regulation, Moore (1981*a*, p. 4) counted the pages in *The Federal Register*, which reports all changes in regulation. He found that "the Republicans expanded regulation almost 50 percent faster than the other party." Even more surprising, perhaps, is the finding of Steven Kelman (1981) in a detailed comparative study of the operations of American and Swedish regulatory agencies concerned with occupational safety that, under the Nixon administration, the American Occupational Safety and Health Administration was more critical of business practices and more stringent in enforcing regulations than its Swedish counterpart under a Social Democratic government. As James Q. Wilson (1981, p. x) summed up Kelman's findings, a Republican administration revealed "in the operations of the Occupational Safety and Health Administration, a disposition to resolve all policy differences to the disadvantage of business and to place the enforcement of these policies in the hands of inspectors with a deep suspicion of business leaders."

THE REAGAN RECORD

Clearly, the record of the first eight months of the Reagan administration is different from that of the previous GOP incumbencies. Representing the *laissez-faire* libertarian wing of the party, Reagan—unlike Eisenhower, Nixon, and Ford—has successfully pressed for cuts in a large number of domestic, welfare oriented programs and an increase in military expenditures. The more moderate Keynesian wing of the party, reduced in electoral strength and congressional representation, has thus far (summer 1981) gone along with Ronald Reagan. Seemingly, for the first time in modern history, the Republicans are attempting a "counterrevolution" to reverse the trends set in motion by the Roosevelt New Deal in the 1930s.

Yet Ronald Reagan should not be seen as a principled, Right-wing ideologue. Like other political leaders, he has accommodated his policies to political pressures and to the findings of the opinion polls. Faced with evidence that the majority of the public perceived his taxation and spending policies as favoring the well-to-do and business, he withdrew some of the proposed tax cuts that would benefit business. He did the same with respect to proposals to cut back on Social Security benefits when these aroused a firestorm of protest among the elderly. The commitment to *laissez-faire* policies has been violated when to do so would alienate important constituencies—e.g., continuation of the Chrysler bail-out and tobacco price supports, restrictions on steel, sugar, and Japanese auto imports, federal aid to New York City, and the appointment of proregulatory chairpeople on some important regulatory commissions.

The compromise character of the Reagan programs may be seen most strikingly in the areas of taxation and regulation. The president himself stressed in his economic message to Congress of 18 February 1981 that it is "important to note that *we are only reducing the rate of increase in taxing and spending.* We are not attempting to cut either spending or taxing to a level below that which we presently have." Assuming the passage of the original Reagan "Kemp-Roth—like personal income tax cut, with 10 percent across-the-board reductions in 1981, 1982, and 1983, as well as accelerated depreciation allowances, which lower corporate income taxes," an economic forecasting team at the University of California, Los Angeles, found that "total federal tax receipts, stated as a percent of GNP, will be higher under

President Reagan than they were under Presidents Truman, Eisenhower, Kennedy, Johnson, Ford or Carter. By this measure, the tax 'bite' under Reagan is projected to be the highest since World War II" (Kimball 1981, p. 6).

In fact, the actual tax bite will be even higher than in the UCLA projection, since the actual tax-rate reduction program passed by Congress did not go into effect until October 1981, involved just a 5 percent cut the first year and, as noted, did not include a number of the reductions in business taxes contained in the original proposals. The administration also tried to drop its original plan to index the income-tax brackets, i.e., to link them to changes in the cost of living. Failure to do so means that inflation will continue to push taxpayers into higher tax brackets, thus effectively canceling out for many the effects of the rate reductions (Rabushka 1981, p. 28). Congressional Republicans, however, objected to this change in scenario and, following Senate adoption of an indexing plan in July, forced the administration to formally endorse the proposal, but the plan adopted will not go into effect until 1985, i.e., after Reagan goes out of office or has been reelected.

Although the president pressed successfully to reduce spending on a number of welfare policies that involve income transfers, under his program transfer payments are anticipated to be higher in 1983—9.0 percent of the gross national product—than in any year before 1974, and "to run nearly double the share under President Johnson's 'Great Society' years" (Kimball 1981, p. 6). The actual expenditure program is likely to be even higher, since the president, reacting to congressional pressures, agreed to moderate some of his proposed cuts. Conversely,

defense spending is predicted to rise as a percentage of the GNP, from 5.0 percent in 1980 to 5.4 percent in 1983. Except for the recent years 1977—80, when the share was about 4.8 percent, this is lower than any year since 1951. The [post-Vietnam] "peace dividend" years of 1973—75 saw an average of 5.5 percent of the GNP devoted to defense expenditures (Kimball 1981, p. 6).

An article written by then President-elect Reagan, published in the *Wall Street Journal* on 9 January 1981, noted the dysfunctional effects of regulation on business growth and productivity. He called for "rolling back various regulations to reduce the non-productive paperwork burden on the private sector" (Reagan 1981, p. 18). Ronald Reagan, apparently, was promising to continue a pattern of deregulation that had begun under Gerald Ford and Jimmy Carter, which had included significant relaxation of controls in the airline, trucking, railroad, and broadcasting industries. But seven months later, in mid-August, the *Wall Street Journal* (1981, p. 22) was to editorialize that "the administration's record on deregulation . . . has been less than sterling and, in some cases, it has backtracked from the inroads made by the previous administration." The paper called attention to new regulatory activity by the Interstate Commerce Commission, the Federal Aviation Administration, and the Federal Communications Commission. Regulatory authority Thomas Moore (1981*b*) also noted that the new administration moved "in exactly the opposite direction" to its pre-election statements, as evidenced by its early policies and its appointments to various regulatory commissions. The new chairman of the Interstate Commerce Commission, Reece H. Taylor, Jr., was "first suggested by Edward Wheeler, the lawyer for the Teamster's Union, which has bitterly opposed deregulation," and was endorsed for the post by the head of the union. According to Moore (1981*b*, p. 4), "the Commission is attempting to construe the Motor Carrier Act in the most restrictive way." The new chairman of the Federal Communications Commission, Mark Fowler, also had a proregulatory record (Moore 1981*b*, p. 4). Before taking office, he had objected to permitting new stations in particular markets.

The Reagan administration, of course, is seeking to relax regulatory controls in areas that do not affect intra-industry competition—e.g., with respect to the environment, occupational safety rules, and affirmative action. The president appears to be following his campaign commitment to appoint members of regulatory commissions "who were less adversarial in their attitudes toward business" (Raines 1981, p. 8). But the realities of politics, the concern to hold or gain support at the margins of his coalition, is leading Reagan to be more cautious than he was in January. Thus, in August 1981, according to Tom Wicker (1981, p. 23), "the Administration has retreated somewhat from its earlier intention to rewrite and water down the Clean Air Act . . . [and has become aware] that a political furor will greet any serious attempt to weaken the network of major environmental protection laws."

There seems to be a general rule, inherent in democratic politics, that governments, whether of the Left or Right, may not make major changes which, though sensible in terms of possible long-range effects, will have short-term, disruptive, economic and political consequences. As a result, politicians generally decide to move slowly so as to avoid creating a situation which will return the opposition to power. Some indication of the way in which such considerations affect the policy of the Reagan administration may be seen in the comments of David Stockman, director of the Office of Management and Budget, at his Senate confirmation hearing. After noting "that the 'windfall profits' tax on oil company revenue resulting from decontrol of oil prices 'isn't sound energy policy,' " he went on to say that "the tax is a 'pretty prodigious producer of revenue,' and that, given the federal government's budget problems, abolishing the tax shouldn't get high priority" (Conte 1981, p. 4.) Thus far, the administration has not recommended the repeal of the tax, although it yielded to pressures from Democratic, oil state, congressmen, whose votes it needed, to modify the levy.

The Democrats have also demonstrated a capacity to adjust their policies in order to rebuild the majority coalition. As Bill Keller (1981, pp. 1132, 1136) noted in the *Congressional Quarterly Weekly*, the 1981 struggle over tax cuts "produced an amazing spectacle: Democrats trying to outbid Republicans for the affections of the business community.... While the public rhetoric of the president and many Democrats has emphasized the shape of tax cuts for individuals, ... the competition for votes in the House has been waged primarily on the question of business cuts." The latter, according to a Democratic congressional tax counsel, followed a deliberate strategy of "showing the business community it is welcome in the Democratic party, too." The House Democrats pressed for a number of provisions in the bill which would give business greater tax breaks than were provided for in the original administration version.

THE FUTURE

The Republicans appear to be riding a trend of growing support, reflecting structural changes in the economy and the population, and an accumulated discontent with the functioning of government and other basic institutions. To these secular trends must be added the future effect of increased financial support for the GOP, which should be enhanced dramatically in 1982 when business-related Political Action Committees concentrate their contributions among Republicans, now that they no longer have to keep in the good graces of powerful Democratic legislators.

The Democrats need not despair, however. As noted, more people still identify with them than with the Republicans, but more important, the Democrats remain committed to the egalitarian values their party has come to symbolize. The majority of Americans favor policies that will extend opportunity to the less privileged and minorities. Seemingly, as of 1981, they give lower priority to this commitment than to efforts to cut back on government expenditures in order to reduce inflation. But in the opinion polls, they voice opposition to many specific proposals which they see as benefiting the well-to-do at the expense of the poor.

Such feelings may underlie the fact that after six months in office, as of July 1981, the 33 percent voicing disapproval to the Gallup poll of President Reagan's job performance was "higher than that recorded for any other president at this point in his administration," while his approval rating stood at 53 percent. Using a somewhat different question, asking respondents to evaluate the job "Ronald Reagan is doing as President"—"an excellent job, a good job, only a fair job, or do you think he is doing a poor job?"—the NBC News–Associated Press poll reported in July that 42 percent judged his performance as only fair or poor, while 55 percent evaluated it as excellent or good. Two months earlier, 33 percent were negative and 62 percent were positive. In late June, when asking about vote choice for Congress in 1982, both the Gallup and Harris polls found that the Democrats led the Republicans by 49 to 45 percent in the former and 50 to 44 in the latter.

Reacting in late June to the drop in the president's approval ratings, Richard Richards noted that

such a decline "happens with all presidents," and was caused in this case by public failure to see results from the president's economic program. And that, he said, is the fault of Congress, for "not doing its job." He conceded that public displeasure with the administration's proposal to cut Social Security benefits also probably contributed to the slump (Furgurson 1981).

Yet Ronald Reagan's ability to mobilize congressional support for his domestic economic package in his first eight months in office has been impressive. It must be noted, however, that post–World War II presidents each lost support in Congress over time. Thus, Eisenhower's percentage of congressional victories on measures he supported fell off from 89.0 in 1953 to 65.0 in 1960; Johnson's declined from 93.0 in 1965, the first year of his elected term, to 75.0 in 1968; Nixon's moved down from 74.0 in 1969 to 50.6 in 1973, his last full year in office; while, curiously, Carter's changed least of all, from 75.4 in 1977 to 75.1 in 1980 (Bibby, Mann, and Ornstein 1980, p. 100).

Ronald Reagan ran on a platform of lower taxes, cutbacks in government functions (military expenditures apart), and criticism of some welfare activities. Regardless of what the polls report or how they are interpreted, he has a mandate to carry out his program. Should he be able to do so, Americans will have to react to these policies in polls and elections. But in spite of what they say or how they vote, the debate as to what they prefer is not likely to end. We may safely predict that they will continue to express ambivalence about the role of government and that experts will differ in interpreting the meaning of their ballots. Was their vote in 1980 a call for a more market-oriented, tax-cutting government, or was it a rejection of a failed presidency which had witnessed or caused severe stagflation? A survey conducted by Yankelovich, Skelly, and White in January 1981 indicates that most voters felt the election results were more "a rejection of President Carter" than "a mandate for more conservative policies." A quarter of those polled, 24 percent, saw the outcome as a conservative mandate, while 63 percent interpreted it as a vote against Carter. Only 34 percent of Republicans and 30 percent of self-identified conservatives believed that the voters had endorsed the new president's conservative program. Other results of this and subsequent surveys reinforce these findings (Frankovic 1981, pp. 113–17; Miller 1981, pp. D1, D5). Most people favored the Reagan program of reducing spending and balancing the budget when presented as one package. But equivalent majorities opposed specific proposals for cuts in federal programs for health, housing, and education.

It is noteworthy that Americans continue to see Ronald Reagan as considerably to "the right" of themselves after observing him in office. In June 1981, 27 percent of a Gallup national cross section identified his views as substantially to the right of center or far right, while only 12 percent placed themselves in these categories. Almost half, 49 percent, described Reagan as to the right of center, compared to 32 percent who saw themselves in this light. The public clearly still thought of itself to the left of the president, a perception which could harm him in the future.

Possibly reacting to the findings of the opinion polls, various spokespeople for the administration have stressed that they are against cuts in most welfare programs and are proposing to increase others. Thus, in a speech delivered on 20 July 1981, David Stockman emphasized that the administration has increased funds for Head Start, the Basic Educational Opportunity Grants, Upward Bound, Summer Youth Employment, public-housing operating subsidies, and low-income energy assistance. He also argued that in reducing other programs such as food stamps, the administration has eliminated benefits for middle-income people—those earning above $16,000 a year—not for lower-income families. And he pointed to various cuts of subsidies to business and farm owners (Stockman 1981).

Seen in the broadest possible light, however, economic events in the last few years have forced the public and politicians to face up to the *costs* of government programs: for most of the postwar period, it seemed that high and increasing government spending did not cost anything; low inflation and high growth kept real after-tax incomes increasing throughout that period until the early part of the 1970s. The last decade, however, has raised the problem of costs, and has thereby forced people to consider the trade-offs. If a way cannot be found to restore the economic growth and rising real incomes that Americans took for granted for most of our history, no amount of social programs or anything else will affect the long-term political trends. Restoring growth has already become the obsessive concern of politicians of both parties. As Bill Keller (1981, p. 1137) notes: "Starting in 1978, Democrats began shifting their emphasis from

redistribution of income toward 'increasing productivity.'
Last year [1980], for instance, Democrats scrambled aboard
the 10−5−3 tax cut in droves." This business depreciation
proposal, included in the 1981 tax bills of both parties, gives
"companies bigger tax breaks by allowing them to write off
more rapidly the cost of new investments."

Richard Scammon commented, following the 1976 election, that there was nothing wrong with the Republican party that a 12 percent inflation rate would not cure. After the
1980 contest, he said there was nothing wrong with the Democratic party that a significant increase in the unemployment rate would not repair. The American electorate has a
funny habit of reacting to the state of the economy. Their
views on specific economic and welfare policies are important, but they rarely determine which party controls
the White House (Tufte 1978; Fair 1978; Hibbs and
Fassbender 1981).

3

S. I. HAYAKAWA

The Two-Party System: A Personal Reflection

Democrats and Republicans—conservative, liberal, and academic. The composition of the two parties. Psychology and rhetoric in politics. Party interaction.

I have thought about the two-party system a great deal, because I have been a member of both parties. It occurs to me how difficult it would be to explain to a foreigner the difference between the Republican and Democratic parties. It is an almost impossible job because, first, few of us have been able to define that difference for ourselves and, second, Europeans as a rule try to understand the difference between one party and another in ideological terms. But ideology does not matter all that much to Americans.

Both parties include, although in different proportions, the rich and the poor, urban people and rural, blacks and whites, industrial interests as well as agricultural. Both parties are highly pragmatic, in the American tradition. Each party borrows ideas freely from the other, so that the great Republican idea of one decade becomes, two decades later, a great Democratic idea, and vice versa.

Hence, the two parties differ from each other, not in composition, or the interests they espouse, or the ideologies they represent, but in psychology. My observations lead me to believe that these psychological differences are clear enough to account for the actions of people who claim party membership.

Republicans, it seems to me, tend to feel a sense of proprietorship toward the economy. That is, to put it bluntly, they act as if they owned the joint. They have the psychology of insiders. Democrats, on the whole, act as though they feel marginal, like outsiders.

These feelings are psychological, and often quite independent of the facts. Some Republicans are on welfare. Some Democrats are insiders, rich and powerful. Nevertheless, this observable psychological difference does serve, in a rough way, to distinguish the modality of the two parties.

Generally, Republicans tend to include insiders in the business system, those who actually own or manage a sufficient portion of the system to give them a sense of proprietorship. That is, they either own a piece of the joint, or act as if they do.

Second, there are those who believe they are about to own the joint, or would like to be mistaken for those who do. Third, there are second and third generation descendants of immigrant families, those described as having upward mobility, who are attempting to expunge from themselves the remaining status of being outsiders, and so they become Republicans. Fourth, there are those who feel that they have benefited from the system sufficiently that, even though they are not insiders in the proprietorship sense, they want to maintain the status quo, so they are Republicans.

In the case of the radical Right, it seems to me that they are those who believe that the joint is rightfully theirs and is being taken away from them by outsiders, often thought to be Communists. And, of course, the Republican party includes thousands and thousands who are Republicans by force of habit, as well as assorted opportunists, chiselers, and punks.

Similarly, Democrats seem to include, first, those who do own the joint or a comfortable percentage thereof, but who are startled at their good fortune and therefore tend to remain identified with those who still look forward to getting their share. Second, Democrats include immigrants and their descendants, at least until the feeling of being outsiders wears off. Third, it seems to me that Southerners, Catholics, Jews, and blacks tend to be Democrats because they believe that Northerners, Protestants, Gentiles, and whites own the joint. Fourth, there are some who succeed in owning a piece of the joint, and know it, who feel duty-bound—perhaps out of guilt feelings—to help the less fortunate achieve the same status, and they become Democrats.

Intellectuals are usually Democrats. Their feelings of being left out are intensified by their conviction that, by rights, they ought to be running the joint. No doubt they are influenced by the philosopher Plato who said that some men are gold, some are silver, some are iron and lead. Of course, women did not count in Plato's world. Imagining themselves to be the "gold" of Plato's definition, intellectuals find it easy to accept his philosophic premise of a perfect republic, governed by philosopher-kings. And, of course, if being an intellectual is sufficient qualification to run the joint, one does not have to scramble and strive to own it.

The Democratic party of course includes thousands and thousands who are Democrats by force of habit; also assorted opportunists, chiselers, and punks.

In the light of these psychological differences, certain rhetorical differences between the two parties assume a clearer significance. For example, for Democrats it is the task of government to do battle with the powerful business interests that are depriving the common people of their economic opportunities and subverting their political rights. For Republicans it is the task of government to help a prosperous nation become more prosperous, so that everyone can share in the good life that results therefrom.

The characteristic Democratic rhetoric is represented by President Franklin Roosevelt, who effectively used such phrases as "princes of privilege," "economic royalists," and "malefactors of great wealth" to rally the people to his side. However inspiring these phrases were to Democrats, they fell harshly on Republican ears. At best, they sounded to Republicans like demagoguery. At worst, they seemed to be a call to class warfare.

On the other side, Republican oratory sounds strangely heartless to Democratic ears. Republicans inveigh against "creeping socialism" and "federal handouts." At the same time as they favor more generous tax write-offs and depletion allowances for industry, they grow furious at what they believe to be an increasing number of "welfare chiselers." Their enthusiasm for "free enterprise" and "individual initiative" reminds Democrats of the elephant who cried, as he danced among the chickens, "Every man for himself!"

The miracle of America is that the poor have been made less poor under legislation often originated by Democrats but endorsed by Republicans. At the same time, industry and agriculture have continued to prosper under legislation often originated by Republicans and endorsed by Democrats.

Additionally, it seems to me that the two parties steal ideas from each other with great regularity, and then claim them as their own. Nevertheless, there is a difference in emphasis between the two parties in the way in which they approach the problems of power. Generally speaking, Republicans prefer to look upon government as a referee, adjudicating and adjusting the conflicting interests of different interest groups, different regions, and different economic blocs.

President Harry S Truman's characterization of Congress in 1948 as a "do-nothing Congress" did not trouble the Republicans, who generally feel that that is precisely what Congress ought to do.

Democrats, on the other hand, tend to think of government as a mover and shaker, the initiator of constructive and necessary social actions. The Social Security Act, the Tennessee Valley Authority, the Rural Electrification Administration—these and many ambitious measures like them are Democratic achievements, strenuously endorsed by the Republicans.

So we come back again to the question of rhetoric.

Democrats are roused to enthusiasm by activist slogans such as Wilson's "New Freedom," Roosevelt's "New Deal," Truman's "Fair Deal," Kennedy's "New Frontier," and Lyndon Johnson's "The Great Society." There is always a touch of euphoria or, in Republican eyes, megalomania, in Democratic aspirations.

Republican aspirations are phrased in more modest terms, even to the point of dullness: "Back to Normalcy," "Keep Cool with Coolidge," "A Chicken in Every Pot," "A Full Supper Pail." The limits of euphoria in Republican oratory were reached in the modest enthusiasm of "I Like Ike."

The two parties are, despite the rhetoric, not opposites, but complementaries, and I trust they will both be around for a long time to come.

II

The Party Systems

4

RICHARD JENSEN

Party Coalitions and the Search for Modern Values: 1820-1970

Development of the two-party political system. Jackson, Hamilton, and the modernizers. The Civil War — before and after. Traditionalism, moral crusades, and voter coalitions. Partisan loyalties and political strategists. Economic influence on party policies. New Deal tactics. The rise of the conservatives. Republican disintegration and current political disenchantment.

Since the 1830s two mass-based parties have dominated American politics. This chapter will argue that if groups of voters are defined primarily by their psychological outlooks and values, the coalitions of voters and interests comprising each party have been quite stable for that century and a half —a long time, indeed, in the world history of democratic politics. The forces that began to confront each other in the 1830s —before industrialization, urbanization, the Civil War, or mass immigration—persisted for so long, despite drastic social and economic changes, because they reflected the two main variations of the predominant American value system. To the extent that the value system itself was giving way in the 1970s, the two parties were decaying or collapsing.

The basic reasons the parties could reflect the society's values were, simply, that everyone could vote freely and that elected officials ran the government. Some qualifications are in order. By the middle or late 1820s (but before Andrew Jackson became president), virtually every white family was enfranchised, regardless of wealth, class, religion, location, or ethnicity. Immigrants in the nineteenth century often could vote before becoming citizens. Black families were en-franchised in the late 1860s, while full woman suffrage had to wait until World War I, as was true for most of Europe. By thinking of families rather than individuals, we can better appreciate the novelty of a society which was 80 to 90 per-cent enfranchised in a world where even 20 percent enfran-chisement was uncommon before the twentieth century. Furthermore, the electors were uncoerced and powerful. The only significant coercion was the systematic disfranchise-ment of Southern blacks from the late nineteenth century to the mid-1960s. The power came from the fact that elected legislators, governors, and other officials controlled most of the powers of government, rather than hereditary officials, lifetime appointees, or permanent bureaucrats. Since the 1950s, however, federal judges (lifetime appointees who almost never are removed or overruled by elected officials)

and tenured civil servants have become increasingly dominant. Before then, the system was highly democratic, with
few exceptions; Virginia and Kentucky, for example, were
controlled by self-perpetuating local oligarchies until the
1850s, and South Carolina, until Reconstruction. The net
effect was that voters were important, and that a majority
coalition of voters could, and did, control local, state, and national government.

The winner-take-all system of American elections forced
politics into a two-party mold.[1] Easy access to the treasury
through high-paying patronage jobs, government contracts,
or inside information provided honey enough for swarms of
eager politicians. The fact that most were drones proved only
a slight burden to society, because the economy was growing
rapidly, the jobs were turned over quickly, and the government, in peacetime, was too small before the New Deal to
have much impact anyway.

A puzzling question is why the same two parties emerged
in every state. The United States always had a very decentralized government, with the states largely independent
of Washington before the 1930s. What was to prevent
different pairs of parties in each state—perhaps with loose,
shifting, national coalitions every four years—to elect a
president? Nothing prevented it; indeed, that was the system
between 1812 and 1832—the "Era of Good Feelings," so
called because the vicious personal attacks of the era seldom
crossed state lines.

THE JACKSONIANS AND THE WHIGS

Andrew Jackson in 1828 won the White House by building a
coalition of highly disparate forces. Powerful state machines
in New York and Virginia formed the core. Old friends from
the militia campaigns helped bring the Southwest in line.

Ideological Jeffersonians brought in the Southeast. Beyond an opportune loyalty to Jackson and expectations of generous rewards, there was little to hold the Jacksonian coalition together. Voters did not show any special loyalty to the national coalition, which did not even have a name until the term "Democrat" gained currency late in the 1830s. Across the country, politicians could label themselves Jacksonians regardless of where they stood. The coalition lacked discipline and a coherent program or platform.

The Jacksonian coalition became a party only after the opposition organized a party. The key issue was modernizing the economy. Jackson and his strongest allies strongly opposed modernization policies, probably because of fear that powerful bankers would wield irresistible political power. The Jacksonians were enamored of a traditional economic order, based on subsistence farming by independent yeomen but also including plantation slavery. The modernizers wanted strong banks, a nationwide credit system, national markets, interregional transportation networks, fast development of fertile western lands, and federal stimuli to the growth of manufacturing in the form of a high protective tariff and a program of technological research. The issue was joined when Jackson set out to destroy the national bank that already was in existence. The modern-oriented business community throughout the nation rose in protest, and used its control of wealth and the press to oppose the White House. Jacksonians responded by closing their ranks to form a tightly disciplined army. They set up conventions to officially nominate legitimate Jacksonian candidates. Anyone who broke the discipline of the convention was an enemy. Taking the name "Democrats" and emphasizing automatic loyalty, the new coalition at last took the form of a modern party.

From the beginning, therefore, the Democratic and Whig parties represented distinct coalitions. The Whigs, as the party of modernization in economy and society, attracted a clear majority of voters with what we can call a "modern" psychological outlook. This outlook was enthusiastic for progress. Science, technology, and expertise generally would solve all of society's problems. Economic progress meant a money economy, national and international markets, industrialization and rapid economic growth. State and federal government had a duty to help build the infrastructure to promote growth—national banks, river and harbor improvements, turnpikes, canals, railroads, tariffs, as well as a favorable legal and tax climate.

Alexander Hamilton had articulated such a program long before the economy was ready for it. By the 1830s the economy was on the verge of takeoff. Bankers, promoters, land speculators, industrialists, investors, merchants, Southern planters, and Northern commercial farmers eagerly joined the Whigs. Modernizers likewise called for social progress. Morals, culture, religion, and family life could all be upgraded. Merit and equal opportunity should replace the traditional ethics of nepotism, male supremacy, and favoritism. Social misfits could be controlled by asylums, prisons, and reformatories. The best guarantee of a modern future would come through education, preferably some form of compulsory attendance at public schools. Social or political evils that threatened to impede progress called for destruction. Thus some modernizers crusaded against saloons, the Roman Catholic church, and slavery. The Whig party supported positive reform movements such as schools and asylums, but had too much acumen to crusade against demons that were well represented at the polls. Slavery posed an awkward problem for the modernizers. As an economic institution, slavery was modern—it was capitalistic, market-oriented, managerial agribusiness. As a social system, however, the master/slave relationship typified the antithesis of a modern, equalitarian, contractual society. The Whigs lived with the dilemma—Abraham Lincoln and Horace Greeley, for example, had no difficulty supporting slave owners like Henry Clay or Zachary Taylor for president.

Modernizers, and hence Whigs, could be found in every section of the country among every class of people. Greeley's *New York Tribune*, for example, deliberately appealed to ambitious mechanics and factory workers who aspired to become shop managers and owners. Empirical voting studies indicate that men who were more successful in the modern economy—that is, men with better jobs, more land or slaves, or greater education—were more likely to be Whigs. Conversely, unskilled workers, traditional craftsmen, and semi-literate subsistence farmers especially were more likely to be Democrats. Geographically, the centers of modernization—in particular, industrializing New England—were Whig; the periphery was Democratic. Hence market towns, transportation nodes, rich and commercial farming areas voted Whig, while the backwoods, scrubland, or frontier areas were Democratic.[2]

The Democrats were more heterogeneous. In general, the party was a coalition of particularistic, traditional groups. They had in common only an opposition—of one sort or another—to modernization. Newly formed city machines, from Tammany Hall in Manhattan to ward operations in Pittsburgh, St. Louis, Savannah, and New Orleans, were likely to affiliate with the Democrats. The machines dealt in favors, graft, payoffs, and patronage, not in modern urban management. Ethnocultural groups that steadfastly clung to traditional folkways or religious practices were—especially if they were in a distinct minority in their area—also likely to seek protection through the Democrats. Thus, Irish and German Catholics throughout the country, the Pennsylvania "Dutch" (Germans), Louisiana Creoles, and small New England sects (like Free Will Baptists) were typically Democrats.

Modernizers could be found in virtually all ethnocultural voting groups, but they were especially predominant among New England Unitarians and Congregationalists, Quakers, Scottish Presbyterians, and English Methodists. Later arrivals, such as Jews and Scandinavian Lutherans, also displayed high predispositions toward modern values. The religious values of other ethnocultural groups, in particular Roman Catholics, German Lutherans, and Southern Baptists, reinforced their historic traditionalism and bound them tighter to the Democrats. Religious outlook and theological values could themselves be modern or traditional. For example, the introspective pietistic theology of Congregationalists, Presbyterians, and Quakers was conducive to faith in progress, education, and social change. The pietistic emphasis on right behavior had a direct bearing on the politics of moral reform. By contrast, the Catholics, Episcopalians, German Lutherans, and Southern Baptists were particularistic about their membership and deeply concerned about ritual, theology, and heresy. These denominations usually avoided contact with the outside world and, conversely, resented attempts by government to impose outside moral standards. The pietists, however, vigorously propagandized their views through missionaries, colporteurs, mass revivals, and an extensive church press.

PRE-CIVIL WAR POLITICAL PRESSURES

Historians have only begun the painstaking process of identifying the causal forces that determined party affiliation before the Civil War. Any analysis of coalitions, therefore, must remain tentative for this period, although there exists more detailed evidence for the last quarter of the nineteenth century. But it is reasonable to speculate that modern psychological values, rather than class, wealth, region, age, ethnicity, or religion, were the primary factors. Not only is this theory consistent with all the evidence at hand, but it also explains otherwise puzzling characteristics of the parties.

The Democratic party, as a coalition of traditional groups whose only unifying force was fear of modernizers, could operate only through strictly imposed discipline. It was open to powerful paternalistic bosses of a type welcomed by traditional men who respected authority, were eager for favors, and did not find special privilege and corruption abhorrent. The bosses learned to mediate between disparate, even hostile elements of the Democratic coalition, thus honing the fine arts of political compromise and leadership. The modern Whig voters were far less willing to tolerate bossism or corruption in any form. Since their ranks were psychologically homogeneous, there was less demand for political leaders who could act as intermediaries and negotiators. Indeed, the leading Whigs were often noncandidates who articulated modern values through newspaper editorials, pamphlets, and books. The Democrats were always splitting into factions, as various traditional groups expressed their mutual hostility. Common fear of the modernizers always brought the factions back together, sooner or later. The Whigs were less prone to factionalism, but never displayed the sort of blind, unquestioning, traditionalistic loyalty that kept the Democrats together. Modern men wanted to think for themselves—not to be pawns of someone else. The weak loyalty augured badly for Whig survival.

In the early 1850s Whig politicians across the country realized that the Democrats, newly reunited, were practically unbeatable. Talented Whig leaders, like Lincoln, abandoned politics for more promising careers in law or business. At the same time, the Whig rank and file took up nonpartisan crusades—for establishment of public schools, prohibition of liquor, or abolition of slavery. Thus the homogeneity of the Whig party was no guarantee of survival, while the antagonistic elements of the Democratic party never strayed too far from home.

The major national and state issues of the 1830s and 1840s can be explained as projections of the values held by the two coalitions of voters. The loudest debates concerned economic modernization through tariffs, banking reforms, money policy, and aid to transportation. As it happened, the Democrats won most of the battles at the national level, but the Whigs more often won at the state level. Thus the state governments provided vast sums of money to help build railroads, turnpikes, and canals long before the federal government began its land-grant program. Despite the furor in Congress, the impact of the federal government on the economy was too slight to affect decisively the course of economic takeoff into sustained industrial growth.

In the 1850s the question of the expansion of slavery put new issues on the national agenda and altered drastically the coalitions. The new Republican party was aggressively modern. It adopted all the modernization programs of the Whigs, and went farther by welcoming the cultural modernizers. Thus the prohibitionists found themselves at home in the Republican party. Most important, the new party denounced slavery as a reactionary force—a "relic of barbarism," as the 1856 platform put it—that was unacceptable in a truly modern society. The emotional fervor of the Republican crusades of 1854 and 1856 against the slavery menace quickened political passions across the country. Ex-Whigs reentered politics in the Northern states, usually as Republicans. Ex-Democrats, particularly those of New England antecedence who had gradually adopted modern values, discovered their old party was too wedded to traditionalism. They switched to the Republicans, giving the new party a majority in every Northern state by 1860. Southern Whigs— modern men too, but proslavery—could not understand the fanaticism of formerly calm Yankees. They wandered in a political wilderness until the new Confederate government was formed on a no-party basis.

THE POLITICAL IMPACT OF
THE CIVIL WAR

The Civil War helped to modernize America. The wartime Republican administration carried out the modernization programs of the Whigs and went further, with homestead laws, land grants to railroads and colleges, high tariffs, national banks, and so on. Despite vigorous Democratic attacks, the basic wartime modernization program remained national policy for the next half century. Traditionalism, as represented by slavery, states rights, and Southern separatism, was destroyed, and the Fourteenth Amendment fixed in the Constitution the basic modern legal principle of equal treatment under the law. Socially and politically, the economic modernizers assumed unchallenged leadership in America.

Despite the victory for modernizers, traditionalism also made certain gains in the Civil War. The destruction of plantation slavery left the South a backward, semicolonial region. Yankee entrepreneurs helped to build and finance a new railroad system for the South—so its raw cotton could be exported and manufactured goods imported. The effect was to retard industrialization and urbanization. Yankee reformers during Reconstruction tried to impose modern systems of public schools and local government, but these efforts were not well received. Southern politics suffered from the worst traditional practices—feuds, violence, assassination, massive corruption, military intervention, fraudulent elections, and routine coercion—all in a pessimistic mood that combined bitter nostalgia and vicious racism. The systematic disfranchisement of black voters, a process that extended from 1890 to 1910, permitted the South to restore its domestic tranquility at the expense of denial of the modern value of racial equality. Disfranchisement techniques, like

the poll tax, also removed a large fraction of the most traditional backwoods white voters—the "hillbillies" and
"crackers." This left the small modern section dominant in
Southern politics throughout the twentieth century, despite
occasionally successful counterattacks by reactionary (i.e.,
traditionalistic) leaders like Huey Long in Louisiana, James
Vardaman in Mississippi, and Tom Watson in Georgia.

Traditionalism also gained in the North—not in the way
society worked or in the policies adopted, for modernization
moved ahead rapidly, but in the style of political behavior
and the composition of voter coalitions. The heroic and hor-
rible memories of war helped to fix partisan loyalty even
deeper into the American psyche. During the war, as even
his critics admitted, Lincoln was "popular with the plain
people, who believe him honest, with the rich people, who
believe him safe, with the soldiers, who believe him their
friend, and with the religious people, who believe him to have
been specially raised up for this crisis." Martyrdom made
him the symbol of national unity and of the Republican party. The Republicans "waved the bloody shirt" for decades,
urging veterans to vote the way they shot (presumably
against Democrats). The Democrats had an array of new
charges, all of which attacked the modernizing thrust of the
GOP and portrayed the Democratic party as the only true
friend of the worker or farmer threatened by forced modernization and of the Catholics harassed by "Puritan" reformers. Orators branded the GOP as the puppet of railroads,
monopolists, even world bankers.

Above all, the Democrats, both North and South, relied on
appeals to white supremacy. The unskilled ethnic laborers in
the towns and cities were terrified that what scant security
they had in their jobs, or protection they could afford their
womenfolk, would be challenged by allegedly inferior
races—especially blacks, but also, on the Pacific Coast, the
Chinese. In the South the appeal for white solidarity dissolved the biracial coalition of Republicans that had

emerged, thanks to federal intervention, during Reconstruction. Southern voter coalitions thus were polarized as black
Republicans and white Democrats, with the latter in complete control of state and local affairs. In the North there
were never enough black voters to have a significant impact
on elections. But there was enough fear of blacks, plus
enough credible evidence, to charge that the GOP was committed to a policy of racial equality and to provide ammuni-
tion for Northern Democrats until the 1920s.

The new traditionalism in the Republican party produced
a decline in moral commitment on the part of the leadership.
The quest for jobs, power, and privilege displaced the crusad-
ing impulse to reform society. The first generation of GOP
leaders retired or was forced out of office by army veterans
whose loyalties to leaders like General Grant had been fused
on the battlefield. In 1872 most of the older idealists in the
party revolted and set up a new "Liberal Republican" movement to express the historic faith in modernization as the
primary mission of the Republican heritage. The movement
was a fiasco. A desperate coalition of losers formed when the
Democrats decided not to run their own candidate in 1872
and instead endorsed the Liberal nominee, Horace Greeley.
An incongruous match it was, for no American had been as
articulate as Greeley in denouncing Democratic traditionalism. The enormous patronage resources of President Grant
and his regulars overwhelmed the Liberals in every state.
The episode strengthened the professional politicians in both
parties, ensuring that government in the last quarter of the
century would work primarily for their benefit.

VOTER PARTICIPATION AND POLITICAL STRATEGY

Voter coalitions were highly stable in the late nineteenth
century. Estimates by historians suggest that normally

fewer than 5 percent of the voters changed parties between elections, or split their tickets to vote for candidates of different parties. Parties were like armies fighting at the polls for the spoils of victory. Politicians were like generals — many had been generals or colonels in the war — whose strategy was to whip up enthusiasm among the rank and file. Parades, speechfests, all-day picnics, and continuous door-to-door solicitation maximized interest and minimized the risk of defections. Newspapers — at the time, the primary medium — were designed to provide a steady flow of detailed information on politics. News columns and editorial pages were hardly distinguishable as editors prided themselves on the red-hot shot they fired at political enemies. The highly politicized electorate, despite its lack of formal education beyond the minimum level for literacy, appreciated the fine points of argument and debate. The typical voter relished an articulate long speech unravelling the complexity of national monetary, trade, or constitutional policy. Like a movie patron of the 1970s who feels a bit cheated if the show does not last at least ninety minutes, the voters demanded orators who both knew their material and could put on a full performance. The intensity of citizen involvement pushed turnout rates to remarkable levels. Even though half the voters were farmers who faced very bad roads at election time, presidential elections typically attracted 75 to 85 percent of the eligible men. Indeed, in the 1880s and 1890s, the turnout in hundreds of counties routinely exceeded 90 percent. Politics was the organized sport of the era.

With partisan loyalties rigidly fixed, political strategists emphasized the turnout of supporters rather than the conversion of opponents. Since the pool of "independents" or nonpartisans was so small, politicians did not waste time trying to discover new issues that might result in new coalitions. The two major parties were evenly matched, with many elections decided by margins of one or two percentage points. Illegal voting, bribery, and fraud, therefore, could determine the outcome, so both parties were on the alert. Corrupt practices were the norm in the South and in the largest cities, particularly for local contests. In major statewide or national elections, however, fraud, coercion, and corruption were seldom decisive. More important was fluctuation in turnout. An intense partisan, who was dissatisfied with the performance of his party or with the specific candidate, would simply sulk at home instead of voting for the enemy. Thorough door-to-door canvassing was needed to identify and head off such problems. If an entire group became dissatisfied, the chance of sustaining a winning coalition dropped. Hence politicians routinely gave nominal recognition to every element of their coalition in the form of patronage and minor nominations.

The GOP and the dominance of modern values

Professional politicians strenuously resisted legislation that might disrupt their delicate coalitions. Thus after 1876, when the issues of Civil War and Reconstruction were finally settled, the main topics of concern were money, tariffs, and prohibition. Modernization was still the underlying issue. The Republicans advocated continued rapid economic development, emphasizing the need for strong banks, national markets, and subsidies to the manufacturing sector. The Democrats, faced with an increasingly industrialized economy in which even farmers produced more for the market than for family consumption, no longer tried to reverse trends. They did, however, try to slow the process. Debates on money and tariffs gave voters a deeper understanding of their society and a chance to match their own values and outlook with appropriate national policies. The modern voter thus could identify with the Republicans as the party of industry and progress, feel proud, and grow optimistic about the future of a country led by statesmen like

James G. Blaine and William McKinley. Prohibition, however, introduced a crosscutting issue that threatened to divide the Republican coalition.

The consensus on economic modernization within the party did not extend to moral issues. The GOP had made significant gains among beer-drinking Germans—a rapidly growing population element concentrated in major states like New York, Illinois, and Ohio. The Germans comprised a majority of the skilled artisans, foremen, and factory workers in industrial centers like Chicago, St. Louis, Milwaukee, Detroit, Buffalo, Newark, and Baltimore. While religious traditionalism, especially among Catholics, pulled the Germans toward the Democrats, aspirations for upward mobility into the Republican middle class were producing significant vote totals the GOP could not afford to forfeit. On the other hand, the core of the party, as always, comprised moralistic, old-stock, British and Scandinavian voters with strong pietistic commitments. Now that the slavery issue was dead, the reforming impulse of the pietistic Protestants inevitably pointed toward the abolition of the saloon, including the prohibition of the manufacture and sale of liquor, wine, and beer. (Drinking itself was never actually prohibited, even in the 1920s.) The professional leadership of the GOP, therefore, had to head off grass-roots movements that threatened to weaken decisively the party coalition. From 1878 to 1892 a struggle raged for power inside the GOP. The pietistic crusaders used the party's decentralized formal structure to gain control of local, county, and state conventions and thus to proclaim official support for temperance and to nominate dry candidates. The crusaders typically were intensely anti-Catholic. Party leaders discovered that compromise and patronage were utterly inadequate to divert the single-minded reformers. As defections mounted and state after state was lost in the early 1890s, the professionals finally turned to crude power politics, crushing the drys and banning the liquor issue from the agenda for another quarter century.

In the process of conciliating all elements of their coalition while beating back the challenge of amateur moralists, the professional Republican leaders developed new principles that would guide the GOP to victory after victory for forty years. McKinley pluralism, to give credit to its outstanding spokesman, attempted to join the needs of American society as a whole with those of the Republican party. The idea was that the GOP would henceforth be a coalition of diverse cultural groups united by a commitment to economic modernization. Intergroup cultural conflict would not be tolerated. Moralists who wanted to get rid of minority customs — beer-drinking, parochial schools, foreign-language teaching, Sunday sports, etc. — could no longer use the party as their vehicle. The GOP would avoid nominating candidates who were blatantly anti-Catholic or racist. Ethnic pluralism would be protected, and in return the ethnics would support the businessmen's economic program. Labor unions would, for the first time, be tolerated and encouraged by the governing party with the understanding that the unions wanted bread-and-butter benefits — higher wages, better conditions, more job security — rather than a revolutionary change in government or economy. Thus McKinley and his successors developed close ties to the trade union movement, and the long, violent strikes that embittered both labor and the middle classes in the 1870s, 1880s, and 1890s gave way to a spirit of compromise that lasted until after the First World War.

Prosperity was the key ingredient. Explicit in McKinleyism was the promise that economic modernization, sustained growth, and further rapid industrialization would guarantee jobs for all, high wages and salaries, good prices for farmers, and handsome profits for business. Nothing sounded better in 1896, when the country had suffered three years of deep depression in every sector of the economy. The depression ended when McKinley entered the White House and, apart from downturns that lasted no more than a year, full employment, rapid growth, high profits, and general prosperity continued to 1929. The Republican premise that a modern economy could be gauged in pay envelopes, and at cash registers and grain elevators, thus remained unassailable by opposition politicians for a third of a century—long enough for the GOP to entrench itself in courthouses and statehouses across the land, not to mention the White House, for seven of the nine presidential terms from 1896 to 1932.

The depth of Republican control is exemplified by the stranglehold on state legislatures. After the 1906 off-year elections, Republicans had large majorities in every Northern state except Ohio (where Republicans held a narrow lead), while the Democrats held the Southern states by equally massive margins. Thus, Michigan sent 127 Republicans and 5 Democrats to Lansing, while Arkansas sent 128 Democrats and 5 Republicans to Little Rock. Only the Border states were competitive (e.g., Kentucky with 65 Republicans and 73 Democrats). Since the North was far richer and more populous than the South, the primacy of the GOP could be threatened only if the party split, as it did briefly in 1912–1914. By 1920, however, the Republicans had healed their splits and returned to the McKinley patterns. The Pennsylvania legislature after the 1926 election thus was Republican by a 236–22 margin, while Tennessee was Democratic by 108–24. The border remained competitive, with the Missouri legislature exactly split 92–92.

The progressives

Turnout fell precipitously after 1896 throughout the nation, as Paul Kleppner's chapter in this volume demonstrates. By 1912 only half the adult men in large Northern cities were voting in presidential elections—with the rest either disfranchised by registration laws or too apathetic to bother. The result was that modern middle-class voters dominated elections everywhere except in the poor ethnic areas of large cities, which were controlled by boss-dominated machines, and in sleepy rural areas that were controlled by courthouse cliques. The middle-class hegemony produced crusades to permanently install modern middle-class values in government at all levels. This was the "progressive" movement. In modernizing government and society at large, the progressives sought to banish all forms of traditionalism — boss control, corrupt practices, big-business intervention in politics, "ignorant" voting, and excessive power in the hands of hack politicians. Efficiency and the application of expertise to public issues led to the enhanced power of technicians—especially municipal consultants, city managers, public health officers, and school superintendents—at the expense of the traditional patronage system. While party affiliation continued to follow the historic divisions, the importance of party itself declined. Nowhere was this more notable than in Congress where, in 1910, progressives succeeded in changing the rules to strip party leaders of their power and hand it to committee chairmen. Henceforth, control of national legislation was gained by virtue of seniority (i.e., experience), regardless of loyalty to the party platforms. The progressives expected that interested experts would stay in Congress long enough to become chairmen, but that party hacks would tire of the game and satisfy their ambitions outside Washington.

On the whole, the system performed exactly as planned. One unexpected consequence, however, was that from the 1930s to the early 1970s the congressmen with the highest seniority were Southerners—experts in legislation, all right, but not necessarily progressive or modern in outlook. The reason was that, for highly talented Southern lawyers and politicians, Congress offered greater opportunities for career advancement than was possible in their poor, rural, home states. The congressional chairmen formed alliances with the business, agricultural, banking, and (occasionally) labor union lobbies, on the one hand, and with the growing bureaucracy, especially the military, on the other. The result was that voters had little representation in Washington except to the extent that their interests were sponsored by one or another organized lobby.

The only interruption of Republican control came in the Wilson years, 1912–1920, when Democrats capitalized on the fissure in the GOP to capture the White House, Congress, and, briefly, some governorships and legislatures in the North. Woodrow Wilson himself was a modernizer who responded more faithfully to the demands of the middle class than to the sentiments of farmers, ethnics, or city machines. The reason is that his base within the Democratic party rested largely on the middle class in the South. Democrats who took power during the era emulated the modernizing programs of the GOP, differing chiefly in their willingness to accord Catholics more patronage. Wilson himself fired the moralism and idealism of the middle classes with his stirring call for a war for democracy, a crusade to modernize the politics of the entire globe. Traditional voters, however, could not identify with the domestic programs implemented during the war, such as prohibition, the draft, woman suffrage, forced "Americanization" of immigrants, and violent attacks on German-American culture. Hence the traditional Irish, German, and Slavic support for the Democrats collapsed in 1920, with ethnic cities like New York, Detroit, Pittsburgh, Chicago, and Buffalo returning massive Republican majorities.

Wilson's leadership in nationwide reform movements created a dilemma for the Democrats that they were unable to resolve in the 1920s. As long as politics focused on local issues, the party was healthy, for its policy positions could easily be tailored to fit the traditionalism of Northern ethnics without disturbing the Southern wing, and vice versa. National issues, especially war and prohibition, however, exposed the incompatible interests in the Democratic coalition, forcing the national party to sway one way or the other,

thus alternating large blocs of voters. The party nearly rup-
tured in 1924 as Northern ethnics and Southern prohibitionists could find no common ground. The nomination of the
Catholic leader Al Smith in 1928, similarly, led to massive
desertions throughout the South, especially in the more
modern-oriented Southern cities.

Socialism

The hegemony of modern values in the McKinley era explains why socialism failed to make inroads in the United
States at the same time it was gaining the political support of
most European workers. In the first place, a large proportion
of the blue-collar labor force was comprised of immigrants
who were disfranchised by citizenship and literacy tests.
Others were staunch Catholics who clung to the Democratic
party as the protector of traditional life-styles. Of course, a
small Socialist party did compete in American elections, but
it never won an office more important than mayor of a small
city. About half of the Socialists were immigrants, especially
Germans and Jews, who were continuing European modes of
protest without regard to the American situation. One of the
strongest appeals of European socialism was its promise of
modernizing society along "scientific lines" (i.e., Marxist
science). Thus it promised to destroy the power of established
churches, entrenched aristocracies, great landowners, and
standing armies.

Such appeals proved ineffective in a society already dedicated to rapid modernization, where emblems of traditional
privilege were weak or nonexistent. (The rich in America
had built their own fortunes—very few had rich grand-
fathers, let alone a titled lineage.) In the handful of cities
where Socialist mayors held power for more than a decade—
Milwaukee, Wisconsin, Rockford, Illinois, and Bridgeport,
Connecticut—success was due to platforms that emphasized
honest government and frugal management, but that never

mentioned a revolution of the proletariat. The small labor-union movement, comprised chiefly of building tradesmen, skilled railroad workers, and coal miners, adjusted to the situation by concentrating on improving wages and working conditions. To accomplish this goal, they struck convenient alliances with local Republican and Democratic leaders and avoided contact with radical causes. The brewery workers' union, entirely German, debated socialism at its conventions, while the rank and file voted Democratic to head off prohibition.

THE DEPRESSION AND THE NEW DEAL

The McKinley coalition collapsed under the deadweight of the Great Depression. All sectors of the economy suffered as the gross national product (GNP) shrank from $3,509 per capita in 1929 to only $2,423 in 1932 (these figures are in 1977 dollars; by contrast, the GNP in 1977 reached nearly $9,000 per capita). At one time or another during the dozen years of depression, nearly half the American population received some form of government relief. Charity was painful—most recipients refused to talk about it later, but all remembered the hunger, the humiliation, the loss of hope that darkened their lives. All classes suffered— the rich lost their assets, storekeepers closed their shops, mortgage holders foreclosed. The worst suffering, however, was felt by men who were economically most marginal. Since even at the worst of times three-fourths of the labor force had employment, job losses fell heavily on the least skilled, the inexperienced young, and the older men no one would rehire. The psychic shock undermined the old faith that industrialization promised higher levels of wealth for all, and that personal inculcation of modern values—ambition, faith in technology, education—guaranteed success in America.

Loss of faith in modernity gave new strength to the ideal of job security, essentially a traditional outlook, as the best hope for men trying to cope with hardship. Thus the ingredients for a radical shift in power, from the more modern to the more traditional world view, were available if only a leader could somehow put together the right combination of ideals, policies, and voter coalitions.

Franklin Roosevelt was that leader. His triumph in 1932 did not, however, mark a realignment of coalitions. Every sector of society had, to one degree or another, recognized that Republican efforts to reverse the downward slide into chaos had failed, and thus every group shifted, temporarily, toward the Democrats. Roosevelt's challenge was to make that uniform, across-the-board shift permanent. Hence the objective of the "First New Deal" (1933–1934) was to discover what every identifiable interest group in America wanted the government to do and then to try to enact it, regardless of the confusion and contradictions that might ensue. During the "Hundred Days" in March, April, and May 1933 legislation was rushed through Congress to help farmers and cities, labor unions and industrialists, bank owners and depositors, importers and exporters, conservationists and dam builders, the unemployed and the stock market investors, the wets and even (by ending bootlegging) the moralists.

The New Deal succeeded in rallying the economy, but it failed to restore prosperity. Unemployment shrank for a while, then flattened out at 16 percent, five times the 1929 level. GNP per capita during Roosevelt's first term averaged 97 percent of the level during 1930–1932. In frustration, the business community deserted Roosevelt's grand coalition by 1935. The erratic multiplication of alphabetical agencies seemed to threaten constitutional government itself—no mean threat in an era of dictators—and cost Roosevelt the support of old Democratic leaders like Al Smith. The New Dealers themselves were nervous about the threat from the left, represented by spellbinders like Senator Huey Long, Dr. Townsend, and Father Coughlin. There is no hard evidence that these men posed any real threat to Roosevelt's reelection chances, but the White House was just as frustrated and worried as Wall Street.

Roosevelt's solution to his political crisis was to revive and extend a theme that had proven effective in 1932—blame the society's troubles on evildoers and crusade against them. In 1931 and 1932 Democrats pinned the blame on Hoover himself, labeling the tin-and-tarpaper shanty towns that had mushroomed up "Hoovervilles," and the newspapers that covered shivering men on park benches "Hoover blankets." They had ridiculed Hoover's reputation as the "Great Engineer" by calling him a "stationary engineer" who had "ditched, drained and damned the country." In 1935–1936 the attack widened to include all men of wealth—"economic royalists"—whose blind greed not only caused the depression, but whose reactionary opposition was now sabotaging recovery.

Powerful rhetoric alone would probably have ensured Roosevelt's reelection in 1936, but the president sought a permanent revolution in the party system that would enshrine the Democrats as the majority party for generations to come. He accomplished this goal by strengthening the loyalties of old Democratic blocks, by purging party leaders who disagreed with the New Deal, and by bringing new groups into the fold. The key elements in the strategy were ethnic voters in large cities, labor unions, and rural Southerners. Roosevelt lavished attention, patronage, and relief funds on the big-city Democratic machines, especially those in Chicago, Jersey City, the Bronx, Kansas City, and Boston. Reformers were aghast, but Roosevelt knew that the traditionalist Catholics comprised a fourth of the potential electorate. The ethnic groups that previously had had low turnout patterns now surged to the polls in record numbers, producing 3-to-1 Democratic margins in industrial neighborhoods around the country. Black leaders were invited to join their old adversary, deserting *en masse* the party of Lincoln. Since a mere 2 percent of the actual voters were black (disfranchisement persisted in the South), the changeover added only a little at a time. When the black electorate finally reached full power in the 1960s, Roosevelt's foresight amply rewarded his party.

Patronage and recognition helped woo the ethnics, but relief money proved an irresistible lure. The vast majority of relief clients voted Democratic. The largest federal relief agency played its payrolls like an accordion in the heat of election dates. The peak enrollment of the Works Progress Administration (WPA), for example, was 3.3 million men, achieved during the month of the 1938 elections. Federal agricultural programs were targeted on cotton and tobacco farmers in the South and wheat farmers in the Midwest. The farmers, in turn, responded enthusiastically in favor of the New Deal. Roosevelt's masterstroke was legislative and executive intervention to build up the labor unions. In 1932 the unions were weak, small, and internally divided. By 1940 they enlisted 12 million members, galvanized into class consciousness through a series of major strikes in basic industries. Unions thus gained the membership, the money, and the motivation to support the New Deal's attacks on business.

Roosevelt miscalculated in his efforts to purge his opponents from power. A thinly veiled attempt to pack the Supreme Court in 1937 revived fears of dictatorship, and suggested that modern faith in the supremacy of an impartial judiciary was anathema to the New Deal. Modernist opponents began calling themselves "conservatives." They defeated Roosevelt on the court issue and turned back his efforts to unseat uncooperative congressmen. The conservatives emphasized that the New Deal meant higher taxes, to be paid by the middle class on behalf of the growing army of reliefers. They also charged that Roosevelt's militant allies in the labor unions were thwarting short-term recovery by their strikes and endangering the managerial control of industry that was a prerequisite for continued economic growth.

LIBERALS V. CONSERVATIVES

By the late 1930s American politics had crystallized along liberal/conservative lines. The liberals emphasized the faults of modernization, the need for federal remedies, and the traditional core value of economic security. The conservatives argued that the modernist ideals of efficiency, progress, and personal achievement were being undermined by the New Deal's antibusiness posture. Class lines came to dominate voting behavior, though a strong residue of ethnic partisan habits persisted. Blue-collar workers in the North voted 63 percent Democratic in presidential and congressional elections from 1936 to 1968. White-collar voters in the same period, however, averaged 57 percent Republican. Northern white Protestants averaged 58 percent Republican, while Catholics averaged 68 percent Democratic. The class and religious components added together, so that Catholic blue-collar workers were 76 percent Democratic versus 52 percent Democratic for Protestant blue-collar workers. Better-educated, higher-income, white-collar voters were more Republican. Thus the average Northern Protestant white-collar voter was 69 percent Republican from 1936 to 1968, while his Catholic counterpart was only 41 percent Republican. The two polar groups in the Northern electorate, therefore, were Catholic blue-collar workers who provided the core of the Democratic party, and Protestant businessmen, professionals, and clerical workers who similarly dominated the GOP. The Jewish vote was never large—about 3 percent of the total electorate—but it was staunchly Democratic.

Northern blacks, a growing segment of the electorate, were consistently Democratic from 1936 to 1962, and after 1964 cast 90 percent or more of their ballots for Democratic candidates. Northern farmers, a largely Protestant, probusiness group of dwindling size, averaged 60 percent Republican during the era.[3]

The fierce conflict between liberals and conservatives dominated national politics between 1936 and 1972. So evenly balanced were the coalitions in that era that the Democrats won six presidential contests and the Republicans four. However, four contests (1944, 1948, 1960, and 1968) were very close; had they gone the other way, the Democrats would have claimed only four to the GOP's six. The Democratic tenure in the White House, however, was largely neutralized by conservative control of Congress. A coalition of Northern Republicans and Southern Democrats overpowered liberal Northern Democrats on most roll calls from 1938 to 1964. The conservative coalition also controlled the key committees during this period. From 1941 to 1948 the conservatives were able to overcome presidential vetoes. They used their power to abolish the more repugnant New Deal agencies, especially the WPA, and to enact legislation to curb labor unions. The conservative cause gained additional momentum during World War II, when the federal income tax grew enormously. Previously, only the richest tenth of the population, a heavily Republican group, paid income taxes; by 1944 nearly all employed families had become familiar with withholding taxes, and therefore listened more closely to conservative arguments that big spending meant smaller paychecks. After the war, the conservatives took the lead in lowering taxes and in abolishing rationing and price controls. The result was that liberals, who hoped to institute centralized planning through federal spending and controls, became thoroughly frustrated. The rapid growth of the private sector of the economy after the war dissipated fears of another depression, and undercut the liberal argument that Republican policies would produce another disaster.

At the state level, the conservative coalitions were dominant nearly everywhere from 1940 through 1958. The larger Northern states usually had Republican governors, while the Southern Democratic governors were conservatives. The state legislatures were the chief bastions of conservatism. The system of district elections, often gerrymandered to neutralize metropolitan population majorities, gave enormous leverage to the conservative businessmen, professionals, and wealthy farmers of the smaller cities, towns, and rural areas. Large liberal majorities in the central cities were thereby rendered ineffective. With wealth increasing, state treasuries had ample new funds without increases in tax rates. The conservative state governments spent heavily on highways, schools, and colleges—modernizing programs that encouraged business growth and favored the middle-class youth who went on to college in large numbers. Welfare spending was kept at a minimum, as were all forms of subsidies to poorer groups. The suburbs, in particular, benefited from these programs as the control cities became more and more dilapidated. The response of Democrats to this adverse situation in the states was to downplay their liberalism, and to adopt policy positions that were distinct from the conservatives only in terms of greater support for the rights of labor unions to conduct strikes. Occasionally a Democrat would win the governorship of a major state—notably Adlai Stevenson in Illinois (1948–1952) and Averell Harriman in New York (1954–1958). Their terms involved few liberal innovations and seldom resulted in reelection.

THE EISENHOWER COMPROMISE
AND REPUBLICAN DISUNITY

The Eisenhower administration offered a blend of modern and traditional values that calmed the intense debates of prior decades. The formula was to pursue moderately conservative programs, supported by appeals to the primacy for national security over individual security. The anticommunist Cold War policies, a direct legacy of Wilson's dreams of modernizing the world, were transmuted into a defense of the American way of life. Eisenhower ended the Korean War and made sure there were no American boys who died on foreign battlefields. The social security system was expanded, with old-age payments in 1956 tripling the level of 1952. Modernizing programs of interstate highway expansion and federal aid to higher education were justified under the rubric of "national defense." Strident rhetoric of left and right disappeared from the land as even Democratic leaders proudly announced they were closer in spirit to Eisenhower than were their Republican counterparts.

Eisenhower's compromises increasingly unsettled modernizers. A conservative revolt demanding return to the pre-bureaucratic modern values of the McKinley era was spearheaded by Senator Barry Goldwater. The 1964 campaign produced a landslide for the Democrats, but it also permanently shifted the GOP toward a more militant antiliberal posture. John Kennedy's administration demonstrated that the Democratic party, including its big-city Catholic wing, had adopted modern values, too. In foreign policy, the shift in the 1960s was toward exerting America's full weight as a modernizing influence throughout the world, especially in Asia. In domestic affairs, the Democrats pushed for more rapid economic growth and full exploitation of the latest technology, climaxed by landing a man on the moon. The drive for civil rights for blacks—that is, full equality under the law regardless of the traditionalism of the rural South—reflected the commitment to a totally modern society.

The Southern and Catholic backlash against civil rights programs demonstrated that ethnocentric traditionalism was not dead in America. Democratic presidential candidates found it increasingly difficult to keep together the

Roosevelt coalition of Catholics, blacks, and white Southerners. Even the Jewish vote, long the most liberal and Democratic of constituencies, began slipping away on the issue of
defending Israel. Richard Nixon's landslide in 1972 marked
the first time a Republican candidate swept every region of
the country. True, Jimmy Carter was able to appeal to
Southern identity in his narrow 1976 victory, but it remains
doubtful whether a Yankee Democrat could again bring the
white South back to the fold.

Republican success at the presidential level reflected more
the disunity of the Democrats than the continued vitality of
the GOP. Demography was destroying the voter base of the
Republican party. From 1940, when 40 percent of the people
identified themselves as Republican, the slide was steadily
downward, until by 1977 only 20 percent were Republican.
The Democratic share held steady at 40 percent, with the
difference representing a rapid surge toward "independent"
status. The effect was most devastating at the state and local
levels, where contests between relatively obscure candidates
typically turn on party identification. After the 1976 elections, the Republicans were left with a mere twelve governors, down from thirty-two as recently as 1968. In only six
states did the Republicans control both houses of the legislature—Colorado, Idaho, New Hampshire, South Dakota,
and Wyoming—and only in New Hampshire did the Republicans have full control of state government, while the Democrats enjoyed this advantage in twenty-nine states. In 1968
Republicans fully controlled sixteen states, including New
York, California, Illinois, and Ohio. Once solid Republican
suburbs—notably those near New York, Chicago, and Philadelphia—increasingly elected Democrats to local office. The
implications were drastic. The GOP had been effectively
destroyed as a governing party on the state and local level.
Only well-funded, well-publicized, glamour candidates could
induce enough Democrats to split their tickets to win
statewide contests. Congress likewise saw a once competitive

Republican force reduced to a 1-in-3 minority. The ray of hope, curiously, was at the presidential level, where the disparate nature of the Democratic coalition itself handed the Republican candidate a good shot if he or she did not identify too closely with the GOP. Richard Nixon recognized the situation exactly when he operated his 1972 campaign quite independently of his party.

TODAY'S CHANGE IN VALUES

Why was the Republican party suffering a demographic disaster while the Democrats flourished? The answer may well involve a systematic rejection of modern values on the part of the well-educated youth of America. The signs started appearing in the late 1950s and early 1960s, growing rapidly after 1963. Youth demanded freedom from the tight psychological self-control demanded by the modern value system. The ideals of ambition, hard study, and upward mobility meant less and less to young people raised in an affluent society. Personal liberation meant marijuana, sexual experimentation, rock music, and radical activism. Patriotism lost its glamour in the mud flats of Vietnam. Ghetto riots, urban decay, support for reactionary dictatorships, were all seen as indicators of the hypocrisy of modern values. Traditional life-styles, especially those of ghetto blacks, cast an irresistible charm.

For a while in the late 1960s a sharp generation gap seemed to be opening. Nixon's appeal to the "forgotten majority," that is, to older Americans who saw their values challenged by the demonstrators on college campuses, proved effective in 1972. But the cultural crisis began to spread rapidly to other age cohorts, abetted in part by the media. The economy seemed out of control; inflation, recession, food shortages, and energy emergencies came so fast that the public lost confidence in the experts of government, finance, and business. Disgrace, scandal, and humiliation tarnished the image of many local politicians, and of the Central Intelligence Agency, the Federal Bureau of Investigation, and even the White House, undercutting the modern faith in the capability of national leadership. Science and technology came under attack, as interest in the occult blossomed. Rigid sex roles gave way, and even the institution of marriage was bypassed. In a word, a loose set of "postmodern" values emerged, drawing support from the best-educated groups that once were the mainstay of modernity and Republicanism. Postmodern politics gravitated toward the Democrats because of the special affinity of the postmoderns toward the poor and dispossessed—traditional groups the Democrats had long championed.

Whether a postmodern political movement will gain force remains to be seen. Certainly, few serious candidates will soon try to reassemble George McGovern's coalition. Perhaps the most important impact of the postmodern challenge lies in the rapid spread of cynicism and apathy. Today fewer people identify closely with political parties than ever before in the 150-year sweep of history surveyed here. Fewer people vote, and fewer people care. The result may well be that government power increasingly is concentrated in the hands of civil service bureaucrats and judges who do not see themselves as duty bound to express the popular will in their decisions. If that comes to pass, the world's first democratic polity will have abandoned its heritage.

5

PAUL KLEPPNER

Coalitional and Party Transformations in the 1890s

Sectional priorities and the third-party system. National Republican dominance and the Democratic South. Pietists vs. antipietist groups. Parties as "political churches." The Prohibition party. Capitalism and the 1893 depression: unemployment, the silver market, the Farmers' Alliance, and the Populists. Cleveland, Bryan, McKinley, and Hanna. The new Republican party.

> ... the Democratic party as we knew it is dead.
>   Grover Cleveland (1900)

Grover Cleveland was accurate—but tardy—in pronouncing the requiem for his old party. The death knell for what the former president regarded as "true Democracy" had sounded at the party's national convention in July 1896.[1] By committing the Democratic party to the Free Silver crusade, and by nominating William Jennings Bryan as the reborn party's standard bearer, the Southern and Western agrarians repudiated both the fiscal orthodoxy of the Cleveland administration and the traditional leadership of the party. They seized control of the national organization and claimed legitimate and exclusive right to use the party label. By symbolically fusing that time-hallowed name with the cause of currency inflation, they at once precipitated a withdrawal of the old-stock "business" Democrats from the ranks of the party managers and opened the party organization at its grass roots to Free Silverites regardless of their former party connections.

While Cleveland correctly diagnosed the condition of the traditional Democratic party, he failed to perceive the operation of similar dynamics within the Republican party. For "McKinleyism" no more represented the Republicanism of the earlier nineteenth century than "Bryanism" did the old-fashioned Democratic faith. The Republican party transformation was accomplished less dramatically. But it was an even more significant change, for it was the redeveloped Republican party which controlled most of the nation's policymaking institutions after 1896.

Even general descriptions of those developments underscore the fact that these *fin de siècle* party battles represented more than a continuation of "politics as usual." Something extraordinary was at stake, and the results had a significance that far transcended most electoral battles. Both of the major parties experienced drastic changes in their coalitional bases, in the balance between their factional formations, and in their policy orientations. While they retained their traditional names, after the mid-1890s neither "Democrat" nor "Republican" represented, tangibly or symbolically, the same groups as each had earlier. The electoral convulsions of the 1890s transformed their political characters as well as their social bases of mass support.

We can begin to understand this party redevelopment by examining the broad contours of the involved electoral shifts and their geographic and social sources. Those examinations can provide clues into the nature and significance of the change in party political characters.

FROM PARTISAN STALEMATE TO REPUBLICAN DOMINANCE

The decade of the 1890s witnessed an abrupt, massive, and durable shift in the competitive balance between the nation's major parties, ending two decades of partisan stalemate in which neither major party regularly commanded the allegiance of a majority of the nation's voters (see table 1). During the 1870s and 1880s, and especially in the heavily populated mid-Atlantic and East-North-Central areas, elections were hard fought and their results determined by margins of a few thousand votes. Overwhelming strength in the ex-Confederate states offset the slight Republican margin in the rest of the country and produced a narrow national lead for the Democrats.

Competitive party struggles and close election outcomes meant that after the mid-1870s neither party was able to exercise control for any extended period over policymaking institutions. At the national level, for example, only once did each party simultaneously control the presidency and both houses of Congress. At the state level, except for the Southern states, partisan control over governorships and state legislatures was remarkably evenly divided.[2]

Table 1
Change in Partisanship and Participation by Regions

Regions[a]	Partisan leads		Shift in competitiveness 1882–1892/ 1894–1904	Turnout percentages		Change in turnout 1874–1892/ 1900–1918
	1882–1892	1894–1904		1874–1892	1900–1918	
New England	8.1R	23.6R	−15.5	56.4	47.9	− 8.5
Mid-Atlantic[b]	0.1R	16.9R	−16.8	67.9	55.1	−12.8
East-North-Central	1.1R	14.8R	−13.7	74.9	61.3	−13.6
West-North-Central[c]	18.1R	23.5R	− 5.4	64.8	61.7	− 3.1
South[d]	32.6D	39.1D	− 6.5	56.1	24.6	−31.5
Border[e]	10.9D	0.6D	+10.3	66.4	65.8	− 0.6
Mountain	11.7R	3.8D	+ 7.9	54.8	74.1	+19.3
Pacific	3.5R	15.5R	−12.0	52.8	43.6	− 9.2
U.S.: Non-South	2.4R	14.5R	−12.1	67.3	57.6	− 9.7
U.S.: Total	3.7D	7.7R	− 4.0	64.8	51.1	−13.7

aExcept as otherwise indicated, these are standard census regions.
bExcludes Delaware.
cExcludes Missouri.

dEleven ex-Confederate states.
eDelaware, Kentucky, Maryland, Missouri, Oklahoma, West Virginia.

However muted they may appear from the data in table 1, there were clear sectional polarities underlying the distributions of party strength during the full course of the country's third-party system (1853–1892). Indeed, it was those polarities, unknown in U.S. politics prior to the mid-1850s, which largely shaped that party system and its associated policy outputs. The sectional swings of the 1850s involved enormous value and interest conflicts between Yankee pietist subculture and white Southern subculture. The resulting reorganization of the party system and its policy outputs along sectional lines produced the eventual extinction of slavery and the displacement, temporarily at least, of the cultural-economic elites who defended it.

At the same time, strident Yankee moralism elicited negative reactions among other Northern groups, and especially among those ethnic and religious groups which did not share the single-minded Yankee compulsion to make their world "holy" and culturally homogeneous. Thus, ethnoreligious conflict, which pitted pietist subcultures against more traditionalist Northern subcultures, constituted a second and overlapping fault line of the third-party system. The narrow margins of electoral contests after the mid-1870s reflected, not the waning of North-South conflict, but the growing relative size of the antipietist groups in the North and their persistent opposition to the "party of great moral ideas."

The electoral shifts of the 1890s ended this era of close elections and altered the bases of partisan cleavage. Nationally, the narrow Democratic lead yielded after 1894 to a comfortable Republican margin, one which was nearly twice as large outside the South. The Democratic party was reduced to the status of a forlorn and noncompetitive minority in the New England, mid-Atlantic, East-North-Central, West-North-Central, and Pacific states.

This Republican electoral dominance enabled the party to control the nation's policymaking institutions. From the 55th through the 61st Congresses, 1897 through 1911, the

Republicans simultaneously controlled the presidency, the House, and the Senate. Between 1894 and 1931 they elected 67.2 percent of the governors in the Midwestern and Western states, and 83.1 percent in the New England and mid-Atlantic areas. And 70.6 percent of the representatives elected to non-Southern state legislatures between 1894 and 1904 were Republicans.[3] The period of party stalemate and divided control over policymaking institutions had ended; an era of Republican party hegemony had begun.

Republican dominance did not spread to all sections of the country; the South and Mountain areas remained unaffected by the contagion. The countermovement of the latter area and the increased competitiveness in the Border region point to the changed nature of the sectional conflict which under-pinned the newly emerging party system. In contrast to the third-electoral era, the South and the West, the nation's two semicolonial regions, were united in *party opposition* to the rest of the country, and especially to its urban-industrial areas. And as black disfranchisement became a legal reality in the South, the Democrats institutionalized their dominance there (Kousser 1974). Surely, memories of the "Lost Cause" still energized the opposition of white Southerners to the Yankee party. But at least among the region's cultural-economic elites, they now became fused with a sense of colonial status shared with the Mountain West. As that occurred, voting for the Democratic party became at once a means of defending "white man's government" and of resisting the encroachments of industrial imperialism.

One final feature of the new party system merits attention. The party battles of the early twentieth century regularly elicited much lower levels of mass participation than had those of the third-electoral era. No region of the country, of course, even approached the level of mass demobilization that characterized the South, but most experienced steep turnout declines. The exceptions were regions where the decline in competitiveness was slight—the

West-North-Central states; or where there was an increase in party competition—the Border and Mountain regions. Whatever the social composition of the new party coalitions, they enlisted the ballot support of lower proportions of citizens than the old ones had.

What were the social characteristics of these new party coalitions? And how did they differ from those of the third-party system? The data in table 1 provide some clues. Sectional swings of the magnitude suggested by those data imply a narrowing of the voting distance among social groups within the polarizing regions. That is, they suggest that whatever factors had earlier pitted one set of Northern voter groups against another set of Northern voter groups faded in importance. As that happened, the partisan distance between the voting behavior of the two sets of groups declined, though typically not to a vanishing point. That this type of voter movement underlay the emerging Republican dominance is indicated by the data in table 2.

Throughout the North, the third-party system had been characterized by ethnoreligious conflict which pitted pietist against antipietist groups. The behavior of Pennsylvania's German and Yankee counties, and of Wisconsin's German and Scandinavian counties, illustrates the types of social-group polarities that were common. So, too, does the fact that the Democrats regularly enjoyed a partisan lead in cities whose voting populations included relatively high percentages of antipietist immigrant groups, and especially of Catholic voters.

The contrast between the 1882–1892 and 1894–1904 electoral sequences is evident. German areas never became bastions of Republicanism; nor did the heavily antipietist cities. But both types of units swung sharply away from the Democrats. While areas of pietist subculture were initially attracted by Bryan's evangelical crusade, they returned thereafter—and with a vengeance—to their original Republican moorings. And both pietist and German rural areas evi-

Table 2

Social Sources of Change in Partisanship and Participation

Social areas	Partisan leads		Shift in competitiveness 1882–1892/ 1894–1904	Turnout percentages		Change in turnout 1874–1892/ 1900–1918
	1882–1892	1894–1904		1874–1892	1900–1918	
Pennsylvania[a]						
German	5.5D	6.6D	− 1.1	76.9	56.8	−20.1
Yankee	10.3R	23.1R	−12.8	69.2	51.1	−18.1
Wisconsin[b]						
German	24.7D	1.6R	+23.1	72.9	61.8	−11.1
Scandinavian	24.8R	45.5R	−20.7	68.8	51.3	−17.5
Cities						
Baltimore	17.3D	5.5R	+11.8	61.0	58.4	− 2.6
Boston	19.7D	3.0D	+16.7	43.9	42.6	− 1.3
Brooklyn	15.6D	0.8R	+14.8	61.8	51.7	−10.1
Chicago	5.6D	12.5R	− 6.9	48.6	52.4	+ 3.8
New York	27.9D	10.0D	+17.9	54.6	38.2	−16.4

aFor the German counties, N = 6; for the Yankee counties, N = 10.
bFor both the German and Scandinavian counties, N = 10.

denced, to an even greater extent than the cities, the sharp turnout decline that was a significant feature of post-1896 politics.[4]

Thus the electoral upheaval of the 1890s altered the partisan balance and created a new structure of social-group partisanship. The emerging coalitions still bore residual traces of the old ethnoreligious conflicts, of course; and under the right circumstances—such as a prohibition referendum—the former patterns reasserted themselves with all of their old-time virulence. But the distinguishing feature of the new political structure was the absence of a clear-cut and persisting correspondence between partisan selections and moralist dispositions. It had been precisely that correspondence which had given shape and substance to party battles and party characters since the mid-1850s. The new party system which emerged in the mid-1890s reflected a deep-seated value and interest cleavage between the nation's urban-industrial imperium and its semicolonial outposts, the South and the West. But what was even more significant, because it was the linchpin of Republican party dominance in the heavily populated imperium, was the fact that there the older politics of ethnoreligious conflict were displaced by a newer politics of "social harmony."

TOWARD THE "POLITICS OF SOCIAL HARMONY"

That displacement was never totally complete, of course. But as a descriptive tag, the phrase "politics of social harmony" accurately encapsulates the central tendencies of mass political behavior after the mid-1890s and, at the same time, draws into focus the principal contrast between that electoral era and the one which preceded it.[5]

Parties as "political churches" before the 1890s

During the second half of the nineteenth century, and among the non-Southern electorate, the principal cleavage line of party oppositions was that which arrayed pietist against antipietist religious groups. The differences between the two sets of groups were frequently expressed as polar attitudes on matters such as prohibition, Sunday-closing laws, foreign-language instruction, and the role of parochial schools. Such conflicts, however, involved more than divergent life-style preferences; they reflected primordial and irreconcilable belief-system differences. These subcultural conflicts attained *political* relevance because the involved groups sought to implement their values through control over public decision-making institutions. They acquired *party* salience because those institutions were manned by elected officials, and because the involved groups perceived the connections between electoral politics, public decision-making, and the values that were important to them. In time, and as memories of specific hostilities faded, parties themselves became objects of habituated loyalty, positive reference symbols which provided cues to the electoral selections of their loyal adherents. Through such complex processes of psychological transference, nineteenth-century American parties came to exhibit the character traits of "political churches."[6]

The Democratic church drew its membership from among antipietist groups—Catholics, confessional German Lutherans, native Calvinists, and salvationist pietists whose emotional religious outlook did not mandate connections between personal salvation and holiness in the world about them. The Republican party was the political church of the pietist groups. It encompassed those native Baptists, Congregationalists, Methodists, and Presbyterians who had internalized the revivalist ethos and who sought actively to purge the world of sin. And it enlisted as well the support of immigrant pietists — especially large segments of the Norwegian, Swedish, and British stock, and less confessional German Lutherans — who shared either the native revivalists' compunction to make holy the world or, at least, their powerful aversion to Catholicism.

In both tangible and symbolic ways, the major parties reflected their coalitional bases. Democrats, in their rhetoric and in their legislative votes, opposed measures which were anathema to their support groups. And, almost as regularly, Republicans favored those measures. To its core supporters, "Democratic" represented "personal liberty" — a toleration and defense of alternative life-styles and values, of *laissez-faire* social ethics, and of a government whose powers were circumscribed so as to preclude positive intervention in the daily lives of its citizens. To pietist enthusiasts, "Republican" symbolized an activist and interventionist disposition, a defense of righteousness, and a government willing and able to use its powers to compel cultural homogeneity as nothing less than a requirement of God's own will.

Of course, no real political party has ever wholly conformed to stereotyped descriptions of it. There are always variations and exceptions. And for political parties operating within the context of a federalized political system, and a system characterized by an asymmetrical distribution of social groups, the exceptions are likely to become increasingly frequent and significant as conditions and population composition change. That was particularly the case for the post–Civil War Republican party.

That party was born in the 1850s of the amalgamation of evangelical Protestantism with rapid abolitionism. For most of the next fifteen years it controlled the nation's policymaking institutions, and shaped national policy to extinguish agrarian and slaveholding opposition to industrial capitalism. But in the 1870s and 1880s its control was challenged by a resuscitated Democratic party. The revitalization of the Democrats involved the end of Reconstruction in the South and the emergence there of a Democratic lead, combined with growth in the relative size of antipietist voter groups in the Northern states. It was the latter development which undermined Republican strength in its antebellum bailiwicks and underlay the increased electoral competitiveness that marked the 1874—1892 period.

The political implications of this demographic change posed a dilemma for the Republican party. For the capacity of that party's modernizing national elites to shape policy ultimately depended upon grass-roots election victories. And at its grass roots the party was unmistakably pietist in social composition and character. Yet as the size of the antipietist voting population increased, pietist zeal for prohibition and anti-Catholic crusades simply guaranteed Republican electoral defeats. Nor were the righteous moralists ever willing to compromise—or even to tone down their strident rhetoric—for the mere sake of election victories.

Therein lay the essence of the dilemma. Pragmatic party managers sought to win elections. To do so they aimed at appealing to some groups of antipietist voters. Such appeals necessarily entailed altering the party's commitment to pristine pietism. Yet any effort to do that invariably produced a countereffort by the party's core support groups, and by the spokesmen within the party organization who responded principally to their demands. It was these distinctive, and ultimately irreconcilable, orientations which underlay Republican factionalism in the 1870s and 1880s.

That conflict in outlook also produced schism within the Republican church. It led to the formation of a separate Prohibition party which ran its own slates and pulled votes from the Republicans. With election outcomes hinging upon a relative handful of votes, the Prohibition danger to Republican victories assumed much greater proportions than the party's comparatively small vote totals might suggest.

The freezing of the cleavage structure of the nation's party system along the dual fault lines of ethnoreligious and sectional conflict had considerable policy significance. Parties which reflected ethnoreligious and sectional interests could not simultaneously aggregate transethnic and intersectional class interests. That the existing parties could not mobilize anti-industrial sentiment and translate it into policy outputs created considerable latitude for maneuver by corporate elites. However valuable that negative safeguard, in itself it was insufficient to satisfy the changing imperatives of a developing corporate capitalism. What these required by the late 1870s was the capacity to intervene actively in order to consolidate and rationalize the corporate system. That intervention needed a degree of political centralization whose attainment was hampered by political parties which had become strongholds of localist resistance to modernizing change. The need, therefore, was to fracture the cleavage lines of the prevailing party system and, ultimately, to displace party as an instrument of popular government.

Economic collapse

The depression of the 1890s provided the necessary opportunities. That economic crisis underscored the need for activist intervention to salvage the industrial system, and created the requisite conditions that made such intervention politically possible.

The economic collapse began as a Wall Street panic in the spring of 1893, and it rapidly deepened into a full-scale depression whose aftereffects lingered to the end of the decade. The immediate political consequence of the depression, apparent in the 1893 and 1894 elections, was a sharp swing away from the Democrats. But those immediate shifts marked only the beginning of the transformation in the political system. How each of the parties responded to the depression, its attendant social unrest and initial political effects, constituted its second and more critical stage.

Soaring unemployment rates, strikes and violence in response to wage cuts and layoffs, demonstrations by the unemployed who demanded relief and public works jobs, and even a march by an "Army of the Unemployed" on Washington—all combined to raise widespread fear of drastic social upheaval. And all of this came on the heels of earlier political manifestations of long-smoldering economic discontent by Southern and Western farmers and Western silver miners.

The sources of that discontent were varied. For silver producers, they lay in the collapse of the market for their product. But it was agrarian discontent that provided the crucial dynamic to a growing sectional restiveness. Farmers were faced with world oversupply problems, long-term price declines, credit shortages, high interest rates, unpredictable weather conditions, and—even worse—exploitive relationships between themselves and their local suppliers and shippers. In the South, the grinding oppression of the farm tenancy system reduced increasing numbers of farmers to a condition of virtual peonage (Goodwyn 1976; Schwartz 1976).[7]

To combat such conditions, leaders of farm opinion sought to organize farmers into what can best be described as self-help and mutual-protection groups. This cooperative movement, spurred by the Farmers' Alliance in the late 1880s and early 1890s, created the secondary-group infrastructure which sustained subsequent support for the partisan expression of agrarian discontent—the People's Party.

It was the absorption of the agrarian and silver Populists by the Democrats in 1896 that altered the factional balance within that party and changed its policy orientation and political character. That absorption, in turn, was facilitated both by the electoral disaster that the party experienced in 1893–1894, and by the victory of McKinleyism within the Republican party.

The depression elections of 1893 and 1894 decimated the Democratic corps of officeholders and discredited its traditional leadership.[8] To have presided over the most severe and extensive anti-Democratic swing in the party's history provided no basis for asserting a continued right to chart its future strategy. The off-year swings created a leadership vacuum at the top and middle echelons of the party. They also broadly diffused the conviction that defense of the Cleveland administration's policies was the route to a repeated electoral disaster in 1896. Conditions thus were ripe for the advent of new leaders, especially of those capable of recruiting the discontented to the party's support.

William Jennings Bryan took advantage of these conditions. For nearly two years prior to the 1896 Democratic national convention, Bryan skillfully ingratiated himself with the silver clubs and farmers' organizations that had become political forces in the West and South. He harnessed the Free Silver panacea, with its overt promise of currency inflation and its implicit suggestion of changed power relationships in the society, to capture the presidential nomination for himself, wrest control of the party organization from its traditional Eastern leadership, and fundamentally alter the Democratic party's social coalition and political character.

In the hands of Bryan and his Populist allies, the Democratic party, the nineteenth-century party of personal liberty and *laissez-faire* ethics, became an instrument of activist intervention on behalf of the downtrodden "producing classes" of society. The aim was to mobilize a broadly based social coalition of farmers and industrial workers—North and South, East and West—in opposition to the "party of the privileged few." Bryan's version of the Democratic creed, as both his enemies *and his supporters* were quick to point out, was not that of the old Democratic party. Its political character no longer resonated emotionally with those of the ethnoreligious groups which had long been the party's habituated supporters. For them it was no longer a party which symbolized defense of their parochial schools, their drinking habits, and their generally antipietist life-styles and values. Instead, it stood for positive government, the very symbolism which for half a century had energized their op-

position. And Bryan, as well as many of his supporters, presented the case to these elements of the "downtrodden
masses" in the idiom of evangelical Christianity, the very
phrases and cadences which these ethnoreligious groups had
long identified with their social and political enemies. More
tangibly, the movement of local prohibition leaders attracted
by Bryan's evangelism—and even, in some localities, of
leaders of the virulently anti-Catholic American Protective
Association—into the ranks as grass-roots party spokesmen
served further to dissipate the appeal of this new Democratic
party to its core of ethnoreligious support groups.

The way in which the Bryanites purposively transformed
the policy stances and character of the Democratic party,
and thereby unintentionally antagonized large segments of
its traditional coalitional base, was the dramatic side of the
political equation. The victory of McKinleyism within the Republican party was its more quiet and significant side.

That victory, and the essence of McKinleyism, cannot be
explained in terms of the party's commitment to the gold
standard in 1896. Surely, that policy stance, one only reluctantly adopted by William McKinley, guaranteed a bolt by
the Western Silver Republicans. That created a support
clientele which could be mobilized by a redeveloped Bryanite
Democratic party, and whose spokesmen could be absorbed
into its leadership. Yet despite all the sound and furor over
the currency question in 1896, McKinleyism has to be viewed
in broader terms. It can best be understood as a political disposition which altered the character of the Republican party.

McKinley, Hanna, and the new Republican party

The unique contribution of McKinley and his *éminence grise*,
Mark Hanna, to the redevelopment of the Republican party
was their commitment to a politics of "social harmony."
Their Republican party tolerated life-style distinctions to
enlist the support of a broad range of ethnoreligious groups.

They accepted cultural pluralism as a condition of the society, and did not attempt to coerce conformity to pietist orthodoxies. In more modern terms, they broadened the social base of the party. To do that, they deemphasized the old culturally divisive questions, and concentrated instead on what they perceived as a natural basis for harmonious relations among otherwise disparate groups—a shared concern for "prosperity."

The depression and its political aftershocks created the conditions which made possible the triumph of McKinleyism within the Republican party. First, the depression elections in 1893 and 1894 resulted in Republican victories in a large number of formerly Democratic constituencies. These new officeholders and party spokesmen increased the size and strength of the pragmatic faction within the party. Not wanting to be single-term incumbents, they consciously sought to minimize ethnoreligious conflict in order to maximize their reelection chances. Second, the size of the Republican margins in the depression elections reduced the impact of the Prohibition party on Republican tactics. As long as election outcomes were very close, Republican tacticians vigilantly guarded against defections to the cold-water cause. As the Republican margins of electoral victory widened, the need to placate the Prohibitionists disappeared, and with that went an impediment to broadening the party's social coalition. Third, and perhaps most significant, the impact of the depression and unemployment reduced the partisan salience of ethnoreligious identifications and increased that of economic concern. It was exactly that pattern which underlay the swing away from the Democrats in 1893 and 1894. To broaden and deepen that pattern was the aim of Republican tacticians in 1896. McKinley's past political experiences, his culturally pluralist outlook, and his public identification with the tariff, made him the logical claimant of the title "Advance Agent of Prosperity."

Political tactics which deemphasized standing eth-

noreligious tensions were no new twist for McKinley. To
secure election to the office of prosecuting attorney in
culturally heterogeneous Stark County, to Congress in a
marginally Democratic district, and to the governorship in
the tightly competitive and highly mobilized state of Ohio,
McKinley had long been attuned to that need. He now
transferred his culturally pragmatic disposition to the arena
of national politics. And when he did, given the prevailing
social and political conditions and the tactics of his opposition, he tilted the balance within the party and the nation to
his brand of Republicanism.

The immediate and obvious result was an enormously
broadened Republican social coalition whose maintenance
inaugurated a period of virtual Republican party hegemony
over the nation's policymaking institutions. That hegemony
had reverberating effects, both on electoral politics and on
the larger political system.[9]

The decline in partisan competitiveness meant that the
basic policy struggles of the early twentieth century would be
fought within the Republican party. For example, questions
of the role to be played by the national government in promoting regional economic development, which were at the
heart of tariff-rate controversies and battles over the allocation of federal funds for internal improvements, pitted
Northeastern against Midwestern Republican factional formations. The increased importance of intraparty factional
strife, in turn, underscored the need to manage and contain
its effects. That coincided with broader popular demand to
find a substitute for interparty competition at the level of
selecting the candidates of the locally dominant party. Both
impulses underlay the institution of the direct primary.
Single-party dominance, and the new significance attached
to the party primary, were factors contributing to that
demobilization of the mass electorate which characterized
post-1896 politics.

The new politics of social harmony also contributed to that
turnout decline. As long as partisanship was rooted in value

differences between competing sets of ethnoreligious groups, it was anchored and reinforced by the involvement of group members in extensive networks of ethnoreligiously exclusive secondary groups. A politics which deemphasized the salience of ethnoreligious identifications eroded the role which that infrastructure had played in sustaining party attachments and eliciting high levels of electoral participation. The new electoral universe reflected the impress of that erosion, both in the form of reduced rates of participation and in lower levels of party-cued voting behavior.

Finally, the cumulative effect of noncompetitiveness and mass demobilization, combined with legal changes downgrading the role of the party as organization, was to lower party effectiveness as a mobilizing agency and thus to reduce its capacity to shape policy outputs. Freeing elected decision-makers from the constraints of the party was a requisite condition to increase the policy-shaping role of other political institutions capable of articulating group interests. As the party's role as a determinant of legislative voting behavior declined, for example, the influence of functionally organized economic interest groups increased.[10] That was accompanied by an accelerated tendency to remove large clusters of policy from even the potential influence of party behavior by shifting decision-making from elected to appointed bodies. Done in the name of "efficiency" and "expertise," the consequence of that removal was further to insulate decision-making from organized mass opinion. That insulation was an indispensable stage in the efforts of cosmopolitan elites to eliminate parties as the critical sources of localist resistance to the centralizing impulses of corporate capitalism.

Thus, the massive coalitional readjustments of the 1890s did more than create a new electoral universe. They altered the factional balances within the parties and transformed their political characters. And they created a set of political conditions conducive to a transformation of the very roles of party and of electoral politics in the political system.

6

JEROME M. CLUBB

Party Coalitions in the Early Twentieth Century

Partisan identification and voting behavior: common and conflicting interests, goals, pressures. Historic periods of political realignment. Republican party dominance, 1890–1930. The 1896 election. Voter participation and patterns of change. The demise of the partisan press. Agrarian discontent. The New Deal.

The common view of American political parties holds that their electoral support is provided by heterogeneous coalitions of population groups. Shifts in the outcomes of particular elections, according to this view, are caused by the defection or loyalty of particular groups, and lasting change in the parties' fortunes, by changes in the composition of the coalitions. It argues that electoral coalitions, and the individual partisan loyalties that underlie them, have historically been shaped and rearranged by periodic "critical" realignments. These realignments are followed by prolonged periods of relative stability during which one of the parties enjoys majority support and relatively consistent control over the major institutions of national government.

Partisan realignments occur during periods of pronounced national tension. The political interests and concerns of the electorate are high during these periods, and attention is focused upon the conditions of crisis and their presumed causes and remedies. Realignments have been identified during the late 1820s and early 1830s, the Civil War years, the mid-1890s, and the late 1920s or early 1930s. In the course of these changes, a new balance of electoral loyalties appeared, and new electoral alignments were formed which dominated national political life until the next realignment. The circumstances of these periods apparently concentrated the attention of the electorate upon a relatively narrow range of issues while temporarily reducing the salience of others. There then emerged a degree of issue consensus which provided the agenda and the symbolic focus for new electoral alignments.

This general view of American political history requires several qualifications. It would be easy to exaggerate both the magnitude of change during realignments and the degree of electoral stability that marked the subsequent periods. There is, in fact, evidence of substantial continuity across realignments, and of significant shifts in the partisan distribution of the popular vote during so-called stable periods. Indeed, these periods are marked by a relatively consistent pattern of change. During the early years, the majority party enjoys consistent and frequently overwhelming majorities in national elections, and highly consistent control over the elective institutions of the national government. The later years of each period, however, are characterized by sharp fluctuations in the popular vote, by the intrusion of minor parties, by indications of governmental deadlock, and by evidence of increasingly unstable electoral support.[1]

The term "coalition" should also be qualified. It is easy to assume that references to partisan coalitions imply a conscious and rational strategy on the part of rank-and-file voters or their leaders, designed to serve goals that transcend mere election of the candidates of a particular party. In fact, however, the partisan identifications and voting behavior of rank-and-file members of the electorate can be seen as based in many cases upon little more than group pressures toward conformity and agreement. Alternatively, the shared partisan orientations of the members of particular groups may be taken as based upon a shared sense, either vague or well defined, of common interest.

Neither of these alternative views implies that the diverse groups that form partisan coalitions necessarily share the same interests and goals where public policy and the conduct of government are concerned. In fact, the component groups are usually characterized by diverse—and often conflicting —goals and interests. As a consequence, electoral coalitions can best be described as involving inherent elements of instability.

REPUBLICAN DOMINANCE

From this general perspective, the early decades of the twentieth century can appropriately be seen as one of the successive electoral eras that have characterized the political history of the United States. During the entire period from the 1890s to the 1930s the majority of American voters undoubtedly was Republican in its partisan identification. The party consistently controlled the presidency and the Congress, save only for the elections that spanned the period from 1910 through 1916. The elections of 1918 and 1920 appear as a restoration of Republican dominance with, if anything, greater electoral strength after a temporary Democratic intrusion. But despite clear Republican dominance, the decade of the 1920s was marked by signs of shifts in the coalitions from which the parties drew their support, of growing electoral instability, and of divisions within the leadership of both parties.

As in the case of other historical realignments, the patterns of electoral identifications and coalitions that resulted from the realignment of the 1890s were characterized by elements of continuity with those of earlier years. The years from the late 1870s through the early 1890s were marked by intense partisan competition, by a narrow partisan balance, and by a highly mobilized and partisan electorate. Partisan loyalties of the electorate were reinforced and sustained by a well-organized party system at the grass roots, and by a heavily partisan press that enjoyed a near monopoly over political information. Those loyalties were rooted, moreover, in the bitter memories of the violence, loss, and destruction of Civil War and Reconstruction, and in basic and intense ethnic and religious cleavages.[2]

These political arrangements, however, were increasingly disrupted by issues and discontents produced by economic change. In the developing economy of the period, staple-producing farmers of the South and West were increasingly disadvantaged, as was the growing and heavily immigrant-stock industrial laboring class of the Northeastern cities. The discontent of these groups was manifested in the efforts of states outside the greater Northeast to regulate the local activities of railroads and other enterprises of national scope, in occasional strikes and industrial violence, and in such organizations and movements as the Farmers Alliances, the

Grange, the Knights of Labor, the Single Tax movement, the Greenback party, and ultimately, the Populist party. With the formation of the Populist party in the early 1890s, and with the onset of severe depression in 1893, tension and discontent reached a high point.

The election of 1896 is usually seen as the critical election of the 1890s' realignment, although a more accurate view would probably see the process of realignment as spanning a more lengthy period. The issues and events of 1896 are richly recounted in other places and are aptly summarized in Paul Kleppner's preceding chapter. But while these issues and events undoubtedly influenced the outcome of the election — and also provided elements of political rhetoric that could be used to sustain a new Republican coalition during the years that followed — a simpler explanation for Democratic defeat can be found in economic circumstances. When the depression of 1893 began, a Democrat, Grover Cleveland, occupied the White House and Democrats controlled both houses of Congress. The usual reaction of American voters in such circumstances is to reject the party in power. That rejection had begun in the congressional elections of 1894, when the Democrats suffered overwhelming defeat. The election of 1896 was a further and, for the time being, final rejection.

The conditions of partisan realignment were clearly present in the 1890s. Tensions were high and the nation was in a state of crisis. The reforms advocated by the Democrat-Populist fusion ticket were radical indeed for the times; when combined with the overtones of violence that were sometimes characteristic of Populist rhetoric, they apparently struck fear into the hearts of businessmen, of business leaders, and of the stable middle class more generally. The Democrats were rejected in the election of 1896, and the characteristics of the campaign and the circumstances of the times were such as to discredit the party. As John L. Sundquist puts it (1973, p. 150), "To the image of the Democrats as the party of rum, Romanism, rebellion, and economic recession was added another R—radicalism." And the addition of still another R, for ruralism, might also be noted. In the election of 1896, Bryan and the Democrats succeeded only in the agricultural and mining states of the South and West; the industrial states of the Northeast were solidly Republican. Recovery from economic crisis during the later years of the decade could be taken as redemption of the Republican promise of a "full dinner pail," as a demonstration of the efficacy of the Republican *laissez-faire* approach to public policy, and the Republicans could be seen as the party of sound and sensible government, prosperity, and progress. Thus the political events of the later 1890s produced a pattern of issues and symbols which, added to those of Civil War and Reconstruction, worked to sustain and reinforce the new partisan alignment during the years that followed.

The new alignment was a modified form of the post–Civil War alignment, with the Democrats in a definite minority. The national distribution of partisan strength was heavily sectional and reflected, in this respect, perpetuation of Civil War cleavages in, if anything, even more exaggerated form. After 1896 the plains and prairie states and, in the main, the Western states that had voted for Bryan, returned to the Republican fold; the greater Northeast remained strongly Republican. Thus most of the states outside the South and the Border were at the least predominantly Republican. As table 1 indicates, aside from the progressive years, Republican candidates for the presidency garnered the lion's share of electoral votes in the North and West throughout the period; Republicans also won the large majority of House and gubernatorial elections in these areas.[3]

The primary bastions of Democratic strength were, as before 1896, the eleven states of the old Confederacy; to a substantially lesser degree, the Border states of Maryland, West Virginia, Kentucky, Oklahoma, and Missouri; and to a still lesser degree, the Mountain states. After 1896, with the culmination of effective disenfranchisement of blacks and

Table 1

The Republican Advantage: Republican Percentages of Regional Electoral Votes, Seats in the House of Representatives, and Gubernatorial Offices 1896–1930, and 1896–1908 and 1918–1930

Region*	Percentage of electoral college		Percentage of seats in the House of Representatives		Percentage of governors	
	1896–1930	1896–1908 and 1918–1930	1896–1930	1896–1908 and 1918–1930	1896–1930	1896–1908 and 1918–1930
New England	82.4	92.1	83.0	87.2	89.2	94.6
Middle Atlantic	88.1	100.0	68.7	72.6	71.9	74.6
East-North-Central	84.2	98.0	73.0	79.6	80.6	89.3
West-North-Central	71.6	86.6	68.8	72.2	75.2	74.5
Solid South	5.1	6.6	2.8	3.2	1.2	1.4
Border states	43.3	55.0	35.5	39.0	37.1	34.1
Mountain states	57.9	76.2	60.3	64.9	43.5	46.1
Pacific states	74.6	96.6	79.9	84.9	74.5	78.6
Nation	60.2	71.1	53.4	57.0	52.9	55.1

*For tables 1 and 2, the regions are defined as:

New England—Connecticut, Maine, Massachusetts, New Hampshire, Rhode Island, Vermont;

Middle Atlantic—Delaware, New Jersey, New York, Pennsylvania;

East-North-Central—Illinois, Indiana, Michigan, Ohio, Wisconsin;

West-North-Central—Iowa, Kansas, Minnesota, Missouri, Nebraska, North Dakota, South Dakota;

Solid South—Alabama, Arkansas, Florida, Georgia, Louisiana, Mississippi, North Carolina, South Carolina, Texas, Virginia;

Border states—Kentucky, Maryland, Oklahoma, Tennessee, West Virginia;

Mountain states—Arizona, Colorado, Idaho, Montana, Nevada, New Mexico, Utah, Wyoming;

Pacific states—California, Oregon, Washington.

Table 2

Sources of the Democratic Minority: Regional Distribution of Democratic Electoral Votes, Seats in the House of Representatives, and Gubernatorial Offices 1896–1930, and 1896–1908 and 1918–1930

Region*	Electoral votes			Seats in House of Representatives			Governors' offices		
	Regional percentage of nation	Percentage Democratic 1896–1930	Percentage Democratic 1896–1908 and 1918–1930	Regional percentage of nation	Percentage Democratic 1896–1930	Percentage Democratic 1896–1908 and 1918–1930	Regional percentage of nation	Percentage Democratic 1896–1930	Percentage Democratic 1896–1908 and 1918–1930
New England	8.4	4.0	2.3	7.4	2.8	2.3	12.7	3.0	1.6
Middle Atlantic	18.6	3.7	0	20.9	14.1	13.6	9.1	5.6	5.4
East-North-Central	18.6	6.2	0	20.4	11.6	9.6	10.6	4.5	2.6
West-North-Central	13.7	9.4	6.5	13.3	8.4	7.8	14.8	8.0	8.7
Solid South	21.9	55.2	72.0	22.0	46.9	50.8	21.2	45.6	48.1
Border states	9.3	14.0	14.5	9.2	13.0	13.2	9.9	13.6	14.8
Mountain states	5.1	5.7	4.1	2.8	2.2	1.9	15.4	16.3	15.7
Pacific states	4.4	1.9	0.5	3.9	1.0	0.9	6.3	3.5	3.1
	100.0	100.1	99.9	99.9	100.0	100.1	100.0	100.1	100.0

*For definition of regions, see note to Table 1.

the completion of the "Southern solution," the solid South became even more solidly Democratic. The dependence of the party on the South is reflected in the large proportion of Democratic electoral votes and of governors and representatives in Congress which the region provided. Table 2 indicates that no other region approached the South in terms of its contribution to Democratic strength, and, as can be seen, Southern support for Democrats far exceeded the region's representation in the nation. Democratic strength in the Border states was significantly more spotty, and in the Mountain states the Democrats were, at best, competitive. When the deviating elections of 1910 through 1916 are excluded, Democratic dependence upon the Border states and the South becomes even more apparent.

Outside the South and the Border, there were also areas of Democratic strength. The most noteworthy of these were in the cities of the Northeast, where Democratic strength has often been seen as related to urban political machines. The party had established strongholds in a number of Northern cities in the earlier nineteenth century, based heavily upon the Irish and, subsequently, upon the "new" immigrants from southern and eastern Europe. In 1896 the Republicans cut sharply into Democratic strength in the cities. In most cases the Democrats promptly recovered; indeed, one of the characteristics of the period was growth of Democratic power in such cities as New York and Boston. In other cities, particularly Philadelphia, the losses of 1896 were more lasting.

It is difficult to go beyond the geographic distribution of support for Democratic and Republican candidates and to identify the specific population groups that comprised the party coalitions. Historical source materials do not allow precise assessment of the degree or consistency with which particular population groups voted for the candidates of one or the other of the parties. Certainly, historical sources do not allow as direct or precise an assessment of the nature and strength of individual identifications with the parties as can be achieved through contemporary sample survey research. The evidence suggests, however, that Republican support came primarily from a coalition of substantial, stable, middle-class, Protestant, and native-stock Americans. To this group could be added blacks, to the degree they were able to vote, and various older immigrant groups. But these additions hardly temper the image of the Republican electoral party as dominated by a coalition of the successful, the respectable, the stable, and, indeed, the privileged elements of society.

The Democratic electoral party was less homogeneous than the Republican. The white Southern core of the party has been noted, as was the shift of industrial labor toward the Republicans in 1896. The new immigrants from southern and eastern Europe who entered the United States in increasing numbers in the later nineteenth and earlier twentieth centuries, and who came to constitute a growing proportion of the urban industrial labor force, present a much more complicated picture. Because of their alien status, and for other reasons that are noted subsequently; many of the "new" immigrants probably did not vote, particularly during the earlier years of the century. It is clear, however, that these groups constituted an element of the support for Democratic machines in many Northeastern cities and, as the period wore on, the new immigrants became a source of both instability and strength for the Democrats.

But the partisan balance did not rest entirely—or, perhaps, even primarily—upon the active electorate. It also rested upon nonvoters, those who were either excluded from electoral participation or who, for other reasons, failed to go to the polls. Indeed, the realignment of the 1890s can be seen, at least in part, as a product of selective demobilization of segments of the electorate rather than as exclusively a matter of the conversion of Democrats. The last half of the nineteenth century was a period of high and—in much of the North—rising voter participation. Although estimates vary, in the presidential election of 1896 more than 90 percent of the eligible electorate voted in Illinois, Indiana, Iowa, Michigan, Ohio, and West Virginia; in few Northern states did participation fall below 75 percent.

It is likely that these estimates of voter participation are inflated to some unknown degree. It is possible that the number of votes recorded as cast during these years was spuriously increased by fraudulent and corrupt electoral practices (Converse 1972; also Allen and Allen [in press]). It is also probable that the censuses of the period tended — again, in some unknown degree — to undercount the national population. As a consequence, available estimates of voter participation may be based upon undercounts of the eligible electorate (Shortridge [in press]). Even so, rates of voter participation declined significantly during the early decades of the twentieth century, and voter participation in the 1920s was low indeed. Only an estimated 49 percent of the eligible electorate voted in the presidential election of 1924, and one estimate places voter participation at less than one-third of the electorate in the off-year congressional elections of the 1920s.[4]

Considerable scholarly effort has been devoted to explaining these declining turnout rates, and the explanations provided have been the center of some scholarly controversy.[5] One obvious explanation was the completion of black disenfranchisement in the South. Here, political participation fell from an estimated 60 percent in the presidential election of 1896 to less than 30 percent in the election of 1904. A second and equally obvious explanation was the enfranchisement of women, which took place at different dates in different states, and was completed with the passage of the Nineteenth Amendment in 1920. Clearly, women were initially slow to implement their newly gained right to participate in elections.

A less obvious explanation lay in patterns of partisan competition. One of the consequences of the 1890s' realignment was to reduce competition. In the South, the realignment and the "Southern solution" effectively eliminated competition in general elections. As a consequence, potential Republicans and dissident Democrats could either compete in the white primaries or simply stay away from the polls. Competition also declined sharply in areas of the Midwest, New England, and the Northeast. Thus, much of the electorate was left in elections without meaningful alternatives, and interest and participation in elections apparently declined. Various "reforms" of the period also worked to reduce effective partisan competition. In California, for example, legislation that facilitated cross-filing worked to eliminate alternative choices at the polls and, hence, stimulus to voter participation.

And other reforms worked, some of them in more subtle ways, to reduce voter participation, in some cases on a highly selective basis. The implementation of personal registration laws imposed an additional obstacle to voting. The fact that these requirements were often applied to the cities but not to the countryside meant that they impacted particularly upon the electoral participation of urban immigrant-stock groups. But even without differential application, registration requirements probably had their greatest effect upon participation of the newer immigrants, who were often poorly acculturated in political terms and poorly motivated to vote, and for whom, as a consequence, the additional hurdle of registration probably most sharply reduced participation.

The party system was also affected. Implementation of direct election of senators and of direct primaries worked to disrupt links between the parties at the national level, on the one hand, and in the state legislatures and at the local level, on the other, while also reducing their role in the nominating process. The parties thus became less effective as agencies of electoral mobilization, and the process was probably further accentuated by the demise of the partisan press. It can be debated whether participation decline reflected widespread popular apathy and alienation from the political system produced by the absence of meaningful alternatives to the business-oriented Republican party. Certainly, however, there was little in the system to stimulate the political interest or electoral participation of large numbers of potential voters.

But for present purposes, explanations of low voter participation are less important than consequences. In substantial numbers, potentially discordant elements of the population were effectively outside the electoral system. Thus, to an unknown degree, the partisan alignment of the times, its stability, and the arrangement, direction, and exercise of political power were based not only upon the commitments and opinions of the active electorate, but also upon the failure or inability to vote of upward to half of the eligible population.

DETERIORATION OF PARTISAN ALIGNMENTS

The partisan alignment of the period, of course, was by no means entirely stable. Both parties drew support from groups marked by potentially conflicting interests and demands. With the passage of the years after 1896, both parties were increasingly faced with internal divisions. Divisions were most obvious among the Democrats, but the Republicans were by no means without them. By the mid-1920s there was clear evidence of the deterioration of both partisan alignments.

The progressive movement marked the first major disruption of the 1890s' alignment, and the disruption came largely within the Republican party. Whatever their impact in other terms, the elections of the progressive era appear primarily as temporary deviations from the normal distribution of the national vote. Wilson's plurality victory in 1912 was a result of Republican division, and suggests little change in the national distribution of partisan identifications. On the other hand, the increase in Wilson's plurality in the next election, from 42 percent in 1912 to approximately 49 percent in 1916, and Democratic successes in the congressional elections from 1910 through 1916, suggest the presence of significant popular dissatisfaction with the prevailing Republican order. Even so, Democratic successes were reversed in the election of 1918, and in 1920 Republicans regained control of both houses of Congress and captured the presidency by landslide proportions. Indeed, the magnitude of Harding's majority could seem to have reinstated the Republicans in power with a larger electoral advantage than ever.

In fact, the events of the progressive years probably reflected lasting divisions within the Republican party. These divisions were most sharply reflected in Congress by the revolt of a small number of Republican senators and representatives from such Western states as Wisconsin, Iowa, Minnesota, Nebraska, the Dakotas, Idaho, Washington, Oregon, and California against the party leadership and its pro-business orientation. These congressmen frequently joined with Democrats to frustrate Taft and the Republican leadership. Subsequently, Republican congressmen from the same states often joined with Democrats to push through the Wilson legislative program that marked the culmination of progressivism at the national level. The agrarian cast of the legislation which they supported was strongly reminiscent of the Populist and Bryan reforms of the 1890s. That orientation, however, was now combined with concern for political corruption and suspicion of the immigrant-stock populations of the cities. It was also combined with advocacy of reforms of the political systems that were justified in terms of extension of popular democracy and responsible government, but which also reflected antagonism to political parties and to the growing role of the cities in national politics.

Manifestations of agrarian discontent did not end with the progressive years. During the 1920s, Republican representatives and senators from these same states of the West and the upper plains and the prairies frequently broke with their party to support, sometimes in isolation and sometimes in combination with Southern Democrats, legislation intended to meet the grievances of their agricultural constituencies.

Nor were signs of agrarian dissatisfaction limited to the actions of a few Republican members of Congress. In the 1920s they also appeared at the grass roots in the formation of political movements under such labels as the National Nonpartisan League or the Farmer-Labor party. In Washington and Minnesota these movements appeared as third parties which, in the latter state, managed to displace the minority Democratic party. In other states they took the form of factions within one or the other of the major parties. In Colorado, Idaho, and Montana they dominated, for a time, the Democratic party, and in North Dakota and Wisconsin they appeared as factions of the Republican party. And it was in this same bloc of states that Robert LaFollette made his strongest showing in the 1924 election as the presidential candidate of a new Progressive party. In 1924 LaFollette cut most sharply into the Democratic party, but the LaFollette candidacy, like the appearance of the Nonpartisan League and the Farmer-Labor party, also reflected dissatisfaction with alternatives provided by the Republican party and was a manifestation of agrarian discontent that neither party could effectively reconcile.[6]

The 1920s, then, witnessed the deterioration of the Republican coalition. That deterioration was most marked in the states of the Northwest and reflected the continuing grievances of agriculture, grievances that were fueled by the depression of the early 1920s and by the depressed farm conditions that persisted long after. Nonetheless, the Republican party continued to dominate national politics, in part because of the even greater disarray of the Democratic coalition.

From almost any perspective, the Democratic alliance between, on the one hand, the rural, Protestant, fundamentalist South, with its nativism and prohibitionist sentiment, and, on the other, the machine-led, immigrant-stock, and heavily Catholic populations of Northeastern cities could only seem unnatural. In the 1920s the alliance became even more unnatural. As growing numbers of the new immigrants attained citizenship, as they became accustomed to the American political system, and as urban politicians devoted effort to improvement of urban social and economic conditions, the Northeastern cities became an increasingly potent political force. The tenuous link between the cities and the national party was reflected in the voting patterns of the largest cities of the nation. In general, throughout the period, Democratic candidates for Congress and, it appears, lesser offices ran better in these cities than did the party's presidential candidates; in the elections of 1920 and 1924 the discrepancy became even more marked (Burner 1967, pp. 20–21). Apparently a presidential ticket conceived for national purposes did not accommodate urban interests.

But in most accounts, the disruption of the Democratic coalition is dramatically symbolized by two events of the 1920s: the Democratic national convention of 1924, and the presidential election of 1928. The convention of 1924 can be described with only a little hyperbole as a rancorous conflict that went on for over 100 ballots, pitted the Northeastern cities against the rural South, wets against dries, immigrant stock against native stock, Catholics against Protestants, and Tammany Hall against the Ku Klux Klan, and led the party to overwhelming defeat at the polls. The election of 1928 symbolized the disruption in a different way. With Alfred E. Smith—a Catholic, a wet, and an obvious product of urban America—at the head of the Democratic ticket, the electorate of the Northeastern immigrant-stock cities turned out to vote in unprecedented numbers, and the Democratic vote rose sharply—in some cases, to landslide proportions.

And the Democrats also made limited inroads into Republican majorities in Midwestern and Western states in Protestant as well as Catholic areas (Sundquist 1973, pp. 174−76). On the other hand, the South defected. Voter participation also rose sharply in the Southern states. But the Democrats failed to carry Florida, North Carolina, Texas, and Virginia, and there were major Republican gains throughout the rest of the solid South and in the Border states.

Smith's successes in Northeastern cities are often seen as the first phase of the Democratic realignment that would be consummated in the 1930s. His most impressive gains came in many of the same cities that would become the urban heartland of the New Deal coalition that emerged in the 1930s, and they apparently came particularly among the immigrant-stock, Catholic groups that would be central elements in that coalition. Undoubtedly, the election of 1928 marked a further step in the political socialization of the new immigrants from southern and eastern Europe. But whether or not the Democratic gains in 1928 would have proven permanent without the intrusion of the Great Depression cannot be determined. The fact that increases in the Democratic presidential vote in these cities in 1928 were not consistently paralleled by commensurate increases in the vote for Democratic candidates for lesser offices suggests that these successes may have been more a tribute to Al Smith than a new-found and lasting source of Democratic strength.

Taken in total, Democratic gains in the Northern cities in 1928, like Republican successes in the South, might better be taken as further indications of the deterioration of the partisan alignments that had appeared in the 1890s. Indications of that deterioration also appeared in Congress. Beginning in the progressive years, the cohesion of both parties in Congress declined, and that decline continued virtually without interruption until a measure of restoration was achieved in the New Deal years (Clubb and Traugott 1977, pp. 375−401). Disruption of the parties in Congress was a reflection of divisions within the party leadership, of diminution of the capacities of the parties to function as policymaking agencies, and of the incapacity of the parties to respond to new and conflicting electoral demands.

By the 1920s a new generation had entered American electoral politics, a generation that had not directly experienced the events of the 1890s, much less those of Civil War and Reconstruction, and for whom, as a consequence, the issues and symbols of the prevailing alignment had less meaning. Among these new voters, attachments to the parties were probably less strong than those of their fathers. The demographic structure of the nation had changed. The rural sector had diminished and the urban sector had grown, bringing with it interests and needs that could no longer be avoided. The "children of the new immigration" were coming of age politically, and constituted a force to which the old alignment had not accommodated. New issues had appeared, and older issues had gained renewed salience. The virtually unbridled power of developed corporate enterprise was one new issue, and the conditions and needs of an urban population constituted a second. The lingering difficulties of the agricultural sector remained. To a degree, the economic concerns of the 1890s had worked to submerge issues of nativism and religion, but with the growth of the cities and the increasing political awareness of immigrant-stock groups, those issues took on renewed virulence.

These developments worked to loosen the bonds of partisan identification and to disrupt the partisan alignment; they provide a partial explanation of the shifting electoral tides and the sometimes bizarre political events of the 1920s. The disruption of the old coalitions and the loosening of partisan identifications did not make a new realignment inevitable, but they did provide the conditions under which realignment could occur.

THE REPUBLICAN ERA

It is by no means farfetched to see the realignment of the 1890s, and the arrangement of political power that emerged, as one of the major turning points in American political history. In the new arrangement, the localistic orientation of nineteenth-century electoral politics was reduced, the weight of events of the distant past was similarly diminished, and the focus of politics tended to shift from local issues and loyalties to concerns of national scope. To these develop-ments the coinciding growth of a national communications system and of business enterprise on a national scale also contributed. The weight of agriculture in the political life of the nation was diminished. The new arrangement removed major restraints on the growth of corporate business and in-dustry, in part, perhaps, through effective nullification of the political voices of potentially dissident groups.

The deterioration in the 1920s of the partisan coalitions that emerged from the 1890s provided the conditions for a new realignment. The arrangement of electoral forces that developed in the 1930s did not mark a complete departure from the preceding decades; indeed, there were marked con-tinuities between the new alignment and electoral patterns of the late nineteenth century. The South remained solidly Democratic, and large areas of the Midwest and of the rural Northeast remained heavily Republican. The principle com-ponent of change was the shift of urban America, industrial labor, blacks, and the poor into the Democratic camp. Even here, there were elements of continuity. There is substantial evidence to suggest that lasting electoral change in the 1930s was not primarily the product of conversion of voters from identification with one party to identification with the other. It appears, instead, that the shift in the electoral strength was heavily the result of mobilization of new and formerly inactive members of the potential electorate into the Democratic party (see Nie, Verba, and Petrocik 1976, chapter 5). But whatever its sources, electoral change in the 1930s was momentous for the nation. Just as the realignment of the 1890s opened the way for the growth of industrial capitalism, the new realignment of the 1930s opened the way for the growth, however halting, of the welfare state.

7

EVERETT CARLL LADD

The Shifting Party Coalitions—from the 1930s to the 1970s

Social change and the unraveling New Deal. The Democrats as the "everyone" party. Voting—presidential and otherwise. New Liberalism and Old Liberalism. The transformation of the South. Class/ideology v. class/party relationships. Dealignment. The presidential referendum.

A political transformation of unusual speed and scope took place in the United States during the 1930s. Its most momentous feature was the emergence of a new reigning public philosophy—New Deal liberalism. But there appeared in response as well a new party system, defined by the Democrats' assuming majority status and by dramatic shifts in the composition of the partisan coalitions. By the end of the 1930s a distinctive set of voting patterns and social group attachments had been firmly established. The "New Deal coalitions" had become a prominent and familiar part of the American political landscape.

Since about 1960, though, the New Deal coalitions have been unraveling in the face of complex social change. The United States has entered upon a new sociopolitical setting most aptly described as "postindustrial"—involving such conditions as a dramatic increase in national wealth, advanced technological development, the central importance of knowledge, the elaboration of national electronic communications processes, new occupational structures, and with them new life-styles and expectations, which is to say, new social classes and new centers of power. The social and political world with which the parties must deal has changed so markedly from what it was in the age of Franklin Roosevelt that the party system could not help but be altered. A different mix of policy issues has been thrust upon the political agenda. Lines of social conflict have shifted. New interest groups have appeared and old groups have found themselves with new interests. And as the Democratic and Republican parties have grappled with this changing environment, they have acted in ways which, inevitably, have increased the impact of the broad external social changes on the composition of their respective coalitions.

Today the party alliances and voting patterns which gave a distinctive stamp to the New Deal era have vanished. Some features of the past, of course, are always embedded in the present. We insist that the New Deal coalitions have left the scene, not because nothing of them remains, but because the alliances, issues, and cleavages which distinguished them are no longer those which demarcate the Democratic and Republican coalitions.

The argument of this chapter with regard to the shifting partisan alliances invokes a common observation about social change. At some point, the differences from earlier periods cannot properly be described simply as "more." The quantitative progression produces qualitative change. The analogy of a small snowball at the top of an inclination gradual at the start and becoming ever steeper is not inappropriate. The ball of snow begins to roll, slowly at first—and with its small mass, it grows but slowly; but as the mass enlarges and the inclination becomes steeper, the growth in size becomes extremely rapid. As it approaches the base of the hill, the innocent little snowball has become a fast-moving boulder of snow. Both the little ball and the boulder have something in common, but a person standing in their respective paths could not fail to detect a real difference. At what point did the little snowball become a boulder? At what point did the New Deal coalitions vanish, to be replaced by new alliances? There is some ambiguity, but it need not concern us here. Now, at the beginning of the 1980s, the decisive transformation of the American party coalitions from their New Deal form has surely occurred.

The objective of this chapter is to review briefly a part of the story of this decisive transformation—in terms of time, that which occurred from the Depression years up to the mid-1970s. The continuation of the shift in the 1980 election is discussed elsewhere in this volume. Obviously, I will not be able, in a single chapter, to examine all important dimensions of partisan change—even for the span of time I am covering. In other works, I have explained much more completely the scope and character of the broad but remarkably coherent partisan transformation through which we have been living (Ladd 1970, 1977*a*, 1977*b*, 1977*c*, 1981*a*, 1981*b*; Ladd with Hadley 1978; Ladd, Hadley, and King 1971).

THE "EVERYONE" PARTY

During the New Deal era, each of the two main parties had its reasonably secure bases among certain social groups. The Republicans were the party of the Northeast, of business, of the middle classes, and of white Protestants, while the Democrats enjoyed a clear majority among the working classes, organized labor, Catholics, and the South. And these sources of respective party strength could be counted upon at all levels of the election process—in voting for president, Congress, lesser offices, and in underlying party identification.

After 1960, however, this condition of relatively secure party bailiwicks defined by ethnicity, class, and region began breaking down rapidly. The Democrats emerged almost everywhere outside the presidential arena as the "everyone" party. The depiction is not intended literally, of course. Rather, it is meant to describe a novel situation in which one party had more, at least nominal, adherents than its opposition among virtually all relevant groups. Since 1960 few social collectivities have given the Republicans regular pluralities either in party identification or in the sweep of subpresidential voting.

An examination of the party identification of various age strata, social groups, and ideological clusters in 1976 shows how far the Democratic surge had carried by that date. The Democrats, for example, were well ahead of the GOP in every age cohort, from the youngest segments of the electorate to the oldest, and their margin was remarkably uniform. The proportion of self-described independents did rise steadily, with movement from the oldest to the youngest voters. The latter had had less time to establish regular preferences. And, of course, college-trained people, more inclined to see themselves as "independent," were more heavily represented in the younger cohorts. Still, there was a big and rather even Democratic lead over the Republicans, one that extended from those people whose earliest political memories go back to the 1910s and 1920s to those who first saw U.S. politics in the years of Kennedy, Johnson, and Nixon.

Tables 1 and 2 testify to the breadth of the Democrats' appeal, as compared to that of the Republicans, by the mid-1970s. Wage workers were less Republican than businessmen and executives, but a *plurality of even the latter identified with the Democrats.* Less than one-third of the business/professional stratum claimed attachment to the GOP. All educational groups showed a Democratic margin. So did all income cohorts—up to the very prosperous. The Democrats led the Republicans in every region, among all religious groups, among virtually all ethnic groups. People from wealthy family backgrounds preferred the Democrats by a 2-to-1 margin.

The Democratic lead extended not only to most of the demographic units, but to the principal ideological groups as well. Survey work by Daniel Yankelovich, for example, showed that the Democrats far outdistanced Republicans among voters who thought of themselves as liberals and moderates, and that they even had a comfortable edge among self-described conservatives.[1]

By 1976 there were only a few Republican bailiwicks left. In defining them, the prominent role of region and ethnicity is striking. White Protestants in the Northeast remained strongly Republican, continuing a regional/ethnic tradition that reaches far back into U.S. history. And no group was more decisively Republican than the "Yankees," if the term is taken to mean white Protestants of British stock residing in the Northeastern states.

Tables 1 and 2 show only party identification. But data on congressional voting reveal the same pattern. The Democrats had surpassed their GOP opponents across most of the social spectrum. The middle classes gave higher proportions of their vote to Republican congressional candidates than did

Figure 1
Party Identification by Year of Birth: The American Electorate in 1976

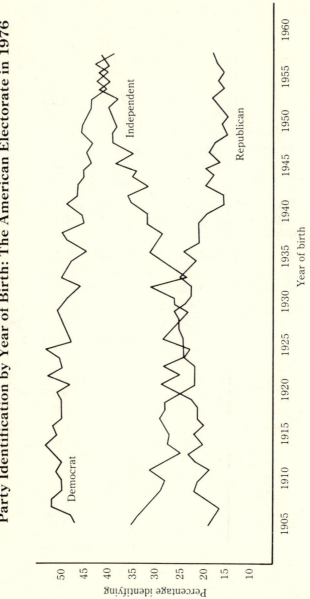

Table 1

Party Identification of Selected Social Groups
(Gallup data, 1976)

Group	Republican	Democratic	Independent
Occupation			
Professionals	27	39	34
Business executives	29	37	34
Sales	29	36	35
Clerical	23	45	32
Skilled blue-collar	17	49	34
Semiskilled, unskilled	15	55	30
Service	18	53	29
Farm owners	36	41	23
Farm laborers	14	59	27
Race and sex			
White males	23	42	35
White females	26	45	28
Black males	5	79	16
Black females	6	79	16
Education			
Less than high school	19	57	24
High school graduate	22	47	31
Some college	26	41	34
College graduate	29	37	34
Religion			
Protestant	27	45	27
Catholic	17	53	30
Jewish	10	59	31
Family income (annual)			
Under $2,000	19	60	21
$2,000–$2,999	17	58	24
$3,000–$3,999	19	56	25
$4,000–$4,999	19	57	24
$5,000–$5,999	18	54	28
$6,000–$6,999	20	54	26
$7,000–$9,999	21	50	29
$10,000–$11,999	21	48	31
$12,000–$14,999	21	45	34
$15,000–$19,999	23	45	32
$20,000 and higher	29	39	31
Region			
Northeast	26	46	29
Midwest	24	41	34
West	27	46	28
South	16	57	28

Source: Combined 1976 data set from American Institute of Public Opinion.
N = 23,086.

Table 2

Party Identification of Selected Social Groups
(NORC data, combined 1972–1976)

Group	Republican	Democratic	Independent
Self-described status			
Lower class	15	61	25
Working class	18	49	34
Middle class	28	38	34
Upper class	38	31	31
Ethnicity			
Irish	21	44	36
German, Austrian	30	34	36
Italian	17	44	39
Scandinavian	30	36	34
Eastern European	13	54	33
English, Scot, Welsh	36	31	34
Other European	24	38	38
Latin American or			
Spanish surname	3	75	22
Black	7	72	21
Family income, age 16			
Far below average	16	61	24
Below average	22	47	31
Average	23	43	34
Above average	27	33	41
Far above average	21	38	41
Other selected groups			
White New England			
Protestants	40	22	39
White Northeastern			
Protestants	45	25	30
Northeast: English,			
Scot, Welsh	52	16	32
Midwest: English, Scot,			
Welsh	38	27	35
West: English, Scot,			
Welsh	36	35	30
South: English, Scot,			
Welsh	27	38	35

Source: Combined data of National Opinion Research Center (NORC), General Social Surveys, each year 1972 through 1976. N = 7,590.

the working classes, but both groups consistently produced large Democratic pluralities.

THE TWO-TIER ELECTORAL ORDER

Over the late 1960s and early 1970s, the United States developed a two-tier system of voting, with one pattern applying at the presidential level and another almost everywhere else. This stood in contrast to the experience of the New Deal era, when presidential voting and that for the lower offices went more or less in tandem. The Democrats came to control by massive margins the Congress, the state legislatures, the governorships, and various lesser offices—reflecting the breadth and inclusiveness of their coalition as described above. But, at the same time, this big majority party had extraordinary difficulties with the presidency. A Democratic presidential nominee received an absolute majority of the popular vote only twice from 1948 to 1976, and only once was there a decisive Democratic victory—Johnson's in 1964. Adding up all of the presidential votes cast from 1948 through 1976, one sees the Republicans actually leading the Democrats, 271 million to 256 million. It is not surprising, considering this, that the presidential coalitions came to differ very substantially from those formed in other contests.

One reason for the sharp and persisting disparity between the Democrats' uncertain performance in presidential elections and their domination elsewhere is that voting for the presidency came to have less and less to do with political party. The parties have been weakened organizationally since 1960, and the American electorate—better educated, more leisured, with more sources of political information, and hence more confident of its ability to judge candidates and programs without reference to their partisan origins—is less strongly attached to the parties and more inclined to vote independently than ever before. The emergence of television as the principal source of information about candidates, especially at the national level where media resources are so great, further transformed contests for the presidency (and a few other highly visible offices in large media-rich states such as New York and California), again reducing the party role. By contrast, in the less visible, less media-attended offices where candidates are not so well known, party is much more influential. Since the Democratic party had more adherents and was more highly regarded than the GOP, the more party emphasis the office received, the better the Democrats were likely to fare.

But it is the special symbolic importance of the presidency that led it to present particular difficulties for the Democrats. The intense public visibility of the office almost requires that various groups and interests attend closely to the style and emphasis of presidential leadership. Presidential contests thus became the principal arena in which were fought out newly emerging policy or ideological differences.

The late 1960s and early 1970s in the United States were a period of extraordinary social change and turbulence. The liberalism that shaped the New Deal state was incorporated into a national consensus, but at the same time a "New Liberalism" emerged—and it was hardly consensual. Comprising such positions as support for new standards of personal morality, cultural values, and life-styles, a questioning of the merits of economic growth on the grounds that growth threatens the "quality of life," and a redefinition of the demands of equality in the direction of "equality of result," the New Liberalism was fraught with danger for candidates who espoused, it, simply because a large majority of the population did not share its enthusiasm for social and cultural change. Dissatisfaction with New Liberalism was especially strong within the white working class. Whereas policy innovation in the 1930s often involved efforts by the working class to strengthen its position vis-à-vis business, in the

1960s and 1970s the New Liberals' projects for social change imposed some significant costs and risks on broad sectors of the working and lower-middle classes, who did not hesitate to make their unhappiness known.

New Liberalism was not, however, without its support, especially among more affluent sectors of the society—even though by 1980 it was decisively out of vogue. The upper-middle class, altered by the infusion of a large professional/managerial, public-sector cohort, had been detached from traditional business concerns. Its perspectives seemed to be shaped far more by the universities and the intellectual community, and many of its members had come to share in some of the critical, change-demanding orientations that had long been associated with intellectual life. These upper strata also had a natural concern about life-styles and cultural change—areas in which the higher-status groups have always been more receptive to change than the traditional middle and working classes. And because they were more secure in their position—less threatened by many contemporary efforts at social change, typically residing some distance from the "front lines"—the upper strata came easily to a more change-supportive posture in such critical areas as race relations.

The Democrats became the primary party of proponents of both liberalisms. The Democratic coalition was thus divided, and over the late 1960s and 1970s the tendency to call attention to this division was far greater at the presidential level than in other contests. The New Liberalism impacted too strongly on the national stage; it was too divisive for the Democrats to be able to package, with any degree of regularity, a ticket which left both New Liberals and Old Liberals comfortably allied. Surely the most dramatic instance of this schism was the 1972 presidential race, in which George McGovern took up the New Liberal banner and was buried electorally by a never especially popular Republican. At the congressional level and elsewhere, however, the party was able to stress the more consensual Old Liberal themes and had little difficulty keeping its massive, heterogeneous coalition together.

THE CASE OF THE SOUTH

A rural, agrarian-radical Dixie was able to rest comfortably within the Democratic party in the context of the economics-dominated Old Liberalism of the 1930s. Contradicting the present picture of their region as the most conservative section, Southerners gave higher approval to the New Deal policies than did the residents of any other region in the country. A newly industrializing, *petit bourgeois* South could not, however, remain securely Democratic as the national political agenda—notably, as it applied to the presidential parties—came to include civil rights and subsequently a host of other extensions of the liberal and equalitarian vision.

Over the 1960s and 1970s, as new issues were thrust upon the political scene, as the South itself was demographically transformed, and as the Southern Republican party was energized and began contesting seriously at the state and local levels, the Democrats' historical ascendency in the region was severely challenged. A virtual decimation of national Democratic allegiance occurred presidentially, within the ranks of Southern white Protestants, between 1940 and 1972. In 1940, 80 percent of this group, the historic center of regional Democratic loyalty, voted for FDR. The Democratic presidential proportion then began dropping off. A major weakening took place around 1948, followed by a kind of plateau, and then virtual collapse in the late 1960s. Only 14 percent of Southern white Protestants voted for George McGovern in 1972.

In 1976, with a Southern white Protestant heading the Democratic ticket—the first politician from a Deep South state to win a major-party presidential nomination since Zachary Taylor of Louisiana in 1848—there was a substantial revival of Democratic support in the South. George McGovern had been completely shut out in the region; yet Jimmy Carter won 118 Southern electoral votes, compared with just 12 (Virginia) for Gerald Ford. The Democratic popular vote in Dixie had been 9.3 percentage points *below* the party's national proportion in 1964, 11.3 percent lower in 1968, and 8.0 percent lower in 1972. Carter, however, won 54.1 percent of the ballots cast in the South in 1976, 4.0 percent above his 50.1 percent share of the national popular vote. This was no return to the massive regional edge enjoyed by the Democrats until 1948—the South had been 18.9 points more Democratic than the country at large in 1932, and 15.7 points more Democratic in 1944—but there was a sharp reversal of the 1964–1972 vote distribution, and a return to roughly the regional advantage of 1948–1956.

Still, Carter failed to win a majority of the vote among Southern whites. Every "Yankee" Democratic nominee from Samuel Tilden through Adlai Stevenson won majority backing among white Southerners—and most did so by overwhelming margins. Southern white Protestants were a loyal and numerically substantial component of the Roosevelt presidential coalition. They gave a higher proportion of their ballots to FDR than any other large, politically relevant, social collectivity. But in 1976 the group was 5 percentage points *less* Democratic than the national electorate.[2] On only four occasions from the Civil War to 1976 did a Democratic presidential nominee lose majority support in the white Protestant South. And these were four presidential elections between 1960 and 1976—all of the elections in this span, that is, except that of 1964. (Again in 1980, Democrat Carter lost the white South.) In many ways, the 1976 results provided even more dramatic proof of the scope and permanence of the presidential realignment than did the McGovern-Nixon contest. If a centrist white Southerner—starting with an extraordinarily high margin of support in his native Deep South state, contesting against the Republican party that had been mauled by the most dramatic political scandal in the country's history and burdened with a poorly performing economy, pitted against a Republican nominee who was the second choice of his own party in the region and was scarcely the most forceful or charismatic of contenders—could not win majority backing in the white Protestant South, what Democratic nominee ever can?

OTHER PROMINENT DEFECTIONS

The Democrats' position nationally as the principal partisan instrument for the New Liberalism brought them a long-term disaffection among other groups that were important parts of the old New Deal majority. Manual workers, big-city dwellers, and Catholics, along with Southern whites, consistently gave much higher majorities during the Roosevelt era to the Democratic presidential nominee than did the public at large. The country was Democratic, and these groups were notably more Democratic than the country. By the elections of 1968 and 1972, however, this Democratic margin had vanished. Blue-collar whites, for instance—12 percent more Democratic than the populace generally in the 1940 election, and again, 12 percent more Democratic in 1948—by 1968 gave the Democrats a proportion of their ballots only 3 points higher than the entire electorate, and by 1972 were actually 4 points *less* Democratic than all voters. There was a comparable decline in the relative margin of Democratic support among such overlapping groups as urban Catholic voters and big-city, working-class whites outside the South (figure 2).

The 1976 vote distribution showed a good bit of similarity to those of other recent presidential elections. The Demo-

Figure 2

Percentage Point Deviation from the Democratic Presidential Vote: Selected Social Groups 1936–1976

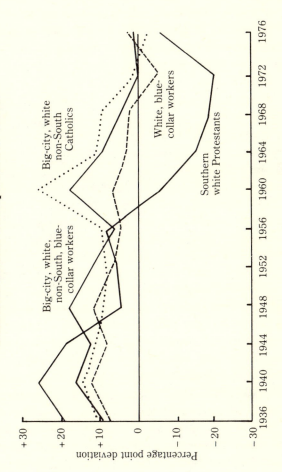

Note: Readings above the "0" line mean the group was (by the indicated percentage) more Democratic than the population generally; readings below the "0" line indicate it was less Democratic.

crats in that year did not regain the large margins within the white working classes which contributed so importantly to their ascendancy in the New Deal era. Urban white Catholics, and blue-collar workers other than those who are blacks and Hispanics, like Southern white Protestants, were somewhat more Democratic in 1976 than they had been in the McGovern-Nixon election, but their electoral standing remained consonant with that of the last decade and a half. There was no return to the Roosevelt-era high Democratic performance.

So the "old New Deal Democratic coalition" was not "put back together one more time" in 1976. Jimmy Carter surely received substantial backing from groups that were the building blocks of the Rooseveltian alignment, and he improved markedly on McGovern's electoral performance, but the Carter coalition had a quite different base than FDR's. Well before the party's 1980 debacle, the character and makeup of the Democrats' presidential coalition had decisively changed.

THE CLASS INVERSION

Class lines were unusually salient in the electoral behavior of the New Deal and immediate post−New Deal years, with groups of lower socioeconomic status markedly more Democratic than the high-status cohorts. This resulted in a relationship involving social class and ideology. That is, the lower-status groups were rather consistently more supportive of liberal programs and policies in the New Deal context than were their high-status counterparts; because the Democrats were the party of New Deal liberalism, they drew their backing disproportionately from among people of lower socioeconomic standing.

Over the late 1960s and early 1970s, however, a pronounced inversion of the New Deal class/ideology relationship occurred—with the result that high-status groups in the United States became more liberal, given the current construction of that category, than the middle-to-lower-status groups across a wide array of issues. This inversion, it must be emphasized, developed around *class* and *ideology*, and it extended to *class* and *party* only in those cases and to the extent that one party was clearly associated with the contemporary extensions of liberalism. The national Democratic party, far more than its Republican opposition, became home in the 1960s and 1970s to the New Liberalism, but the extent of the latter association varied with the individual candidates put forward in each election.

In the presidential elections of 1968 and 1972, the issues of the New Liberalism were unusually prominent, and the Democrats suffered a marked falling off in their relative standing among lower-status groups as compared with their support among high-status cohorts. There was something approaching an actual inversion of the familiar New Deal class/party alignment. In many instances in 1968 and 1972, groups at the top were more Democratic in their presidential voting than those at the bottom.

Table 3 reviews the classic pattern of class voting as it persisted throughout the presidential elections of the New Deal era and into the early 1960s. What had been well established as the traditional configuration held neatly for the several sets of groups represented in this table, and indeed, for all the various socioeconomic groupings which can be located with survey data. Thus, only 30 percent of all white Americans of high socioeconomic status voted for Democratic nominee Harry Truman in 1948, compared with 43 percent for Truman among middle-status whites and 57 percent among low-status white voters. In the 1960 Kennedy-Nixon election the same relationship can be seen, with Kennedy backed by just 38 percent of the high-status group, by 53 percent of the middle-status, and by 61 percent of those of low socioeconomic standing.

Table 3

Democratic Percentage of Presidential Ballots, White Voters by Socioeconomic Position (selected years 1948–1976)

Voters	1948	1960	1968	1972	1976
All					
High SES*	30	38	36	32	41
Middle SES*	43	53	39	26	49
Low SES*	57	61	38	32	53
Women					
High SES	29	35	42	34	41
Middle SES	42	52	40	25	46
Low SES	61	60	39	33	53
Under 30 years of age					
High SES	31	42	50	46	46
Middle SES	47	49	39	32	48
Low SES	64	52	32	36	52
College-educated	36	45	47	45	44
Noncollege	56	49	33	30	51

Source: Data from the following American Institute of Public Opinion surveys: (1948) numbers 430, 431, 432, 433; (1960) numbers 635, 636, 637, 638; (1968) numbers 769, 770, 771, 773; (1972) numbers 857, 858, 859, 860; (1976) numbers 959, 960, 961, 962.

*SES: socioeconomic status. High SES includes persons having upper white-collar and managerial occupations who have had college training; middle SES includes persons having lower white-collar or skilled manual occupations; low SES includes persons having semiskilled and unskilled occupations, service workers, and farm laborers.

By 1968, however, the relationship had changed markedly. Humphrey was supported that year by 50 percent of high-status whites under thirty years of age, but by only 39 percent of their middle-status age mates and by just 32 percent of young, low-status electors. The newly emergent conformation was even clearer in 1972, when the somewhat distorting factor of the Wallace candidacy was removed. Among whites—for blacks constitute a deviating case of voters who are disproportionately in the lower socioeconomic strata but overwhelmingly Democratic—those with college training were more Democratic than those who had not attended college; persons in the professional and managerial stratum were more Democratic than the semiskilled and unskilled work force; and so on. McGovern was backed by 45 percent of the college-educated young, but by only 30 percent of their age mates who had not entered the groves of academe. Comparing 1948 and 1972, we see a reversal of quite extraordinary proportions.

We may conclude, without need of extensive elaboration, that the McGovern candidacy of 1972 distinguished itself far more than the 1976 Carter candidacy by a commitment to the style, programs, and constituencies of the New Liberalism. The tendencies to an electoral inversion paralleling those of class and ideology, then, should have been more pronounced in 1972 than in 1976. And so they were.

But the elements of an electoral inversion so clearly seen in 1968 and 1972 were not wiped away in the Carter-Ford contest. There was a fairly steady increase in the Ford proportion with movement up the socioeconomic ladder, however socioeconomic status is measured. But there was no return to the class voting of the New Deal years. Louis Harris found that grade school—educated whites were about 14 percentage points more Democratic in 1976 than were their college-trained counterparts. Whites from families earning less than $5,000 a year were approximately 16 points more for Carter than were whites with annual family incomes of

$15,000 and higher. Data made available from the Election-Day "exit" polls of the *New York Times*, CBS News, and NBC News show similar distributions. In the 1930s and 1940s, by way of contrast, high-status and low-status whites were separated by between 30 and 40 percentage points in presidential preference.

The Gallup data presented in table 3 reveal the same thing. Lower-status cohorts were relatively more Democratic, compared with their upper-status counterparts, in the contest between Gerald Ford and Jimmy Carter than in either of the two preceding elections. But the Democratic contender in 1976 did not regain the big relative margin among lower-class voters enjoyed by his Democratic counterparts in the New Deal years, nor that which Kennedy achieved as late as 1960. Carter ran a campaign which minimized rather than heightened the "social issue" concerns of lower-status whites. And it should be noted that actual social conditions in 1976 made it far easier for a Democratic nominee to accomplish this than it had been in 1968 and 1972. Still, the altered meaning of liberalism—and hence of the national Democrats as the liberal party—together with the changed social position of the white working classes and the professional/managerial groups, had precluded a return to the class voting patterns of the New Deal epoch.

College-trained professional and managerial people, especially the younger age groups, remain consistently more liberal than the noncollege blue-collar groups on a wide range of social and cultural issues. On matters of economic policy, however, they are often more conservative, although much less decidedly so than during the New Deal. The Democratic party came, in the 1960s and 1970s, to be associated with both the new social liberalism and the old economic liberalism, and as a consequence it evoked contradictory responses within both the upper and the lower socioeconomic categories. The decline in class distinctiveness in voting, and the tendencies toward inversion, came as a result—among white Americans. Black Americans must be treated separately, because their electoral choices have not been accounted for by the class/ideology dynamics we have been describing.[3]

DEALIGNMENT

Since the 1980 presidential balloting, a lively debate has ensued over what the election results actually mean and what their long-term consequences are likely to be. Some have argued that a marked ideological change has occurred in the United States in recent years—the populace has "swung to the Right"—and that Ronald Reagan and the Republicans are building what is likely to be a lasting new majority on the more conservative public mood. Others maintain that the election was simply the rejection of an ineffective president who had to confront some intractable problems, and that at most the GOP won "an opportunity" to show that it could govern successfully.

That this argument has centered on whether a new realignment burst upon the U.S. political scene in 1980 seems to me most unfortunate because it is so untheoretical. As noted, new alignments have been emerging in response to broad social changes ever since the New Deal, and especially since 1960. The 1980 balloting signalled the continuation and the elaboration of these changes, not some sudden new departure. And it has been evident over the 1970s that the primary direction of these shifts is toward *dealignment*, not *realignment*.

A realignment encompasses the movement of large numbers of voters across party lines, establishing a stable new majority coalition. In a dealignment, by way of contrast, old coalitional ties are disrupted, but this happens without some stable new configuration taking shape. Voters move away from parties altogether; loyalties to the parties—and to their candidates and programs—weaken, and more and more of the electorate "comes up for grabs" each election. Over the 1970s an impressive body of theory and data developed which supports the argument that the present era in American electoral politics is one of dealignment and party decay, which specifies the sources of this development, and which identifies its implications for American political life. The progress of dealignment has been giving recent electioneering its distinctive cast.

During the late 1960s and early 1970s one began noting, with increasing frequency, signs of a vast transformation of the political parties and of the nature of voters' attachments to them. For one thing, the national party organizations, never notably robust, experienced a major decline and loss of functions. Within the Congress and in the conduct of presidential nominations, political individualism triumphed over institutional and collective requirements. I have described these developments in some detail elsewhere (Ladd 1979, 1981c).

A weakening in public attachment to the parties has contributed to their institutional decline as much as it has resulted from that decline. Increasing numbers of voters think of themselves as independents, and regularly cross party lines with abandon in election contests (Ladd 1978, pp. 320–33). The proportion of the public lacking confidence in both of the major parties has grown substantially (Ladd 1981a, pp. 3–7). The electorate is less shaped and located by stable partisan loyalties now than at any time in the last century.

An electorate thus "cut loose" is potentially much more volatile than one held in place by the anchors of party. This potential for volatility that party dealignment creates was amply realized over the 1980 presidential campaign, but it had been apparent for at least the preceding decade (see Ladd 1981a, 1981b).

CONCLUSION

Writing in 1971, Samuel Lubell argued that the Republican coalition showed little prospect of becoming majoritarian and that "there does not seem to be much chance of reestablishing the New Deal coalition in its old form" (Lubell 1971, p. 278). He saw party loyalties becoming ever more lightly held, and party fading into the background before what he called "total elections"—those in which presidents utilize their power in economic and foreign affairs in an attempt to orchestrate electoral results. When things go wrong in this setting, the president is blamed massively and is banished from office. Thus, the United States had arrived, Lubell argued, at an age of plebiscitary presidencies. These developments, contributing to an inability to establish any long-range resolution of conflicts dividing the country, had produced "a new alignment of two incomplete, narrow-based coalitions polarized against each other," with the bulk of the populace dealigned and responding afresh every four years to the presidential "referendum" (Lubell 1971, p. 278). Lubell was right.

The changes occurring in the parties and in the public's loyalties to them over the 1960s and 1970s thus were not building to a "critical realignment" of the sort that took place in the late 1920s and 1930s. The changes were momentous enough, and they brought about the dissolution of the New Deal party system, but they were not yielding a coherent new majority. Old attachments were being disrupted without, for the most part, new ones being built in their place. The full impact of electoral dealignment was to be felt in the volatile, party-free voting of 1980.

III

Contemporary Politics

8

NELSON W. POLSBY

Coalition and Faction in American Politics: An Institutional View

The value of coalition politics. Institutional arrangements which force coalitions: elections and the use of the electoral college, nontyrannical majorities. Factions. History, tradition, and analysis of the two major parties. Changes in public policy. Factions and coalitions in Congress. The relationship between Capitol Hill and the White House.

It is a commonplace to observe that American national politics is coalition politics. Any political system of much size

153

or scope is likely to contain within it a population sufficiently diverse as to provoke the formation of factions, each pursuing its own interests. So long as these factions obey majoritarian rules in their dealings one with another, and so long as no faction is by itself large enough to constitute a stable majority, coalitions are necessary. Without coalitions it is impossible to enlist the machinery of government in behalf of the goals of any faction. Consequently, the making and tending of coalitions become central tasks of democratic politics.

All this, as I have said, is commonplace. It applies not only to American politics, but to the politics of any polity meeting the conditions of diversity (i.e., no faction large enough to be itself a majority) and majoritarianism (i.e., policy is made by methods that entail the consent of representatives of more than 50 percent of the populace). Institutional arrangements among polities meeting these conditions vary widely, however. This essay will review the main institutional arrangements in use in the contemporary American political system, exploring the ways in which they tend to facilitate, hinder, and channel the formation of coalitions in government.

COALITION-FORCING INSTITUTIONS

Chief among these institutions is the system of winner-take-all elections. Seats in Congress are contested one at a time, one in each constituency. This means that there is absolutely no incentive built into our system for coming in second, as would be true in a multimember electoral arrangement. In principle, all the congressmen from a state could run in an at-large election, and the top three or eight—whatever number the state was entitled to—would be declared elected. Such a system puts a premium on differentiation among politicians rather than on coalition-building among them. Each contestant tries to find his own special constituency, and tries, not to gather up a majority, but simply to get enough firmly committed votes to end up on the list of winners.

This is not, however, the way we do things. Congressional candidates are obliged to win elections by assembling pluralities, and all those coming in behind the first-place candidate are losers.

In the race for the presidency, the same logic prevails. One of the hidden virtues of the electoral college system—with its aggregation of votes state by state, and the custom of casting all the electoral votes of a state for the winner within the state—is that coalition-building within each state, looking toward the assembly of a majority vote, is encouraged. Under a direct election system, incentives would run in the opposite direction. Instead of pressing politicians toward coalitions looking to a majority in each state, factionalism would be encouraged. Each new entrant into the presidential race, carrying with him an unknown potential for capturing the loosely attached votes of a front-runner, creates an invitation for the next presidential hopeful and the next until, in a crowded electoral field, differentiation—however marginal—and not consensus-building would provide the best chance for victory.

In some states, gubernatorial races and primary elections are designed in this fashion, with free-for-all primaries; in these states, factional warfare is frequently at fever pitch. When the incentives are weak for politicians of divergent opinions to work together, they rarely overcome their natural antipathies. Thus the poisonous political strife of such places as Texas. In such unlikely places as Connecticut, meanwhile, where ethnic rivalry is the engine of politics, "balanced" tickets and mutual accommodations are the norm, owing to nomination processes that make heavy use of such consensus-forcing institutions as state party nominating conventions.

The revolution in the presidential nomination process that has taken place over the last decade has to some extent weakened the capacity of this process to encourage coalition-building. This, surely, is one immediate lesson to be drawn from the difficulties Jimmy Carter experienced in confronting a Congress overwhelmingly controlled by members of his own party. Carter's pathway to the party nomination did not entail making peace with the congeries of political organizations that nominated the congressmen and senators with whom he served. On the contrary, many of the newly minted provisions built into the presidential nomination process required him to build his own organization, state by state and primary by primary. His task was not to assemble a majority, but to come out ahead of the other contestants as frequently as he could. Whoever wins the most important of these trial heats—as judged by the news media and by other political observers—gets the nomination under contemporary rules. The requirements for coalition-building (as contrasted with the activities that go into charming the mass media) have been somewhat relaxed.

Abolition of the electoral college, if this were to come to pass, would relax these requirements even more. It would do so by making the official nomination of a party convention somewhat less valuable, and by encouraging popular candidates to stay in the general election race even without an official party endorsement, in the hope of appealing to enough voters on a cross-party basis to make it into the runoff election.

Much of the preceding discussion has hinted at a proposition that needs to be stated explicitly: that coalition-building is the central task of American political parties. Where party organizations are strong, coalition-building flourishes; where they are weak, the politics of factional rivalry prevails. The great struggles for the dominance of our leading national political parties can be seen as attempts to write the rules of the game so as to favor coalition-building on the one hand, or factionalism on the other. And, as I have said, in recent years coalition-forcing rules in national politics have been weakened.

In Congress, however, the politics of coalition-building is still relatively strong, and this in part explained the sharp differences that observers noted between President Carter and the congressional Democratic majority. Coalition-forcing rules in Congress include the need to build successive majorities, first in committee, then on the floor in each house for each and every measure passed there. Authority over diverse subject matter is widely allocated, and the building of consensus around any particular course of action requires enormous effort. Moreover, each such effort must be viewed in the context of all other similar efforts proximate to it in time. And that, of course, is what coalition-building is all about. The different conditions of men, as James Madison saw—their differing perceptions of what is in their own interest, of what is good, what is better, what is important—provide the raw material out of which nontyrannical majorities might be created.

The creation of nontyrannical majorities is not a bad description of what actually must be done in Congress in order to move the business that comes there. Here, once again, the institution of party eases the considerable friction of the process. Party loyalties provide a basis for common action among disparate members. Party leaders are, by the norms of the place, granted legitimacy to move among the members, to establish schedules and orders of priority, to ask for assistance in orchestrating a program. The fiction is widely subscribed to in Congress that the party program they pass or fail to pass somehow determines each member's own electoral future. Yet the numbers of senators and representatives who actually run on the congressional record, and who stand or fall on what Congress as a collectivity does, must be exceedingly small. Even so, while they are in session, the piety of members toward their party responsibilities is a help in ensuring the passage of many bills.

Electoral rules, political and constitutional structures, the institution of the parties, I have argued, all facilitate coalition-building in American national politics. I have given only brief mention, however, to the material out of which coalitions are formed—namely, factions.

FACTIONS

Coalitions, however necessary they may be for the operation of democratic government, are somewhat unnatural constructs. They arise, not out of the natural bedrock interests of people, but out of their capacity to calculate their advantage over a protracted period, and their ability to see their best interests in the light of the complexity of the political world in which they exist. American coalition-forcing institutions are products of the wisdom and ingenuity of constitution-makers, and reflect a political theory that explicitly attempts to balance the just claims of the political system as a whole against those of its constituent parts.

Factions are the name for the natural parts of a complex political system such as that prevailing in the United States. Factions organize interests, the felt needs of individuals which are seen to be in some sense capable of satisfaction by means of governmental policy. And in order to be more than "interest groups" or "pressure groups," they must exist to some substantial degree in and through the party system, providing a mass base, an ideological format, an organizational matrix, or all three, for the expression of interests by means of party policy or party effort.

Like interest groups, the resources of factions may differ greatly, depending on such things as (1) whether they are composed of many or few members, (2) whether they are concentrated geographically or dispersed thinly over the entire map, (3) whether they represent major resource investments of members or only relatively minor investments, (4) whether, in particular, the social status–giving characteristics of members (such as race or ethnicity) are prominent in factional concerns, and (5) whether their main ideas or policies are fashionable, or popular with the mass media, and thus capable of assuming an aura of self-evident correctness.

These are, of course, only resources; they can be deployed with or without skill, diligence, or dedication to the tasks of influencing party policy. At any given moment in history, some resources may count for more than others. Most competent observers, for example, would concede that the dominant branch of the U.S. labor movement, led by AFL–CIO President Lane Kirkland, contributes greatly in money and in coordinated volunteer effort to the fortunes of the national Democratic party. Yet it was labor, then led by the redoubtable George Meany, that lost the conflict with another faction of the party—activist women's groups and some black groups enjoying a high level of approval from the news media—over the identity of the secretary of labor in the cabinet of the new Carter administration. This illustrates the difficulties of predicting which resources at any given time will prove most effective in shaping party policy.

How factions arise and come to affiliate with one or another political party appear mostly to be accounted for by accidents of history. The Republican party arose in the mid-nineteenth century in part as a result of strongly felt anti-slavery sentiment in the North. The Republican-administered post–Civil War Reconstruction in the South as much as anything made the South solidly Democratic for almost a century after Reconstruction ended in 1876. Black voters—predominantly in the North, where they were not systematically prevented from voting as was true in the Democratic South—were almost always Republican, partisans of Abraham Lincoln, and it took the hardships of the Great Depression of 1929–1933, the mass migration to the

North during and after World War II, and the growth of American prosperity under Democratic auspices to turn American black voters into overwhelmingly Democratic voters in national elections.

In the upper Midwest, it is said, voters of German-American heritage cling to Republican affiliations in part because America fought two world wars against Germany under the leadership of the Democratic party. It was possible to hear an appeal to an echo of this sentiment in Senator Robert Dole's nationally televised reminder, during the 1976 presidential campaign, of the American casualty rate in the "Democrat wars" of the twentieth century.

CONTEMPORARY AMERICAN FACTIONS

One consequence of the grand sweep of American history, and of the different ways that history has affected the different sorts and conditions of Americans, has been the creation of a factional structure in each of the major political parties that is extremely complex. Although some groups have recently voted overwhelmingly for one party (e.g., Jews for the party of Franklin Roosevelt, blacks against the party of Barry Goldwater), it is possible to find, high in the counsels of both parties, prominent members of virtually every group into which Americans divide. Even under rules that relax the pressure for coalition-building, such habits die hard in American politicians, and all but the youngest of them have seen enough turns of the wheel to know that it makes no sense arbitrarily to write off potential allies.

It is nevertheless true that the major factional groupings of both parties can be described with a broad brush as containing a five-faction system. The Republican party has always had two main wings, one representing Main Street, the other, Wall Street. Vermont farmers and Ohio hardware store owners are among the prototypical Main Street Republicans, who were thought to embody homely American virtues of self-reliance and frugality, and therefore to oppose entanglements abroad and big government at home. Main Street Republicans are moralistic about politics and disapprove of professional politicians as a breed. They view government as an intrusion upon the real business of life.

There is a sizable jump from the cultural milieu of the Norman Rockwell painting, represented by this strand of the Republican party's heritage, to the Museum of Modern Art and the sophisticated internationalist moneyhandlers and entrepreneurs who adopted the Republican party as their own because of its permissive—indeed, encouraging—view of economic development. For the last thirty-five years Republicans have been entertaining observers of their presidential nomination politics with fights between these two wings of the party. Usually, at this level, the moderns have won out over the traditionalists; their strongest candidates—Willkie, Eisenhower, Nixon, Ford—have invariably blurred the conflict by somehow bridging the gap between the two wings. Candidates who have traded on the cultural gap or emphasized it—Dewey, Taft, Goldwater, Rockefeller—have suffered accordingly.

Over the years, the modernist wing of the Republican party has shrunk dangerously, and more and more the party is entirely in the hands of its most traditionalist—and frequently its most conservative—remnant. In an era of restricted suffrage, such a posture might be barely tenable. As more and more groups of citizens mobilize effectively and make their demands through the government, as government more and more deploys itself to meet these demands and to compel compliance throughout the private sector, the residuary legatees of the Republican party seem likely to become increasingly alienated from practical politics and decreasingly able to offer effective opposition to the Democrats on a nationwide basis. When they succeed in electing a president, as they did in 1980 with Ronald Reagan, it may be presumed that their success is largely the product of disarray within the Democratic party.

Thus, in some respects, the factional struggle within the Democratic party seems likely to demand the closest attention of serious students of politics. For the Democrats are the true weathervane of American politics; where they point, the rest of the nation, willy-nilly, follows. And here at least three main factions can be identified.

Since the great consolidations of the Roosevelt-Truman years, all mainstream Democrats are, at least nominally, internationalists, welfare-statists, and proponents of civil rights. Yet the variations on these themes create the great conflicts within the party. Contemporary internationalism, for example, was a response to the "lessons" of World War II; to this day, in the rhetoric of some Democrats, these are expressed as a desire to prevent the repetition of the debacle of Munich. The first great cleavage in the party is between Munich-oriented internationalists and those for whom the great lesson is Vietnam. The "lessons" of Vietnam are manifold and varied. No more Vietnam means, to some, no more land wars in Asia; to others, it means no more commitment of U.S. troops anywhere abroad, at least for the time being. To some, it means no more pax Americana; to others, it means all American activity overseas is morally tainted. To some, it means better and more careful consultation with Congress before important actions in foreign policy are undertaken; to others, it means a vast scaling down of all unilateral foreign activity and an increased reliance on such international instrumentalities as the United Nations, whether these international organizations are friendly to U.S. interests (which are regarded as having dubious legitimacy in any event) or not.

The latter halves of these paired comparisons capture at least some of the sentiment expressed by New Left critics of U.S. internationalism in the Kennedy-Johnson-Nixon years.

Many of these critics have been active in Democratic politics and have found allies among established Democratic politicians of national stature. This branch of the party has sought to emphasize so-called "North-South" relations, and to urge that American policy, at a minimum, dissociate itself from activities in which U.S. enterprises invest for profit in nations whose living standards are low or in which right-wing elites control the government. At the same time, they urge a deemphasis upon so-called "East-West" relations. Rivalry with the USSR, the capacity of the Soviet Union to inflict unacceptable damage on the United States, the security of the U.S. "sphere of influence" in Western Europe are, according to this school of thought, problems that have too long constrained the imaginations of U.S. policymakers.

In the field of welfare, there have been two major Democratic dissents from the mainstream. One was George Wallace's quasi-populist complaint about big government, welfare chiselers, and "pointy-headed bureaucrats," a sentiment that resonated rather well with Jimmy Carter's 1976 anti-Washington campaign for the presidency. These views have always coexisted in the South with sentiments favoring big armies, rural electrification, and farm price supports; so the temptation exists to describe Southern populism as a mobilization of more generalized resentments that people at a geographic or social periphery often harbor against those in control of institutions at the center. That these resentments are expressed mostly through the Democratic party rather than through third-party voting is a tribute to the coalition-forcing character of our electoral processes.

The second dissent from the welfare-statist Democratic mainstream is very elitist in its origins, and consists of intellectuals dissatisfied with the results of New Deal through Great Society legislation. Now virtually all economists, including ardent Democrats, embrace the heresy that minimum wages contribute to unemployment. It was Charles Schultze, a liberal Democrat of impeccable credentials, who

torpedoed the original Humphrey-Hawkins public employment bill on the grounds that it would quite likely be
counterproductive.

A skeptical posture vis-à-vis social and economic legislation
is, on the whole, a luxury that Democratic politicians
do not permit themselves, and so the success of intellectuals
in persuading politicians to share their misgivings is likely to
be mixed. In the society at large, the main force working in
their favor is a growing perception that the national government is beginning to approach an upper limit on its capacity
to levy taxes on personal incomes, traditionally the main
source of federal funds. A consciousness of limits on the dis-
posable income of the government promotes an interest in
the cost effectiveness of programs; in these circumstances,
the good report of dispassionate analysts is likely to become
one among many resources on which advocates of programs
will come to rely.

Finally, even in civil rights the Democratic party is in conflict. This has come about in part because the earlier goals of
the party's mainstream have been largely achieved. But as
barriers to equal opportunity have come down, the spirit of
amelioration has moved forward to a new goal, sometimes
described as equality of results. Until recently, keeping
records of Americans according to their race or religion or
national origin was discouraged or outlawed so as to prevent
discrimination. In many areas of national policy this very
practice is now required so as to provide proof that adequate
proportions of previously disadvantaged classes of people are
represented.

This change in the thrust of public policy has not been
unanimously favored by Democrats. In particular, Jewish
groups, for whom the memory of Nuremburg laws is still
green, have dissented from the mainstream Democratic
movement toward benign quotas and affirmative action.
Their main recourse has been to the courts, however. In the
counsels of the party their cause is, for the most part, lost.

Democratic politicians do not align themselves with perfect precision in respect to all these issues, so that a position on one predicts a position on another. On the whole, however, the three main factions of the party have adopted the following dispositions: "New Left" Democrats have been mainly concerned with the lessons of Vietnam, have embraced affirmative action, and have been indifferent to issues of the welfare state. Traditionalist Democrats with strong labor union affiliations have, by and large, retained a keen interest in international East-West rivalry and have defended the welfare state against its critics, while adopting a position of indifference or mild disapproval toward affirmative action. Wallaceites, a shrinking proportion of the whole, have never favored civil rights in any form, and consider affirmative action merely a further occasion for the elaboration of their negative views of the welfare state. In foreign affairs, they are ritualistically anti-Soviet.

It is an instructive anomaly that Jimmy Carter, the last Democratic president, was a member of none of these broad factions and was firmly allied with none of them. His strategy for gaining the nomination relied heavily on making a strong showing in early caucuses and primaries, thereby capturing the attention of the media, and in portraying himself as an anti-Wallace Southerner, thereby enlisting the help of Southern black politicians.

In 1976 this strategy was enough to gain the nomination in a situation where the rules of the game made coalition-building among established politicians relatively unimportant. As his failure to be reelected in 1980 suggests, it was clearly not enough to resolve the main factional conflicts within the party, or to supply the newly elected president with a mandate to which a Democratic Congress felt obliged to respond. And so, evidently much to his surprise, President Carter had to learn to build coalitions in Congress. In this endeavor, his success was not great.

FACTIONS AND COALITIONS
IN CONGRESS

The factions with which any president must contend as he turns his attention to Congress mirror, in most respects, the ideological map of the national party electorates sketched above. Members of Congress—representatives and senators alike—are elite political actors, however; they are not masses reachable only by television. They are nominated and elected in their own right, and, quite properly, take seriously their constitutional duties. As Congress has decentralized its authority structure in recent years, giving more power to the party caucuses, to subcommittee chairmen, and to rank-and-file committee members, the task of a president—or any lobbyist—has become far more complex. Instead of dealing with a handful of institutional kingpins, presidents must now deal with multitudes of influential members, each in his sphere a leader of a committee or a subcommittee, each holding a little piece of discretion over policy and hence, for a president's purposes, power.

There is also the institutional fact of bicameralism, a condition that runs far beyond constitutional formalities. The Senate is no somnolent upper chamber of aged notables, but rather a working body of elected politicians, eager for publicity, many of them alive with presidential ambitions, well supplied with personal staffs and with committee assignments that focus their appetites and their energies. The proper image is not the contemporary House of Lords, but the collection of barons that met at Runnymede.

The House, the far more structured and less individualistic chamber, has always exploited the considerable advantage of numbers to divide labor, and hence to capture decision-making prerogatives through the narrow expertise of its many specialist members. Recent reforms have, if anything, accentuated these institutional differences. The barons of the Senate have voted themselves armies of staff aides whose careers depend on gaining for their principals in one or more policy arenas a position that requires interest groups, national constituencies, and executive-branch bureaucrats to take account of them. The decentralizing reforms of the House have spread to larger numbers of members the opportunity to make their mark on one or another policy process.

As the Congress has decentralized structurally, symbols of ideological commitment have become more important as rallying points for coordination and leadership. Thus, when the House decreased the power of committee chairmen and increased the power of subcommittees and *their* chairmen, it did so through the previously moribund party caucuses —especially on the Democratic side—thus giving to their elected party leaders within the House a set of leadership tools that had lain disused since the days of Joseph Gurney Cannon at the turn of the twentieth century. Now the Speaker and the Democratic caucus invoke, as a condition of committee leadership, stricter norms of party loyalty—ideological tests—than have been institutionally possible since the advent of the seniority system around World War I.

The political precondition of this interesting turn of events was the emergence in the last few elections of a numerically dominant mainstream coalition in the congressional majority party, the Democrats, and the decline of the South in the Democratic congressional caucus. These, in turn, are evidently consequences of reapportionment and the growth of the Republican party in the South.

The factional structure which these changes have affected has maintained its main outlines since Reconstruction:

On the Republican side, as I have noted, there are the two main groups. By far the larger of the two consists of conservative Republicans. This faction includes at least three regional groupings: foremost among them are still the representatives of traditionalistic "rock-ribbed" constituencies dominated by small and middle-sized towns and their rural hinterlands in the Midwest and, to a decreasing extent, along the margins of the East Coast megalopolis. Gerald Ford represented one such constituency, Grand Rapids, Michigan, as did his two predecessors in the Republican leadership, Charles Halleck of rural northern Indiana, and Joseph W. Martin, Jr., of North Attleboro, Massachusetts, and the current minority leader of the House, Robert Michel of Peoria, Illinois. Ford's immediate successor, John Rhodes of Arizona, is an example of the second regional group. Rhodes, like many of his constituents, was born and educated in the Middle West and moved as an adult to Phoenix. As Rhodes illustrates, affluent retirees, ranchers, and the dominant white Anglo, urban and suburban, middle classes throughout the Southwest have sent Republicans to Congress. This has also been true in much of Southern California, from San Diego through Santa Barbara. Meanwhile, in the South, a third conservative regional group has grown up as mass migration and its consequent strain toward the nationalization of ideological perspectives have slowly transformed conservative Democratic congressional seats into conservative Republican seats. Perhaps the most startling example of this process in recent years is the Mississippi Gulf Coast seat held for forty years by a Democrat, William Colmer of Pascagoula. In 1972, on Colmer's retirement, his former administrative assistant, Trent Lott, won the seat as a Republican. As of the 98th Congress, elected in 1980, 39 Republican representatives come from formerly Confederate states, three or four times the number of Southern Republicans as late as a decade ago and a sizable component in the Republican caucus.

Liberal Republicans exist in Congress, but they do not flourish there; as a group they are small and uninfluential. To be embedded in a minority of a minority is painful for politicians of normal ambitions, and consequently some of the most ambitious Republican liberals—John Lindsay of New York, Donald Reigle of Michigan, Bradford Morse of Massachusetts, are examples—have left the House of Representatives for greener—or, at least, other—pastures. Two of the three just mentioned changed their party affiliations, a very rare event among political activists, and the third took a vow of political silence at the UN secretariat.

Other liberal Republicans, representing mostly "silk stocking" or affluent suburban or exurban constituencies from the Berkshires of Massachusetts and Fairfield County in Connecticut to Palo Alto, California, hang on in Congress. Only one, the remarkable (but not excessively liberal) John Anderson of Rockford, Illinois, got very far in the leadership of his party in the House, but he disappeared from Congress after his run for the presidency as an independent candidate in 1980.

In recent congresses, Democrats have outnumbered Republicans by sizable majorities, sometimes by better than two to one. And so any coalition-builder who means to pass laws must attend primarily to the four main factions of the congressional Democratic party. These factions can be distinguished in three ways: by their regions, by their ideologies, and by the nomination processes that sent them to Congress. Not all the Southern seats, for example—indeed, not even a majority of them—have turned Republican. Those sixty-odd congressional districts in the South that continue to return Democrats to Congress are still mostly dominated by Wallaceite white electorates—conservative about federal spending (except for farm subsidies and military construction), and antipathetic to civil rights and to the federal imposition of rules of social conduct. But not all Southern Democratic constituencies are obsessed with matters of race. Andrew Young, for example, represented an Atlanta district having more white than black voters.

The tradition of Southern liberalism goes back a long way, especially in the poorer rural Southern areas that never supported plantations, such as produced Sam Rayburn and Wright Patman in Texas, James Trimble and William Fulbright in Arkansas, and Carl Elliott, Albert Rains, and Bob Jones in Alabama. When these districts are added to Southern districts dominated by urban working folk (e.g., in Houston or New Orleans), or by Northern liberal migrants or underprivileged minorities (e.g., in South Florida or San Antonio), perhaps one-quarter of the Southern Democratic districts are accounted for by mainstream Democrats. More precisely, 25 of the 106 seats allocated to the eleven states of the former Confederacy were held after the 1980 election (which knocked off 5 Southern liberals) by congressmen who voted more than two-thirds of the time with the mainstream of the Democratic party in the preceding Congress.

A little arithmetic can reveal how time has worked against conservative Southerners. So long as the parties were fairly evenly divided in Congress, the South made up nearly half of the Democratic caucus and, in league with conservative (i.e., most) Republicans, it could control the flow of legislation. This was the underlying coalitional structure of the famous "conservative coalition" which dominated Congress from 1938 to the 1960s, and may again as elections change the numbers of members in the various categories. As Democrats increased in Congress overall, the proportion of Southern Democrats, of course, declined, since there were so few Republican Southern seats to take over. In the South the trend went the other way, in fact, and Republicans began in the 1960s to eat into Southern Democratic—mostly conservative—seats. So by the 1970s the Southern conservative voice in the Democratic caucus had diminished sharply.

Just as the homogeneity of the South disappears under scrutiny, so does the uniformity of the Northern and Western Democrats. Here it is useful to invoke variations in nomination processes as a key explanatory variable. In their voting behavior, most of the time, Northern and Western Democrats have indistinguishably supported the New Deal, the labor movement, civil rights, and presidential leadership in foreign affairs. Yet some have led and others have lagged in each of these domains. Some have provided intellectual leadership, tilted at windmills, eschewed temporary alliances with their enemies, and some have not. In general, where strong local party organizations have controlled the nomination process, congressmen have had a strong "practical" streak, and have been followers rather than innovators in policy matters. Where nomination processes have relied heavily on self-starting candidate-oriented organizations, congressmen have tended to be more ideologically committed, more entrepreneurial and experimental in policy matters, more ready to innovate (as well as to ride hobbyhorses) and less ready to compromise. These two groups—urban, frequently ethnic, products of political machines and ideologically liberal self-starters—have not always seen eye to eye.

In the House, the first group is frequently identified, incorrectly, as big-city Democrats, because Chicago, Boston, Philadelphia, Baltimore, and New York City once provided prototypical examples. But embedded within most of these cities have been exceptions to the rule: Abner Mikva of Chicago, Paul Sarbanes and Barbara Mikulski of Baltimore, for example, are or were big-city congressmen but not big-city congressional types, and New York of late has spawned a whole raft of reform-oriented machine-wrecking congressmen. Meanwhile, small and middle-sized communities like Hartford, Connecticut, and Reading and Wilkes-Barre, Pennsylvania, have sent pragmatic mainline Democrats to Congress with great regularity.

DEMOCRATIC DILEMMAS

After the landslide election of 1958, liberal Democrats in the House expected to move their twenty-year-old agenda of

social reform through Congress without difficulty, and instead met with frustration and, for the most part, failure.
Out of this experience grew the impetus for an organization
of liberal Democrats, the Democratic Study Group, which
over the next fifteen years was a major influence in shifting
the leadership of the Democratic congressional party away
from a posture of acquiescence toward the conservative
coalition and toward programmatic coherence around New
Deal/Fair Deal/New Frontier/Great Society proposals. The
leadership of Lyndon Johnson in the White House, and the
Democratic landslide of 1964, provided the added components necessary for success—a friendly president, and
enough votes to win in committee, in caucus, and on the floor.

The Vietnam War, however, drove a wedge through the
mainstream Democratic coalition—organization congressmen retaining their loyalty to the Johnson war policies,
reformers, and those without strong local party organizations tending toward disaffection. Fortuitously, one of the
few dovish congressional party regulars—Thomas P. O'Neill
of Cambridge, Massachusetts—found himself in line for the
speakership when Speaker Albert went into retirement in
1976, thus holding out the promise of a renewed alliance between the two largest factions of the congressional Democratic party.

Historically, alliances among these various factions have
been subject to continuous negotiation. In 1910–1911 a
group of big-city Democrats sided with stand-pat Republican
Speaker Cannon in his fight against the insurgent
progressive wing of his own party. But the insurgents and
the rest of the Democrats, led by Champ Clark of Missouri,
were too numerous on that occasion. The conservative coalition, which I have mentioned, has been an extraordinarily
successful long-term collaboration between conservative
Democrats and Republicans over a forty-year period, yet in
1964 it broke down over an issue dear to the heart of the
South when Republicans deserted the coalition to support

the civil rights bill. Traditionally, Southerners would trade their votes on reclamation projects to pick up Western support on procedural matters surrounding civil rights bills. In organizing the Democratic party in the House, an alliance was formed between Southern moderates and party regulars of the North that has produced virtually all the leadership combinations of the last forty years (Rayburn [Texas]/ McCormack [Massachusetts], 1940–1961; McCormack/Albert [Oklahoma], 1962–1970; Albert/O'Neill [Massachusetts], 1972–1977; O'Neill/Wright [Texas], 1977–), the only exception being the short majority leadership of Hale Boggs (Louisiana, 1970–1972, in combination with Albert of Oklahoma). Each time, however, these alliances have had to be renegotiated, and ideological affinity is always subjected to the inexorable discipline of numbers.

These historical examples of coalition formation within Congress illustrate some of the diverse patterns that successful congressional alliances are capable of taking. It is important to stress that those coalitions are by no means confined within party lines, and that they are based on calculations of factional interest no less astute than those calculations that inform the alignments producing presidential nominees. But owing to the differential institutional contexts within which each set of factions must work, presidential and congressional coalitions, even when dominated by the same party, are bound to differ in their compositions and consequently in their priorities. Recent reforms of the presidential nominating process seem likely to accentuate these differences by further divorcing Democratic presidential nominees from the party organizations that nominate congressmen. Increases in the capability and willingness of congressional Democrats to apply simple ideological tests to their institutional leaders work in a conciliatory direction. But the long-run capacity of Congress and the president to work together—harmoniously, at least—under Democratic auspices is heavily dependent upon (1) the maintenance of the coalition within Congress between the program-oriented, liberal-on-principle, independently nominated faction of the party and the moderate, pragmatic, party-organization nominated faction; (2) the election or reelection of a sufficient number of Democrats in each category to defeat the resurgence of the conservative coalition; and (3) the willingness of a Democratic president, whose route to power differs so much from that of his most likely congressional allies, to match his goals and shape his rhetoric so as to respond constructively to the political constraints with which congressmen must grapple. Elizabeth Drew remarked that Jimmy Carter had said so often that he owed his election to nobody, that nobody on Capitol Hill felt he owed anything to Jimmy Carter. Only a conscious and concerted effort is likely to overcome this emerging weakness in the ability of our institutions to encourage and sustain the building of a Democratic coalition that can govern successfully.

REPUBLICAN OPPORTUNITIES?

One major consequence of the reforms of the presidential nomination process chiefly inspired by the Democratic party has been the failure of the Democrats to win three out of the last four presidential elections. This has given new impetus to the perennial speculation that the grand coalition which has made the Democrats the nationwide majority party since 1932 is finally crumbling. Republican landslides at the presidential level in 1956 and 1972 failed to elect Republican congressional majorities. In the 1980 election, however, the Democrats yielded a dozen Senate seats and, for the first time in twenty-six years, lost control of the Senate itself. In the House their majority shrank from 114 to 51.

There seems to be no doubt that Ronald Reagan was elected president with the help of a large number of Democratic votes. The question is whether this many Democratic votes will continue to be available to Republican candidates, not only for president but farther down on the ticket. If so, then analysts, by hindsight, will presumably consider 1980 to have been a "critical election" in which a fundamental shift in the electoral bases of party politics took place.

Alternatively, in the light of future elections, 1980 may come to be seen as just another Republican blip in the midst of a Democratic era, caused by Jimmy Carter's unpopularity and by the Democratic party's inability to get itself organized reliably to nominate presidential candidates widely supported by Democrats. Of course, such an inability, neglected long enough, can result in a great deal of Republican success at the polls.

The critical election interpretation implies the broadening of the Republican coalition from its rather narrow base of true believers; the blip theory implies no such expansion of the Republican party, merely Republican electoral success under conditions that are bound to be unstable over the medium term.

Present evidence, while imperfect, points more toward systemic inertia than toward the fundamental change preached by Ronald Reagan's well-wishers. A skeptical reading of the signs produces the following points:

(1) While it is true that Ronald Reagan won the presidency in 1980 by a handsome margin of popular votes, greatly magnified by the arithmetic of the electoral college, there is evidence that he was the beneficiary of anti-Carter sentiment rather than the leading edge of a Republican or a conservative landslide. Most of those eligible to vote did not consider themselves either conservative or Republican. Indeed, the Reagan victory does not seem to have materially altered mass political attitudes or party allegiances very much. Opinion polls did not disclose a shift away from popular support for a variety of public expenditures and social attitudes opposed by President Reagan.

(2) This does not mean that President Reagan will be unable to create and capitalize on one of those "rolling waves of sentiment" that sometimes grip Washington, D.C., on behalf of his program. There are plenty of historical precedents. Much was done in Washington in the wake of Sputnik that was unrelated to the perceived Soviet challenge. The underlying electoral justification was slight for the panic that Senator Joseph McCarthy engendered in Washington. Reagan is greatly aided by Republican recapture of the Senate, and by the resurgence in the House of the rudiments of an alliance between conservative Southern Democrats and Republicans.

(3) It will, no doubt, be part of the Reagan administration strategy to read the congressional election figures optimistically, yet the claim of an overwhelming electoral ground swell will not survive scrutiny. In the election of 1980, a strongly Republican result was achieved in the Senate without a Republican landslide. In fact, without counting votes cast for the unopposed Democrat Russell Long, almost 3 million more people voted for Democratic candidates for the Senate than voted for Republicans. Republicans won 21 out of the 33 Senate seats up for a decision in 1980, but mostly by small margins. Of the fifteen races where the winner won by the biggest margins, nine were won by Democrats. Democratic liberals beat Republican conservatives for two of the five open Senate seats (in Illinois and Connecticut). A Republican liberal, Arlen Specter of Pennsylvania, won a third. Republicans won three seats (in Alaska, Florida, and Alabama) where Democratic incumbents had been knocked off in bitterly contested primary elections. The most conservative Republican winners, on the whole, barely squeaked through: D'Amato of New York with a resounding 45.0 percent of the vote, Goldwater reelected with 49.4 percent, East of North Carolina, Kasten of Wisconsin, and Denton of Alabama getting barely 50.0 percent of the vote. While six prominent Democratic liberals were beaten in the general election (McGovern [South Dakota], Magnuson

[Washington], Bayh [Indiana], Culver [Iowa], Church [Idaho], Nelson [Wisconsin]), six other Democratic liberals (Inouye [Hawaii], Glenn [Ohio], Cranston [California], Eagleton [Missouri], Hart [Colorado], Leahy [Vermont]) survived, half of them by handsome margins. Not all Republican winners were conservative: Mathias of Maryland was reelected with two-thirds of the vote, and Packwood of Oregon, Gorton of Washington, and Rudman of New Hampshire all ran as moderates. Not all Democrats defeated were liberal—for instance, Talmadge of Georgia and Morgan of North Carolina.

All of these observations taken together cannot nullify the fact of Republican and conservative gains in the Senate as the result of the 1980 election. They do, however, give ample grounds for doubt that the 1980 electorate was particularly conservative in its outlook, or indeed greatly different from the electorates that produced quite different senatorial results in other years when it was liberals rather than conservative candidates who were squeaking through.

(4) In the House, an even more straightforward interpretation is available that argues for persistence rather than drastic change. Since the election of 1974, disapproval of Watergate had swollen the ranks of House Democrats. The election of 1980 returned the partisan alignment in the House to the numbers that resulted after the 1972 election, when another unpopular Democrat ran for president. In that year, the most plausible interpretation of the results was that George McGovern had single-handedly held off a Democratic landslide. The 1980 senatorial election figures suggest only weakly that other factors beside Jimmy Carter's unpopularity were at work favoring the Republican side, so the question remains: if 1980 was a genuine landslide for the Republicans, why were they not able to win control of the House outright? Nearly 2 million more Democratic than Republican votes were cast for House candidates. In addition, in

eleven unopposed seats—seven of them held by Democrats—the votes were not counted.

(5) In the state houses and state legislative assemblies, the Republicans have made great gains under the leadership of a gifted and sophisticated national chairman, Bill Brock, deploying an opulent war chest. Yet even here, what resulted by 1980 were Republican gains over a previously dismal situation, not Republican dominance. After the 1980 elections, roughly twice as many state legislative assemblies were controlled by Democrats as by Republicans, and Democratic state legislators outnumbered Republicans by 4,497 to 2,918.

Thus, by the measures of overall electoral results, party identification, and policy preferences within the American populace, the political foundations for Republican presidential dominance are weak. A Republican president is now serving at the pleasure of disaffected Democrats. His principal long-run political task is to broaden the base of the Republican party. Over the short run, good management of the considerable political resources of the presidency can produce much in the way of programmatic results. The sands of time run swiftly for any president, however, and the historic pattern of midterm congressional elections is to sap, not to augment, the president's party in Congress. Trends in reapportionment may assist President Reagan here, but they will have to do heroic work to reverse the longer-term pattern.

The main source of disaffected Democrats—the fuel which evidently powers Republicans into the presidency—remains the Democratic party itself and its presidential nomination processes. Only so long as the Democrats are unable either to agree overwhelmingly on a consensus candidate or to evolve a nomination process that embraces rather than alienates its disparate factions can Republicans enter each election season expecting to win without compromising the political principles that they hold in common—but do not share with most Americans.

9

WILLIAM SCHNEIDER

Democrats and Republicans, Liberals and Conservatives*

The three partisan systems in modern U.S. electoral history. The forces that affect voting behavior. Alignment and realignment. Partisanship and ideology. Political geography: the effect of economic, social, and cultural issues. Radicals, liberals, and conservatives. Party coalition and conflict. The patterns of congressional voting.

*This research was supported by a National Fellowship at the Hoover Institution, Stanford, California.

The geographic patterns of modern American voting behavior suggest two distinct issue dimensions: a *partisan* dimension related primarily to economic issues, and an *ideological* dimension reflecting social and cultural conflict. State-level election returns reveal that these two dimensions account for the nationwide pattern of the vote in presidential and congressional elections since 1900, with each dimension representing a historically continuous alignment.

The relative importance of the two dimensions changes over time, as do the parties' positions on them. These changes reflect periods of realignment in American electoral history. Three different "party systems" can be identified: (1) the "system of 1896," which preceded the New Deal, (2) the New Deal system, and (3) the "system of the 1960s," which has characterized presidential elections since 1964. Each system shows a distinctive pattern of partisan and ideological conflict.

CHANGING PATTERNS OF POLITICAL BEHAVIOR

Since the early 1960s, following the tradition of *The American Voter* (Campbell et al. 1960, especially chapters 5 and 6), political scientists have measured and analyzed the partisan alignment, elaborated theories concerning the transmission of partisan loyalties within groups and across generations, and traced in minute detail every palpitation in the conventional indicators of partisan allegiance.[1] All would agree with Everett Ladd's general conclusion (Ladd with Hadley 1978, p. 271) that "as we have moved from the New Deal party system to that of the postindustrial era, we find continuities aplenty, the persistence of many traditional patterns in social group distributions. Changes defining the new party system are nonetheless impressive."

The most dramatic changes have been the defection of the South from its historic Democratic allegiance; the emergence of black voters as a major political force; the "law-and-order" backlash among white working-class voters in many urban centers; and the emergence of activist ideological movements on both the Left and the Right. On a more detailed level, Ladd finds evidence of a partial inversion of the New Deal class relationship in the repeated defections of many working-class Democrats from the more liberal nominees of their party, accompanied by the increased attraction of certain upper-middle-class voters to these same candidates (Ladd with Hadley 1978, p. 271).

These discontinuities in the demographic sources of the vote have been accompanied by impressive changes in political behavior, mostly in the direction of decreasing partisan regularity and increasing issue orientation. Nie, Verba, and Petrocik (1976, p. 346) summarize the most important findings:

Citizens are less committed to the political parties. The Independents represent the largest group in the society. . . . Furthermore, even among those with a partisan identification, the ties of partisanship are much weaker. Voters have become more likely to desert their party to vote for the opposition candidate in both national and local elections; and citizens in general are dissatisfied with the performance of the political parties, including their own. At the same time, the electorate has developed a more coherent set of issue positions and uses those issue orientations as guides in voting. The result is that voters in presidential elections are more likely to vote for a *candidate* on the basis of the candidate's personal characteristics and/or the candidate's issue positions than they are to vote on the basis of long-term commitment to a political party.

Most researchers agree that these sociological and behavioral changes have been significant (see, for instance, Burnham 1970, pp. 119–34; Ladd with Hadley 1978, pp. 319–61; Miller and Levitin 1976, pp. 255–66). There is much less agreement on what they mean —whether they signify a temporary aberration, a partial realignment, a trend toward party decomposition, or a reinvigoration of the New Deal party system.

ALIGNMENT

Studies of voting behavior emphasize "alignment"—a stable and persistent pattern of voting across different elections. With a partisan alignment, votes for candidates of the same party should be positively correlated. Republican candidates for different offices and in different elections, for example, should do *relatively* well in strongly Republican areas and strongly Republican population groups; they should do *relatively* poorly in strongly Democratic areas and strongly Democratic social categories. The word "relatively" is emphasized. A party may nominate a candidate whose inadequacies are so universally recognized as to cause him to lose in every geographic area and within every population group, from the strongest Democrats to the strongest Republicans; but the notion of a partisan alignment means he will do relatively well among his own strong partisans, even if he loses them along with all the others.

The correlation coefficient (r) expresses in standardized form the relationship between two votes.[2] By examining correlational patterns, we are implicitly distinguishing between long-term and short-term influences on voting behavior. A popular candidate like Eisenhower appears to have won large "personal" majorities in the 1950s without disturbing the underlying patterns of party identification (Nie, Verba, and Petrocik 1976, pp. 28–35). On the other hand, Lyndon B. Johnson's landslide victory of 1964 disrupted traditional patterns of party support, most obviously in the massive defection of the Deep South from the Democratic party.

The test of a realignment is its endurance. In the case of

the 1964 Johnson vote, there is at least *prima facie* evidence of persistence; the Deep South continued its defection from Democratic presidential candidates in 1968, 1972, and 1980.

An alignment represents a particular pattern of division — by class, ideology, religion, generation, region, or party, for example. These divisions emerge from conflicts over what Stokes has called "position issues" (1966, pp. 170–71) — issues on which there are legitimate opposing sides.[3] These he distinguishes from "valence issues," which produce no fundamental disagreement over alternative values: peace, prosperity, and good government are examples.

Valence issues, on which candidates compete by claiming to stand for the same universally desired values, often have a determinative effect on electoral outcomes. The desire for change may be more meaningful to voters than ideological differences or class or ethnic conflict. The important characteristic of valence issues is that they affect voters across the board, and not differentially by geographical area or social category. As a result, they may have a powerful effect on a candidate's overall performance but absolutely no impact on the underlying pattern of correlations. In looking at correlations, we are making a conscious decision to exclude valence issues and short-term forces in order to focus on enduring sources of conflict.

TWO DIMENSIONS

The following analysis will describe the alignment structure of modern American voting behavior and offer an interpretation of the period 1960–1980 in terms of broader historical patterns.

Our working hypothesis is that a dual alignment has emerged since 1960 — a partisan alignment (Democrat, Independent, Republican) and an ideological alignment (liberal, moderate, conservative). The partisan alignment represents the "New Deal system" of partisanship, with the Democratic and Republican parties differentiated primarily in class terms, but with a strong overlay of religious and regional loyalties long antedating the New Deal. This is the dimension measured by the standard "party identification" question first analyzed in depth in *The American Voter* (Campbell et al. 1960): "Generally speaking, do you usually think of yourself as a Republican, a Democrat, an Independent, or what?" The most important characteristic of this alignment has been the continuing predominance of Democratic party identifiers, who have usually outnumbered Republican identifiers by about 2 to 1 (that margin has been diminishing to about $1\frac{1}{2}$ to 1 in 1980–1981 surveys).

The ideological alignment represents a dimension of conflict that has come into prominence since the mid-1960s. It is usually described as "liberal" v. "conservative," although these terms have been used in American politics for much longer than the past fifteen years. In the past decade "liberal" and "conservative" have acquired a new currency because of their association with opposite sides of the great political conflicts of the 1960s—race, the Vietnam War, and social and cultural radicalism. By now it is conventional to use a two-dimensional classification to describe both voters and politicians—"liberal Democrats," "moderate Republicans"—a usage that implies the inadequacy of party labels alone to depict political beliefs and issue positions. The Democratic party has a large and powerful liberal wing, while conservatives predominate within the Republican party. Yet there remain many moderate and conservative Democrats and a small but resilient number of liberal and moderate Republicans, as well as substantial numbers of liberals and conservatives who profess no partisan allegiance at all. Thus one may treat the two dimensions, partisanship and ideology, as conceptually distinct, though empirically correlated.[4]

The data for this analysis consist of the percentage votes,

by state, in each presidential election from 1900 through 1980 and in each congressional election from 1896 through 1980. These time spans include roughly equal periods before and after the New Deal realignment of the 1930s. The 89 votes (46 presidential votes and 43 congressional votes) were subjected to a factor analysis. Two factors—which I have called ideology and partisanship—were found to fit the data quite well.[5]

Figure 1a plots the correlation of every Democratic presidential vote, 1900 through 1980, with the two factors. Figure 1b does the same for every Democratic congressional vote, 1896 through 1980. Table 1 displays the actual factor loadings for presidential votes from 1960 through 1980.

The three 1968 presidential votes shown in table 1 help to identify the two factors. Factor I sharply differentiates the Humphrey vote and the Wallace vote. Nixon's vote in 1968 shows no correlation in either direction. This pattern corresponds to the polarization over social and cultural issues in the late 1960s, with Humphrey's vote defining the "liberal" direction and Wallace's vote, the "conservative" direction. Nixon's 1968 vote was ideologically "centrist." Factor I is labeled "IDEOLOGY" in figures 1a and 1b and is represented by a dotted line.

The second factor in table 1 contrasts the Humphrey vote with the Nixon vote, thereby differentiating the candidates of the two major parties. The vote for the Independent candidate, Wallace, is in the middle, showing a slight correlation in the "Democratic" direction. Factor II is labeled "PARTISAN-SHIP" in figures 1a and 1b and is represented by a solid line.

The two-factor solution thus defines the 1968 Humphrey vote as liberal Democratic, the 1968 Nixon vote as centrist Republican, and the 1968 Wallace vote as conservative Independent—all very much in line with conventional interpretations.

This definition of the two factors is consistent with the rest of the data. In figures 1a and 1b, a positive correlation with

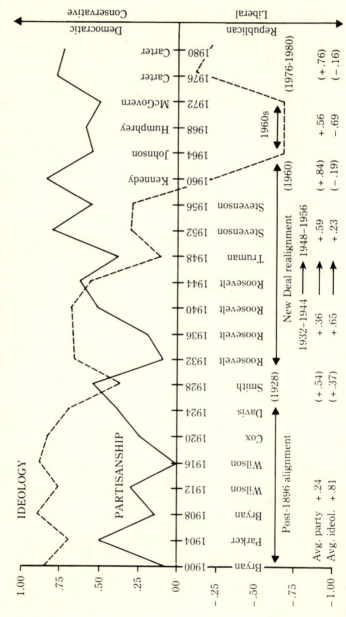

Figure 1a

Factor Loadings:

Democratic Presidential Votes, 1900–1980

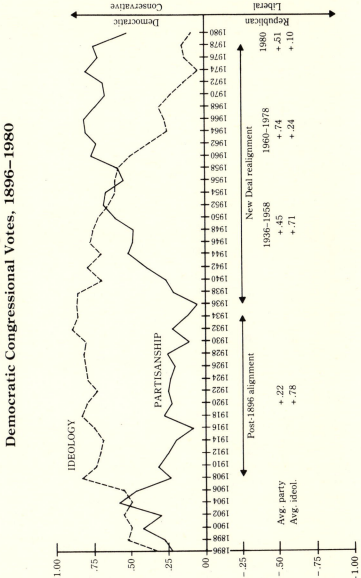

Figure 1b
Factor Loadings:
Democratic Congressional Votes, 1896–1980

Table 1
Factor Loadings of Presidential Votes 1960–1980

Presidential votes		Factor I Ideology + Conservative − Liberal			Factor II Partisanship + Democratic − Republican		
1960							
Kennedy (50%)	D	−.19			.84		
Nixon (50%)	R		.01			−.87	
1964							
Johnson (61%)	D	−.68			.55		
Goldwater (38%)	R		.68			−.55	
1968							
Humphrey (43%)	D	−.69			.62		
Nixon (43%)	R		−.01			−.91	
Wallace (13%)	I			.80			.19
1972							
McGovern (38%)	D	−.69			.50		
Nixon (61%)	R		.68			−.43	
1976							
Carter (50%)	D	−.11			.78		
Ford (48%)	R		.15			−.76	
1980							
Carter (41%)	D	−.18			.74		
Reagan (51%)	R		.40			−.71	
Anderson (7%)	I			−.57			.06

Note: Varimax rotated factor matrix* (partial results)

Weighted N = 37 non−Southern states (excluding Alaska and Hawaii), plus 11 Southern states weighted equal to 1.

*For 1900−1976 matrix, see Schneider 1978, pp. 264−67, table A−2.

partisanship is defined (arbitrarily) as Democratic, and a positive correlation with ideology is defined (arbitrarily) as conservative. The negative directions are therefore Republican and liberal. Every Democratic presidential vote in figure 1a and every Democratic congressional vote in figure 1b is positively correlated with the partisanship factor.

In figures 1a and 1b, the positive correlations between Democratic votes and partisanship increase steadily after 1936. Only one out of ten Democratic presidential votes prior to 1940 reached a correlation with the partisanship factor of over .50—the Al Smith vote in 1928, a vote often taken as a portent of the New Deal realignment. From 1940 to 1980 only one Democratic presidential vote failed to correlate at least .50 with the partisanship factor. That was the Harry Truman vote in the 1948 election, when Truman and Strom Thurmond, the States' Rights candidate, shared the traditional Democratic vote (Truman .39, Thurmond .35). The New Deal appears to have consolidated the previously weak and irregular partisan alignment.

Ideology shows a more complex pattern. Figure 1a reveals a shift in the ideological complexion of the presidential vote across the twentieth century. In the early part of the century, between 1900 and 1924, the Democratic presidential vote was strongly conservative and the Republican vote, correspondingly liberal. The ideological distinction between the major-party presidential votes remained fairly strong in the 1930s and 1940s (about .65 for the Democrats and −.65 for the Republicans) but by the 1950s had become insignificant at the presidential level.

The important shift came in the 1960s. The ideological differentiation between Democrats and Republicans increased markedly, but in a direction exactly the reverse of the historic pattern. Democratic presidential votes between 1964 and 1972 became significantly liberal: −.68 for Lyndon Johnson and −.69 for Hubert Humphrey and George McGovern. Republican votes for Barry Goldwater in 1964 and for Richard Nixon in 1972 were correspondingly conservative. In 1968 it was George Wallace who captured the conservative vote. Nineteen seventy-six saw a temporary respite from the ideological polarization of the 1964–1972 period. The ideological difference between the Carter and Ford votes was relatively slight—about the same, in fact, as the difference in 1960 between Kennedy and Nixon. Figure 1a suggests that ideology had little effect in 1980 as well; that is because only Democratic votes are displayed in that figure, and the Carter vote in 1980, as in 1976, was not significantly liberal or conservative. But ideological differences did make a partial comeback in 1980. They can be seen in table 1, in the contrast between the Reagan vote (which correlated .40 with ideology) and the Anderson vote (−.57).

How should this pattern of ideological change be interpreted? Each of the great confrontations of the 1960s— Goldwater v. Johnson, Humphrey v. Wallace, Nixon v. McGovern—can be described as intensely ideological, in that the issues and candidates tended to split voters along liberal/conservative lines. In each of these three elections, there was one candidate whose appeal was strongly ideological—the Republican in 1964, the Independent in 1968, and the Democrat in 1972. When an ideological candidate runs against a moderate in a two-way race, the nature of the choice becomes ideological.

In the three-way contest in 1968, it was Humphrey and Wallace who polarized the vote along the ideological dimension. Nixon, whose vote was notably centrist in 1960 and 1968, drew a decidedly conservative vote in 1972, when his opponent was a liberal Democrat and there was no third-party conservative to draw off votes. In 1972 Nixon did best in those states where Wallace had done best in 1968—in the South. Indeed, Nixon's worst state in 1968—Mississippi, where he won only 13.5 percent of the vote—was his best state in 1972, giving him no less than 78.0 percent.

The ideological factor appears to have been weak in presidential elections between 1952 and 1960 and again in the 1976 election. The 1950s are often described as a period of low ideological conflict in American politics, and the 1960 election was widely perceived at the time as offering a "Tweedledee-Tweedledum" choice (Miller and Levitin 1976, pp. 52–53; Pomper 1975, pp. 166–85; Nie, Verba, and Petrocik 1976, pp. 14–42). And in 1976, both Carter and Ford were regarded as moderates in the contexts of their respective parties, especially when compared with the candidates who came in second for each party's nomination, Morris Udall and Ronald Reagan. The weakness of ideological differences in 1976 may also have been due to Carter's appeal to white Southerners as a Deep Southerner and fundamentalist Protestant himself.

However, the 1980 election demonstrated that the impact of "the 1960s"—namely, ideological polarization—was not a transitory phenomenon. The Republicans nominated a real social and cultural conservative who had established his appeal in the late 1960s as a "law-and-order" spokesman, while the Anderson candidacy essentially punished the Democrats for failing to nominate a *bona fide* liberal.

The most striking characteristic of the ideology factor is the change over time in party positions. From 1900 to 1956 the vote for every Democratic presidential candidate correlated positively with the ideology factor, while every Republican presidential vote correlated negatively. Figure 1b shows this pattern continuing to the present in congressional voting. The data would lead us to conclude that, historically, the Democratic vote has been conservative and the Republican vote, liberal. This pattern has declined in significance over the twentieth century in both presidential and congressional voting. But the change has occurred at different rates; the conservative-Democratic, liberal-Republican pattern became insignificant at the congressional level after 1960. The presidential alignment reversed during the 1960s; the Democrats became the liberal party, and the Republicans, the conservative party. As of 1980 this reversal had not occurred at the congressional level.

The ideological alignment is strongly sectional. The conservative presidential candidates in the 1960s—Goldwater, Wallace, and Nixon in 1972—all showed disproportionate strength in the South. The ideology factor is not merely a sectional alignment, however. A truly sectional factor would have differentiated Wallace from both Humphrey and Nixon in the 1968 election, since Nixon's 1968 vote was also relatively low in the South.[6] The 1968 conflict between Humphrey and Wallace to capture traditionally Democratic white working-class votes can better be described as ideological. The two candidates split those votes mostly along lines of racial ideology—a split that did indeed have strong overtones of sectionalism, since "Southernism" was associated in all parts of the country with racial prejudice and, consequently, with support for Wallace (Lipset and Raab 1978, p. 391).[7]

In the recent American context, partisanship relates primarily to economic issues, while ideology signifies social and cultural conflict. Thus it can be argued that Democratic partisanship represents economic liberalism in the Progressive and New Deal sense—attitudes sympathetic to a stronger government role in the economy and antagonistic toward business (although not toward free enterprise).[8] If this interpretation is correct, the increase in the importance of partisanship during the 1940s and 1950s was a response to the economic conflicts associated with the New Deal.

Social and cultural issues tap such values as tolerance, authoritarianism, and support for social change. Thus, a liberal social attitude is usually depicted as tolerant, nonauthoritarian, and supportive of change—characteristics more frequently found among better-educated and higher-status individuals.[9] Race has been the most persistent source of social conflict in U.S. history. The 1960s saw a sharp increase in the salience of racial issues as civil rights became a nationwide conflict. Other social issues also emerged during the 1960s: the Vietnam War, which produced deep divisions over military values and interventionism, as well as social and cultural radicalism (student protest, civil disobedience, women's rights, environmentalism, and conflicts over sexual freedom, drug use, and conventional morality). These issues, which split the electorate on a different sociological axis than that of economic conflict, intensified after 1964. The Democratic party became identified as relatively more sympathetic to social and cultural liberalism, at least at the national level. According to figure 1a, the Democratic presidential appeal in 1964, 1968, and 1972 was liberal in both the economic and the sociocultural sense.

The main problem of interpretation relates to the ideological factor prior to the New Deal. Figures 1a and 1b suggest that the Democratic party before the New Deal was the party of social and cultural conservatism, and that the Republicans were relatively liberal on this dimension. Between 1896 and 1932 the Democrats' electoral base consisted of the Solid South and the Catholic- and immigrant-dominated political machines in many Northern cities, plus some remaining Populist adherents in the West, mainly in the silver states. The Republicans were "the party of the urban middle class ... from which Progressivism sprung," a party "far more involved in a cosmopolitan than a local world. ... The party of the national idea as embodied in the enterprise of industrial nation-building" (Ladd with Hadley 1978, p. 38).[10] The Republicans were the party of the industrial and cosmopolitan center; the Democrats, the party of the political hinterland and the urban lower class.

Liberals on social and cultural issues have often been economic conservatives. Both values were characteristic of the Northeastern Republican Establishment before the New Deal. Economic radicalism, on the other hand, usually flourished in a culturally backward, provincial, lower-class milieu. The New Deal consolidated the definition of the Democratic party as the party of economic liberalism without, for a time, disturbing the party's traditional cultural conservatism. It was not until after the New Deal era that the Democrats became the party of social and cultural liberalism as well. It was a slow transformation; Adlai Stevenson and John F. Kennedy obeyed the party tradition of naming Southern Democrats as their vice-presidential running mates.

In contrast to the middle class, lower-status voters tend to be liberal on economic issues but socially and culturally conservative. The Democrats' shift to the left on social and cultural issues has gained the party many liberal middle-class supporters at the cost of much of the white working-class vote. Conversely, the Republican party has alienated many of its high-status liberal adherents in the hope, so far unrealized, of consolidating "a new majority" around themes of moral and cultural conservatism. Hence one of the widely reported trends in recent presidential politics—namely, that ideological "clarification" of party support has produced sociological confusion, as in the partial class inversion found by Ladd (with Hadley 1978, p. 271).

It was noted that both alignments might be called ideological, though with reference to different substantive issues. This is exactly why the terms "liberal" and "conservative" are inherently ambiguous: one can be liberal or conservative on either, or both, dimensions.

In the 1930s and 1940s the distinction between liberals and conservatives referred to one's position on the New Deal. Liberals were pro—New Deal, pro-Roosevelt, and pro-labor. Conservatives were anti—New Deal, anti-Roosevelt, and pro-management.[11] The terms have since shifted their primary meaning to the new social and cultural conflicts of the 1960s and 1970s. It is, however, a bothersome but unavoidable fact that the old meanings have not vanished. Hundreds of thousands of voters consider themselves liberal in the older sense but are bewildered by what liberalism has now come to mean. And there are as many traditional conservatives who find themselves horrified by the excesses of the New Right.

The decision to label one factor "partisanship" and the other "ideology" does nothing to resolve these ambiguities. It merely represents an effort to conform to prevailing current usage. Partisanship, to most voters, is an "old" cleavage, and strong partisans tend to be significantly older than the rest of the electorate. Ideology is seen by most voters as a "new" cleavage—the New Politics of the Left, the New Right activists—and the data show that many young, well-educated voters who eschew partisan labels will readily identify themselves as liberal or conservative.[12]

PERIODS OF REALIGNMENT

The trend lines in figures 1a and 1b indicate that there have been three national party systems in twentieth-century American politics.

The post-1896 alignment, or the "system of 1896" as E. E. Schattschneider (1960) identified it, characterized presidential elections between 1900 and 1924 and congressional elections between 1908 and 1934. For the seven presidential elections between 1900 and 1924, the major-party votes show uniformly high correlations with the ideology factor —Democratic votes in the conservative direction and Republican votes in the liberal direction. The partisanship factor during this period displays a weak and irregular pattern; all the Democratic correlations are positive, but most are statistically insignificant. The system of 1896 has been described as a strongly sectional alignment in which sociocultural distinctions between the major parties predominated. Economic differences were of secondary importance.

The second party system is that associated with the New Deal. In figure 1a, the gradual New Deal realignment can be seen in presidential elections between 1932 and 1960. That realignment had two simultaneous components: a decline in the salience of ideology and an increase in the salience of partisanship. The traditional sociocultural distinction between the major parties, which was the dominant characteristic of the "system of 1896," tended to dissolve, particularly after Roosevelt. At the same time, the partisan differentiation of the presidential vote—that is, class-related partisanship in the New Deal sense—became increasingly important.

Two stages of realignment can be identified: (1) the four Roosevelt elections between 1932 and 1944, in which the ideological effects remained stronger than the partisan effects; and (2) the Truman and Stevenson votes between 1948 and 1956, in which the partisan effects became stronger than the ideological effects. The two-factor representation of party alignments thus delineates two sources of political change after the New Deal: the Democrats lost their traditional association with social and cultural conservatism and gained a clearer definition as the party of economic liberalism.

One aspect of the New Deal realignment in figure 1a remains puzzling. The partisan correlations did not become significant until the 1940s and 1950s, well after the period of the most intense economic conflict and class polarization. Moreover, survey data from the 1940s and 1950s reveal that class polarization in presidential voting actually decreased after 1948 when the aggregate data used here show the partisan alignment rising in importance. Ladd and Hadley (1978, pp. 73–74), for instance, cite "the secular decline in the salience of class differentiations in electoral behavior since the Roosevelt and Truman years.... The high and low [status] cohorts were much more sharply distinguished between 1936 and 1948 ... than they have been at any time since." Campbell and his coauthors (1964, pp. 201–3) also found a decline in status polarization outside the South in 1952 and 1956.

It appears that the increase in the salience of partisanship was a delayed reaction to the Depression and the New Deal. *The American Voter* explains this lag as follows (Campbell et al. 1964, p. 201):

Circumstances may arise in which status polarization outside the political order is inadequately reflected in matters of political partisanship. This pattern of events is most likely to characterize a period of rising polarization in a political system bound to traditional parties. If status polarization continues to mount, we would expect either that (1) new parties will break through institutional barriers, or that (2) events will force the existing parties to a clearer class alignment.

It was the second possibility that materialized during the New Deal realignment. The period of the most intense class conflict—1936 through 1944—was "a period of rising polarization in a political system bound to traditional parties." While the New Deal economic alignment grew increasingly prominent, the Democrats remained the party of cultural conservatism. The full New Deal alignment became predominant only after the old sociocultural alignment had largely dissolved in the 1950s.

Indeed, there was substantial continuity between the two alignments. It has been noted that both economic liberalism and cultural conservatism tend to be associated with lower socioeconomic status. Among many voters, the New Deal realignment confirmed an existing partisan predisposition, giving it a new and stronger substantive basis. For example, the New Deal tended to solidify the traditional Democratic partisanship of white Southerners and urban Catholics, groups that included large proportions of low-status voters. The New Deal realignment as depicted in figure 1a did not reverse the major-party positions so much as it shifted the prevailing basis of partisanship from one dimension to the other.

Once a political alignment becomes established, partisanship acts as an inertial force to maintain political polarization long after social or economic polarization has declined. Thus the partisan alignment predominated during the 1950s, which was a period otherwise characterized by declining class polarization as well as low ideological intensity. As stated in *The American Voter* (Campbell et al. 1964, p. 201): "When polarization is receding and no major conflicts of another nature arise to realign the parties on a different axis, the strength of party allegiances may maintain polarization in political partisanship above that which we would otherwise predict."[13]

The 1960 election shows the predominance of partisanship over ideology most clearly; John F. Kennedy's vote correlated +.84 with the partisanship factor and −.19 with the ideology factor, the first Democratic presidential candidate whose vote showed even the faintest contours of sociocultural liberalism. In this sense, the 1960 vote was both a culmination of the New Deal trends and a hint of things to come.

The third party system, that of the post-1964 period, saw the Democratic presidential vote become significantly liberal on the ideology factor in response to the sociocultural conflicts over race, Vietnam, and the radicalism that dominated the politics of the late 1960s. Figure 1a indicates that the New Deal partisan distinction between Democrats and Republicans diminished somewhat during the three presidential elections between 1964 and 1972, when economic issues temporarily lost prominence. But partisan differences continued to be significant and, indeed, revived in importance as the economic crisis of the 1970s set in. Unlike the "system of 1896," which was predominantly defined by ideology, or the New Deal system, in which partisanship came to be the prevailing alignment, the system of the 1960s was distinctively two-dimensional. Any explanation of the "shape" of presidential votes during this period must take into account both factors.[14]

The three Democratic presidential votes between 1964 and

1972 had approximately the same political profile—liberal (−.68, −.69, −.69) and Democratic (.55, .62, .50). The 1964–1972 period also saw the emergence of predominantly upper-middle-class ideological movements on both the Left and the Right, plus a predominantly lower-status "populist" protest, the Wallace movement. One may think of the ideological conflicts of the 1960s as cutting across the New Deal class alignment: both middle-class and working-class voters were divided between the political Right and Left. The Goldwater movement, which captured the Republican nomination in 1964 and has continued to exercise strong influence in the Republican party ever since, was largely upper-middle class in origin. So were the McCarthy and McGovern movements in the Democratic party. On the other hand, Hubert Humphrey and George Wallace split the white working-class vote.

The growing predominance of ideological issues between 1964 and 1972 had the effect of confusing the class basis of partisan choice. Class differences were notably weak in the 1968 and 1972 elections (Ladd with Hadley 1978, p. 73). Middle-class liberals found a home in the Democratic party, while lower-status "backlash" voters refused to support liberal Democrats. The presidential party system of the 1960s was in a state of tension between conflicting ideological and partisan pressures. "The Democratic party," Ladd notes (Ladd with Hadley 1978, p. 290), "is associated with both 'social liberalism' and 'economic liberalism,' and as a consequence it is evoking contradictory responses within both the upper and the lower SES groups."

Democrats gained support among affluent, upper-middle-class suburban voters outside the South. These "New Politics" voters cannot abide the reactionary social conservatism of the new Republican party. On the other hand, the Democratic party lost much of its traditional support among white Southerners, conservative Catholics, and blue-collar voters who feel threatened by social and cultural change.

The realignment trend has been clearest in the South, where the Republican party has become dominant in presidential voting, competitive in statewide contests, and increasingly important in local elections. The Democratic presidential ticket failed to carry the South in 1964, 1968, 1972, and 1980; even in 1976, according to network exit polls, most white Southerners voted for Ford.

The mid-1970s temporarily reversed this realignment trend. There were three reasons: (a) Watergate, (b) the most severe recession since the 1930s, once again under a Republican administration, and (c) the nomination in 1976 of a Democratic candidate who was culturally conservative— and, as it turns out, out of step with his party.

In the 1964–1972 period, most white blue-collar voters were cross-pressured between economic insecurity and racial fear. Racial fear predominated, and many of them defected from their traditional party loyalty to vote for law-and-order Republicans and backlash candidates. In 1974 and 1976 economic insecurity brought most of them back to the Democratic fold, a move made easier in the presidential election because Jimmy Carter did not seem to threaten them on social and cultural issues. The return of many renegade Southerners and "white ethnics" seemed to give the old New Deal party a fresh breath of life.

The 1980 election, however, has confirmed the larger realignment trend. The continuing economic crisis kept traditional partisan differences at a very high level in 1980, while ideological differences reappeared. Anderson presented a direct challenge to Reagan's conservatism on sociocultural issues—as well as a warning to the Democratic party that it could not ignore the New Politics constituency with impunity. The dual alignment characteristic of the "system of the 1960s" was once again in evidence. Voting differences by class and religion—the traditional bases of the New Deal partisan alignment—were weaker in 1980 than in any year since 1952 (Schneider 1981, p. 260). And despite the renomination of Jimmy Carter by the Democrats, the South resumed its characteristic behavior in the "system of the 1960s" and went Republican once again.

The "X" pattern of the New Deal realignment also shows up in the congressional vote in figure 1b. Between 1936 and 1952 the ideological difference between the parties that had characterized the "system of 1896"—conservative Democrats and liberal Republicans—declined somewhat in importance, while the partisanship factor became much more significant. The shift was completed between 1952 and 1980, as partisan differences became predominant and ideological differences tended to dissolve.

It should be noted, however, that at no time from 1964 to 1980 did the Democratic congressional vote take on a liberal ideological cast. Instead, the period after 1964, and particularly the period between 1968 and 1972, was one in which the traditional ideological coloration of the congressional vote— conservative Democrats and liberal Republicans—rapidly attenuated. Partisanship was the dominant factor in the congressional vote from 1960 through 1980. The partisan effect did diminish slightly in 1980, but there was no accompanying upsurge in ideological voting. An ideological difference may appear, however, if the Democrats purge the conservative "boll weevil" faction that has been supporting the Reagan program in the House of Representatives—or if these conservative Democrats defect to the Republican party on their own.

In sum, ideological conflict has had a stronger impact at the presidential than at the congressional level. Congressional voting has tended to be more strongly determined by partisanship and therefore has been more stable, nationwide, than presidential voting. The Republican party has not elected a majority to the House of Representatives since 1952; even in the 1980 Republican sweep, the Democrats maintained a slight edge in the nationwide House vote.

POLITICAL GEOGRAPHY OF THE UNITED STATES

What do the two alignments look like? Which states are the most liberal and the most conservative? Which are the most Democratic and the most Republican?

The factor scores show the relative positions of the states on the partisanship and ideology dimensions. Since factor scores are standardized, a score of zero represents the mean for all states.*

Figure 2a classifies each state according to its factor score on partisanship. Figure 2b provides a key for interpreting the map in figure 2a; it also shows the distribution of states and of the population across the categories of partisanship. Figures 3a and 3b present the same information for ideology.

Figure 2a suggests a general "East versus West" configuration for the partisanship cleavage. This is clearer in table 2, where the states are grouped into regions and the regions ordered by partisan inclination. The most conspicuous feature of the New Deal Democratic vote is the alliance between the urban Northeast and the South — which, together, represent "the East." The core Republican vote is in "the West"—the Farm Belt and the Mountain states. There are two swing areas: the industrial Midwest (that is, the Great Lakes states—Ohio, Michigan, Indiana, Illinois, and Wisconsin) and the three Pacific Coast states. Six of these eight swing states are marginally Democratic,

---

*The eleven Southern states were, as usual, weighted equal to one state. Alaska, Hawaii, and the District of Columbia were excluded because of too much missing data; they have participated in federal elections since only very recently. All factor scores were multiplied by 100 for ease of presentation. Therefore, a score of +100 on partisanship indicates a state which is typically 1 standard deviation above the mean on the partisanship scale. A score of −50 indicates a state half a standard deviation below the mean.

while Ohio and Indiana are marginally Republican. It is worth noting that four of the nation's ten largest states are in this swing category.

The cultural diversity of the New Deal Democratic coalition is obvious. The two core areas of traditional Democratic strength are the heavily rural and Protestant Deep South (Georgia, Louisiana, Mississippi, and South Carolina), and heavily Catholic, urban, and industrial New England (Massachusetts and Rhode Island). Democratic loyalties weaken as one moves outward from these core areas. One might add a third, somewhat weaker area of New Deal Democratic support—the old Progressive states of the upper Midwest (Wisconsin, Minnesota) and the Pacific Northwest (Washington). These states, particularly their poorer, rural, Scandinavian areas, were hotbeds of economic radicalism during the Progressive era.

What these areas have had in common is the experience of class conflict, poverty, and extreme vulnerability to economic depression. The deeply divisive economic policies of the New Deal fused several different traditions of economic radicalism—the trade union movement of the urban industrial working class in the North, the agrarian protest tradition of poor white farmers in the South, and the economic radicalism of rural Progressive voters in the upper Midwest and Northwest.

The anti–New Deal Republican vote is concentrated in predominantly rural states marked by relatively high economic and cultural homogeneity. Republicanism is strongest in Nebraska (factor score of 216), followed by Kansas (178), Idaho (139), Vermont (132), North Dakota (124), Wyoming (104), and South Dakota (102). Nebraska and Kansas are archetypal Farm Belt states—overwhelmingly agricultural and white Anglo-Saxon Protestant, and not marked by major class or cultural stratification. For instance, the largest foreign-stock group in Nebraska, Kansas, and the Dakotas is German, but the Germans in these states are mostly Protes-

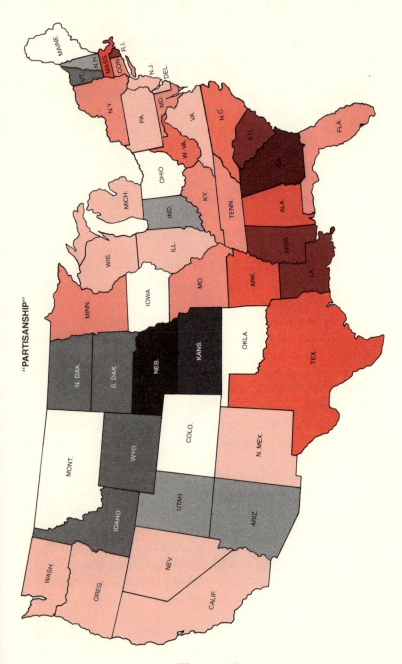

"PARTISANSHIP"

Figure 2A

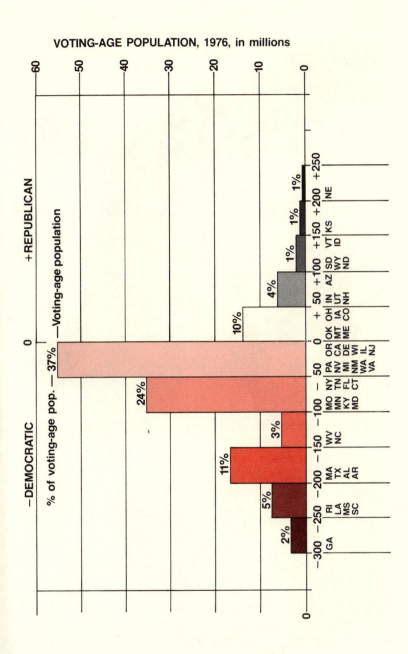

Figure 2B

"IDEOLOGY"

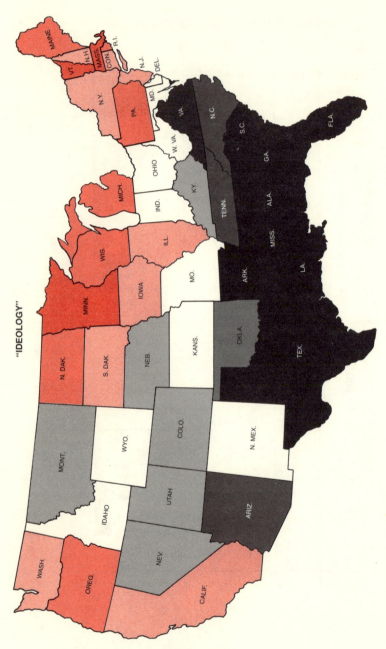

Figure 3A

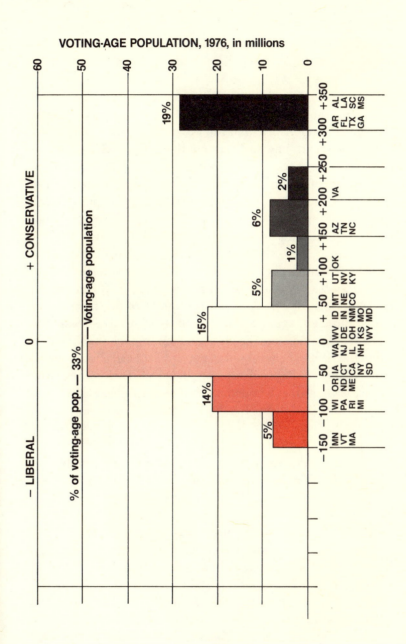

Figure 3B

tant (Lutherans and Mennonites), whose culture is close to that of their Anglo-Saxon neighbors (Phillips 1970, pp. 361, 380).

The Republican Farm Belt and Mountain states did not experience the same level of internal class conflict as did the Northeast, the South, and the Progressive states during the late nineteenth and early twentieth centuries. This is not to say that these states were immune to economic radicalism. One form of economic radicalism was deeply rooted in the historic experience of these states—namely, Populism. The Farm Belt and the Mountain states were the strongest supporters, outside the South, of William Jennings Bryan's crusades in 1896, 1900, and 1908. But the reasons had little to do with internal class divisions. The Mountain states were silver states for whom Bryan's Free Silver platform had an obvious appeal. The agrarian radicalism of the farm states was directed against outside conspiratorial forces—the banks, railroads, monopolies, goldbug financiers, big cities, and the East in general—and not against local class enemies like Yankee Republicans or Bourbon Democrats. The Populist movement undeniably offered a radical critique of industrial capitalism. But being limited almost entirely to the native-stock agrarian milieu, the movement never developed a distinctively Left-wing "class" constituency.[15]

There is still a sense of sectoral protest to the Republicanism of the Farm Belt and Mountain states. Since the New Deal, their resentment has been directed, not at the East in general, but at the federal government in particular. The Republicans have held these states by appealing to a powerful anti-Washington sentiment, as in the recent "sagebrush rebellion" against federal control of undeveloped land.

Franklin D. Roosevelt did well initially in all areas of the Farm Belt, but the Democrats did not find in the old Populist states a tradition of class conflict on which the party could build a lasting base. The Democrats did better in the more urban and foreign-stock farm states where the party appealed to the economically radical wing of the Progressive movement.

Another reason why the Farm Belt did not remain within the Roosevelt coalition was the region's historic isolationism. The Democrats suffered massive losses in the 1940 election in the Mountain states and in the German-dominated areas of the Farm Belt because of distaste for the Democratic administration's obvious sympathy for the Allied cause. The Progressive movement had long been characterized by a dual commitment to economic radicalism and isolationism. The New Deal and World War II split what Samuel Lubell called "the leftist-isolationist alliance," with the largely Scandinavian radical wing going to the Democrats and the more heavily German and Irish isolationist wing moving toward the Republicans.[16] The Republican loyalties of Farm Belt and Mountain state isolationists were undoubtedly reconfirmed by subsequent "Democratic wars" in Korea and Vietnam.

Figure 3a shows the distribution of the states by ideology. If the impression conveyed by figure 2a was roughly that of an East v. West division, the basic geographic pattern of figure 3a is even clearer: North v. South. Democratic partisanship unites the Northeast and the South, while differences in social and cultural ideology set the two Eastern regions profoundly apart. The line separating the liberal Northeast from the conservative South is the Mason-Dixon line. Table 3 shows the mean ideological score in each of the seven regions of the country. Whereas in table 2 (partisanship by region) both the Northeast and the South were inclined toward the Democratic party, in table 3 they are at opposite extremes of the ideological spectrum.

The relatively strong Democratic partisanship of the South is more than matched by the region's social and cultural conservatism. For instance, the five states of the Deep South — Louisiana, Mississippi, Alabama, Georgia, and South Carolina — averaged 230 points more Democratic than

Table 2
Mean Partisanship Factor Scores by Region

Region	Partisanship: mean score	Number of states
Most Democratic		
South	−159	(11) = (1)*
Border	− 86	(4)
Northeast	− 37	(10)
Pacific	− 22	(3)
Industrial Midwest	7	(5)
Mountain	35	(8)
Farm Belt	83	(7)
Most Republican		
All regions	0	(48) = (38)*

*Weighted, South = 1.

Table 3
Mean Ideology Factor Scores by Region

Region	Ideology: mean score	Number of states
Most liberal		
Northeast	− 61	(10)
Pacific	− 52	(3)
Industrial Midwest	− 30	(5)
Farm Belt	− 14	(7)
Mountain	25	(8)
Border	44	(4)
South	366	(11) = (1)*
Most conservative		
All regions	0	(48) = (38)*

*Weighted, South = 1.

the mean for the country. But these same states averaged no less than 481 points more conservative than the national mean. In other words, the Deep South is more than twice as strong in its conservatism as in its Democratic partisanship. The eleven states of the old Confederacy are the eleven most conservative states in the union. In ideology, much more than in partisanship, the South is a region apart.

What are the core liberal areas of the country? First, it must be noted that there is not a single Northern state as liberal as *any* Southern state is conservative. The least conservative Southern state, Tennessee, is 171 points more conservative than the mean; the most liberal state in the country, Minnesota, scores 148 points in the liberal direction.

Liberalism is strongest in three specific areas: New England and the Middle Atlantic states above the Mason-Dixon line; the northern tier of the Midwest from Michigan to North Dakota; and the Pacific states, particularly Oregon. What these areas have in common is a particular cultural heritage: they are the areas of Yankee settlement and influence which share the peculiarly moralistic political heritage of New England Protestantism. Yankee New Englanders and their kinsmen in the upper Midwest and the Pacific Northwest were the most zealous abolitionists and Unionists during the Civil War period. The Republican party was widely perceived in the late nineteenth century as a predominantly Yankee party, and the Civil War, a Yankee war. Yankee areas were the strongest supporters of the Republican party from the Civil War through the "system of 1896." It is precisely these Yankee areas that have trended liberal in their voting behavior over the past fifteen years. This has meant in many cases a significant trend toward the Democrats in areas like Maine, Oregon, and Vermont, which had maintained staunch Republican loyalties throughout the entire New Deal realignment.

It is not unfair to characterize Yankee culture as profoundly anti-Southern in its moral and political outlook;

Yankees were anti-Southern in the Civil War period, and their anti-Southern bias was revived in the recent era of civil rights. This bias is one of the unifying features of "the Yankee environment," along with cold and wet weather, a scarcity of white Southerners and blacks, and a history of Yankee/Catholic antagonism. One of the most interesting aspects of this Yankee/Southern animosity, so vividly depicted in figure 3a, is that it is a historic conflict between two white Anglo-Saxon Protestant groups. Liberal/conservative conflict represents, in part, a deep-seated cultural division within American Protestantism.[17]

In the Northeast, the most liberal state is Vermont (factor score of −135), the one state with a homogeneous, rural, Yankee culture almost undisturbed since the early nineteenth century, followed by Massachusetts (−121), Pennsylvania (−86), Rhode Island (−85), and Maine (−74). These, of course, were the states of bedrock Republicanism before the New Deal. These same states showed a distinctly liberal trend during the 1964−1972 period. Barry Goldwater, who carried 38.5 percent of the vote nationwide in 1964, did somewhat worse than this in the hitherto hard-core Republican states of Vermont (34.0 percent) and Maine (31.0 percent). Hubert Humphrey in 1968 did slightly better than his nationwide total in Vermont and considerably better in Maine, because Senator Edmund Muskie was his running mate. What was most striking about the 1968 New England vote was George Wallace's paltry performance—2.0 percent of the vote in Maine, 3.0 percent in Vermont, and 4.0 percent in Massachusetts, New Hampshire, and Rhode Island. In 1972, not only did George McGovern carry Massachusetts, but he did better than his nationwide percentage in all the New England states, including Vermont, New Hampshire, and Maine. And in 1980, New England was by far John Anderson's best region. Anderson—who was very much in the mold of a traditional liberal Yankee Republican—carried 14.0 percent of the New England vote, which was twice his share of the vote in the rest of the country.

The liberal-conservative division in the Midwest corresponds almost precisely to the Yankee and Southern settlement patterns of this region of the country. Kevin Phillips, for instance, divides the farm states into two ethnocultural traditions: "Iowa, Wisconsin, and Minnesota were the states of pre—Civil War Yankee settlement. In Kansas and Nebraska, not only were persons of foreign stock less numerous, but the Anglo-Saxon population had a substantial Southern element" (Phillips 1970, p. 360; also p. 295 [map 30]). Moreover, the foreign stock elements which populated the northern tier of the Farm Belt tended to reenforce the liberalism of the original Yankee settlers: "It is safe to say that the large, progressive Swedish, Norwegian and Finnish population is one of the principal reasons why Minnesota is the most liberal and Democratic-minded of the Farm states" (Phillips 1970, p. 382).[18] It might be noted that John Anderson, the model of a liberal Republican, is a Midwesterner of Swedish descent.

The pattern suggested by figure 3a is the "Sun Belt phenomenon": a conservative coalition of Southern and Western states against the liberal Northeast and its allies. Three of the states that typify the Sun Belt population boom—Arizona, Texas, and Florida—are strongly conservative, according to this analysis. The Sun Belt is usually taken to include California as well, but always with the warning that California is really "two states" and only Southern California qualifies as Sun Belt country. Unfortunately, the historical election statistics do not recognize this political reality. The result is that California appears on both maps as a swing state, marginally Democratic and marginally liberal over the course of the twentieth century.

Thus, our analysis confirms the notion that a new sectionalism has been emerging in recent American politics, specifically at the presidential level. The increasing relevance of the Sun Belt v. Snow Belt cleavage can be explained by the increasing relevance of ideological considerations in

presidential politics. The analysis here suggests an important modification: this sectional alignment is by no means
new. It is the same alignment that characterized the "system
of 1896," but with the parties now switching positions.
Yankee liberalism v. Southern conservatism is the consistent pattern; the difference is that during the "Sun Belt era"
the Democrats have become the party of Yankee liberalism.

According to our two-dimensional theory, the Sun Belt
alignment in figure 3a materializes only when partisan
differences are weak. Partisanship cuts directly across the
Sun Belt alignment. For instance, table 1 shows that the
Kennedy vote in 1960 and the Carter vote in 1976 were
almost entirely partisan. Both Democrats had an appeal that
cut the Sun Belt in half, the Eastern half voting Democratic
and the Western half, Republican (Carter carried Florida
and Texas but lost Arizona and California). In congressional
voting, where partisanship continues to predominate, the
Sun Belt theory has almost no relevance. In recent presidential voting, where ideological polarization has emerged, the
Sun Belt alignment has modified the traditional East-West
partisan configuration.

Figure 4 plots the location of each state on both factors
simultaneously; the vertical axis represents partisanship
and the horizontal axis, ideology. The ideological dimension
extends from Mississippi and South Carolina at the conservative end to Minnesota and Vermont at the liberal end. The
most Democratic states are Georgia and Rhode Island, and
the most Republican states are Nebraska and Kansas. The
circle at the center of the graph encloses those states that
are within half a standard deviation of the mean on both
dimensions. These are true swing states. They show no significant partisan or ideological inclination. Three of the five
largest states in the country—California, Illinois, and
Ohio—fall into this swing category.

The entire South is in the conservative Democratic quadrant of figure 4, with the Deep South states more Democratic

Figure 4
Partisanship and Ideology
(48 states)

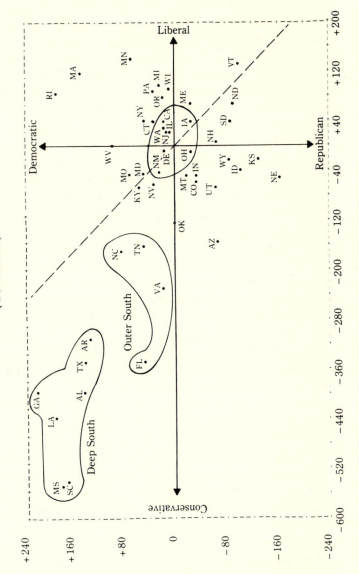

and more conservative than the Outer South states. The other states in this quadrant are rather easy to characterize —they are the Border states, including Oklahoma, Kentucky, Missouri, Maryland, and West Virginia.

Rhode Island and Massachusetts stand out as the most liberal Democratic states; as New England states, they have a strong Yankee cultural tradition, and as industrial states, they have a large, predominantly Catholic, urban working class. They are the states where the New Politics and the old partisanship meet (but do not necessarily merge). Minnesota, the most liberal state in the union, is less solidly Democratic. Also in the liberal Democratic quadrant are several large industrial states of the Snow Belt—New York, Pennsylvania, Michigan, and Wisconsin.

Arizona, one of the fastest growing states in the nation and the archetypal Sun Belt state, comes closest to occupying the conservative Republican position, although the state's conservatism has been somewhat stronger than its Republicanism. Otherwise, what one finds in the conservative Republican quadrant is the rural heartland of America—most of the Rocky Mountain states, the inner core of the Farm Belt, and, Indiana, the most rural Great Lakes state. These states share the moderate conservatism of the Border states but are more Republican (i.e., less Southern).

Two areas fall within the liberal Republican quadrant: rural northern New England (Maine, New Hampshire, and Vermont) and the Dakotas. (Iowa, the most liberal and Yankee-dominated of the farm states, is also in the liberal Republican quadrant, although its scores are not significant.) Not only does this quadrant contain a small number of states, but the states within it contain very few people: less than 2 percent of the population in 1970.

At the end of Kevin Phillips's *The Emerging Republican Majority* (1970, pp. 472–73 [map 47]), a map is drawn to show the contours of a projected Republican majority coalition. Phillips classifies the states into four categories: "projected bastions" of the new Republicanism, "contingent bastions," "battlegrounds," and the Yankee Northeast (New England, New York, and Michigan), which is hopeless for the coalition Phillips has in mind. How does the two-dimensional representation in figure 4 fit into Phillips's 1969 projection of an emerging Republican majority?

One can see the relationship by adding a diagonal axis to figure 4 from the northwest corner (conservative Democratic) to the southeast corner (liberal Republican). Every state that Phillips classifies as either a "projected" or a "contingent" bastion of the emerging Republican majority falls below the diagonal. These states are of three types: (1) all states in the conservative Republican quadrant, (2) those states in the conservative Democratic quadrant that are more conservative than Democratic (the South), and (3) those states in the liberal Republican quadrant that are more Republican than liberal (the Dakotas). Almost all of Phillips's "hopeless" and "battleground" states fall above the diagonal. Only a few "battleground" states fall below the diagonal and therefore on the side of Phillips's new majority (Ohio, Indiana, and Kentucky). One state considered hopeless by Phillips—New Hampshire—is actually below the diagonal. With the exception of these four states, the correspondence between Phillips's game plan and the diagonalization of figure 4 is complete.

A strict division of states along the diagonal produces, in terms of the 1980 electoral college, 243 electoral votes below the diagonal and 285 electoral votes above the diagonal. If Hawaii and the District of Columbia are added to the states above the diagonal and Alaska to the states below the diagonal, there is a majority of 292 to 246 votes against Phillips's emerging Republican majority. Phillips's projection, as he himself realized, depended upon the Republicans' winning many of the "battleground" states (Phillips 1970, p. 473).[19] In his analysis, as is the case here, the overall outcome depends on how the swing states swing.

Both Phillips and the academic realignment theorists recognized that something new was happening in American politics beginning in 1964. The analysis here has defined that phenomenon as the emergence of an ideological alignment. Ideological polarization has occurred in response to social and cultural conflicts—particularly over racial issues—and has stimulated a renewed North-South sectionalism in American politics. It has also reversed traditional party positions on social and cultural issues, with liberal Republicans and conservative Democrats becoming conspicuously out of place in their respective parties. So far, the most important characteristic of the "system of the 1960s" is the dual salience of traditional (economic) partisanship and new (sociocultural) ideology. These two historically continuous alignments vary in importance, depending on the issues that dominate at a particular time. In 1974 and 1976 it appeared that the conflicts of the 1960s had disappeared and that the notion of an "emerging Republican majority" was a quaint historical anachronism. The 1980 election, though dominated by economic issues, revealed that the ideological forces unleashed in the tumultuous years between 1964 and 1974 had not entirely spent their force and had, indeed, made enduring changes in the American party system.

THE POLITICAL PARTIES

How has the "system of the 1960s" affected the political parties?

The essence of the recent realignment is that the Democratic party has been moving to the Left and the Republican party to the Right on the ideological dimension. This process began with the emergence of upper-middle-class protest movements in the 1960s that saw themselves as Populist and anti-Establishment. The first step was taken in 1964, when Barry Goldwater mobilized conservative activists to attend Republican caucuses and outmaneuver more moderate party regulars. Their ultimate objective was to wrest party control from the liberal Eastern Establishment. Foreign policy was a principal theme in the Goldwater movement—the view that administrations of both parties had not been vigorous enough in opposing Communism.

The Left protest movement emerged with the antiwar candidacy of Eugene McCarthy in 1968, again with foreign policy as the main motivation. In 1972 liberal activists mobilized their strength in the primaries and caucuses to defeat the party Establishment that had "stolen" the Democratic nomination from them four years earlier. Thus, both conservatives and liberals waged war against their respective party Establishments, and both, essentially, have won.

The two great ideological conflicts of the 1960s, civil rights and Vietnam, were fought out among warring factions of the Democratic party. The center wing of the party consisted of "regular" Democrats led, in the 1960s, by Lyndon Johnson and Hubert Humphrey. The regulars stood in a direct line of descent from Franklin Roosevelt through Harry Truman and John F. Kennedy. They were the party Establishment, and they stood for three substantive commitments: the pro-labor social welfare liberalism of the New Deal, the anti-Communist interventionism of the Truman Doctrine, and the racial liberalism of the civil rights era.

The commitment of the Democratic party to racial liberalism represented a courageous—and costly—decision by the party regulars (Kennedy, Johnson, and Humphrey) to end the party's historic evasion of the issue out of deference to its powerful Southern wing. That decision brought the first challenge to the party Establishment. It came from the Right, as George Wallace ran against Lyndon Johnson in the 1964 primaries and brought the politics of racial backlash from South to North. The second challenge, as noted, came from the Left in 1968. While favorable to the party regulars' civil rights position, the New Politics liberals were galvanized by opposition to their interventionist foreign policy.

The basic logic of party conflict during this period was not the Left against the Right, but the Left and the Right against the center. The regulars found in 1968 that they could not survive the defection of both the Wallace constituency and the New Politics liberals. The liberals took over the party in 1972, only to find that they could not hope for victory without the support of the party regulars and the traditionally Democratic white working class. Once the Vietnam War ended in 1975, there was reason to expect that the regulars and the liberals would reconcile around a new party consensus. A kind of "deal" would be made: the liberals would accept the big-government economic programs and commitment to organized labor of the party regulars, and the regulars would admit their error in Vietnam and accede to a less-interventionist foreign policy.

This coalition failed to materialize in 1976 until it was too late. The problem was that the liberals and the regulars put up competing candidates in the Democratic primaries that year—Jackson for the regulars and Udall for the liberals. The most salient feature of Jimmy Carter's candidacy was that he had no base in any of the party's three historic factions. Carter was ideologically moderate like the regulars, but he was an outsider and an anti-Washington candidate who, like McGovern and Wallace before him, opposed the party Establishment.

Carter took on and defeated the party's Right, Left, and center factions in the 1976 primaries one at a time, each on its own turf: Wallace in Florida, Jackson in Pennsylvania, and Udall in Wisconsin. It was only late in the 1976 primaries that the liberals and the regulars realized that, by pooling their strength, they could defeat a common enemy— Carter. That was when the anti-Carter coalition formed behind Jerry Brown and Frank Church and managed to win several late primaries. But it was too late. Carter already had the delegates he needed to win the nomination.

Edward Kennedy led precisely this same anti-Carter coalition of liberals and regulars in 1980. Kennedy's roots are deep in the regular tradition, but he has moved substantially to the Left, notably on foreign policy, in order to win a following among New Politics liberals. Kennedy, in fact, symbolizes the "deal" described above to redefine the Democratic party consensus. The battle between Kennedy and Carter was essentially over the issue of party control, with the Kennedy coalition presenting itself as the rightful inheritor of party leadership and opposing Carter as an outsider and an impostor.

Some of the tensions within the liberal-regular coalition were evident in the 1980 primaries. Many liberals were unhappy with Kennedy's big-government philosophy. They drifted toward John Anderson, a much purer New Politics type, who was unencumbered by that concession to Democratic party orthodoxy. Also, President Carter managed to reclaim many regular Democrats during the early primaries because of his conversion to a more hard-line foreign policy.

But in the end, it was Carter's economic policies that violated the essence of party tradition: Democrats do not create recessions. The onset of a recession in the late spring handed Kennedy the issue he had been waiting for. He ran against Carter by championing the most traditional of Democratic causes, opposition to unemployment and compassion for—in what became the litany of the Kennedy campaign—"the senior citizens, the working people, the poor, the minorities, and the young people of this nation." Kennedy offered his antirecession program as the long-awaited issue basis of his campaign and the focus of his platform challenge at the 1980 Democratic National Convention.

The most notable fact about Kennedy's candidacy in 1980 was not its failure, but that he did so well against an incumbent president. While Kennedy lost the nomination, he won the argument that Carter was not a "real" Democrat and that he, not Carter, represented the true soul and spirit of the Democratic party. The panicky Democratic officeholders behind the open convention movement were really seeking a candidate without Kennedy's personal flaws who represented the same ideological consensus. Jackson was a bit too regular for the liberals, and Udall was a bit too liberal for the regulars. Mondale and Muskie were ideal, but both were personally committed to the Carter administration. The point is that the anti-Carter coalition, not the Carter constituency, defined the essential values and philosophy of the Democratic party—that is, the old economic and the new social liberalism—and will probably inherit party control with Jimmy Carter now out of the way.

In the Republican party, foreign policy has long been a central issue of contention. The Eastern and Midwestern wings of the party fought each other bitterly over isolationism in the 1940s. The battle came to a head in 1952, when the isolationist Midwestern wing, led by Robert Taft, was defeated by Eisenhower, the candidate of the internationalist "Wall Street" wing of the party (also represented by Thomas E. Dewey, Wendell Willkie, and John Foster Dulles). Most Midwestern Republicans like Arthur Vandenberg and Everett Dirksen came to accept internationalism once the Cold War put the United States on the "right" side in world affairs.

The protest faction of the Republican party that emerged in 1964 with Barry Goldwater's candidacy came from neither the East nor the Midwest. It appeared quite suddenly in the suburbs and boom towns of the Sun Belt, an area that had never in the past been a significant center of Republican strength. Indeed, the South and the Southwest, where Goldwaterism was strongest, had been areas of conservative Democratic strength. The idea of realignment is supported by the fact that the Sun Belt wing of the Republican party has tended to pick up much of its support from conservative former Democrats. John Connally, Strom Thurmond, S. I. Hayakawa, Jesse Helms, and Ronald Reagan were all Democrats at one time.

In 1964, Goldwater challenged and defeated the Eastern wing of the party, led by Nelson Rockefeller and William Scranton. Many centrist Republicans like Senator Dirksen were willing to go along with the Goldwater nomination, although without great enthusiasm. In 1968, Richard Nixon won the nomination as a party centrist against challenges from Ronald Reagan on the Right and Nelson Rockefeller on the Left. By 1976 the Eastern and Midwestern wings of the party had formed an alliance, symbolized by President Ford's selection of Nelson Rockefeller as his vice-president in 1974. In the 1976 campaign, Reagan used a foreign policy issue— détente—to challenge this alliance. Ford barely won the nomination, and only after he let Reagan have his way on the foreign policy section of the party platform.

Reagan's victory in 1980 confirms the Republicans' shift to the right. In 1980, unlike 1964, Reagan was endorsed for the nomination by party regulars in all sections of the country, including a few Eastern liberals like Jacob Javits. Moreover, the leading moderate candidates in 1980, George Bush and Howard Baker, moved noticeably to the Right in order to make themselves acceptable to party conservatives. Indeed, Bush's campaign strategy was to make himself indistinguishable from Reagan on the issues and, therefore, acceptable to the party's now-dominant conservative wing as a younger, fresher, and more "electable" version of what Reagan stood for. The Reagan-Bush ticket symbolized the newfound unity of the Republican party—a unity based on the unchallenged supremacy of the conservative consensus.

In both parties, the former protest factions have amassed considerable strength. Reagan's nearly successful challenge in 1976 to an incumbent president in his own party showed how powerful and assertive the conservative forces in the Republican party had become. In losing the nomination that

year, the Reagan campaign claimed victory on the party platform and vowed to win the nomination four years later. They
did just that. Kennedy's nearly successful challenge in 1980
to an incumbent president in his own party shows how
powerful and assertive the liberal forces in the Democratic
party have become. In losing the nomination, the Kennedy
campaign claimed victory on the party platform and vowed
to win the nomination, for Kennedy or for another candidate
of the same persuasion, in 1984. They may do just that.

The realignment process involves more than the victory
(or imminent victory) of the protest factions. It is also
denoted by the reconciliation of moderate and ideological factions within each party. That is the meaning of the afore-
mentioned coalition between regular and New Politics Democrats embodied by Kennedy—a shift of regular Democrats to the left, particularly on foreign policy issues. The
Reagan-Bush ticket represents a similar reconciliation on
the Republican side, with Bush, the candidate of the formerly
dominant moderate wing of the party, acceding to the more
muscular and Populist conservatism of the Sun Belt. Liberal
and conservative activists have become "regulars" in their
respective parties. The situation is far different from 1964,
when Goldwater activists saw themselves as an outside force
attempting to overthrow the party Establishment, or 1968,
when Eugene McCarthy's followers fought the Democratic
party Establishment in the streets of Chicago.

A final piece of evidence for realignment is the elimination
of anomalous party factions—liberal Republicans and conservative Democrats. Both factions continue to exist, but
they face diminishing influence in the two parties.

Liberal Republicans have become an isolated and
demoralized force, almost totally without influence in the Republican party. They have managed to hang on in a few
areas (New England, Oregon) only because of the ability of
particularly attractive candidates to draw support from
liberal Democrats and Independents. But that is becoming

more difficult, as liberal Democrats find that they have more attractive candidates in their own party (the defeat of Massachusetts Senator Edward Brooke) and as liberal Republicans are faced with primary opposition from the Right (the defeat of New Jersey Senator Clifford Case). John Anderson, the current voice of liberal Republicanism, won not a single Republican primary in 1980. The homeless quality of liberal Republicanism is aptly demonstrated by Anderson's decision to run for president as an Independent.

Conservative Democrats continue to have a base in the South. Since the New Deal, however, Southern conservatives have been an anomaly in the Democratic party. As noted, one of the most noticeable characteristics of the "system of the 1960s" has been the repeated defection of Southern voters to Republican presidential candidates. In Congress, the old guard of conservative Southern Democrats has gradually been dying off and is being replaced by younger, more-moderate Democrats and by Republicans. Conservative Democrats have become an even more conspicuous anomaly in the Ninety-seventh Congress. An organized faction of "boll weevil" Democrats, mostly Southerners from districts that Ronald Reagan carried by overwhelming margins in 1980, has provided the Reagan administration with an ideological majority in the House of Representatives. The status of these Democrats in the Democratic caucus is very much in question, and the Reagan administration has signaled its intention of trying to persuade conservative Southern Democrats to affiliate openly with the Republicans in the next Congress by voting for a Republican Speaker of the House. Both sides argue that that may be where conservative Democrats really belong.

Outside the South, conservative Democrats have a more difficult time. Occasionally they may win on the basis of protest votes, but—as in the case of "cop candidates" like former Philadelphia Mayor Frank Rizzo—they usually have tense relations with party regulars. When Robert Short, a conservative Democrat, won the 1978 Democratic-Farmer-Labor (DFL) primary for senator from Minnesota as a tax-revolt candidate, the DFL party organization refused to endorse him and he subsequently lost the election. The future of conservatives within the Democratic party does not look bright. Even neoconservatives, the rump faction of party regulars who refuse to accept the "deal" with liberal Democrats on foreign policy, seem to be increasingly isolated within the party, and many of them openly endorsed Ronald Reagan in 1980.

In sum, the ideological polarization associated with the "system of the 1960s" has become institutionalized in the party system. For instance, instead of performing their traditional role of advertising the philosophies of the party nominees, the party platforms in 1980 pulled the candidates apart ideologically. The Democratic platform was markedly to the left of Jimmy Carter on both economic and social issues, and the nominee had to state his objections to several platform provisions in writing. The Republicans in Detroit managed, remarkably, to write a platform for their party that was to the right of Ronald Reagan on many points. The factor analysis of presidential and congressional votes revealed a lag between the intense class polarization of the 1930s and the institutionalization of the New Deal partisan alignment in the 1940s and 1950s. A similar lagged adjustment may now be occurring for the "system of the 1960s"—the ideological conflicts of the 1960s are only now becoming institutionalized in the party system of the 1980s.

1980 AND BEYOND

Did the Republicans destroy the New Deal Democratic majority in 1980, and are they in the process of creating a new majority coalition on economic issues?

The 1980 election was certainly a triumph for the Republican party, and economic issues can be shown to have dominated public concerns to an unusual degree during the 1980 campaign. The factor analysis presented in this essay argues for the preeminence of the economic-based partisan alignment in 1980. It is also true that the electorate rejected Jimmy Carter principally because of his perceived incompetence in managing the economy. (See Schneider 1981 for a more detailed discussion.)

Around the time of the 1972 election, the prevailing theory of realignment was that the Republicans could build a new majority by shifting the political focus from economics—where the Democrats had a natural advantage—to social and cultural issues, including foreign policy. The Republicans' traditional economic conservatism—pro-business, anti-government, anti-labor—had never gotten the party very far, while the Democrats had torn themselves apart over race, Vietnam, and cultural radicalism. The Democrats' commitment to New Deal social-welfare liberalism was what carried the party through the bad times. It very nearly got Hubert Humphrey elected in 1968. It brought massive numbers of traditional blue-collar Democrats back to the party fold in 1974 and 1976, when the Republicans presided over the worst recession since the 1930s. The economic issue seemed to hold the normal Democratic majority together, while the social issue appeared to be the Republicans' great opportunity.

That is why the 1980 election was so devastating for the Democrats. When the Republicans got the Democrats in 1980, it was not on race or foreign policy or corruption, but on the economy. In other words, the Republicans got the Democratic party where it lives. The 1980 election destroyed the one position in the Democratic party consensus—"economic protection"—that had always held the party together; indeed, that had created the party in the 1930s. In 1980 the social-welfare liberalism offered by the party of the New

Deal no longer meant "economic protection" to most voters. It meant "big government."

That shift in meaning is in large part attributable to inflation. By 1980 inflation was felt to have become a more serious problem than unemployment, and the electorate consistently singled out "big government" and government spending as the principal cause of inflation. Inflation was the single issue that most preoccupied the voters in 1980, and Ronald Reagan held a consistent lead as the candidate best able to handle it. The Democrats also gave up their natural advantage on the unemployment issue. By bringing about a recession in the spring of 1980—and announcing it long in advance—Jimmy Carter weakened the economic ties of blue-collar Democrats to their party. The Democrats could no longer claim to offer the "economic protection" that had worked time and again to bring their traditional constituency back home. With economic self-interest no longer a compelling reason to stick with the Democrats in 1980, a majority of blue-collar voters and Catholics did not.

One of the basic facts about the 1980 election is that the Democrats lost more than the Republicans gained. That can be seen in the aggregate election results: between 1976 and 1980 the Democratic presidential vote went down by 9 percentage points, but the Republican presidential vote increased by only 3 points. The rest went to John Anderson. Jimmy Carter's share of the vote went down in every single state and in every major category of the electorate except blacks. In the Northeast and upper Midwest, Anderson picked up most of Carter's loss; in the South, most of the votes that Carter lost went to Reagan. The support that Carter lost among women, the college-educated, young voters, Protestants, higher-status groups, Republicans, independents, and non-Southerners tended to go disproportionately to Anderson. Carter's losses accrued mostly to Reagan among Democrats, labor-union families, manual workers, Southerners, Jews, Catholics, older voters, and the noncollege-educated (see Schneider 1981; Orren and Dionne 1981). In other words, Carter lost everywhere, but some of his losses went to the Left and some to the Right, depending on the underlying predispositions of each social group or geographical area.

Thus, the political meaning of the 1980 election is that Jimmy Carter's administration was widely judged a failure. The ideological meaning of the election is less clear. The voters were voting for a change, and they were certainly aware that the type of change Reagan was offering was going to take the country in a more conservative direction. They were willing to go along with that, not because they were convinced of the essential merits of the conservative program, but because they were willing to give conservatism a chance where liberalism had failed.

The conventional wisdom about realignment in 1981 is that economic issues now represent the Republican party's great opportunity to build a new majority, while social issues —anti-abortion, anti-feminism, religious fundamentalism—threaten to tear the party apart and destroy its hopes for the future. The evidence on these points is not decisive. Certainly, the Democrats have, for the time being, lost their traditional advantage on economic issues, although it is not clear that the New Deal social welfare consensus has been demolished; more likely, it has simply been laid aside until inflation is brought under control. The public has continued to support Reagan's economic program, even though the polls show that many of its specific provisions are unpopular; people seem to feel that we must take whatever measures are necessary to get the economy back on track. On the social issues, the majority shifts, depending on the specific issue and the mood of the electorate. Most Americans approve of the Equal Rights Amendment, the Voting Rights Act, and a woman's right to have an abortion. But most Americans also approve of school prayer, capital punishment, and a stronger military posture. The truth seems to be that social issues are inherently divisive and can do as much damage to the Republican party as they have done to the Democrats.

The analysis presented in this essay does not argue that either party is destined to have a natural majority in the years to come. It does point to the fact that the "system of the 1960s" has brought ideological polarization into our politics and has moved the parties farther apart. It has enabled the Republicans to pick up support in hitherto solidly Democratic areas—the South, most noticeably—while the Democrats have also realized gains in such historically Republican constituencies as affluent Northern suburbs. Realignment simply means a shift in the parties' bases of support, not necessarily a new majority. That shift has been under way since 1964.

The most interesting realignment prospects continue to lie in the economic area. There are already signs of strain within the Republican party over how to interpret the party's apparent success in demolishing the Democrats' fifty-year-long hegemony over economic policy. Many traditional Republicans see the current economic crisis as finally justifying the ideological position the party has been committed to since the 1930s—namely, rolling back big government and curtailing the federal government's social welfare role. The new wave of "supply-side" thinking, however, argues that the purpose of Republican policy should be to reinvigorate capitalism by using the tax system to stimulate productivity in the private sector. In this view, it is dangerous and unnecessary for the party to wage a holy war against the New Deal. The problem is that the Republican party has been steadfastly antigovernment for fifty years, and that position remains the core element of party orthodoxy.

But there is an even older party tradition—namely, the Republicans as the party of economic growth and technological progress. That tradition once helped make the Republicans the nation's normal majority party. If the Reagan economic program succeeds, it may do so again. The question is whether that tradition can be reconciled, not only with the party's antigovernment ideology, but also with the new and aggressive forces of social conservatism.

IV

The 1980 Campaign

10

RICHARD B. WIRTHLIN

The Republican Strategy and Its Electoral Consequences

Tracking the national vote in 1980. Coalitional strategy and its modifications. Appraising key voter groups: three major campaign themes. Leadership style. Demographic and geographic factors. Targeting. The Anderson threat. The question of realignment. Reagan's mandate—"change." The future.

On Monday, 3 November 1980, the Reagan campaign covered a lot of territory. We made five major stops that day in three states—Illinois, Oregon, and California—closing, of course, in the governor's home state. The last stop, the one we had all been looking forward to for more than two years, was a rally in San Diego. We couldn't have daydreamed a better finale—30,000 people jammed a shopping-center parking lot to give a last rousing hurrah to candidate Ronald Reagan.

Despite those successes, however, the day had not been a good one for Nancy Reagan—she had an encounter with some extremists in San Francisco and was clearly fatigued when we returned to the plane. In the front cabin, the crew had surprised us with champagne and a large bowl of iced shrimp; a fitting and pleasant culmination to the campaign. After the governor gave a toast, Nancy turned to me and asked, "Dick, are we really going to win tomorrow?" I said, "Yes, Nancy, we really are going to win."

My confidence was not based on wishful thinking. The signs of victory had been clearly evident since mid-October, and we distinctly felt the rumblings of a landslide on the previous Friday when our last strategy meeting was held. At that time, our tracking showed Ronald Reagan with 45 percent of the vote, Jimmy Carter with 36 percent, John Anderson with 8 percent, and 10 percent of the electorate still undecided (table 1).

But results that were generated from our Political Information System (PINS) gave us even more confidence than our latest national tracking survey. PINS provided continuous readings on how the electorate from each of the fifty states would vote. Unlike the political pundits and the public, we had never been preoccupied with our overall national standing; rather, right from the beginning, our campaign goal had been to secure a minimum of 270 electors. PINS not only gave us an immediate assessment of the campaign in each of the fifty states and the status of our "win coalitions," but also enabled us to run the campaign hypothetically under a wide variety of different assumptions. By Friday morning, 31 October, we had run the election hypothetically almost 400 times.

Table 1
National Presidential Ballot:
March 28/November 3, 1980

Survey date 1980	Reagan margin	Reagan	Carter	Ander-son	Un-decided
March 28	− 7	36	43	15	6
June 25	2	36	34	20	10
July 25	25	48	23	15	14
September 30	6	42	35	11	12
October 11	1	40	39	11	10
14	− 2	39	41	11	9
17*	4	41	37	10	12
18	8	43	35	9	13
19	7	43	36	8	13
20	8	43	35	9	13
21	5	42	37	9	12
22	6	43	37	10	10
23	6	44	38	9	9
24	8	44	36	10	10
25	5	42	37	11	10
26	5	43	38	10	9
27	5	43	38	10	9
28	7	44	37	10	9
29	5	44	39	8	9
30	7	44	37	10	9
31	8	45	37	8	10
November 1	10	45	35	9	11
2	10	44	34	9	13
3	11	45	34	9	12

Source: National surveys conducted by Decision/Making/Information.

*National tracking began October 17 — estimates based on three-day moving averages (N=1,500).

At earlier campaign strategy meetings, I would give an average estimate of the number of electors we could expect to win at that time. In addition, I would give optimistic and pessimistic estimates. At the last strategy meeting held Friday, 31 October, with the campaign director and deputy directors, it was somewhat different. We had run PINS about five minutes before the meeting, and once I glanced at the results, I decided to give the other directors only one estimate—namely, the most pessimistic one. It showed us locking up 290 electors—20 more than we needed to win the presidency. The moderate estimate gave us about 350, and the best-case estimate gave us over 400. By Monday afternoon our simulations under the "worst case" scenarios were showing 405 electors.

That electoral projection reflected the successful culmination of our coalitional strategy, initially drafted in March of 1980. Our October tracking surveys showed the geographic coalition coming nicely into place. The West held rock-solid; we had an excellent chance of both sweeping the large Midwestern states and cracking Carter's South. The gains since August among our key demographic groups—union, blue-collar, Hispanic, Catholic, and middle-aged voters—also were most encouraging, which meant, in turn, that on Friday, 31 October, we were gathering strong support from moderate, independent, and soft Democratic voters.

How did that coalitional strategy evolve? What were the issues and the themes that were selected to help piece it together? What were the critical elements of that win coalition? What did the vote reflect? And what does the 1980 presidential election portend for the future? These are the questions addressed below.

THE EARLY REAGAN
COALITIONAL STRATEGY

Pieces of the Reagan coalitional strategy were already in place when I was asked to assume the position of director of planning and strategy in February 1980. John Sears had already targeted the Catholic and blue-collar voters as key elements in our win coalition.

In a March 1980 strategy memorandum, I noted that the survey research conducted in the primary states showed that Ronald Reagan was winning among Republicans, not because his ideological positions were congruent with the electorate, but rather, in spite of a substantial ideological gap between himself and the average Republican. The extent of that gap was remarkable. In Illinois, Wisconsin, and Pennsylvania, Ronald Reagan was further from the average individual's ideological position than even Congressman John Anderson.

Clearly, to win a general election, that ideological gap had to be closed perceptually and/or issues and themes had to be developed to override ideology as a vote determinant. It was very evident from the outset, however, that we had no opportunity to win the general election unless we pulled substantial numbers of moderates and ticket-splitters into our vote column. The key groups most attractive to us for making inroads were the somewhat less affluent and less educated voters, union members, blue-collar voters, and middle-aged voters.

By the end of June we had pretty well solidified the plan that provided the basic frame of reference for the campaign through the November election. Elements of that plan, however, were modified by later strategy memos.*

---

*Vincent Breglio, Richard Beal, and Craig King assisted in the drafting of the campaign plan and also provided some of the later memos.

The general election campaign was launched under the basic assumption that there had been considerable erosion in the Democratic coalition that elected Jimmy Carter in 1976—the same coalition that dominated national politics since the 1930s. It was our view that the glue that bound that coalition together was the economic issue. We assumed from the beginning that the Carter campaign would no longer be credible in claiming that "the Democrats are the only ones who can control the economy," for not only was inflation reaching almost unprecedented rates, but the rate of unemployment was running higher than expected across the country.

Such dismal economic factors, we felt, would continue to erode the solidarity of the Democratic coalition; hence, the basic thrust of the Reagan for President 1980 Campaign was focused on strategies that would attract those voters most directly and negatively affected by the economic failures of the Carter administration. Many of the working-class voters who were drawn into Roosevelt's New Deal, we found through our survey research, were now dissatisfied with the Democratic party and the president's handling of the economy. On the other hand, it was also evident that these voters would not switch to Reagan if Carter successfully demonized the former California governor.

But looming large over the 1980 campaign was a second factor which conditioned both our coalitional targets and, specifically, the themes and issues we used to impact them: the *fluidity* of the voters' political preferences. During the primary, large blocs of voters moved back and forth between available political candidates. Not only did they appear firmly committed to one candidate one moment and equally committed to another by the next, but they were prone to make these massive shifts in allegiance very abruptly. We had been conditioned by our experience in New Hampshire. Immediately after Iowa, we saw a 6-point lead turn into a 19-point deficit in less than ten days; thus, we felt we could not take any constituency for granted. This represented both an opportunity and a challenge. We were firmly convinced that the New Deal appeal was no longer relevant to many independent and Democratic voters, but many of them remained both uncertain of where to go politically and suspicious of Ronald Reagan personally. To overcome those suspicions, the campaign forged a set of issues and themes that were designed to appeal to our target coalitions and simultaneously to reinforce our base support.

THEMES AND ISSUES USED TO FORM THE REAGAN WIN COALITION

Two strategic thrusts were used to crosscut the 1976 Democratic coalition in favor of Ronald Reagan—the economic issue, and an appeal for strong, moral, and optimistic leadership.

In June of 1979 Decision/Making/Information conducted a national study focusing on the values and aspirations of several key voter groups. The interview was lengthy and the sample heavily stratified to provide us with an understanding of the interaction between voter personality, personal values, opinion, and anticipated political behaviors. We were attempting to pinpoint particular things which met three criteria: (1) values that were consistent with the candidate and the candidate's past positions; (2) values and aspirations that appealed to our key coalitional groups; and (3) already established perceptions of Ronald Reagan's values that would not alienate our Republican/conservative base.

We found that Ronald Reagan, more than any other candidate measured, polarized the voters on more than a dozen personality and interpersonal style variables. We examined in fine detail not only present, but also potential, Reagan supporters (union members, blue-collar workers, those with moderate or slightly low incomes). We found, as we expected, that they were concerned about the size and efficacy of the federal government, and that they generally held a more individualistic outlook than other voters.

But we were somewhat surprised to learn that our key win coalition reflected certain values more strongly than the average. We grouped these values under three headings: the traditional ethics factor, the strong-leader appeal, and a "Can Do, America" vision.

Traditional ethics

Our coalition expressed a strong commitment to established values, and a sense of deterioration in the standards and traditional patterns in modern life. This perception was combined with a strong inclination to refute the idea that old values are gone, and the belief that established standards are still worth maintaining. The majority in our target groups also rejected the belief that values are relative and that decisons should be guided by circumstances rather than by established concepts of right or wrong. Those in our target groups were more likely than nontarget groups to accept as true statements about the desirability and need to help others, to be generous, to be forgiving, to obey the dictates of one's conscience, to be virtuous, to maintain old friendships and form new ones, to be loyal, to be humble, to conform to custom, and to maintain faith. Furthermore, this group expressed a higher degree of what we call "religiosity"; namely, the belief that God exists in the form in which the Bible describes Him, and that this country would be better off if religion had a greater influence in daily life.

The data gave conflicting signals about the influence on the vote decision of what was identified as the "Moral Majority" (those who had at some time "made a special personal commitment to Christ that changed their lives"). Contrarily, there was no question that the groups and coalitions that we were trying to move were attracted to Reagan because of the religious traditionalism as broadly defined in the above terms—especially after Carter's negative personal attacks that were launched around the first of October.

Strong leader appeal

The target groups reflected a high commitment to obedience, honor, and willpower, and support of strong leadership. Further, our target groups expressed the feeling that respect for authority and obedience to it are important personal values.

"Can Do, America!" vision

When we tested various concepts about feelings toward the United States today, two of them were rated very appealing by the majority of the entire sample on the dimensions of wise, strong, interesting, and believable, but our key groups—soft Democrats, the middle-aged and lower-income voters, union members—rated two concepts even more favorably than the average. These two—the first reflecting optimism and the second, strength—were:

A problem-solving country. America is built on the motto, "Can do!" We've put a man on the moon and explored the deepest parts of the seas. We can cook food in seconds and fly all the way across the country in only hours. We have solved problems that other countries believed had no solutions. Sure, we've got some problems right now with energy and pollution. But American ingenuity can solve these problems, and our children can enjoy an even better life than we've had.

A strong leader. We're tired of suffering insults at the hands of other nations. We need a president who will stand up for the United States even if the rest of the world doesn't approve. We're tired of a Congress that seems to be going nowhere. We need a president who can unite the Congress and get something done—even if he has to use political pressure to do it. Give us a leader who will restore our pride in being Americans.

These elements—strength, optimism, traditionalism —were naturals for Reagan. They were used as the basic frame of reference for both speeches and our media themes. President Carter's "malaise" speech provided almost the perfect foil for these specific leadership themes which were sounded from the beginning right through the end of the campaign.

We found it necessary to play primarily to these positive themes of our campaign through the second week in October. By the first week in October we saw that the voters, while they did not want Carter, still had serious reservations about Ronald Reagan. The race on October 11 was virtually dead even (see table 1).

In early October Carter himself provided us with a major break. In Chicago, he asserted that electing Reagan would divide North from South, Christian from Jew, and rural from urban. Reagan responded more in sadness than in anger, saying "[Carter's] reaching a point of hysteria that's hard to understand." President Carter's overblown attack rhetoric stuck him with the tag "dirty campaigner" for the duration, and he lost credibility. In the second and third weeks of October the campaign achieved something close to a role reversal. By election day, Ronald Reagan was viewed as more "presidential" than the president himself. This change in image was accompanied by a sharp drop in the number of individuals who said they knew "very little" about Ronald Reagan and his views. Thus, by mid-October the governor had the necessary credibility to launch the frontal attack.

It was at this point that Ronald Reagan started to ask the question with which he closed the debate a week later:

"When you go to the polls, you will make a decision. I think when you make that decision, it might be well if you ask yourself, 'Are you better off now than you were four years ago?'"

Thus it was important for the campaign not only to develop themes focusing on a particular style of leadership which contrasted sharply with that offered by Jimmy Carter, but also to tie that leadership issue to the burning issue of the day—the economy. We felt it was important (if we were to utilize this issue to build a broad coalition) for Ronald Reagan to do two things: first, to present to the American voters a comprehensive, credible, and proprietary economic program; second, to take this program beyond the isolated treatment of inflation to a comprehensive proposal for curing the nation's major economic ills, inflation and unemployment. Voters were well aware of the dual demons of inflation and unemployment and wanted leadership that would cope with both. While inflation was onerous to most Americans, the ravages of high unemployment were being borne more heavily by precisely those groups whose swing support was most needed to elect Ronald Reagan to the presidency: the less educated, the less affluent, the blue-collar, the union members, and the Hispanic voters. We recognized that these groups might not understand arcane economic theory; but they did understand that, while the economic issues were complex and not subject to facile resolution, they were nevertheless subject to *some* resolution. Therefore, the Reagan economic proposal, while remaining straightforward, had to convince our swing coalitions, in particular, that it dealt effectively with the spectrum of economic ills, and held a promise for positive change not found in the record or the program of Jimmy Carter.

We now turn to review how the Reagan campaign themes and Reagan's treatment of the economic issue impacted moderates, Catholics, Hispanics, blue-collar voters, and union members as played against the Carter strategy.

Table 2

Changes in Reagan Vote Support by Key Groups*

	June (%)	August (%)	Early October (%)	Late Oct/Nov tracking (%)	Difference** Oct/Nov minus June (%)	Post-election (%)
Ideology				*Political groups*		
Very conservative	54	65	57	61	+ 7	71
Somewhat conservative	50	50	49	53	+ 3	64
Moderate	26	36	31	38	+12	41
Somewhat liberal	20	24	24	27	+ 7	28
Very liberal	19	20	31	19	0	20
Partisan strength						
Strong Republican	83	86	85	88	+ 5	91
Weak Republican	62	64	69	67	+ 5	83
Lean to Republicans	57	67	70	76	+19	83
Independent/ no preference	33	36	38	41	+ 8	52
Lean to Democrats	19	15	18	14	− 5	22
Weak Democrat	24	30	24	30	+ 6	35
Strong Democrat	10	11	7	10	0	15
Age			*Demographic groups*			
17–20 years old	24	37	39	37	+13	46
20–24 years old	34			34	0	
25–29 years old	24	38	40	36	+12	48
30–34 years old	32			43	+11	

						**
35–39 years old	42	46	40	46	+ 4	54
40–44 years old	44	43	42	48	+ 4	55
45–49 years old	51	41	38	48	– 3	53
50–54 years old	40	41	38	45	+ 5	49
55–59 years old	29			45	+16	
60–64 years old	39			44	+ 5	
65 and over	36			45	+ 9	
Education						
Some high school or less	34	34	28	37	+ 3	41
High school graduate	33	42	41	43	+10	51
Some college/vocational	41	43	39	45	+ 4	45
Postgraduate	30	37	44	42	+12	52
Income						
Under $5,000	31	24	23	NA	NA	39
$5,000–$9,000	28	39	37	NA	NA	40
$10,000–$14,000	32	41	38	NA	NA	46
$15,000–$19,999	36	42	42	NA	NA	49
$20,000–$29,999	39	40	38	NA	NA	52
$30,000–$39,999	45	46	46	NA	NA	54
$40,000 or more	48	55	55	NA	NA	67

Sources: Unless otherwise noted, all surveys were conducted by Decision/Making/Information. June national survey (in person), N=1,500; August national survey (telephone), N=7,200; early October national survey (telephone), N=1,300; tracking surveys (aggregate; telephone), N=10,000; post-election survey, November 5–8 (telephone), N=3,000.

*Question: "If the full ticket for the presidential race in November were (ROTATE) Ronald Reagan–George Bush, Republicans; Jimmy Carter–Walter Mondale, Democrats; and John Anderson–Patrick Lucey, Independents, for which ticket would you vote?"

**This difference measure is based on independent estimates for the universe of registered voters — October/November minus June.

DEMOGRAPHIC COALITIONS

By the time I answered Nancy Reagan's question, "Are we going to win?" I knew almost for certain that the demographic coalitions we needed to elect her husband to the presidency were ours.

Between June—when our data showed Reagan 36 percent, Carter 34 percent, and Anderson 20 percent—and late October/early November, we had made significant gains among all ideological groups except the "very liberal" (see table 2). Our biggest gains were scored among the moderate voters. Similarly, our partisan strength increased across the board, with the largest gains coming from independents leaning Republican, and true Independents.

While we strengthened our support among older voters, it was a most pleasant surprise to see that the campaign had also impacted young voters favorably. Similarly, our biggest gains accrued from those with just a high school education, but Reagan also picked up considerable marginal strength between June and November from that small proportion of the electorate who had undertaken postgraduate work.

Between August and the election, our key target groups had also responded extremely well. We realized our major gains occupationally among craftsmen/foremen, union households, and veterans (see table 3).

While the forging of our demographic coalitional strategy rested heavily upon the development of themes and issues that would appeal to the key swing groups, our geographic coalitional strategy was one implemented by efficiently allocating our scarce resources: the candidate's time, media dollars, and organizational efforts.

Table 3

Change in Vote Support Among Key Target Groups
Between August and the Election

	Key target groups	
	August (%)	Postelection (%)
Occupation		
Clerical/sales	48	48
Craftsmen/foremen	38	44
Union households	34	43
Veterans	48	56
Sex/age		
Younger women	39	46
Older women	40	49
Younger men	39	53
Older men	47	56
Religious groupings		
"Born-again" Protestant	46	50
High-church Protestant	47	61
Other Protestant	35	49
"Born-again" Catholic	34	49
Roman Catholic	35	50

THE REAGAN GEOGRAPHIC
COALITIONAL STRATEGY

Initially, only the South was conceded to Carter. In March of 1980, when the race seemed close from both the electoral and popular point of view, we estimated Carter's solid base at 78 electors (see table 4). That base was Southern, but it included the Northern states of Massachusetts, Minnesota, Rhode Island, Maryland, and Hawaii.

Reagan's base of 77 electors ranged mostly through the agricultural Midwest and the Rocky Mountain states, plus Indiana, New Hampshire, Vermont, and Alaska. Thus, even before the primary was well under way, it appeared that we should allocate our limited resources—to just twelve key states which, with our base, would provide a rather slim 285 electoral win.

These targeting decisions were heavily based upon both winnability and potential yield in electoral votes. Other things equal, states with larger numbers of electoral votes and reasonable potential for victory received disproportionately larger allocations of limited resources, according to an allocation formula developed for the Reagan campaign.

The following elements guided the state-targeting process carried out under the direction of Vincent Breglio:

- Establish a data base of historical and current survey information coupled with the judgment of campaign professionals to profile each state.

- Provide interactive access to this data base, creating a dynamic environment capable of responding to the most current survey and/or professional judgment inputs.

- Identify Reagan base states—those states where the probability of a Reagan victory is equal to or greater than 70 percent.

Table 4

March 1980: First Cut at State Targets

Carter electoral base	Votes	Reagan electoral base	Votes	Reagan key states	Votes
Georgia	12	Nevada	3	**Large states**	
Alabama	9	Idaho	4	California	45
Massachusetts	14	Montana	4	Texas	26
Minnesota	10	Wyoming	3	Illinois	26
Rhode Island	4	Colorado	7	Ohio	25
District of Columbia	3	New Mexico	4		(122)
Hawaii	4	Utah	4	**Medium states**	
West Virginia	6	Arizona	6	Florida	17
Arkansas	6	North Dakota	3	New Jersey	17
Maryland	10	South Dakota	4	Virginia	12
		Nebraska	5	Missouri	12
Total electoral votes	78	Kansas	7		(58)
		Indiana	13	**Small states**	
		New Hampshire	4	Oklahoma	8
		Vermont	3	South Carolina	8
		Alaska	3	Iowa	8
				Maine	4
			(77)		(28)
				Total electoral votes	285

Source: Strategy memorandum, March 1980.

- Identify Carter base states—those states where the probability of a Reagan victory is equal to or less than 30 percent.

- Give priority to the remaining states in descending order of their victory potential, and segment them according to size (based on number of electoral votes) and region of the country (based on eight geopolitical groupings of the fifty states).

- Develop priority targets among large, medium, and small states. Provide enough flexibility to generate two or more combinations of target states leading to the minimum required number (50 percent plus 1) of electoral votes from each state-size category.

Table 5 displays the original geographic coalition of states developed from the June targeting effort. It also shows the number of electoral votes targeted within each size category, identifies the key battleground states, and specifies the changes in target states that occurred during the campaign. A "battleground" state was defined as one targeted for a disproportionately larger share of campaign resources—organizational funds, candidate time, and media placement concentration.

A perusal of table 5 reflects the evolution of our geographic coalitional strategy. It went through three stages. In March, our base states held solidly through the campaign. Many of these states were not battleground states because our margins within seemed sufficiently high to permit us to focus resources elsewhere. This occurred, for example, in Indiana, Virginia, and virtually the entire bank of small states. In the West, only the Pacific states of California, Oregon, and Washington remained final battleground states through the last cut.

The early September and early October targeting schemes excluded most of the Southern states as a battleground area.

However, during the first week of October, just at the time when our media budget was very anemic and we seemed to lose momentum in the large industrial Midwestern states, our tracking effort picked up some attractive targets of opportunity in the South. First, Tennessee was added to our list of targets, and then Kentucky and Mississippi. By mid-October we added North Carolina, Alabama, and South Carolina to our battleground list; by late October we added Missouri and New York, and the last state to be listed for a disproportionately large dose of resources was Arkansas.

In sum, while we kept a good deal of pressure on the big seven states as the campaign progressed, we shifted resources into Carter's Southern base as we observed his vote support erode there, at first marginally, around the first week in October, but then significantly, as the month closed. Note that Carter did not win a single state outside of the initially defined set of ten states we identified as his base in March. On the contrary, he lost three of those ten — Alabama, Massachusetts, and Arkansas.

THE IMPACT ON THE REAGAN COALITION OF THE CANDIDACY OF JOHN ANDERSON

Just at the time we were putting the final touches on the campaign plan, our latest national survey showed Ronald Reagan with 36 percent of the vote, President Jimmy Carter with 34 percent, and John Anderson with 20 percent. Given that rather large bloc of Anderson supporters, we seriously considered his potential impact on our candidate. We questioned the statement often heard then that Anderson hurt Carter more than Reagan. It was clear from our surveys that the issue was considerably more complex than was initially supposed.

Table 5

Evolution of the Reagan Geographic Coalitional Strategy

Inventory of all states in Ronald Reagan's geographic coalition*	March targets	June	Early September	Early October	Mid-October	Late October	Final battleground
Large states							
California (45)	CA	CA	CA	CA	CA	CA	CA
Illinois (26)	IL	IL	IL	IL	IL	IL	IL
Texas (26)	TX	TX	TX	TX	TX	TX	TX
Ohio (25)	OH	OH	OH	OH	OH	OH	OH
Pennsylvania (27)	–	PA	PA	PA	PA	PA	PA
Michigan (21)	–	MI	MI	MI	MI	MI	MI
New York (41)	–	NY	–	–	–	NY	–
Medium states							
Indiana (13)	IN	IN	IN	IN	IN	IN	–
Virginia (12)	VA	VA	VA	VA	VA	VA	–
Tennessee (10)	–	–	–	TN	TN	TN	TN
Florida (17)	FL	FL	FL	FL	FL	FL	FL
Maryland (10)	–	MD	MD	–	–	–	–
New Jersey (17)	NJ	NJ	NJ	NJ	NJ	NJ	NJ
Louisiana (10)	–	LA	LA	LA	LA	LA	LA
Wisconsin (11)	–	WI	WI	WI	WI	WI	WI
North Carolina (13)	–	–	–	–	NC	NC	NC
Missouri (12)	MO	MO	–	–	–	MO	MO

State (electoral votes)*	1	2	3	4	5	6	7
Idaho (4)	ID	ID	ID	ID	ID	ID	–
South Dakota (4)	SD	SD	SD	SD	SD	SD	–
Wyoming (3)	WY	WY	WY	WY	WY	WY	–
Vermont (3)	VT	VT	VT	VT	VT	VT	–
Utah (4)	UT	UT	UT	UT	UT	UT	–
Nebraska (5)	NE	NE	NE	NE	NE	NE	–
North Dakota (3)	ND	ND	ND	ND	ND	ND	–
New Hampshire (4)	NH	NH	NH	NH	NH	NH	–
Kansas (7)	KS	KS	KS	KS	KS	KS	–
Montana (4)	MT	MT	MT	MT	MT	MT	–
New Mexico (4)	NM	NM	NM	NM	NM	NM	–
Nevada (3)	NV	NV	NV	NV	NV	NV	–
Arizona (6)	AZ	AZ	AZ	AZ	AZ	AZ	–
Oregon (6)	–	OR	OR	OR	OR	OR	OR
Alaska (3)	AK	AK	AK	AK	AK	AK	–
Iowa (8)	IA	IA	IA	IA	IA	IA	–
Colorado (7)	CO	CO	CO	CO	CO	CO	–
Washington (9)	–	WA	WA	WA	WA	WA	WA
Maine (4)	ME	ME	ME	ME	ME	ME	ME
Connecticut (8)	–	CT	CT	CT	CT	CT	CT
Oklahoma (8)	OK	OK	OK	OK	OK	OK	OK
Kentucky (9)	–	–	–	KY	KY	KY	KY
Mississippi (7)	–	–	–	MS	MS	MS	MS
Alabama (9)	–	–	–	–	AL	AL	AL
South Carolina (8)	–	–	–	–	SC	SC	SC
Arkansas (6)	–	–	–	–	–	AR	AR

Source: Internal strategy memoranda and campaign strategy book.

*With electoral votes indicated in parentheses.

We felt that Anderson posed a threat to the Reagan campaign because he was a centrist candidate who claimed a large pool of our potential voters. He was an "Independent"; his attraction was primarily based on his representing an alternative for the protest vote against both Reagan and Carter. When Anderson garnered 20 percent of the vote, he altered the traditional coalitions of the major parties by cutting across the customary political alignments in a fashion which potentially could have more adverse effects on Reagan than on Carter because the Democratic coalition was composed of diverse but reasonably large constituencies of the population. The Republican coalition, on the other hand, was more homogeneous and relatively smaller; hence, it was more vulnerable to erosion from a third-party candidate who had his roots in the Republican party. Anderson, however, was not able to sustain that high level of support we observed in June, and by the first week in October it was evident to us that his support was fading in the stretch. For our end-game coalitional strategy, we assumed his base to be no larger than 6–8 percent and his impact almost a wash. As it turned out, the marginal impact of his vote did affect, in our opinion, the New York and Massachusetts outcomes, and ended up ballooning our electoral support.

THE VOTE AND ITS IMPLICATIONS

By viewing the vote through the prism of change between 1976 and 1980—the shift between the Ford-Carter vote in 1976 as compared with the Reagan-Carter vote in 1980—we can highlight coalitional anomalies. As the following table clearly reflects, the Reagan campaign successfully attracted large numbers of union members, high school graduates, both younger and older voters, behavioral Democrats and, more specifically, conservative Democrats to its ranks (see table 6). Perhaps more important than these marginal changes, that reflect in key demographic and political groups, was the strong support Ronald Reagan received in the South. This crack of Carter's hold on the Southern states may portend considerable promise for future Republican presidential aspirants who can make the same kinds of appeals that Ronald Reagan initiated.

THE FUTURE OF ELECTORAL POLITICS IN THE 1980s

Did 1980 signal a realigning election? It is too early to answer that question definitively. However, there is strong evidence that the 1980 presidential election might well be considered to have initiated a "rolling realignment." The forces set loose in that election are still undergoing the process of confirmation and reinforcement. There still remains the question, "Will those voters who cast their first ballot in some time for a Republican president vote for a Republican the second time around?" We cannot answer that question now. But it is evident that what happens to the union blue-collar worker, to the younger and the Hispanic voter, and to those attracted to the Reagan banner because of their commitment to a leader who reflects traditionally oriented values and who initiates a new set of policies to deal with inflation and unemployment, will answer that question.

Contrarily, there is little doubt that the 1980 election triggered a set of forces which provides the Republican party with considerably more strength than it has ever enjoyed in almost five decades. As table 7 shows, Decision/Making/Information measured a 21-point gap between those identifying themselves as Republicans and Democrats. A year later that gap has closed to only 2 points.

Table 6

Marginal Changes in Presidential Choice Among Key Demographic and Political Groups Between the 1976 and the 1980 Elections

	Ford-Carter 1976 Difference[a]	Reagan-Carter 1980 Difference	Net Shift[b]
Sex			
Male	− 2	+18	+20
Female	− 1	+ 3	+ 4
Labor union			
Yes−union member	−21	− 5	+16
No−not union member	+ 6	+16	+10
Religion			
Baptist	−24	−12	+12
Other Protestant	+17	+40	+23
Roman Catholic	− 9	+ 7	+16
Jewish[c]	−44	+ 6	+50
Other	+ 8	+ 2	− 6
Race			
White	+ 5	+18	+13
Black	−65	−73	− 8
Other	− 7	−17	+24
Education			
Less than high school	−27	−15	+12
High school graduate	− 8	+ 8	+16
Some college/vocational	+12	+16	+ 4
College graduate	+11	+24	+13
Postgraduate	+ 3	+18	+15

	Ford-Carter 1976 Difference[a]	Reagan-Carter 1980 Difference	Net Shift[b]
Age			
18–24 years old	−13	+ 5	+18
25–34 years old	+ 2	+ 8	+ 6
35–44 years old	− 1	+16	+17
45–54 years old	− 3	+16	+19
55–64 years old	− 6	+12	+18
65 years and older	+ 5	+ 1	− 4
Vote behavior			
Behavioral Democrats	−67	−45	+22
Ticket-splitters	+12	+20	+ 8
Behavioral Republicans	+84	+78	− 6
Ideology			
Conservatives	+33	+34	+ 1
Non-ideologs	− 9	− 5	+ 4
Liberals	−60	−22	+38
Party/ideology			
Conservative Democrats	−43	−25	+18
Conservative Republicans	+77	+79	+ 2
Liberal Democrats	−77	−48	+29
Liberal Republicans	+55	+65	+10

Source: Data based on Decision/Making/Information studies of 2,000 voters interviewed immediately after the 1976 and 1980 presidential elections.

[a]The positive/negative signs designate the Ford-minus-Carter and Reagan-minus-Carter support.

[b]The net shift reflects the algebraic sum of differences in the support level of 1976 and 1980, respectively.

[c]Small sample size.

Table 7

Change in Party Identification* Between June 1980 and May 1981

	Republican			Independent			Democrat		
	June 1980	May 1981	Chg	June 1980	May 1981	Chg	June 1980	May 1981	Chg
Aggregate	30	39	+ 9	19	21	+ 2	51	40	−11
Sex									
Male	29	41	+12	21	23	+ 2	50	36	−14
Female	33	38	+ 5	16	20	+ 4	51	42	− 9
Age									
18–24	29	43	+14	28	15	−13	43	42	− 1
25–34	25	36	+11	24	25	+ 1	51	39	−12
35–44	33	39	+ 6	16	23	+ 7	51	38	−13
45–54	35	44	+ 9	16	19	+ 3	50	38	−12
55–64	28	36	+ 8	15	18	+ 3	57	46	−11
65 and over	36	41	+ 5	13	24	+11	51	35	−16
Education									
Less than high school	24	26	+ 2	14	21	+ 7	62	53	− 9
High school	25	41	+16	21	22	+ 1	54	37	−17
Some college	35	38	+ 3	20	23	+ 3	45	39	− 6
College graduate	38	49	+11	18	18	0	44	33	−11
Postgraduate	38	44	+ 6	18	19	+ 1	44	37	− 7
Geographic 4-pt									
Northwest	32	43	+11	18	19	+ 1	50	38	−12
Midwest	31	38	+ 7	20	26	+ 6	49	36	−13
West	35	38	+ 3	17	25	+ 8	48	37	−11
	33	39	+16	19	16	− 3	58	45	−13

Born again

Yes	30	38	+ 8	17	20	+ 3	53	42	−11
No	31	39	+ 8	20	22	+ 2	49	39	−10
Income									
Under $5,000	24	22	− 2	14	27	+13	62	51	−11
$ 5,000–$ 9,999	25	31	+ 6	13	11	− 2	62	58	− 4
$10,000–$14,999	23	32	+ 9	20	27	+ 7	57	41	−16
$15,000–$19,999	26	38	+12	23	24	+ 1	51	38	−13
$20,000–$29,999	34	41	+ 7	19	19	0	47	40	− 7
$30,000–$39,999	36	47	+11	21	20	− 1	43	33	−10
Above $40,000	54	52	− 2	14	20	+ 6	32	28	− 4
Ethnicity									
White	34	43	+ 9	19	22	+ 3	47	35	−12
Black	4	7	+ 3	14	6	− 8	82	87	+ 5
Hispanic	16	21	+ 5	11	17	+ 6	73	62	−11
Other	25	42	+17	25	25	0	50	33	−17
Labor-union family									
Yes	20	32	+12	21	20	− 1	59	48	−11
No	34	42	+ 8	18	22	+ 4	48	36	−12

Source: Data based on two samples of 1,500 eligible voters interviewed by Decision/Making/Information by telephone in June 1980 and May 1981.

*Questions: "In politics today, do you usually think of yourself as a Republican, a Democrat, an Independent, or what? (IF REPUBLICAN OR DEMOCRAT, ASK:) Would you call yourself a *strong* (Republican/Democrat) or a *not-so-strong* (Republican/Democrat)? (IF INDEPEN-DENT/OTHER/NO PREFERENCE, ASK:) Do you think of yourself as closer to the Republican or to the Democratic party?" Note the "Independent leaners" have been collapsed into Republican or Democratic categories.

It is also instructive to assess where the change in party identification occurred. Note that the largest single gains stem from those aged 34 or younger. While the youngest age cohort (18 to 24) shifts directly from the Democratic category, it breaks from the independents to the Republicans. At the other end of the age spectrum (over 65), voters who hold long and well established partisan allegiances are also leaving the Democratic party in large numbers to become independents.

Other strong gains in Republican identification come from those with a high school education, from the South, from middle-income voters, and from union families. I do not believe it is coincidence that these groups were precisely those that were most dramatically impacted in the Reagan-Carter contest.

The Republican party also has made significant gains perceptually as the party best able to handle a wide array of issues (see table 8). Note, in particular, that on the three key issues—fighting inflation, holding down taxes, and maintaining world peace—the Republican party, for the first time in decades, is viewed as better able to deal with these key issues than the Democratic party.

Furthermore, using the standard thermometer scale to assess attraction to various institutions and individuals, Decision/Making/Information's study completed 18 August 1981 showed the Republican party with an average thermometer score of 61°, which was fully 6 points above that given to the Democratic party. Our postelection studies in November 1980, using this measure of approval, showed the Democrats and Republicans even.

Control of the House of Representatives may be a bridge too far for the Republicans to cross in 1982. Nevertheless, it appears very possible that we will be able to observe next year something that has occurred only one other time in American political history since the close of the Civil War— an increase, in the off-year, in the number of congressmen

Table 8
Which Political Party Is Best Described
by the Following Phrases?

	Republicans (%)	Democrats (%)
Cutting inflation	62	17
Maintaining military strength	65	19
Controlling government spending	68	17
Increasing energy supplies	39	33
Maintaining world peace	41	36
Holding down taxes	60	22
Decreasing unemployment	40	39
Balancing the budget	62	16
Protecting equal opportunities for minorities	17	63
Helping the elderly/retired	20	63

Source: Results of survey conducted for the National Congressional Campaign Committee by Market Opinion Research, 1 June 1981.

who are of the same party as the president. This, as much as
any other factor, will confirm or deny whether the rolling
realignment is real.

THE 1980 MANDATE:
AN OPPORTUNITY TO ESTABLISH
A NEW GOVERNING COALITION

Ronald Reagan's mandate is "change."

Traditionally, Americans have viewed their president as
the catalyst for progress. It was this key theme that under-
pinned our campaign strategy. Jimmy Carter's failed presidency, juxtaposed against Reagan's unique appeal to the
hope that things could change for the better, lies at the very
base of the 1980 victory. Thus, the 1980 presidential election
should be viewed as a major political event initiating an opportunity to redraft the policy agenda of this country.

The election was not a bestowal of political power, but a
stewardship opportunity for the Reagan administration to
reconsider and restructure the political agenda for the next
decade. The win coalitions of the Reagan campaign may well
have sanctioned this search for a new public philosophy to
govern the United States.

In sum, Governor Reagan won because he, not Carter or
Anderson, articulated an approach to governance, reflected
an awareness of the role of leadership in motivating masses
of individual citizens, and provided a sense of vision about
America's future direction. Political leaders in the United
States reduce uncertainty about the future, not because they
have ready-made solutions for all problems, but rather,
because they give expression to the essential tenets of an
overall approach to both public policy and governance—an
expression that strikes a responsive chord among a broad
swath of the electorate because of the values it embodies.

The central features of Reagan's basic approach that built the 1980 electoral mandate were:

- Trust the values of American society that are largely responsible for sustaining its *growth.*

- Treat America's leaders, public and private, as account-able stewards responsible for living up to those commonly shared traditional values of family, work, neighborhood, peace, and freedom.

- Recognize the inherent value of individual initiative, and the operating premise of a representative democracy that government—federal, state, and local—should not per-form functions that are better handled by individual citizens on their own behalf.

- Generate solutions to the major problems now besetting our society by explicitly recognizing that three major con-ditions have darkened the visage of America. Specifically, those conditions are:

  - A sluggish economy and double-digit high inflation, principally caused by excessive government spend-ing, taxation, and an overregulated private en-terprise sector;

  - The federal government's size and cost, which have exceeded what is reasonable and have led the govern-ment often to do what is unnecessary and frequently to miss the mark on what is really needed;

  - The acquiescence of a once-proud and powerful America to a secondary role in the world.

The specific mandate calls for an amelioration of these three conditions.

After the election, Carter noted that, "One of the anomalies of this election is that things on which I worked the hardest were the ones that were politically counterproductive." He then cited the Panama Canal, the Mideast peace talks, and human rights policies as particularly damaging to him politically.

More to the point, however, may be the fact that four years ago, when Mr. Carter arrived in Washington, he committed himself to a sweeping consolidation of many federal agencies into a few. Instead, he ended by adding the departments of energy and education to the cabinet. He was going to save millions with "zero-based budgeting." He was going to reform a tax system that was "a disgrace to the human race." He hoped, in his inaugural address, that "nuclear weapons could be eliminated from the face of the earth." Hence, Jimmy Carter established in the first few months the foundation for the shearing comparisons between his promises and performances by the way he uniquely shaped and created expectations which fueled the antagonisms that helped to defeat him.

In sum, the Reagan administration, four years hence, will be judged on the basis of what it accomplishes as well as on the expectations it generates. But ultimately its success will ride on whether things by 1984 "have changed for the better"—when more Americans, perhaps, will answer "Yes!" to the question, "Are you better off now than you were four years ago?" If so, that mandate will have been met, and perhaps will have also established a set of new coalitions that could dominate national politics in the 1980s.

11

PATRICK H. CADDELL

The Democratic Strategy and Its Electoral Consequences

Five points to explain the 1980 election. Voter survey results on Election Day weekend. A referendum on Carter. "Weak" Democrats, independents, and ideology. Iran and public opinion, 1979–1980. Democratic strategy. The debate. Defections. Population shifts. Future partisanship realignment.

The Democratic party suffered a major defeat in 1980, significant enough to pose the question: does this election signal the demise of its status as America's majority—or, better put, plurality—political party?

Both major parties have gradually weakened throughout the last two decades, and each has experienced periods trying enough to prompt forecasts of extinction. The latest in a stream of death notices—this time, for the Democrats—appeared soon after 4 November. Liberalism was finished; the Democrats had lost touch with the people; the teetering New Deal coalition had finally been toppled, and another "emerging Republican majority" sighted. The evidence for these judgments expanded quickly from the election itself to include all sorts of public opinion polls, pet theories, and Washington mood-ring colorations that, in their beholders' eyes, spell great and perhaps fatal trouble for the Democrats' future.

The reaction, in so many ways extreme, has led me to conclude that there is at work in politics a law that may be summarized as follows: "The greater the surprise on Election Day to political elites, the greater the propensity (by some exponential factor) for those same elites to find cosmic and earth-shaking causes and consequences in that election." The 1980 election—anything but unsurprising—is a classic example of the law.

The American voters paint an extraordinary portrait of their country and of politics in national elections. A careful review of the available election data suggests that while the Democratic party was soundly defeated and is clearly on the defensive in the administration's first year, 1980 does not mean that the Republicans have staked a majority claim, nor will they in the near future. The Republicans, like other winning parties, have been granted an opportunity and little more. Indeed, combining smart politics and a little luck, the Democrats could conceivably stage a comeback in 1982 and 1984.

FIVE CENTRAL ARGUMENTS

There are five points central to understanding the 1980 election that this essay will discuss.

1. By Election Day, the vote had become essentially a referendum on the incumbent—a circumstance that the Carter campaign had successfully prevented all year.

2. While the country has become more conservative, the Reagan victory cannot be categorized as an ideological victory. Indeed, President Reagan may be no more successful in molding a long-term majority coalition in support of his policies, personality, or party than other recent occupants of the White House.

3. The Iranian crisis and the performance of a struggling economy dominated the campaign's chronological course. A confluence of these two issues, which saw increased economic concerns triggered in part by developments in Iran, contributed significantly to the late Reagan surge and the ultimate dimensions of the GOP landslide.

4. The dramatic Democratic loss of the Senate and the heavy losses in the House of Representatives were in actuality less startling than they appear and were directly tied to Carter's sharp decline in the closing days. These results may signal a return to a pattern of coattail party voting in presidential elections.

5. The election offers the Republicans an opportunity to achieve political dominance in the 1980s if their programs and policies prove successful in addressing America's problems. Such dominance has not yet been established; 1980 was a passing of initiative not unlike that presented to the Democrats in 1976.

THE CANDIDATES AND VOTERS
ON ELECTION DAY

Cambridge Survey Research (CSR) conducted full national surveys on each of the last three nights preceding the election. The survey conducted on Monday evening, 3 November, showed Reagan's lead ballooning to 10 points—his eventual victory margin. It also found only a bare plurality of voters, 49 percent, holding a favorable opinion of Ronald Reagan as a person, with 46 percent unfavorable. While superior to President Carter's rating, this score was vastly inferior to the personal support accorded Richard Nixon just before his 1972 landslide or Jimmy Carter in 1976.

Some further evidence on Reagan's mixed ratings:

- By only a slim plurality, 46 percent to 42 percent, did voters feel that Reagan had the vision to provide solutions for the nation's problems.

- Forty-six percent felt it would be a risk to elect Reagan president—only 49 percent disagreed.

- On the positive statement that, as president, "Reagan would keep the country out of war," only 32 percent agreed and 41 percent disagreed, with a large 27 percent unsure.

- Sixty percent agreed that Reagan "shoots from the hip too much without thinking things through."

- Similarly, 59 percent felt that Reagan "hasn't told us what he would do as president."

In addition, the electorate rated Carter over Reagan on a number of key qualities, including "best qualified," "trustworthy," and "cares about people" (see table 1). One would have thought, given these doubts about Reagan, that Jimmy Carter might be poised for reelection. Instead, our data pointed to an avalanche defeat rooted in the campaign's definition and dictated by that definition.

Table 1
Comparative Measures on Personal Qualities

	Carter	Reagan
The following phrase best describes which candidate:		
Would keep us out of war	51%	20%
Is best qualified	47%	38%
Is trustworthy	43%	29%
I respect more	42%	38%
Would best handle an international crisis	42%	40%
Cares about people like me	41%	31%

CHOICE V. REFERENDUM

For over a year, through primary and general elections, President Carter's campaign was tied to a single overriding premise: that the election had to be defined by the voters as a choice between two men and not as a referendum on the incumbent administration. The thrust was always to keep attention directed to the future and not to the past, due to Carter's uneven record.

Carter had enjoyed success in the early primaries when Democratic voters were forced to make a general election—like choice for president between Senator Kennedy and himself. In the later rounds, Carter struggled as his record became the focus of more classic primary voting and as his opponent became a rallying point of protest.

The Carter defeat by Ronald Reagan reflected the preeminence by Election Day of the referendum definition. The incumbent's record became the decisive factor for millions of uncertain swing voters. While such a development follows normative political theory, which argues that elections are supposed to render judgments on an incumbent's record, the reality of recent presidential elections has often been somewhat different. The late stages of closely contested presidential elections have been organized around the choice model, with a greater burden and scrutiny being placed on the challenger.

During the fall, the Carter campaign had been fairly successful—particularly with swing voters—in advancing the definition of choice. As choice gave way to referendum by election eve, Carter's political fortunes fell. By Election Day a slight majority regarded him unfavorably as a person, and his job performance scores demonstrated even greater weakness (see figure 1). Most voters also thought Carter lacked vision, and questioned his strength, decisiveness, and effectiveness. In these leadership areas, the GOP challenger held significant edges, just as "challenger" Carter had in 1976 against incumbent Gerald Ford.

More important, Reagan held his greatest comparative margins over Carter on economic issues (table 2). His margin increased on every economic comparative after the Cleveland debate. Additionally, importance of economic measures in a voting calculus had grown relative to personal and leadership characteristics, exceeding even that of party.

These results illuminate a changed character of the election over the last week. The debate aftermath and the reentrance of the hostage issue focused critical attention on the Carter administration, specifically, for many previously uncertain voters, on economic management.[1]

Table 2

Comparative Measures on Economic Issues

	Carter	Reagan
Which phrase best describes which candidate:		
Would do the best job controlling inflation?	26%	56%
Would do better reducing unemployment?	28%	51%
Would best manage the economy?	30%	55%

Figure 1

Carter Job Ratings, 3 November 1980

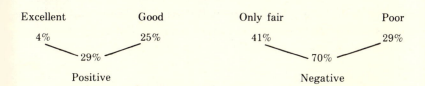

Excellent	Good	Only fair	Poor
4%	25%	41%	29%

29% Positive   70% Negative

Approve: 38%
Disapprove: 54%

WHO "MOVED"?

In the wake of a landslide, particularly one that occurs sud-
denly and catches pundits off guard, there is always the tendency to see "everyone" moving. Of course, this is never the
case. The Reagan landslide was caused primarily by the
defection of two vital groups in the electorate: "weak" Democrats and independents (see table 3).

Reagan made minimal gains in the last week among Republicans and strong Democrats, but improved with independents and weak Democrats by 20 and 26 points, respectively.
The losses among independents were large enough to seal
Carter's fate, but his decline among his own partisan supporters set a landslide in motion. In an era of weakened party
allegiance, defections from weak partisans are unsurprising.
The timing of the defections—at the end of the campaign
when a party tug is strongest—is unique.

The weakly affiliated Democrats were almost all white,
primarily middle class, both blue-collar and white-collar, and
heavily Catholic. This bloc, particularly the Catholic voters,
had been of concern to Carter strategists throughout 1980.
Carter had led Reagan by 10 points among Catholics before
the debate, but eventually lost this traditional Democratic
group by 11 points.[2]

The loss of "weak" Democrats cannot be explained away
for reasons of ideological differences. Although less liberal
than other Democrats, these voters were quite moderate, and
they consistently placed themselves closer to Carter than to
Reagan on an ideological continuum.

IDEOLOGY AND THE
REAGAN MANDATE

Following the 1972 election, there was an outpouring of
academic theory that proclaimed the emerging dominance of

Table 3
1980 Movements in the Electorate

	Pre-debate 24–26 October	Election eve 3 November
Democrats		
Carter	72	64
Reagan	15	24
Carter margin	+57	+40
Independents		
Carter	30	20
Reagan	40	50
Carter margin	−10	−30
Republicans		
Carter	9	9
Reagan	78	82
Carter margin	−69	−73
Weak Democrats		
Carter	55	42
Reagan	25	38
Carter margin	+30	+ 4
Strong Democrats		
Carter	85	80
Reagan	7	13
Carter margin	+78	+67

ideology in presidential voting. In the wake of the Reagan landslide, once again the banner of ideology has been raised by many observers. Such explanations form the core of the "mandate" theory of Reagan's victory. However, a review of the 1980 data should inspire caution.

Throughout the fall, survey data consistently found Carter viewed as not only a more "centrist" candidate than Reagan, but usually as closer to voters' own ideological self-perceptions (see table 4).

Almost every self-designated liberal considered Carter as moderate or liberal, and 60 percent saw Reagan as conservative; most moderates thought Carter also moderate and Reagan conservative; only the quarter of the electorate calling themselves conservative placed Reagan closer to them ideologically. And one-third of the electorate placed Reagan on the extreme conservative end of this scale.

Furthermore, even a cursory view of the electorate's attitudes on issues raises questions about a Reagan policy mandate. The National Opinion Research Center reported that in 1980 large majorities of Americans supported increases or no change in the levels of federal spending on nine of eleven major issues, such as the environment, cities, defense, and education.

Such findings hardly support the notion that Election Day 1980 found the public articulating a demand for elimination or even reduction of effort in most federal programs. Suspicion of government effectiveness and overall spending policy did not translate into specific calls for cuts in 1980.

However, what most post-election surveys clearly suggest is that the election was far more a rejection of Jimmy Carter than an endorsement of Ronald Reagan's platform. The *New York Times*/CBS News Election Day Exit Survey found that an overwhelming plurality of Reagan voters cited dissatisfaction with the incumbent as the cause of their decision. A post-election survey by *Cambridge Reports* discovered 47 percent of the Reagan voters volunteering anti-Carter

Table 4
Seven-point Liberal/Conservative Continuum
October 1980

(A)	Liberal	1	2	3	4	5	6	7	Conservative
The voter		8	8	11	28	16	12	13	4
Carter		11	11	18	34	10	7	6	3
Reagan		5	4	4	14	12	24	32	5

(B)	Liberal (1,2)	Moderate (3,4,5)	Conservative (6,7)
The voter	16	55	25
Carter	22	62	13
Reagan	9	30	56

comments as the reason for their choice, while 27 percent cited aspects of Reagan's personality, and only about 20 percent raised Reagan's positions on the issues, his ideology, or similar qualities as the major factor in their vote. Finally, in January the Yankelovich, Skelly, and White survey for *Time* magazine found that 63 percent of the electorate felt that the outcome was "a rejection of President Carter" while 24 percent labeled it "a mandate for more conservative policies." In that survey, only 30 percent of the self-defined conservatives and 34 percent of the Republicans chose the "mandate" response.

CAMPAIGN CHRONOLOGY

In the summer of 1979, before the appearance of serious announced opposition, Jimmy Carter was an unpopular president, reaching historic lows in the polls. A large majority of Democrats preferred Edward Kennedy as the party's next nominee. This was the first of several poll "landslides" awarded to various candidates. Like the Queen in *Alice in Wonderland,* the polls gave prizes to all: Kennedy in the summer of 1979, Carter in the late winter and spring of 1980, and on 4 November 1980 Ronald Reagan received the one that counted most.

By January 1980 Carter's and Kennedy's fortunes had reversed, for two reasons: the hostage crisis, and a shaky start by the challenger. Carter's rise in popularity was swift after the embassy seizure. Kennedy's campaign floundered, and the Carter efforts to make early primaries and caucuses choices instead of referenda soon proved successful. Carter's new strength was not purely a "rally around the flag" phenomenon; most Americans were deeply impressed with his responses to the crisis that fall and winter. Many voters changed their assessment of his leadership character, finding a strength and decisiveness where formerly they had perceived only weakness and indecisiveness.

Ironically, this altered assessment of Carter contained great risk for the president. Previous low ratings had reflected more disappointment in Carter than anger or hostility. There was new concern that any new negative turn in the president's popularity would develop a bitterness and anger connected to the belief that somehow Carter had tried to "fool" the electorate. When hope for a hostage release faded and economic troubles grew, Carter's popularity sank again.

Indeed, by early summer, Carter occupied a more precarious position than he had pre-Iran. In almost every late primary state, majorities of Democrats agreed with the proposition that Carter had shown "he can't handle the job, we'd be better off trying a new president." The president was counseled in June that, in the abstract, "the American people do not want Jimmy Carter as their president," and that further slippage could make victory in November nearly impossible.

An unstable public opinion turned again, and despite a large Reagan lead following his convention, the Billy Carter scandal, a tumultuous Democratic conclave in New York, and consistent unpopularity, Carter on Labor Day had drawn almost abreast of Reagan. This reversal in fortunes had two causes: a return to the party standard by many Democrats and persistent doubts about the Republican nominee. In short, as the fall campaign began, Reagan still faced an "acceptability" test applied without regard to the incumbent, which traditionally focused greater attention and pressure on the challenger.

The Democratic strategy

FIRST, and foremost, *the campaign had to be a question of the future, not the past. It had to be a choice for president, not a referendum on the Carter administration.* To this end, we wanted to focus on the presidency itself, to stress the importance and extreme sensitivity of the office, and to emphasize the question of which individual might better be trusted with the responsibility.

SECOND, it was imperative that the perception of Carter's job performance be improved, and that the incumbency be used to the best advantage. "Hard" news—governmental, noncampaign actions and results—was more valuable than softer, campaign news.

THIRD, Carter had to be portrayed as a president who had learned and who would be a better president in a second term. Polls indicated that most voters accepted this argument, and we believed that if Reagan faltered, many would need to utilize this rationale in voting for the president.

FOURTH, the campaign wanted to portray the president as being in the mainstream of American political beliefs, in contrast to Ronald Reagan.

FIFTH, the issue had to be Ronald Reagan. Nineteen eighty was a negative political year when every contender was burdened with high negative ratings. It was imperative that Reagan, his positions, and his weaknesses be the focus of public attention. This was particularly true on the issue of "war and peace"—the most "presidential" of issues.

SIXTH, the Democrats must be united. Carter was the nominee of the majority party. His chief electoral problems, many stemming from the primaries, lay among Democratic constituencies: liberal, blue-collar, union, Catholic, Jewish, and weak-preference Democrats.

SEVENTH, the South and Northern industrial states were of necessity the core of the electoral college strategy. Those two regions elected Carter in 1976, and would have to do so again in 1980. Carter's regional appeal had to be capitalized upon. Initial efforts had to be directed to the North, and particularly to the suburbs, where Carter had run poorly in 1976 but where Reagan was highly suspect.

EIGHTH, John Anderson had to be weakened. Anderson's independent candidacy initially hurt Carter among key constituencies in most major Northern states.

The Democratic strategy enjoyed mixed results until the Cleveland debate. The greatest failure occurred in improving the perception of the president's job performance. Throughout the fall there was little disastrous news, but also precious little positive news from events or administration actions. Nor was the effort to paint Reagan as a candidate outside the mainstream very successful, in part due to Reagan's success at moderating his position, an effort aided by his personality.

On the other hand, there was steady if unspectacular success through October in attracting wavering Democrats and in weakening John Anderson. Furthermore, in the period just prior to the debate, 60 percent agreed that "Carter had learned a lot and would be a better president in a second term." By late October, Carter had made crucial gains in the Northern states, particularly in key suburbs. These gains, however, were balanced by stubborn resistance in many economically depressed Democratic urban areas.

Reagan, as had Carter in 1976, stumbled in his first general election appearances, making a series of impolitic remarks. Carter narrowed the margin further, but attention was soon diverted to the Anderson-Reagan debate in Baltimore. The president refused to participate, despite harsh press criticism, and thereby avoided a simultaneous grilling by both opponents. John Anderson "won" the debate according to instant polls, but the real winner was Ronald Reagan who mollified some concerns of key voter groups.

In the campaign's next stage, stretching through mid/late October, Carter gained steadily, moving ahead in some polls. During October, Carter utilized the "war and peace" issue to inflict serious damage on the Reagan candidacy, while at the same time he was put on the defensive by press criticism that he was running a "mean" campaign.[3] The small decline in Carter's high marks for honesty, trustworthiness, and decency was an affordable trade-off for the heightened concerns about Reagan's riskiness, hip-shooting, and impulsiveness in foreign policy. By late October the Carter campaign had succeeded in turning the electoral focus to Reagan.

THE CLEVELAND DEBATE AND THE NATURE OF PRESIDENTIAL DEBATES

While the Carter campaign moved to cut off any possibility of a debate with Reagan, the Republican nominee reversed his earlier position and accepted an invitation for a one-on-one debate scheduled for exactly one week before Election Day.

Meanwhile, several promising signs had emerged. By the weekend prior to the debate, Carter's personal rating had finally surpassed Reagan's, and the sizable bloc of undecided voters viewed Reagan more negatively than Carter, as did the remaining Anderson supporters.[4]

Carter's usual advantages on comparative measures (keep us out of war, international crisis, best qualified, etc.) had reached a peak, and Reagan's margins on economic comparisons had dwindled to their smallest points. A majority agreed for the first time that it was "a risk to make Ronald Reagan president," and by a wide margin (46 percent to 26 percent) voters disagreed that "as president, Ronald Reagan would keep us out of war." In addition, better than 60 percent felt that Reagan shot from the hip and failed to explain what he would do as president.

The reluctance of the Carter camp to debate—particularly, late in the campaign—rested on three chief premises:

A late debate would interfere with the traditional surge in the last week of the incumbent primary which had occurred in every election since 1948, with the exception of the landslide elections in 1964 and 1972.

The debate offered Reagan a significant forum in which to rebut the damaging charges raised by Carter and to reassure millions of voters who had been affected by those attacks.

Presidential debates are the vehicles of challengers, not of incumbents.

The last two points are closely related. Voters do not approach presidential debates as a sporting match. Historically, debates serve to strengthen candidate support, regardless of who "wins." Voters utilize debates to resolve doubts—few look to be converted. Since doubts generally are greater for a challenger than for a well-known incumbent, the former is better positioned to assuage the specific concerns of voters even if he loses a debate on points. John Kennedy and Jimmy Carter both probably could not have been elected with debates.

For these reasons, the Carter campaign was baffled throughout the fall by Reagan's refusal to accept a head-to-head debate. We had always assumed that Reagan approached the debates with an edge. His task was singular: to allay the fears raised by Carter that he was reckless and impulsive on foreign policy issues. A victory for Reagan was possible by a credible performance of the sort he had made throughout 1980. For Carter, to achieve a real victory required a "knockout," a clear demonstration of intellectual leadership and substantive superiority not easily achieved over a man with the skills possessed by Ronald Reagan.

THE LAST WEEK

Within forty-eight hours, the extent of Ronald Reagan's debate victory had become evident. Not only did he "win" the debate, but he also moved into an immediate 5-percentage-point lead. More important, Reagan had registered striking improvement on a number of the key candidate-quality questions.

On the Sunday before the debate, a slight plurality of voters were unfavorable to Reagan on the personal rating questions; by Friday, the positive was 5 points greater than the negative. In addition, Reagan gained 11 net points on the projective statement "that he has not told us what he would do." The perception that Reagan "shoots from the hip" declined 17 points. On the crucial questions pertaining to "risk" and to "keeping the United States out of war," Reagan improved about 8 points. Finally, on the entire range of comparison qualities between the candidates, the challenger consistently gained 5 to 6 points. These changes in voter preference and perception clearly reflected the impact of Reagan's performance.

The dawn of the campaign's last weekend found grave concern in the upper echelons of the Carter campaign. However, two factors permitted some last-minute hope. First, our polls in 1976 found that within several days of first changes in voter attitude toward the winner of each debate (Ford in the first, Carter in the last two), candidate preferences moved back toward the level which existed just prior to the debate. Second, the administration was beginning to receive signals that the Iranian parliament might be moving to resolve the year-long hostage crisis.

CSR conducted a full national survey of 1,200 interviews on Saturday, 1 November. Late Saturday night, an anxious campaign received the results: the race had returned to a dead heat—the postdebate "bounceback" to Carter had seemingly materialized.[5]

But by dawn on Sunday that hope had faded. As most of the country slept, the president's political and governmental high commands began to react to news from Iran that the Majlis had announced conditions for the release of the hostages. Thus, two days before the election and the anniversary of the embassy seizure, the tenuous focus once again began to shift from political choice to the unfolding drama in Tehran.

Deciding that the uncertain situation could not be handled away from the capital, the president cancelled campaign activities and returned to the White House amidst great speculation that the hostages would soon be freed. But by Monday, when the campaign resumed, an immediate release was obviously not forthcoming. Unlike any presidential election in recent history, the network television news that night focused primarily, not on the morrow's crucial election choice, but on long accounts of the developments in Iran. Each network also ran anniversary retrospectives of the entire crisis—moving accounts of rioting in Tehran, Desert One, the ordeal of families, and all the anger and frustration linked to the episode. For the Carter campaign, only faint traces remained of the strategy to refocus on Reagan as the issue uppermost in the electorate's mind. As events passed from the campaign's hands, its own polls told the story (see table 5).

A review of survey data on post–World War II presidential elections yields a consistent finding: Every presidential election which polls indicated to be close on entering the last weekend resulted in a close election. Only in 1980 did the margin of victory expand significantly in the campaign's waning hours.

Our extensive surveys over the last weekend suggest that the atypical movement toward Reagan was directly attributable to a major event—the hostage crisis. This analysis does not suggest that events in Iran "caused" defections from Carter. Instead, the renewed focus on this saga served first to turn voter attention almost exclusively toward Carter, casting the election once more as a referendum. Second, that attention began to reach beyond the reignited crisis to Carter's greatest area of vulnerability—the economy.

Table 5
Voter Preference 30 October/3 November 1980

	Reagan/Carter	Reagan margin
Thursday/Friday	44%/39%	+ 5
Saturday night	41%/41%	0
Sunday night	45%/40%	+ 5
Monday night	46%/36%	+10

Ironically, voters thought that Carter handled the immediate situation fairly well. That did not help him, however. American frustration over Iran came to a boil, and voters said, in effect, "Jimmy Carter is doing his best—but that isn't good enough."

FIRST-STAGE DEFECTION

The first major shifts to Reagan took place Sunday night, after a day of exciting and upbeat news. Nonetheless, the vote movement was clearly to Reagan.

Between the Sunday and Monday night surveys, when Reagan's margin increased from 5 percent to 10 percent, we found significant movement in the challenger's direction on many of the comparison questions (particularly economic), and on questions concerning Reagan himself. However, at the initial stage of movement—Reagan's 5-point vote surge on Sunday—there was slight or no pro-Reagan movement either on comparisons of the two candidates or on questions relating to Reagan, the individual.

Instead, most of the Carter questions revealed serious declines—on a day when the hostage news appeared positive, and when Carter was personally monitoring the crisis from the White House.

In that one day, Carter lost 10 net points on his job performance rating, 8 points on being a "safe choice," and 9 points
on "has learned and would be a better president in a second
term." Interestingly, voters did give Carter a 51 percent approval rating to 38 percent disapproval on his handling of the
immediate hostage situation. Of the issues, only one question
showed major movement from Saturday to Sunday, a question that had elicited stable figures all year, including most
of the prior week. That question asked voters to rate the position of the United States in the world (see table 6).

SECOND-STAGE DEFECTION

A comparison of the surveys taken Sunday and Monday, as
Reagan's lead jumped to 10 points, indicated not only Reagan
gains on voter perceptions, but significant movement on
issue questions as well. Two clusters of issues, Iran and the
economy, were the most significant.

Iran

Our battery of Iran crisis questions showed contradictory
movements. Questions involving Carter's handling of the
crisis, and the notion that he was playing politics with the
crisis, were quite positive to him. However, his political position was collapsing. Two questions dealing with the specifics
of the crisis—the reasonableness of the Iranian conditions
and the timing of a possible hostage release—underwent
radical change, and doomed the president (see table 7).
Neither voter defection nor increased negative personal perceptions seemed linked to Carter's direct handling of the
crisis on that weekend.

Voters were asked whether the conditions set forth by the
Iranian parliament were reasonable or not, and on Sunday a

Table 6
Voter Rating of U.S. Position in the World

	Rating*	Margin
Pre-debate, 24–26 October 1980	40% P/58% N	−18%
Pre-election:		
29–30 August 1980	40% P/59% N	−19%
Saturday, 1 November 1980	39% P/59% N	−20%
Sunday, 2 November 1980	34% P/64% N	−30%

*P = positive (excellent/good); N = negative (only fair/poor).

Table 7
Reaction to Hostage Issue

	Rating*	
	Sunday (2 Nov. 1980)	Monday (3 Nov. 1980)
Carter's handling of Iran crisis	51% A/38% D	53% A/39% D
Carter's using hostage issue for political gain	37% A/56% D	28% A/65% D

*A = approve/agree; D = disapprove/disagree.

plurality of 10 percent called them unreasonable. A day later the margin had risen to 27 percent. Similarly, on Sunday, when asked when the hostages might be released, 34 percent of the voters said, "Within a week" and 48 percent responded, "Two weeks or longer." By Monday, those saying "Within a week" declined to 20 percent, and the responses of "Two weeks or longer" increased to 61 percent. Thus, in one day, there was a 27-point margin increase of pessimism. One can, I think, accurately suggest that these questions reveal a sharp increase of frustration, even anger.

Economy

Although the general Iranian questions suggest an environment charged with frustration and anger, the vote calculus does not indicate that Iran was directly responsible for the late vote defection. Rather, this calculus points to Iran as a trigger for dramatic changes in attitude concerning the economy.

Reagan's margins on the three standard economic comparisons (handling inflation, unemployment, and the economy in general) all increased about 10 points in the campaign's last hours. The last of the comparisons—"Best manage the economy"—was by far the most significant factor in voter decisions. Indeed, of all the factors—economic and noneconomic—measured in the vote calculus, it increased the most in absolute importance between Sunday and Monday. This strongly suggests that the late defection was connected to frustration about the management of the economy and a desire to change it.

Iran appears to have focused the voters' general unhappiness with the Carter regime. For voters in motion, Reagan became the alternative for expressing that displeasure. At that point, the debate—and the lessened public concern about Reagan caused by the debate—proved decisive.

None of this analysis suggests that Carter would have been

reelected, absent the events of the final weekend. There is only a slim possibility that he could have won. A stronger case can be made that, with no debate, Carter stood a good chance of reelection, given the electoral movements in the period immediately before the debate and an expected late incumbent-party gain. The data most definitely demonstrate that, without the events of the last weekend triggering a referendum psychology, Carter's margin of loss would have been much smaller. That margin probably would not also have included the late Monday defections which might have significantly altered the outcome of the Senate and House elections.

THE CONGRESSIONAL VOTE

If the magnitude of the Reagan landslide surprised political experts, then the Senate and House results were shocking by comparison. Perhaps nothing has lent more impetus to the notion of *Götterdämmerung* than the capture of the Senate by Right-wing Republicans and the heavy losses suffered by Democrats in the House of Representatives.

However, a careful election analysis of the voting at this level suggests that the congressional results were deeply intertwined with the late movements in the presidential vote and may not be attributable to a national conservative tide.

Throughout the turbulent election year, the national vote for Congress as reflected in the polls was an island of stability. The results only tended to confirm the decade-long phenomenon of detaching the presidential vote from the congressional vote.

From summer through late fall, the Democrats' lead on congressional voting varied at most a few points, seemingly impervious to presidential fluctuation (see table 8). During most of the final campaign week, as major shifts in the presidential vote were recorded, the likely vote for Congress remained stable. That is, until the last day (see table 9).

Interestingly, the congressional vote did not change at the first stage of Carter's decline. However, as Carter lost an additional 5 points to Reagan on the campaign's last day, so the Democrats in Congress lost 5 percent to their challengers — after almost five months of absolute stability!

The nature of defection from congressional Democrats to Republicans mirrored the presidential movement. "Weak" Democrats slipped 13 net points in Democratic congressional preference, more than twice the overall decline and by far the largest of any group.

This point is further reinforced by examining the voting by House "classes." After Watergate, the Democrats captured 48 House seats in the 1974 election. That election featured Democratic successes in a number of suburban and often traditionally Republican seats. One could naturally assume that these old Republican seats would be at the heart of 1980 Republican gains.

Yet a careful post-election analysis finds little Republican resurgence in those seats. In districts captured by Democrats since 1972, the aggregate Democratic vote percentage fell only 1 point from 1978 to 1980. However, the results are quite different in the incumbent Democratic seats held prior to 1974.

Most congressional elections prior to the 1974 Democratic sweep produced little turnover in partisan control. The Democratic seats won in the 1960s and early 1970s constitute a base group of traditional Democratic strength. From 1978 to 1980 the Democrats suffered an aggregate 6 percent decline in electoral performance in these pre-1974 Democratic seats. The 1980 losses thus occurred mainly in the bloc of seats that, in the previous decade, were by far the most Democratic.

The dichotomy can be highlighted with specific examples: on Long Island, New York, the Democrats retained the key

Table 8
Congressional Preference

	Democrats	Republicans	Democratic margin
July 1980	38%	28%	+10%
August 1980	45%	32%	+13%
September 1980	39%	27%	+12%
October 1980	46%	35%	+11%

Table 9*
Congressional/Presidential Preference

	Congress		President	
	Demo-crat	Repub-lican	Demo-crat	Repub-lican
Pre-debate	46%	35%	41%	40%
Saturday, 1 November 1980	50%	36%	41%	41%
Sunday, 2 November 1980	50%	36%	40%	45%
Monday, 3 November 1980	47%	38%	36%	46%

*These preference figures for congressional vote do not precisely reflect the final House of Representatives vote which was almost evenly split between the parties. Such questions cannot factor the personalities of candidates or the confusion with Senate voting. However, the marginal movements over time are more significant.

Republican district in Suffolk County captured by Tom Downey in 1974, and lost the more Democratic Nassau seat held sixteen years by Lester Wolff. In the Republican farm Fifth District of Iowa, Tom Harkin retained the same strong vote level he had registered in 1978, while the more Democratic Fourth District Democratic incumbent, Neal Smith, saw his percentage drop from 65 percent to 54 percent.

The implications of this analysis for 1982 are crucial. The Democrats from these suburban moderate GOP districts have adapted themselves well to their constituencies, working from the moment of election to secure a hold on vulnerable seats. The approach, which has permitted survival, may offer important clues for a successful Democratic future. If the Democrats who survived a Republican tide in 1980 can maintain their hold on these base Republican seats, then the historical impulse toward out-party off-year gains could place the Democrats in far better shape to contest the 1982 House elections. This possibility is strengthened if defecting Democrats, unburdened by an unpopular Democratic president, return home in an off-year election. The Democrats could gain in their traditional strongholds while holding their own in the Watergate districts. Indeed, depending on the vagaries of reapportionment, gains of 10 to 15 seats would not be all that surprising. Certainly, the Republicans' task of gaining control of the House would seem to be more difficult than commonly imagined.

The Senate result, while undeniably impressive and startling, was a near thing. More than a third of the Senate races were decided by less than 4 percentage points, and of those, the Republicans won ten and the Democrats, two. Seven of the Republican margins were 2 points or less. Only one of the Republican victories was by a GOP incumbent, two were open GOP seats, five were held by incumbent Democrats, and two were open Democratic seats.

Thus, if one assumes that the last day saw the 5-point defection from Carter and the congressional Democrats extended to the Senate races as well, then the loss of the Senate could hang on the coattails of those negatives. This does not diminish other factors that worked to the detriment of the Democrats—whether the targeted efforts by Right-wing groups like the National Conservative Political Action Committee, or the historic vulnerability of incumbent senators in their third terms, or the more recent focus of protest voting at the Senate level, or idiosyncratic local issues or events.

In summary, the congressional results seem at least as much an overflow of the Carter repudiation as they do an ideological or partisan GOP triumph. The late, and generally decisive, switchers were mostly Democrats. "Time for a Change" seems to have reached beyond the hapless president to his congressional party as well.

LOOKING TOWARD THE FUTURE

This essay has analyzed the 1980 elections from the viewpoint of a Democratic strategist. My purpose was not to offer excuses or to rationalize what was a great debacle for the Democratic party and its president. However, since much of today's conventional wisdom seems predicated on superficial analyses and an emotional reaction to the events of 4 November 1980, a concrete understanding of what really did and did not happen in 1980 is crucial to all involved in the national political process.

The 1980 election year was as complicated and intricate as any in recent years. As with all elections, it had something to do with historical movements, and it had much to do with actions, circumstances, events, and luck—right decisions, wrong decisions, and nondecisions by the participants and the uninvolved alike. As with every election in which I have worked, the last contained underlying truths that have been lost in its debris. It also signalled less than is often claimed.

Probably more than most elections, it was a transition election—but one that closed an old era rather than defined a new epoch.

Ronald Reagan and the Republican party were granted an opportunity, as have been others in the last twenty years. If there was a mandate, it was not for any specific set of policies or ideological dogma, but to solve a host of problems that have bedeviled the American people for a generation. First and foremost, those problems are economic.

In truth, Reagan and his party have a mandate to build a mandate as big as they dare, provided their policies prove successful. For those who grant this opportunity are increasingly impatient and irascible, hardened by skepticism, and cynical from decades of failed promises.

In his first year, Reagan won a string of impressive political victories while simultaneously accumulating the highest negative rating of any modern president who is six months into his term. Perhaps no president in the modern era has been elected with so many negatives, so many doubts, so many concerns. Perhaps Reagan's most impressive feat has been to hide that reality from the political and media elites. In his sleight of hand, he has been aided by events, confusion, and misperception of political change, as well as by the attractiveness of his considerable political skill.

But the president and his adherents can dominate American politics in the future only if they are successful at solving the problems which defeated Jimmy Carter, and only if the incumbent performs this feat without simultaneously raising a host of unforeseen issues that could easily undo him. The wreckages of the last four presidencies are not merely the product of accidents. The collective debris stands as solemn testimony to the limits of American patience with seemingly intractable problems and uncontrollable historical forces.

The test for Reagan will take place only when the efforts of his policies are experienced by the public many months after enactment. This is particularly true with regard to his budget proposals which, until the arrival of the fiscal year, remain an abstraction to most voters. Moreover, Reagan has skillfully huddled a variety of quite conservative program and issue initiatives under the umbrella of "economic revitalization." Many of these ideologically motivated initiatives, especially in the environmental and energy areas, are completely at odds with the attitudes of a lot of voters, and in some cases are possible only because those voters are willing to yield ground on these lesser issues in the hope of broad economic success. Voter reaction when that rhetorical umbrella blows inside out is unpredictable.

CHANGED LANDSCAPE

At the presidential and congressional levels, the Republicans probably will benefit from population shifts to the South and West and away from urban centers. The GOP is expected to dominate the growing Southern and Western states as a presidential party. Indeed, many observers, surveying the electoral map, point out that the West is solidly GOP, that X out of Y states have not been cornered by a Democratic presidential candidate in Q number of years, that the Sun Belt states are gaining electoral votes while the Frost Belt Democratic states are not, and so forth. Certainly, there is enough truth in these arguments to worry Democratic strategists.

U.S. politics, however, is in fact often quite different from the heady expectations of our theories. The assumptions of Republican dominance of the electoral college, for instance, could be upset if heightened regional self-interest drives the Northeast and the industrial Midwest into a Democratic electoral bloc, perhaps in reaction to a GOP Sun Belt strategy. Since federal budget cuts will affect disproportionately not only the Democratic-leaning Northeast but the large Midwestern states as well, it is possible that the Democrats' small electoral base could easily expand into a very strong electoral posture. Whether this particular scenario happens or not, the point remains: actions in politics provide counteractions; strategies targeted to particular areas or constituencies are never played out in a vacuum.

1982 elections

To predict the results of the 1982 elections at this point would be foolhardy, for the conditions and contexts that will determine those decisions have not yet been determined by events.

In the House, next year's elections may be among the hardest fought in decades. Republicans believe that the three Rs—reapportionment, resources, and Reagan—can propel the GOP to majority control. Democrats can counter by citing the historical pattern of off-year setbacks for the incumbent presidential party as well as the analysis of internal voting patterns expounded earlier in this discussion.

Four factors are important when speculating on the 1982 House elections:

FIRST, the success of Ronald Reagan. No other factor or combination of factors is likely to be as crucial. For the moment, the GOP has intertwined its fortunes completely with Reagan's fortunes. If his programs are viewed as successful—or at least give a sense of improvement—then Republican candidates will prosper. A perception of failure, more than a real failure, will almost certainly spell defeat for the GOP. Simply put, the central factor in 1982 will be more a matter of perceived substance than of presidential folksiness or style.

SECOND, reapportionment. Seventeen seats are shifting from the Northern industrial belt to the boom states, West and South. Even in the North, urban seats will be lost to suburbs and small-town areas. It is obvious that the movement is away from Democratic strongholds to Republican territory. However, the process of reapportionment itself is anything but obvious. The expansion of national party strength is important, but it is rarely the primary motivation for state officials or individual incumbents. Ambitions, tradition, localism, horse trading, and an irrational desire for total political safety often produce redistricting that is hardly a pure reflection of population movements. The key redistricting will take place in states mostly under Democratic control.

And that brings us to the real irony in the last election. When the election year began, the national Republican party did not target its major effort at the presidency, the U.S. Senate, or even the House of Representatives. Its major effort in money, time, and candidate recruitment was directed at the winning of hundreds of legislative seats in order not to be counted out in reapportionment. The poorer Democratic national party could not compete with this effort. Yet, on Election Day, while the GOP surpassed even its wildest expectations at the federal level, it won fewer legislative seats than expected at the year's start or anticipated in the wake of a national landslide. Politics is never as clear as it appears.

THIRD, resources.   The Republicans have always been the "rich" party in resources, particularly in money. Under recent campaign laws written by their own party, the Democrats have seen an increase in the disparity of wealth. Nineteen eighty-two promises a Republican financial advantage that may become almost incomprehensible. In addition to its wealthier constituency base, the GOP controls a money magnet in the White House. Furthermore, the Republican seizure of the Senate means that many business political action committees (PACs), which routinely gave to powerful majority-party candidates, may no longer feel the need to balance their gifts and may follow their ideological and party fancies. Early reports indicate that the GOP committees are out-fundraising their Democratic counterparts by 13 to 1, and that the Republican House Campaign Committee has already raised over $16 million, compared with the Democrats' $700,000. Republican spending advantages of 5 to 1 or more are an incalculable factor in the equation of 1982.

FOURTH, the Democratic appeal. The possible policy failures of the Republican administration, while certainly benefiting the Democrats, do not insure massive Democratic gains or a certain restoration of voter affection. A Republican setback will return the game to "deuce." Real Democratic success will depend on the party's ability to forge a program that speaks to the future.

Unlike 1980, the 1982 Senate elections hold little promise of political excitement. In all probability, the Republicans will retain control of the Senate in 1982 (law of averages— 20 Democratic incumbents face reelection, along with only 12 Republicans and 1 independent). A persistent majority is a more tenuous prospect. Incumbent senators have become the most vulnerable politicians in the new era of big-issue, mostly negative voting. Heretofore, the electorate's ire has been directed toward Democrats, and mostly toward liberals; but a failed Reagan administration could put Senate Republicans on the exposed flank of American politics.

In sum, the 1982 elections are anything but predictable. The environment in which those contests will be resolved has been sketched only partially, and will depend to an extraordinary degree on the effect of policies and events. One thing does seem clear, though. The elections will take place at a point in history where party loyalties and partisan behavior are in great flux.

A RISE OF PARTISANSHIP?

"Every man for himself" has been the battle cry of battalions of candidates in recent years. Stressing personality and constituency service, fashioning ad hoc campaign organizations staffed by professional technicians, and heralding their "independence," these candidates have campaigned with few links to national party structures or platforms.

The 1980 elections may have signaled the beginning of a reversal in the success of such strategies. The apparent return of coattail voting, discussed earlier, runs counter to the trends witnessed in the last three previous presidential elections. Many Democrats campaigning behind the familiar barricades of personal appeal, past accomplishments, and constituency service found themselves overrun by opponents, often barely recognizable, riding vehicles of big-issue frustration. Increasingly broad national issues and party positioning played a major role in 1980; the prospect for 1982 may be more of the same. A continuation of this trend could be a positive development for both parties, and an opportunity for one or the other—or even both—to strengthen its weak grip on the public.

THE SHAPE OF PARTISANSHIP —REALIGNMENT?

The most significant and fascinating political development in the aftermath of the Reagan victory has been the change measured in partisan self-identification by voters. Almost all surveys have indicated gains in Republican affiliation and declines in Democratic preference. Some surveys have, in fact, shown the Republicans pulling even with the Democrats.[6] The greatest Republican surge has come in the South and the West, regions where many have predicted a Republican ascendancy.

The striking change in partisan identification has been coupled with an apparent reversal of party role on key questions. Gallup polls in mid-1981 indicate that the Republican party has taken a 41 percent to 28 percent lead over the Democrats on the question of which party can "do a better job of keeping the country prosperous." This change in perception may well be at the heart of the party instability questions, for this issue is the *raison d'etre* of the Democratic party. At the same time, by a margin of 39 percent to 26 percent, the electorate selects the Democrats as the party "best able to keep the peace," an issue the GOP has consistently dominated for years.

Some have pointed to changing survey results as evidence that a major party realignment is under way. However, before a permanent Republican majority is proclaimed, it might be wiser to consider the following. These striking Republican gains of 1980 may well be tied to an expectation of Republican success on the economy. The very "newness" of attitudes measured in recent polls suggests the tentative nature of such attachments. Persistent double-digit inflation, 20 percent interest rates, or a major recession in 1982 would probably make a shambles of these current GOP gains.

Changing party preference data probably do reflect a willingness to move party affiliation and allegiance—if earned. They suggest the enormity of the opportunity presented to the Republicans for success. But if this sea change in party loyalties were already in place, we would certainly have found far greater evidence for it in our 1980 election analysis.

THE BABY BOOM—THE KEY?

When one reviews the most recent party-preference data, the Republicans improve with most demographic subgroups. However, the most striking gains take place with the 18 to 35-year-old age cohort, the post—World War II baby-boom generation. An April 1981 *New York Times*/CBS News survey discovered overall preference figures of 49 percent Democratic/41 percent Republican (compared with a 53 percent/34 percent edge in 1980).[7] Among 25 to 34-year-olds, the largest segment of the baby-boom generation, the preferences had moved from 55 percent Democratic/30 percent Republican to 44 percent Democratic and 43 percent Republican—a 24-point margin gain for the GOP.

America's largest age cohort, 18 to 35-year-olds, comprise 41 percent of the adult population. Yet their voting participation has remained very low, even as many have entered their 30s.[8] Millions are still nonparticipants in American politics and have been for ten years or more. Of all age groups, they have demonstrated the weakest attachment to party when they did vote. In recent years, political analysts have speculated over the baby boom's behavior and potential if activated. This cohort, by its size alone, could reshape the face of American politics for a generation. A first glimmer of activity is now apparent, and it could signal movement of historical significance.

However, the Republicans may not be the natural recipients of this group's votes. On many issues, young voters have opposed the stands of their parents and grandparents. To oversimplify, their elders have been classic New Deal liberals on economic issues and traditional conservatives on social and cultural issues. For some years, the baby-boom cohort has displayed strongly anti–New Deal economic instincts, coupled with liberal social and cultural attitudes.

The *New York Times*/CBS survey seems to suggest that the initial Reagan appeal to this group is economic. Most of their adult life has been spent under the burden of double-digit inflation. It may be that Reagan's unorthodox economic approach has struck a predisposed nerve.

However, the situation is more complex. The baby-boom generation is also pro-environment, pro-abortion, anti–nuclear power, and pro-ERA. On foreign policy, its instinct is quite "dovish." It is hostile to big government and equally hostile to big business. Although moving into family life, it is culturally still the most liberal and tolerant group in the United States on life-style issues. These beliefs, if threatened by a Reagan/New Right/Religious Right coalition, could easily serve to move this cohort counter to the GOP.

Against such a background, the Republican preference surge should at best be judged as tentative. To capture young Americans, Reagan must not only be successful economically, but he must avoid driving them away on issues crucial to his basic conservative constituency. In truth, neither party has been able to fashion a program that reaches across this cohort's broad set of views without threatening older base constituencies. It could be argued that some of the neoliberal, Democratic voices recently rising out of the Senate may be far better attuned to this battleground group.

In their brief lives, by force of numbers and sometimes of views, the children of the baby boom have rocked the United States at every stage of growth. In the 1950s they prompted massive educational initiatives. In the 1960s they turned campuses upside down, music inside out, and their elders ashen with their mores. In the 1970s they pushed into the job market and changed the economic arena with their preference for small cars, leisure goods, and nonsaving behavior. So, in the 1980s, as they reach their maximum numerical dominance in the adult population, today's voters under 35 years of age appear to be a good bet to profoundly alter, in ways yet to be determined, the future of American politics.

V

Realignment in the
1980 Election

12

E. J. DIONNE, JR.

Catholics and the Democrats: Estrangement but Not Desertion

Catholics and the appeal of the major parties. The cleavage within the Catholic community. Differences by class, region, and age. Voting in 1976 and 1980. Floating voters in presidential and congressional elections. Abortion, social conservatism, and the economy. Partisan strategy for the future.

The story is told of Mrs. O'Reilly being taken to the polls by her son James. Mrs. O'Reilly, who is seventy years old, has cast straight Democratic ballots in every election she has ever voted in. Her son James, who is forty-five and has enjoyed some financial success, votes Democratic more often than not; but, like most members of the middle class, he believes in splitting his ticket.

On the way to the polls, James asks his mother how she plans to vote, and she replies, predictably, "Straight Democratic."

"Mom," says a frustrated son, "if Jesus Christ came back to earth and ran as a Republican, you'd vote against Him."

"Hush!" replies Mrs. O'Reilly. "Why should He change His party after all these years?"

For decades, loyalty to the Democratic party has been something on the order of a theological commitment for a large share of America's Catholic community.[1] As Richard Jensen has shown, religion has long been a mainspring of American political alignments. Going back to the Jacksonian era, Irish-Catholic migrants to America's large cities found a home in the heterogeneous Democratic party (Jensen 1978). Later Catholics found little to cheer about in the Republican party of Abraham Lincoln; the party brought together abolitionists, who hailed from Protestant denominations long hostile to Catholic interests, and nativists, for whom anti-Catholicism was the *sine qua non* of political activism (Lipset and Raab 1978, pp. 47–57).

Catholic support for the Democrats was by no means unanimous in the post–Civil War period. For one thing, new Catholic migrants, such as the French Canadians in New England and the Italians in New York City, often joined the Republicans in reaction to Irish domination of the Democratic party. As Kevin Phillips put it, these groups "disliked the exclusionary brogue of the Democratic Party" (Phillips 1970, p. 144). In addition, William McKinley, Mark Hanna, and their followers had some success in broadening the Republican appeal beyond the confines of moralistic Protestantism.

But Al Smith's presidential candidacy in 1928 strengthened the ties that bound Catholics to the Democratic party. Even in years between 1928 and 1952, Democratic hegemony in the Catholic community was not always complete—Italian, German, and some Irish Catholics bolted to the Republicans in 1940 in reaction to Franklin Roosevelt's foreign policy, which they saw as pro-British more than anti-Nazi. But the Democratic party's share of the Catholic vote was consistently high throughout the period.

Since 1952, however, voting analysts have wondered how long this primordial relationship between the Church of Rome and the Party of Smith could last. Large numbers of Catholic Democrats defected to Eisenhower in 1952, though Adlai Stevenson still carried 56 percent of the Catholic vote. In 1956 Stevenson's share dropped to about 50 percent. John Kennedy's showing in 1960 among Catholics was, of course, spectacular: roughly 4 Catholics in 5 cast their ballots for America's first Catholic president. But even in 1960, as Kevin Phillips has pointed out, Nixon did remarkably well in middle- and upper-middle-class Catholic areas; and Daniel Patrick Moynihan noted that, while the students at Fordham University gave Kennedy a narrow majority, "it appears it was the Jewish students at the College of Pharmacy who saved that ancient Jesuit institution from going on record as opposed to the election of the first Catholic President of the United States" (Phillips 1970, p. 164; Glazer and Moynihan 1970, p. 272).

In 1964 Catholics voted almost as overwhelmingly for Lyndon Johnson, but the Catholic vote fell back to roughly 60 percent for Hubert Humphrey in 1968. And in 1972 the Democratic share of the Catholic vote fell to 48 percent, making Richard Nixon the first Republican to win a clear Catholic majority since at least the 1920s. Jimmy Carter restored the Democrats' majority among Catholics in 1976, but his 54 percent was actually less than Stevenson's 1952 vote, and it was also below Humphrey's 1968 showing.

And the Catholic Democratic share in 1980 fell to its lowest point since the turn of the century, with Carter winning but 40 percent of Catholic ballots. Even more striking is the fact that, while Carter in defeat in 1980 ran 3 points *ahead* of George McGovern nationwide, he ran 8 points *behind* McGovern among Catholics. Put differently, although a majority of Catholics rejected McGovern in 1972, Catholics were still far more sympathetic to his candidacy than was the rest of the country. In 1980, on the other hand, the voter surveys suggested that the Catholic vote exactly mirrored the vote in the electorate at large.

AN END TO CATHOLIC PARTICULARISM?

There can be no doubt that America's Catholic community has undergone a political sea change in the last three decades. What is very much at issue is whether the change is permanent, and whether the changes among Catholics differ much from those in the country as a whole.

In his broad range of writings, Andrew M. Greeley has insisted rightly that, for all the changes in the Catholic community, Catholics still remain more liberal and more Democratic than the mass of white Americans—which, in effect, means America's white Protestants (Greeley 1978, pp. 271–95; idem 1974, pp. 187–216). Data gathered by Greeley and others make this point rather convincingly. Even in 1976, for example, when Jimmy Carter's public expression of his born-again religious convictions—and his Southern roots—strengthened his appeal to white Protestants, Catholics were more likely to support him than were Protestants. A CBS News poll in 1976 found that Catholics supported Carter by 54 to 44 percent over Gerald Ford, while white

Protestants preferred Ford by 57 to 43 percent. And in 1980 Catholics were again more likely to support Carter than were white Protestants. The *New York Times*/CBS News survey of 15,201 voters as they left the polls found that, while Reagan carried the white Catholic vote 51 to 40 percent, with 7 percent going to Anderson, he carried the white Protestant vote even more convincingly, 62 to 31 percent, with 6 percent going to Anderson. White Protestants were 13 points more Republican than were Catholics in 1976, and 11 points more Republican in 1980.[2]

In 1980 these religious differences held up across class lines. The greatest disparities were among those of lowest income; but even at the highest income level, Catholics were still 10 points more Democratic (see table 1).

But it is also clear that a sharp class cleavage has opened within the American Catholic community. Catholics earning less than $15,000 annually voted Democratic by about 5 to 4; those earning over $25,000 voted Republican by about 2 to 1.

The results of the 1980 election lend support to Scott Greer's theory that the movement of Catholics out of the working class and lower-middle class would lead them toward Republican alliance (Greer 1961, pp. 611–25). But it is important to see this change not only as an effect of Catholic upward mobility, but also as part of an important change within the Catholic upper-middle class. In the 1936 presidential election, for example, white non-Southern Protestants of high socioeconomic status cast only 35 percent of their ballots for Franklin Roosevelt. But upper-status Catholics cast some 69 percent of their votes for Roosevelt (Ladd with Hadley 1978, pp. 52–53). In the 1930s Catholic loyalties to the Democratic party overcame class pressures toward the Republicans. By 1980 class had largely—if not completely—overcome the traditional religious bond.

There were other factors, however, weakening Catholic loyalties to the Democratic party. Table 2 summarizes Protestant/Catholic differences by region. The largest

Table 1

Religion, Income, and the 1980 Presidential Vote

(A) Income range:	Under $10,000		$10,000/$15,000		$15,000/$25,000		$25,000/$50,000		Over $50,000	
(N)	White Prot. (801)	Cath. (441)	White Prot. (994)	Cath. (512)	White Prot. (2,066)	Cath. (1,073)	White Prot. (1,846)	Cath. (1,021)	White Prot. (326)	Cath. (149)
Carter	38%	51%	38%	47%	31%	41%	25%	32%	15%	25%
Reagan	57%	38%	55%	42%	62%	50%	67%	60%	78%	68%
Anderson	4%	9%	6%	8%	6%	9%	7%	6%	7%	6%
Other	1%	2%	1%	3%	1%	1%	1%	2%	0	1%

(B) Difference:	Protestant % more Republican	Catholic % more Democratic
Under $10,000	+19	+13
$10,000/$15,000	+13	+ 9
$15,000/$25,000	+12	+10
$25,000/$50,000	+ 7	+ 7
Over $50,000	+10	+10

differences were to be found in the Northeast and Midwest, where the Catholic/Protestant political divide began to grow in the nineteenth century. In the South, Catholics were actually *less* Democratic than white Protestants. In the West, Catholics were more Democratic than were Protestants, but one is still struck by the substantial lead enjoyed by Reagan among Western Catholics.

Looking only at Catholics, by region the substantial split is even more striking. Catholics in the older parts of the country, the Northeast and Midwest, gave Reagan a lead of only 5 points, but Sun Belt Catholics preferred Reagan by 25 points. The regional divisions among Catholics contrast with the fairly regular regional pattern among white Protestants.

It is true that more than two-thirds of America's Catholics live outside the Sun Belt. But Catholics, like other Americans, are migrating to these newer parts of the country, where traditional ties of church and ethnic group bind less tightly. This, too, portends badly for Democratic hopes among Catholics.

Table 3 offers further evidence of difficulties for the Democrats. Looking at the religious split by age, the strongest divisions are among the oldest voters. This age cohort came to political maturity when the political divide among Protestants and Catholics was largest. The smallest religious differences are found among those aged 30 to 59. A large proportion of this group came to politics in the 1950s, when the religious differences were ebbing. Interestingly, the religious differences became large again in the 22-to-29 age group; it is possible that these younger Catholics will replace the oldest Catholic group as the loyal carriers of the Democratic tradition. In the meantime, those who make up the largest share of the Catholic voting population—the middle-aged—appear to be behaving remarkably like their white Protestant brethren.

Table 2
Religion, Region, and the 1980 Presidential Vote
(whites only)

(A) Region:	Northeast			Midwest			South			West		
	Prot.	Cath.	Jewish	Prot.	Cath.	Jewish	Prot.	Cath.	Jewish	Prot.	Cath.	Jewish
(N)	(1,137)	(1,375)	(347)	(2,075)	(999)	(65)	(2,118)	(500)	(145)	(1,115)	(595)	(169)
Carter	28%	43%	49%	31%	44%	26%	34%	29%	43%	26%	36%	46%
Reagan	63%	48%	36%	60%	49%	55%	64%	65%	42%	64%	52%	37%
Anderson	9%	8%	14%	7%	6%	19%	2%	5%	14%	8%	10%	14%

(B) Difference:	Protestant % more Republican	Catholic % more Democratic
Northwest	+15	+15
Midwest	+11	+13
South	− 1	− 5
West	+12	+10

Table 3
Religion, Age, and the 1980 Presidential Vote

(A) Age range:

(N)	18/21 years Prot. (233)	18/21 years Cath. (228)	22/29 years Prot. (837)	22/29 years Cath. (621)	30/44 years Prot. (2,073)	30/44 years Cath. (1,129)	45/59 years Prot. (1,693)	45/59 years Cath. (868)	60 years & over Prot. (1,563)	60 years & over Cath. (592)
Carter	37%	39%	29%	43%	29%	34%	31%	37%	32%	49%
Reagan	53%	43%	60%	42%	63%	57%	64%	56%	63%	46%
Anderson	10%	14%	10%	11%	7%	7%	4%	6%	4%	3%

(B) Difference:

	Protestant % more Republican	Catholic % more Democratic
18/21 years	+10	+ 2
22/29 years	+18	+14
30/44 years	+ 6	+ 5
45/59 years	+ 8	+ 6
60 years and over	+17	+17

CATHOLIC VOTING: DEALIGNMENT, NOT REALIGNMENT

The weakening of Catholic loyalty to the Democrats is clear; so are the persistent differences between Catholics and white Protestants.

But if Catholics have moved away from the Democrats, they have hardly embraced the Republicans with enthusiasm. Indeed, if one uses consistency or ardor as a measure, Catholics are even more Democratic relative to white Protestants than the raw figures would suggest.

The *New York Times*/CBS News 1980 survey asked voters how they had cast their ballots in 1976. The results produced a somewhat inflated total for Carter, since voters have an uncanny tendency to remember having supported the winner. But there is no reason to believe that these results have any religious bias, so the findings retain an interest.

Table 4*a* summarizes choices by religion. Voters who supported Carter in both elections constituted 43 percent of the Jewish electorate, 36 percent of the Catholic electorate, but only 26 percent of the white Protestants. Consistent Republicans, on the other hand, made up 47 percent of the white Protestant electorate, compared with 32 percent of Catholics and 21 percent of Jews. Among consistent partisans, table 4*b* indicates that only 36 percent of the white Protestant voters cast Democratic ballots in both elections, compared with 53 percent of Catholics and 68 percent of Jews. This 17-point difference between Catholics and white Protestants is much closer to the old religious divide.

Table 4 also points to substantial electoral shifting—and the shifting is especially great among Catholics and Jews. Some 37 percent of Jews, along with 33 percent of Catholics and 27 percent of white Protestants, reported that they had moved from one party to another (or to Anderson) between

Table 4

Religion and the Presidential Vote in 1976 and 1980
(whites only)

(A) Vote by religion: (N)	Protestant (5,542)	Catholic (2,871)	Jewish (637)
Carter 1976 Carter 1980	26%	36%	43%
Ford 1976 Reagan 1980	47%	32%	21%
Carter 1976 Reagan 1980	17%	21%	19%
Ford 1976 Carter 1980	5%	5%	3%
Carter 1976 Anderson 1980	3%	4%	12%
Ford 1976 Anderson 1980	2%	3%	3%
(B) Party support among consistent party voters:	**Protestant (4,077)**	**Catholic (1,932)**	**Jewish (404)**
Democratic	36%	53%	68%
Republican	64%	47%	32%

1976 and 1980. This huge group of floating voters suggests that the political future of all groups—but particularly that of traditionally Democratic Jews and Catholics—is very much up for grabs.

The tentative nature of the Catholic shift to the Republicans is suggested by two other findings from the *New York Times*/CBS News survey. The poll asked voters when they had decided to vote as they did. Among white Protestant Reagan voters, some 47 percent said they knew all along that they would vote for the Republican nominee. Only 39 percent of Catholic Reaganites shared that certainty. The survey also asked voters how they had cast their ballots in the congressional elections.[3] The poll suggested that about 17 percent of white Protestant Reagan supporters, but 28 percent of Catholic Reagan supporters, backed Democrats for Congress. Most of the Catholics, it should be noted, were voting outside the South for moderate to liberal Democrats. Many of the white Protestants, on the other hand, cast congressional votes in the South for conservative Democrats whose views—as the results of President Reagan's budget fights showed—were rather close to those of the Republican party. This only serves to underline the major difference between Catholic and Protestant supporters of President Reagan's election.

Overall, the data suggest the importance of a distinction drawn by Everett Ladd between dealignment and realignment (Ladd 1980). Catholic ties to the Democrats are undoubtedly weaker, but there has yet to be a clear conversion of Catholics to the Republican cause.

ABORTION AS A PERIPHERAL ISSUE

In view of the Roman Catholic hierarchy's ardent stand against abortion, it is hardly surprising that so central a role would be assigned to one issue in explaining Catholic defections to the Republicans. This tendency is reinforced by President Reagan's strong stand against abortion, and the support he received from leaders of the Right-to-Life movement.

Yet the evidence suggests that abortion played only a bit part in 1980 voting. And insofar as the issue was important, it appears to have been equally so for Catholics and white Protestants.

In fact, Catholic attitudes on abortion are rather similar to those of white Protestants. Table 5 summarizes the results of a variety of surveys on the abortion issue. The table suggests that insofar as there is a consensus on that issue, it is a consensus that opposes government involvement, either positively or negatively. On the one hand, majorities of both Protestants and Catholics oppose an across-the-board ban on abortions. But both groups also oppose government financing of abortions. On each issue, Catholics are slightly more "pro-life" and Protestants, "pro-choice." But the differences are not large, and majorities of both groups take the consensus view.

In August of 1980 the *New York Times* and CBS asked a sample of Americans two questions on abortion: one probed opinions on a Constitutional amendment to ban abortions, the other, opinions on an amendment "protecting the life of the unborn child." Both, of course, were different ways of asking about the so-called "human life" amendment. The disparities suggest how important the wording of survey questions can be. Those who answered consistently on the two questions can be regarded reasonably as those with the most firmly held views on the issue. The results, also shown on table 5, still show a plurality of Catholics opposed to the amendment, though Protestants are slightly more opposed. Again, however—especially in view of the attention focused on Catholic opposition to abortion—one is struck more by the similarities than by the differences between the two groups.

Table 5
Religion and Attitudes on Abortion
(whites only)

		Protestant	Catholic
June 1980: Making abortion illegal	(N)	(832)	(358)
Favor		34%	40%
Oppose		58%	54%
Don't know/no answer		9%	6%
November 1980: Government paying for abortions for poor women	(N)	(1,414)	(702)
Favor		37%	32%
Oppose		57%	62%
Don't know/no answer		6%	6%
August 1980: Constitutional amendment			
— to ban abortions	(N)	(989)	(449)
Favor		28%	31%
Oppose		63%	60%
Don't know/no answer		9%	9%
— to protect life of unborn child			
Favor		46%	54%
Oppose		42%	37%
Don't know/no answer		11%	9%
Consistently pro-choice*		39%	34%
Consistently pro-life*		25%	28%

*"Consistently pro-choice" respondents are those who opposed a constitutional amendment regardless of how the question was posed; "consistently pro-life" respondents are those who favored the amendment regardless of how the question was worded.

Richard Wirthlin, President Reagan's polling analyst, has argued that, while majorities disagreed with Reagan's position on abortion, the issue actually helped him, because abortion foes were more likely to cast ballots on the basis of a candidate's stand on that one issue. Other data suggested that this was the case—and that Jimmy Carter was also hurt by the fact that many of the voters most strongly in favor of legal abortion cast ballots for John Anderson (Dionne 1980). Also helping Reagan was the fact that abortion foes are concentrated in the social groups most likely to vote Democratic—the less well-to-do and the less educated. The issue thus helped Reagan cut into the Democratic base.

Still, the effect of the issue was limited. In their exit survey, the *New York Times* and CBS asked voters to list the two issues that were most important to them. Only about 7 percent of white Protestants and Catholics checked a box on the survey marked "Abortion/ERA." These voters were more *pro-Carter* than the rest of the electorate, as table 6 indicates, with Catholics who checked the issue being especially sympathetic to his candidacy. This should not be taken as indicating that the abortion issue helped Carter; other parts of the survey suggested that most voters who checked this box were mainly concerned about the Equal Rights amendment. But the results do indicate the limited impact of abortion on either Catholic or Protestant voters, and most of the surveys indicated that abortion had an equal effect on Protestants and Catholics. If anything, in fact, white Protestant voters who described themselves as "born again" Christians were *more* likely than Catholics to be affected by the issue.

There is, of course, a more general level on which social conservatism helped move voters toward Ronald Reagan. Reagan was well aware of this when he spoke in defense of the values of "family, work, neighborhood." These themes rang true with many Catholics, as with many Protestants; many voters were prepared to respond to an appeal to a return to social stability following a time of intense challenge

Table 6
Abortion, ERA, and 1980 Voting by Religion
(whites only)

		Protestant		Catholic	
		All	ERA/abortion*	All	ERA/abortion*
(N)		(6,444)	(444)	(3,468)	(254)
Carter		31%	43%	40%	51%
Reagan		63%	47%	51%	41%
Anderson		6%	10%	7%	5%
Other		1%	—**	2%	3%

*Said ERA or abortion was important issue.

**Less than 1%.

to traditional values. But this appeal transcended denominational lines; and, as Greeley has shown, Catholics are relatively liberal on social questions. Protestants were probably even more ready than Catholics to respond to these issues.

As has been repeatedly pointed out in this volume, Reagan's victory must be seen as primarily the result of voter dissatisfaction over the performance of the economy under Carter. And the data suggest that bread-and-butter discontent was especially important in moving Catholics to the Republican side. Table 7 shows that, in both religious groups, voters' decisions were strongly affected by their perceptions of economic well-being. Among Catholics who felt financially better off at the end of the Carter years, the Democratic nominee enjoyed a substantial lead over Reagan. (White Protestants who felt better off were much more Democratic than their coreligionists, but even this group backed Reagan.) Catholics who felt their economic situation had not changed also gave Carter a lead, albeit a narrow one. Reagan actually led Carter only among those Catholics who said their economic situation had worsened, but here his lead was overwhelming.

Another indication of the relative importance of economic issues to Catholics is the fact that, while Catholic and white Protestant perceptions of their economic fortunes were nearly identical in the electorate as a whole, Catholic Reaganites were more likely than white Protestant Reagan voters to say their economic situation had worsened.

THE DEMOCRATS' CATHOLIC PROBLEM

Whatever else is true of the Catholic vote, it is clear in the wake of the last four elections that straight Democratic voters like Mrs. O'Reilly are no longer the Catholic norm. It is also clear that upward mobility has pushed a substantial minority of the Catholic community toward fairly regular Republican voting habits.

But the Democrats still have major opportunities to restore clear majorities among Catholics—even if Catholic Democratic voting is never likely to approach the levels reached by Al Smith or John Kennedy. Between 33 and 40 percent of the Catholic vote is still reliably Democratic, and another third is prepared to vote Democratic. If Jimmy Carter had won just those Reagan-voting Catholics who supported Democratic congressional candidates, he would have won a substantial Democratic majority.

The difficulty for the Democrats is that their party was victorious in the past when it won overwhelming majorities within blocs of minorities, particularly Catholic. The Republicans, on the other hand, have such a solid base among white Protestants that they need pick off only minority shares of the ballots cast by Catholics, Jews, blacks, and other minority groups to keep winning national elections.

Table 7
Religion and the 1980 Presidential Vote
by Economic Situation
(whites only)

Question: "Compared to a year ago, is your family's financial situation:
better today? ———
worse today? ———
about the same? ———"

(A)

Response:	Better		Same		Worse	
(N)	Prot. (1,002)	Cath. (530)	Prot. (2,826)	Cath. (1,466)	Prot. (2,435)	Cath. (1,352)
Carter	46%	58%	37%	48%	18%	25%
Reagan	49%	35%	58%	44%	75%	67%
Anderson	6%	7%	5%	7%	7%	8%

(B) Candidate:

	Protestant		Catholic	
(N)	Reagan supporters (3,958)	All (3,263)	Reagan supporters (1,751)	All (3,348)
Better	12%	16%	11%	16%
Same	42%	45%	37%	44%
Worse	46%	39%	52%	40%

If the Reagan economic program succeeds, there is a good chance the Republicans will be able to do this for a long while. But there is an important caveat relating to the zealous religiosity of the share of President Reagan's coalition that has rallied behind groups such as the Moral Majority. In the past, it is precisely this sort of Protestant religious enthusiasm that has driven so many Catholics — and Jews—to the Democrats. As Richard Jensen put it, the Democrats were seen even back in the nineteenth century as the defenders "of alternative life-styles and values, of *laissez-faire* social ethics, and of a government whose powers were circumscribed so as to preclude positive intervention in the daily lives of its citizens" (Jensen 1978, p. 51). Catholics will certainly be drawn to the values of "family, work, and neighborhood." They have been traditionally unenthusiastic, however, about enforced social homogeneity, and they are not likely to become more enamored of it in the 1980s.

13

ALAN M. FISHER

Jewish Political Shift? Erosion, Yes; Conversion, No*

The appeal of Carter and Reagan. Support for liberal candidates. The Anderson vote. Polling the presidential and congressional votes. Ideological identification. The Leftist/Rightist tendencies. Demography, geography, and party competition.

*Special thanks are due to the following people for making the data available without which this paper could not have been written: the Gallup organization, Mark Schulman of Louis Harris, Kathleen Frankovic and Solomon Barr of CBS News, Ann Robinson and Charles Franklin of the Center for Political Studies, Fay and Lester Braunstein of B'nai Brith. They are not responsible for the manipulations, analyses, and interpretations found here.

Since the early 1970s, a growing number of observers have been convinced that the Jews are finally becoming Republican. As a group, Jews are considerably above the average income, and high income is still one of the best predictors of a Republican vote. Jews have escaped the ghettos and the unskilled jobs where they were natural targets for Democratic—New Deal politics; thus, the argument that attachment to the Democratic party is just a political lag, now wearing off as it apparently has for other white ethnics. By acting on their real political/economic interests, Jews are switching parties.

Yet although the economic condition of most Jews has risen constantly, support for the Democrats has not unilinearly declined. Strongest during the Franklin Roosevelt years and then again in the 1960s, Jewish Democratic voting has increased and decreased twice since the advent of the New Deal. Therefore, we should be circumspect about predicting an inevitable upsurge in Republican support resulting from a rise in socioeconomic status.

Although Jews are slightly less than 3 percent of the population, their voting patterns are of great practical and academic interest. Jews are still concentrated in populous states with large electoral college votes, and their political influence is amplified by their high turnout, their campaign contributions, and their other political activity. Since the white Catholic vote has become increasingly marginal, when the Jews become Republican the (white) New Deal will have been completely dissolved. Can we finally abandon that coalition?

POLITICAL CONTEXT

In 1980 the two major-party candidates did not represent the stereotypical dichotomy between New Deal liberals and moderate conservatives. Jimmy Carter's domestic economic policies were basically conservative, attacking inflation, not unemployment. Only in basing his foreign policy on support for human rights was Carter consistently liberal, and even here some slippage occurred. Carter was a rural, agricultural, Southern, reborn Baptist—hardly typical of that which supposedly attracts Jews. Jews had opposed him in all the 1976 primaries; their support for him against Ford was weak, and they consistently felt that he was doing a poor job in office (Orren 1978, pp. 151–61; Fisher 1979, pp. 107–9).[1]

Among the major Democratic candidates, Carter was the least attractive to Jewish voters on Jewish issues. He won some support by speaking out on behalf of the Soviet dissident movement. He helped Egypt and Israel to achieve a breakthrough—perhaps the only major accomplishment of his regime. But he also pushed for extensive arms sales to Saudi Arabia—over which his "Jewish liaison," Mark Siegel, resigned—and made public overtures to the Palestine Liberation Organization via UN Ambassador Andrew Young. Generally, Carter's Middle East policies were less popular among Jews than those of any president since Dwight Eisenhower. In addition, Carter suffered the embarrassment of his brother's buffoonery, which particularly nettled Jews, not only because of its style, but because of its anti-Israel overtones and anti-Semitic undertones.

For the Republicans, Ronald Reagan had solid conservative credentials, although as the campaign progressed—when many voters were still deciding—he moved to the center. For only the second time since the New Deal, the Republicans made a special effort to attract the Jewish vote, counting on general economic and international problems, on Reagan's consistent support of Israel, and on some politically disenchanted Jewish leaders (Rosenbaum 1981).

METHODS

Problems of data collection create difficulties in ascertaining exact Jewish voting statistics. It is only of limited utility to look at "Jewish precincts," because relatively few precincts are more than 75 percent Jewish, especially outside New York, and these areas are not typical of all Jewish voters. Few reputable national surveys are large enough to contain a Jewish subsample with acceptably narrow confidence limits. These problems are endemic, but in 1980 they were exacerbated by significant differences in the findings of various polls.

This divergence is resolved by averaging seven different polls (Gallup, Harris, *New York Times*/CBS News, ABC, NBC, Center for Political Studies, and California Field), and weighting for sample size and overall accuracy. This is probably the most accurate projection available.

FINDINGS

Dissatisfaction among Jewish Democrats with the president's performance was translated into anti-Carter votes in the primaries. Jews were more likely than other Democrats to vote for Edward Kennedy, who had long been identified with Jewish causes such as Israel and Soviet Jewry—although Jews, like other Americans, were suspicious about his character. Without additional questions, it is impossible to differentiate a vote for Kennedy from a vote against Carter; but we do know from the 1976 primaries that Jews tended more than non-Jews to support the liberal candidates except for Henry Jackson, the most committed pro-Israel senator (Orren 1978, pp. 151–60; Fisher 1979, pp. 107–11).

In a Gallup poll during May 1980, Jewish respondents preferred Mondale over Reagan by 64 percent to 14 percent, compared with 40 and 47 percent for all respondents.[2] A parallel finding in July was that, of Jewish Democrats indicating a specific preference, 75 percent named Kennedy, Mondale, or Muskie.[3]

Although Jews continued to vote in greater proportion than others, their overrepresentation in the general election declined (Himmelfarb 1981, p. 29). Most of the Jewish non-voters were Democrats who felt uncomfortable voting for Carter. The Jewish vote would have been significantly more Democratic if a traditional liberal, like Kennedy or Mondale, had been running.

One of the most striking findings is John Anderson's strength among Jews (17 percent), almost three times greater than among non-Jews. Jewish Republicans disproportionately preferred Anderson early in the year, and when he first announced his independent candidacy, Anderson was the clear favorite among all Jews, scoring higher even than Kennedy.[4] In part a protest against the two major-party candidates, Anderson ran well among Jews even when alternative candidates were presented. If the early polls and primaries are correct, he might have won a plurality if not the majority of the Jewish vote in November, had his candidacy been more viable then. Anderson may well be the quintessential candidate for the Jews in the future: liberal on social issues and supportive of civil liberties, moderate in economics, humanitarian, erudite, and a friend of Israel.

The remaining findings depend on how we redistribute the Anderson vote. On the basis of income, education, party affiliation, and self-identification, I estimate that the vote should be split about 12 to 5 for Carter. Among the general population, the split was about 6 Democrats for 4 Republicans. But Anderson received a disproportionate share of support from self-defined liberals (Pomper 1981*b*, p. 71); Jews, more than others, see themselves as liberal. Jews were

Table 1

Democratic Primaries, 1980

	Massachusetts			Florida			New York		
	State	Non-Jews	Jews	State	Non-Jews	Jews	State	Non-Jews	Jews
Carter	29	31	17	66	70	50	41	51	22
Kennedy	66	64	74	22	20	30	59	49	78
Other	3	3	3	7	8	3	–	–	–
No preference	2	2	3	5	3	15	–	–	–

Source: Figure for Jews are from *New York Times* /CBS News Election Day Polls and *Los Angeles Times* Election Polls. State figures come from the *Los Angeles Times*. Non-Jewish figures are estimated from state and Jewish figures, accounting for the approximate percentage of primary voters who are Jewish.

Table 2
1980 Presidential Vote

	Reagan	Carter	Anderson	Others
Nation	51.0	41.0	6.6	1.4
Whites	55.0	36.0	8.0	1.0
Jews	34.0	47.0	17.0	2.0

Source: National figures from *World Almanac and Book of Facts 1981*, p. 42; whites from an adjusted *New York Times* /CBS News Election Day Poll (Pomper 1981, p. 71); Jews from a weighted average of seven different polls (see text under "Methods").

Table 3
Early (1980) Campaign Presidential Preference Polls

	Reagan	Carter	Anderson	Don't know
Nation*	32	39	22	6
Jews*	6	30	43	20
Jews**	19	23	59	–

Sources: *Combined AIPO (Gallup) Polls Nos. 155 (13 May) and 157 (10 June). The earlier poll is weighted twice that of the later.

**Harris Poll (May), cited by Rosenbaum (1981, p. 14). The "don't knows" have been redistributed.

more likely than others to see Anderson on the Left.[5] Most important, partisan differences are widest for middle-income people. Jews are relatively more likely to vote on their social and political preferences and needs, whereas (white) non-Jews tend to vote with their pocketbooks.

If the 12-to-5 split is accurate—and this is an essential assumption—several additional findings become clear. First, the 60-to-40, two-party split in the Jewish vote is within the normal range, if we take the 1950s as the base decade (see figure 1). Compared with both 1972 and 1976, it means that Jewish support for the Democrats has eroded, but not that there has been a major realignment. The Republicans have made inroads, but this is not unprecedented, and they are far from becoming the majority party. The difference between the Jewish and white non-Jewish vote is similar to what it has been in the recent past (figure 1, indirectly), arguing against discontinuity. Jews are subject to the same forces as other people in this society and they respond in comparable ways—they just start at different points.

The congressional vote presents the same methodological problems, but the findings are easier to interpret. There are fewer polls, and they all agree that Jews still support Democratic candidates, considerably more so than do other Americans. The dearth of data makes exact comparisons difficult, but the trend is clear; there is no discernible decline in the Democratic Senate vote, and although the House vote is dropping, it is still very high. Schneider (1978, p. 216) notes that congressional voting lags behind presidential changes, which might explain why the Jewish Democratic vote is still high even while alignment is occurring, except that the same phenomenon does not occur among (white) non-Jews. Their congressional vote has declined.

In spite of Reagan's unexpectedly large victory, Election Day data on party identification give no indication of major realignment (see table 5). Party identification of Jews has been notably stable over the last decade. Recent mid-1981

Figure 1

Presidential (Two-Party) Vote
1952–1980*

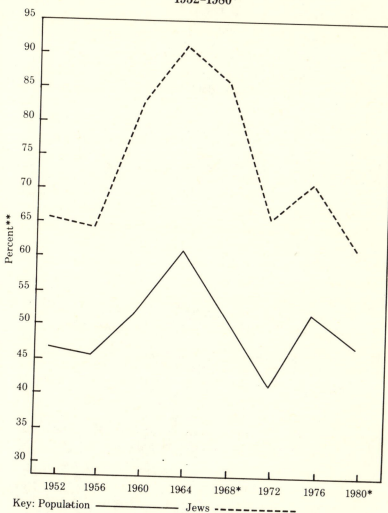

Key: Population ————— Jews ----------

*For both 1968 and 1980, the third-party vote has been redistributed, but not simply according to the two-party proportion since they did not draw evenly from Democrats and Republicans. The calculation examined third-party support in terms of income, education, party affiliation, and race, and redistributed accordingly.

**Percentage of two-party vote for Democratic candidates.

Source: For 1952–1976, see Fisher 1979, p. 100.

Table 4

1980 Congressional Vote

	House of Representatives*			Senate**	
	Demo-crat	Repub-lican	Other/don't know	Demo-crat	Repub-lican
National	54	41	5	52	48
Jews	69	24	7	91	9

Sources: *Center for Political Studies (CPS) and AIPO Nos. 162 (9 September) and 164 (4 November).

**CPS. The Jewish number polled is only 22, making this a highly problematic figure.

Table 5

Political Party Identification, November 1980

	Democrat	Republican	Independent
National	43	24	32
Jews	61	13	28

Source: AIPO Polls (October/December 1980), cited in *Gallup Opinion Index* (December 1980, p. 65); *New York Times*/CBS News Election Day Poll; Center for Political Studies.

polls indicate a changing, more evenly balanced partisan distribution for the entire nation (Clymer and Frankovic 1981, pp. 42–47).[6] The Jewish samples are small, and therefore not published; but based on the geographical and demographic groups which have changed, one can estimate that it is not the Jews who have been switching.

One further measure of political opinion is ideological self-identification. Here, too, there are few signs of significant change over the last few years. Jews are less likely to see themselves on the far Left than they were twenty years ago, but they are still noticeably more likely to call themselves liberal than is the rest of the population (Himmelfarb 1981, p. 28).[7]

CONCLUSION

If the American political system of coalitions is undergoing a major change, it will permeate all levels of voting and personal identification. Although, nationally, some signs of a realignment appeared in 1980, they were barely visible among Jews. The presidential vote is problematic because of Anderson's strong showing. Moreover, we still face a basic question of interpretation: is it *only* or *fully* 60 percent of the Jewish vote which is Democratic? When and with whom does one compare? The explanation and prediction are partly a function of the reading—*only* or *fully?*

It might be argued that Reagan attracted Jews to the Republican party. Although findings were mixed, some polls indicated that Jews were slightly more likely than other Americans to list inflation as the nation's greatest problem.[8] Caught in a tight economy with proliferating federal spending, middle-income Jews listened closely to Reagan, who articulated these concerns more effectively than did Carter. In addition, apparently more Jewish public leaders endorsed the Republicans than in recent history. Yet this is insufficient evidence for the realignment hypothesis.

A safer interpretation is that we *may* be entering a transition, but no clear change has (yet) occurred. Some commentators were presaging the attenuation of the Jewish-Democratic link in 1972, but that attachment has survived the least attractive candidacy the Democrats could have chosen in 1980 (Horowitz 1972; Evans and Novak 1972). The Jews voted Democratic, although almost all other ethnic, regional, sexual, and age divisions switched to the Republicans. They have done so in spite of economic duress, international setbacks, and an unpopular president with an alien style who accomplished very little in office and who faced a challenger perceived as much more pro-Israel. These unpropitious circumstances have produced the minimal rather than the normal Democratic vote.

Realignment of the Jewish vote is theoretically a simple process—it requires only that Jews think like other people with similar incomes. In the last century, that happened only when the Jews were poor. Forces which might disturb traditional affiliation include a coalescence of anti-Semitic forces, Jewish demographic changes, and normal party competition.

Most explanations of Jewish liberalism trace its origin to anti-Semitism of the Right, not just in the United States but throughout the Western world (Himmelfarb 1973, pp. 3–62; Lipset and Raab 1978). In the late 1960s—when the Left became increasingly visible and increasingly critical of Israel while the racist Right seemed to wane—Jews, particularly militant Zionists, began to reassess their allies. In the decade since, there has been a resurgence of the traditionally anti-Semitic Right and a decline of the virulent Left. At the same time, however, support for Israel has found a vocal new source in the evangelical Christian Right and in several conservative leaders in government, while sympathy for the Palestinians is occasionally expressed by Left-oriented churches and some liberal Republicans.

A distinction needs to be drawn between mainstream conservatives and the Ku Klux Klan, of course. Reagan has denounced hate groups and he is not a racial Rightist. Moreover, the neoconservative intellectual movement includes Jewish Old Leftists, and criticism of government inefficiency is widespread among Jews. Nevertheless, old allegiances persist. Jews are still overrepresented in liberal groups, and Jewish concerns—e.g., Israel—are strongly supported by most liberals. When a politically conservative church leader proclaims that God does not hear the prayers of Jews, and when strong Reagan backers argue that public schools should be made more explicitly Christian, then Jews are bound to be wary. Mass media presentation of the Holocaust and current anti-Semitic vandalism reinforce their fear of the Right. Unless liberal congressmen entirely relinquish their support for Jewish issues—and for reasons of ideology and of monetary and constituency support that seems highly improbable—the existence of the Klan and the evangelical Right will keep Jews on the Left.

A second factor worth considering is demographic development. As a statistical group, Jews are economically advantaged; but this fact alone does not necessarily reduce their support of the Democrats. They have been advantaged since 1945, without any major realignment, and there is still a sizable group of Jewish poor who retain their New Deal mentality. Within the Jewish middle class, the contemporary pattern is to move into white-collar occupations rather than into individual or family businesses. Given the high proportion of Jews in human services and in salaried professional jobs which may be unionized in the future, even middle-income Jews may see the Democratic party as most representative of their economic interests. In any case, economic class since the New Deal has generally become less powerful as a determinant of partisan choice. Ladd exaggerates the case for class inversion, but if he is on the mark in suggesting that the middle class is becoming more liberal and more Democratic, then middle-income Jews will not be changing their political partisanship (Ladd 1978, pp. 96–102).

The last special demographic feature of American Jewry is its geographical concentration. Although those who could afford to do so have left the inner cities, most Jews still live in or near the Northeastern urban areas. Those who moved to the Sun Belt have gone to growing metropolitan areas like Los Angeles or Miami–Fort Lauderdale, and not to rural areas with strong Republican majorities. For most of this century, the Democrats have had stronger ties to big cities than the Republicans, and there is no immediate prospect that this will change.

The third significant factor is party competition. Democratic theory does not require that a party always nominate the most popular candidate, but if voters are regularly dissatisfied, a breakdown results. One option is to switch parties; another is to stay home on Election Day. Both have been happening. The Democrats have not been nominating candidates who are especially attractive to the white New Deal coalition, so that vote has been slipping away. An even more radical change would have occurred had the Republicans offered someone who could appeal strongly to labor, white ethnics, or urbanites. When a Republican John Anderson runs against a Democratic Jimmy Carter, the Jews will indeed switch. That is, however, unlikely to occur in the near future, given the success and strength of the conservative Republican wing and given the role of Jewish activists within the Democratic party. But in the last decade, in fact, the Jewish Democratic leaders have not been very successful at the presidential level.

The Jewish vote is not as firmly liberal and Democratic as it once was, though it is stable and substantial at the sub-presidential level. Unless an external force causes it to move, it will stay predominantly moderate-liberal Democratic. Except for Israel and anti-Semitism, the immediate force will be the success of the Republican administration in improving the economy, reducing social malaise, and regaining a sense of national pride. We may have a clearer picture in 1984.

14

MARTIN P. WATTENBERG

ARTHUR H. MILLER

Decay in Regional Party Coalitions: 1952–1980

Split-ticket voting and the independent voter. Long-term/short-term factors in the normal vote. The South; the Mountain West; the Northeast and Midwest. The public's image of the parties on issues. Volatility in current politics.

The election of Ronald Reagan marked the fifth time in the eight presidential elections since 1952 that the Republican party captured the White House. As with the elections of Eisenhower and Nixon, Reagan's victory has prompted speculation about an impending major realignment in American politics, a realignment which some commentators believe will produce a Republican majority in the electorate for the first time in nearly fifty years. In particular, attention has once again been focused on the South as a potential source of large permanent gains for the Republicans. Jimmy Carter's 1976 wins in thirteen of the fifteen Border and Deep South states are now being written off by many as a temporary aberration from the trend toward a Republican-dominated South.

However, we believe that the reports of impending minority status for the Democrats—both in the South and nationwide—have been greatly exaggerated. Since 1952 there has been a slow process of regional convergence in terms of partisanship, but with the net result being little change in the ratio of Democrats to Republicans nationwide. Thus, if the question is whether there has been a realignment similar to that of 1928–1936, in which the minority party became the majority party and vice versa, then the answer is quite clearly, "No." However, if the question is whether there has been a gradual sectional realignment, in which there have been durable changes in regional party loyalties, then the answer is "Yes." The deterioration of the old regional (and religious) cleavages makes the appearance of a new alignment more likely, but as of the 1980 election, the potential for a profound shift in the national partisan balance had not been fulfilled.

PARTY IDENTIFICATION AND THE NORMAL VOTE

If one were to examine the character of American electoral behavior solely on the basis of presidential election returns from 1952 to 1980, one would undoubtedly conclude that Americans have been highly volatile in their party loyalties. After all, except for the elections of 1952 and 1956, no two successive elections have produced anything approaching similar results. Close elections have alternated landslides and Democratic victories with Republican victories.

However, survey data from the SRC/CPS* National Election Studies indicate a remarkable stability in the relative strength of the parties nationwide in terms of psychological identification. In each election since 1952, respondents have been asked, "Generally speaking, do you usually consider yourself a Democrat, a Republican, an Independent, or what?" Unlike the Gallup party-affiliation question, which begins with the phrase, "In politics, as of today, . . . " the Michigan question purposely aims at tapping long-term loyalties rather than short-term intentions, and hence shows far less vacillation from year to year. As figure 1 demonstrates, Democrats have consistently outnumbered Republicans by an average ratio of approximately 1.7 to 1.0. The only change of any lasting substantive significance has been the growth of Independents from about 23 percent in the 1952–1964 period to roughly 35 percent between 1972 and 1980.[1]

This decline in party identification, along with the marked increase in split-ticket voting, has provided the parties with a far greater number of potential swing voters. Yet it has not caused much change in the estimate of the expected normal vote, which can be calculated on the basis of the direction and strength of party identification in the electorate, adjusted to reflect historical differences in turnout and defection rates.

The normal vote, according to Converse (1966a), is the aggregate vote which would have been cast if the long-term force of party identification were the only political factor

*Survey Research Center/Center for Political Studies, University of Michigan.

Figure 1

Party Identification in the United States
1952–1980

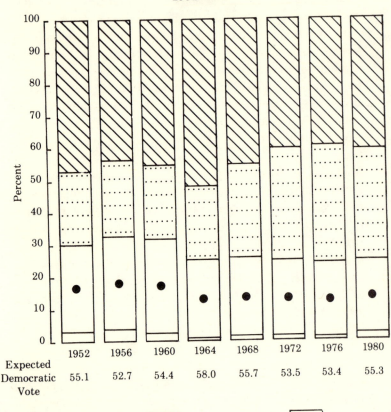

Expected Democratic Vote	55.1	52.7	54.4	58.0	55.7	53.5	53.4	55.3
	1952	1956	1960	1964	1968	1972	1976	1980

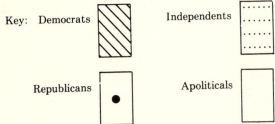

Key: Democrats

Independents

Republicans

Apoliticals

Source: SRC/CPS National Election Studies

relevant to the electoral outcome. Of course, each specific election is subject to the influence of idiosyncratic short-term factors such as the unique personalities of the candidates and the issues of the day. Party alignments, however, are presumably more enduring—lasting across many elections and affecting how voters respond to the more transient issues of the day. The normal vote concept is therefore much better suited to an investigation of shifts in party coalitions than observed voting patterns, as it provides a simple summary measure which isolates only the long-term forces which represent the basis of the party coalition.

In addition to its conceptual and empirical advantages, the normal vote offers a concise summary value which is readily interpretable and which enables us to parsimoniously compare the partisanship of a wide variety of groups. From the estimates of the national normal vote presented at the bottom of figure 1, one can clearly see that, despite some minor fluctuations, there has been a great deal of stability across time. The national normal vote values of roughly 54 percent Democratic and 46 Republican thereby reconfirm what we have already noted above—namely, that Democrats have consistently outnumbered Republicans nationally at approximately the same ratio for the past three decades.[2]

REGIONAL CHANGES IN THE NORMAL VOTE

In spite of the stability in the national normal vote, substantial regional changes have taken place. The sectional trends shown in figure 2 offer a striking contrast to the national picture.[3] In the Southern and Mountain states, one can see a distinct trend favoring the Republicans, while the trends in the Northeastern and Midwestern sections of the country have favored the Democrats. Only in the Pacific Coast states has there been anything approaching the consistency of the national normal vote.

The South

The most notable of the regional trends has been the decline of Democratic strength in the South. From Reconstruction through World War II, the South rarely wavered a bit from its solid support of the Democratic party. In 1948, however, the liberal Democratic platform on civil rights seriously called into question for the first time whether such a pattern continued to make any sense. The defection of many Southern Democrats to Strom Thurmond's States' Rights ticket clearly demonstrated that, given the right issue appeal, the South would not vote so solidly Democratic.

Yet the expected rapid Southern conversion to the Republican party did not occur. When data on party identification were analyzed in the 1952 SRC Election Study, partisanship in the South was found to be overwhelmingly Democratic, yielding an expected normal Democratic vote of 71.7 percent. It soon became apparent that long-term partisan loyalties in the South were far less susceptible to change than the temporary defections in the presidential vote might imply. The support for civil rights among Northern Democratic leaders may have concerned many Southern voters, but they could take comfort in the fact that their own local Democratic senators and representatives would vigorously oppose any change. The Democrats still retained their image as the party most likely to provide jobs and to benefit the common man, both of which continued to be distinct advantages, given that the South remained relatively poor.

Indeed, in examining the decline of the expected Democratic vote in the South between 1952 and 1960, Converse (1966b) found little evidence of partisan change among native Southerners, but rather traced the increasing Repub-

Figure 2

Expected Democratic Normal Vote by Region
1952–1980

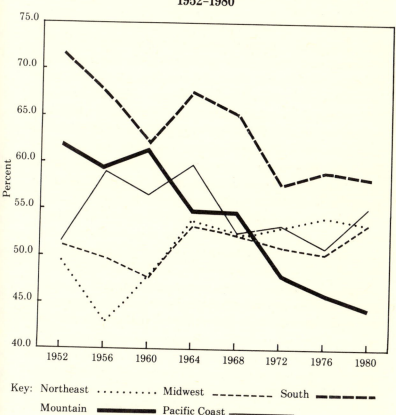

Key: Northeast ·········· Midwest ———————— South ▬▬▬▬▬▬
Mountain ▬▬▬▬▬ Pacific Coast ————————

Source: SRC/CPS National Election Studies

lican support to population migration. In 1960 the estimate of the normal Democratic vote for migrants to the South was less than half the estimate for native Southerners, at 30.3 percent. As Converse noted, this migration consisted largely of professional workers—a predominately Republican group—either transferred to a developing Southern city or moving to a warmer climate to retire. However, since the early 1960s the impact of migration has clearly diminished. The migration has not slowed, but its occupational character has changed. Of the Southern immigrants in the 1960 sample (excluding housewives), only 12.0 percent were blue-collar employees, but by the late 1970s this had tripled. Not only have young blue-collar workers been moving to a rapidly industrializing South; migration Southward after retirement is no longer largely limited to the most affluent white-collar workers, but it is increasingly becoming common for retired blue-collar employees as well. Thus, while the expected Democratic vote for migrants to the South could once be estimated to be at 30.3 percent, by 1980 the comparable figure had reached 46.0 percent.

A more complete understanding of the decline in Democratic strength in the South requires the identification of two distinct periods during which the explanations for the decline differ. The first, occurring between 1952 and 1960, provides an example of the realignment process, as the change which took place can be traced largely to a compositional shift in the electorate produced by the influx of Northern Republican migrants. Much previous research (Converse 1972; Andersen 1979) suggests that realignment occurs due to population replacement rather than to conversion—i.e., individuals shifting their loyalties from one party to the other. The earlier period of change in the South thus provides a prime example of such a realignment.

In contrast, the second stage, occurring between 1964 and 1972—*after which there has been no further change*—can best be described as an example of dealignment, in which es-

tablished partisan loyalties dissolve without new attachments arising in their place. By 1972 Republican affiliation
in the South was still only 19 percent compared to 18 percent
in 1960. However, the 1964–1972 period saw two major
changes in partisanship which significantly weakened the
Democratic position in the South. First, Independents increased from 17 percent in 1964 to 30 percent in 1972. And
secondly, Southern Democrats became much less likely to
say that they strongly identified with the party. In 1964, 55
percent of the Southern Democratic bloc stated that they
considered themselves to be strong partisans; by 1972, this
figure had fallen to just 35 percent.

This two-stage explanation can best be illustrated by examining over time the images of both parties in the South.
One limitation of the party identification scale is that it can
only tell us which party the respondent generally prefers and
how strongly—it does not necessarily imply how positive or
negative respondents feel about each party. For example,
people can be weak Democrats because they like both parties but are slightly more positive toward the Democrats, or
alternatively because they *dis*like both parties, but the Democrats slightly less. Fortunately, time-series data are available concerning how citizens feel about each of the two major
parties individually. Since 1952 election-study respondents
have been asked in an open-ended fashion what they liked
and disliked about both of the parties. By counting the number of likes and then subtracting the number of dislikes, it is
possible to construct indices of net affect toward both the
Democrats and the Republicans.[4]

Such indices represent the affective images which citizens
have of the parties. These images are naturally less stable
than reports of party identification, given that they contain a
substantial amount of short-term references to the particular issue stands and leadership of the parties in each individual year. Furthermore, party identification is a
relatively stable and enduring attitude which is generally

maintained, even in the face of short-term negative feelings about one's preferred party or positive images of the opposite party. Given that party images will reflect such temporary changes in affect, one should not expect partisanship to perfectly mirror trends in party images over time. However, if the changes in the images of the parties persist over a substantial period of time, then identifications are more likely to change as part of the general psychological need to achieve a state of cognitive consistency.

Figure 3 displays the changes which have occurred in party images of white and black Southerners from 1952 to 1980. In the early stage—from 1952 to 1960—it is clear that the more positive image of the Republican party was primarily associated with the decline of Southern Democratic partisanship. While the Democratic image remained fairly level, the Republican image improved steadily. However, the positive image which the Republicans had in the South in 1960 among whites and blacks has not since been equalled for either. Southern blacks turned sharply against the Republicans as the national Republican leadership came out against civil rights and social welfare legislation in 1964. Yet the Republican hopes for improving their image among Southern whites were not realized. While the Republican image among white Southerners has benefited some from comments concerning the general conservatism of the party, such responses have generally been offset by negative perceptions of the Republicans as the party of big business and the upper class.

Rather than being due to any continued improvement of the Republican image, figure 3 indicates that the change in the normal white Southern vote after 1960 can be attributed primarily to the decline in affect toward the Democrats, which plunged sharply between 1964 and 1968. Much of this decline was clearly issue motivated, with the most common theme being discontent with wasteful big-government spending by the Democrats—the effect of which was further

Figure 3

Party Images in the South
1952–1980

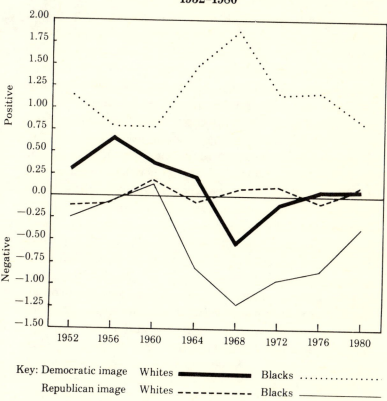

Key: Democratic image Whites ▬▬▬▬ Blacks ....
Republican image Whites ‒ ‒ ‒ ‒ ‒ Blacks ──────────

Source: SRC/CPS National Election Studies

exacerbated by dissatisfaction with civil rights policies and Democratic proposals for handling the Vietnam War. This issue dissatisfaction undoubtedly provided the basis for the sizable Wallace protest vote in the South in 1968. Furthermore, the Wallace movement accentuated the underlying divisions within the Democratic party, thereby making it all the more difficult to restore a consistent positive image of the party among white Southerners.

Since 1968 the data show a gradual recovery in the Democratic party image among Southern whites. However, the Democrats have not been able to restore the edge which they held in party images over the Republicans from 1952 to 1964. Young Southerners entering the electorate after this period have thus experienced a far different partisan socialization than their elders. Therefore, the 55 percent margin which the Democrats continue to hold as of 1980 in the white Southern normal vote is probably susceptible to future change toward the equilibrium level through the inevitable process of population replacement. Indeed, among white Southerners who entered the electorate after 1964, one finds an expected Democratic vote in 1980 of only 51 percent. As this generation continues to replace the New Deal cohort, whose identifications are still heavily influenced by the once highly favorable image of the Democrats in the South, the normal Democratic Southern vote is likely to gradually slide yet further, even in the absence of any possible improvement of the Republican image among Southern whites.

Nevertheless, the South is more likely than not to remain predominately Democratic for some time to come, due to the solid support given to it by the black segment of the population. As shown in figure 3, Southern blacks have consistently had a much more favorable image of the Democrats than of the Republicans. Interestingly, whites and blacks in the South may have been separate in many ways through the 1952–1960 period, but their images of the parties were remarkably similar. But since then the two races have come to view the parties quite differently. For example, while 1968 represented the low point in Southern white affect toward the Democrats, it marked the high point among Southern blacks. Although the data indicate a good deal of convergence since then, the racial polarization in party images which occurred in the 1960s has had long-lasting consequences for Southern partisanship. In particular, one should not interpret the trends in the party images of black Southerners since 1968 as indicating any real weakening of their identification with the Democratic party. Rather, these trends reflect the declining saliency of the issues which caused the polarization to take place. Blacks are likely to remain strongly Democratic as long as social programs continue to be important to them and they see the Democrats as more favorable toward such programs. And given that they number roughly one-fifth of the Southern population and now turn out at virtually the same rate as whites, blacks are likely to provide the Democrats with a cushion in the normal vote in the South for some time to come.

The Mountain states

While the South may continue to be the most Democratic region, the Mountain West is likely to be the most Republican region for the foreseeable future. Returning to the sectional trends in the normal vote displayed in figure 2, one finds that the Mountain region was second only to the South in Democratic partisanship between 1952 and 1960. However, due to the large shift in the Mountain states from an expected Democratic vote of 61.4 percent in 1960 to 44.2 percent in 1980, the two regions now stand at opposite poles from one another.

Unlike the changes which have occurred in Southern partisanship, this sharp trend in the Mountain West has largely escaped academic notice to date. One possible reason for this neglect may be the sparsity of the region's population. After all, residents of these eight states (Arizona, Colorado, Idaho, Montana, Nevada, New Mexico, Utah, and Wyoming) cast only 5 percent of the vote in the 1980 presidential election. Furthermore, the small population makes it difficult to obtain many interviews in the region as part of any national representative sample. Even if one is sufficiently interested to examine the Mountain West separately, there are very few cases with which to do so. Our data are no exception to this rule, as none of the SRC/CPS studies contain more than one hundred interviews in the region. Thus, they must be interpreted with a fair measure of caution.

Nevertheless, we feel that these data are quite plausible empirically, and are potentially very significant. The Mountain West may cast only 5 percent of the popular vote for president, but in the U.S. Senate its representation is inflated to 16 percent. And this representation has changed just as one would expect from the normal vote figures over the last twenty years. In 1960 the Democrats held 12 of the 16 seats from these states, but since then this figure has gradually declined to the point where they now hold only 5. The results of the 1980 election, in which the Republicans established a slim majority in the Senate, have clearly demonstrated the importance of such a shift. With a strong base in the Mountain region plus the weakening of Democratic support in the South, Republican control of the Senate may prove to be more than a transitory phenomenon.

Historically, the attachment of the Mountain West to the Democratic party can be traced to William Jennings Bryan and the system of 1896. The populist, agrarian appeal of the Democrats, plus their support for Mountain silver interests, made them more palatable to voters in the region than the Northern, business-oriented Republican party of the time. Isolated from the political, cultural, and economic power centers of the country, the affiliation of the Mountain West with the Democratic party fits neatly under the rubric of a center/periphery cleavage. Senators from the region were sent to Washington primarily as ambassadors to the federal government to seek aid for economic development, rather than as ideological representatives.

However, thanks to the advent of television, peripheral regions such as the Mountain West and the South are by no means as isolated as they once were. As late as 1952, figure 4 shows that only 4 percent of those interviewed in the Mountain states and 27 percent in the South reported that they had followed the campaign on television, compared with over 60 percent elsewhere in the country. By 1964, though, these regional differences had largely disappeared, as television came to virtually permeate all areas of the country. The instantaneous transmission of political news provided by television has had an unparalleled effect toward integrating American life, and thus may also have contributed to the decline in long-standing regional political cleavages.

Yet the decline of traditional partisan loyalties in the Mountain West and the South, despite a similar downward trend for the Democrats in both, has resulted in the South's remaining the most strongly Democratic region, while the Mountain states have come to be the most Republican in the nation. One possible interpretation of this is that the Democratic declines in both regions simply represent parallel trends with a different starting point. Given that the Mountain states were always less solidly Democratic than the South, one would naturally expect that they would move into the Republican column sooner under similar pressures. As such, the 1980 normal vote in the Mountain region might be seen as an indication of the future position of the South.

However, in examining the change in the demographic composition of the regions displayed in table 1, it is apparent that the two trends have reached different points by 1980, largely because the pressures toward change have been different. In the Mountain states, demographic changes have clearly benefited the Republicans. In contrast, Southern demographic trends favored the Republicans only during the

Figure 4

Percent Following the Campaign on Television
1952–1980

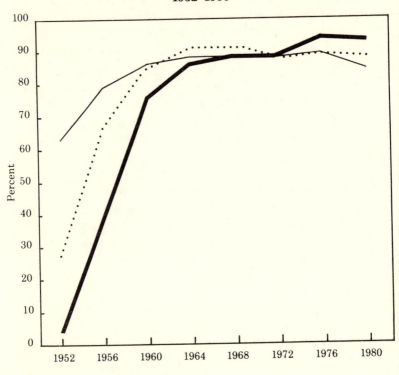

Key: Mountain ▅▅▅▅▅   South ·········   Other regions ─────

Source: SRC/CPS National Election Studies

initial period of Northern white-collar migration described above. In the South one now finds the largest proportion of blue-collar workers in any region, while in the Mountain states one finds by far the largest proportion of white-collar workers. Similarly, the proportion of Catholics in the South has more than quadrupled from the 1950s to the 1970s, while in the Mountain region Catholics declined from about one-third to one-quarter. And finally, the educational levels of all regions increased during this period, but the relative position of the South remained about the same, while education levels in the Mountain West increased from far below the national average to far above it.

Yet even with all of these favorable demographic trends, the Republican party is still not as strong in the Mountain West as one might expect. Independents currently outnumber Republicans in the region, and the Republican party image is only very slightly positive. Thus, the Republicans are clearly in a much better position than the Democrats in the Mountain states, but they are still far from completely dominating the area.

The Northeast and Midwest

Up to this point we have closely examined only the sectional trends which have favored the Republicans. However, in the Northeast and Midwest—where nearly half of the population resides—the changes which have occurred have worked to the advantage of the Democrats. Close two-party competition has been the rule throughout the 1952–1980 period in these Northern regions, but between 1952 and 1960 the Republicans generally had a slight edge in the normal vote, while since then the Democrats have maintained a slim majority.

What is most interesting about this change is that it is the product of the decline of two traditional, partisan group

Table 1
Change in the Demographic Composition of the Regions: A Comparison of the 1950s and 1970s

	Northeast		Midwest		South		Mountain		Pacific Coast	
	1950s	1970s	1950s	1970s	1950s	1970s	1950s	1970s	1950s	1970s
Education										
Grade school	33	17	35	19	44	23	51	11	22	8
High school	52	54	49	51	40	50	38	46	54	45
College	15	29	16	30	17	27	10	43	24	47
Occupation										
White collar	31	39	24	36	22	32	15	59	32	43
Blue collar	25	34	22	31	19	37	24	22	30	29
Unskilled labor	7	3	7	2	12	2	10	3	6	3
Farm labor	2	1	9	5	11	3	11	0	3	2
Housework	35	23	38	26	36	25	41	16	30	23
Religion										
Protestant	49	41	75	71	92	76	57	68	72	64
Catholic	40	44	21	23	4	18	34	25	21	21
Jewish	9	7	2	2	1	1	0	2	2	1
Other and none	2	8	2	5	3	6	9	5	6	13

Source: SRC/CPS National Election Studies for 1952, 1956, 1972, and 1976.

loyalties which have long dominated the politics of the North—the Catholic identification with the Democrats and the white Protestant identification with the Republicans. In 1960, at the height of the presence of religious issues in politics during recent times, figure 5 shows that the difference between the normal vote for Northern white Protestants and Catholics was slightly over 30 percent. However, the difference since then has narrowed considerably, to only 14 percent, as Catholics have become less Democratic and white Protestants have become less Republican.

For Northern white Protestants, this change occurred rapidly between 1960 and 1964, as religion ceased to be the major issue it had been prior to the Kennedy presidency, and as Goldwater ousted the traditional Eastern-Establishment Republicans from power. The lasting impact of this shift has enabled the Democrats to maintain their slight majority in the North ever since. In contrast, partisan change for Catholics has been much more of a gradual process, and represents the declining attraction of the Democrats much more than it does any positive Catholic attraction to the Republicans. In fact, only 16 percent of Northern Catholics identified with the Republican party in 1980 compared with 17 percent in 1964. Like Southern whites, their image of the Republican party has not improved much over time, while their image of the Democrats has fallen substantially.

Accompanying this convergence in Protestant and Catholic party loyalties has also been a decline of the polarization in how each group rates its own group relative to the other. Between 1964 and 1976 the national election studies asked respondents to rate both "Protestants" and "Catholics" on a feeling thermometer with a range from 0 to 100 degrees. In 1964 Northern white Protestants and Catholics rated each other an average of 20 points apart. Figures for subsequent years, however, have shown a substantial decline, with the difference in group ratings being only 11 points in 1976.

The rise of evangelical groups such as the Moral Majority

Figure 5

Expected Normal Democratic Vote for
Northern White Protestants and Catholics
1952–1980

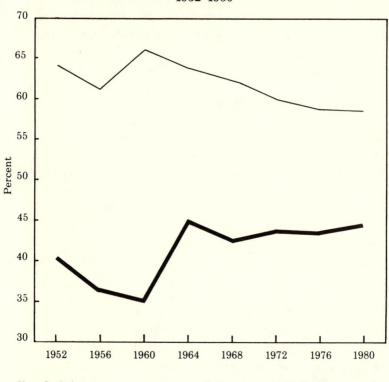

Key: Catholics ———————— Protestants ▬▬▬▬▬▬

Source: SRC/CPS National Election Studies

may bring religious questions back into politics, but they are unlikely to restore the polarization between Northern white Protestants and Catholics, as such fundamentalist issues cut across the traditional cleavage between the religions. Rather, as Protestants and Catholics come to be more and more alike both politically and socially, the long-standing Northern pattern of close two-party competition becomes more vulnerable than ever, as it is increasingly possible for one party to establish a positive image among both major religious groups.

PROSPECTS FOR FUTURE CHANGE: THE FRAGILITY OF THE CURRENT ALIGNMENT

Perhaps the most often employed term to describe the likely character of American politics in the 1980s has been "volatility." The old cleavages which once provided a sense of continuity and stability have been slowly dissolving, and there seem to be few issues capable of establishing new coalitions. The fragility of the current alignment nationally is best illustrated by the lack of substance in respondents' party images as revealed in the 1980 election study, which shows remarkable regional similarities. As table 2 demonstrates, the only major advantage enjoyed by either party is the Democrats' positive image concerning the groups which they represent. Similarly, the only major disadvantage for either party is the negative image which people have of the groups popularly associated with the Republican party. These feelings—that the Democrats are the party of the common working man, while the Republicans are the party of the upper class and big business—represent virtually the last surviving remnant of the party images which developed during the New Deal era.

Table 2
Images of the Political Parties, 1980

	Like Democrats (%)	Dislike Democrats (%)	Like Republicans (%)	Dislike Republicans (%)
Because of:				
The groups they are for or against	25.5*	4.2	4.3	19.3
Economic/welfare policy stands	6.2	10.0	8.1	3.9
Social issue stands	0.8	0.7	1.0	1.1
Stands on general philosophy of government activity	8.1	8.2	11.1	5.1
Their ability to manage the government	2.5	9.7	7.2	2.0
Foreign policy	4.2	6.3	7.4	4.5
Carter	0.6	1.9	–	–
Reagan	–	–	1.1	1.5

Source: SRC/CPS National Election Study, 1980.

*Table entries represent the proportion of the sample offering each given type of response.

Table 3
Images of the Political Parties, 1952

	Like Democrats (%)	Dislike Democrats (%)	Like Republicans (%)	Dislike Republicans (%)
Because of:				
The groups they are for or against	33.1*	4.7	3.2	20.3
Economic/welfare policy stands	31.9	16.3	22.1	22.4
Social issue stands	–	–	–	–
Stands on general philosophy of government activity	11.4	8.7	11.0	5.8
Their ability to manage the government	2.3	26.6	18.0	4.3
Foreign policy	4.1	17.1	12.3	3.4
Truman	1.0	7.6	–	–
Eisenhower	–	–	7.7	1.8
Stevenson	1.3	0.9	–	–

Source: SRC/CPS National Election Study, 1952.

*Table entries represent the proportion of the sample offering each given type of response.

Table 3 presents an examination of the party images found in the 1952 election study which can be directly compared to the percentages displayed in table 2 for 1980. The comparison indicates that there has been a marked deterioration of images which once were highly favorable to the Democrats as well as of those which once greatly benefited the Republicans. Aside from the traditional images concerning which parties favor which groups, the electorate simply no longer has much to say when asked what it likes and dislikes about the two parties.[5]

For example, in 1952 nearly a third of the respondents stated that they liked the Democratic party because of its economic or welfare policies, while 22 percent made similar negative comments in reference to the Republicans. With memories of the Great Depression now in the distant past, it is probably not too surprising to find that the comparable figures in 1980 were only 6 and 4 percent, respectively. Many observers, however, may not expect to find that positive comments about the Republican party's economic/welfare policy stands were also more numerous in the 1952 sample than in 1980 (22 compared with 8 percent). Moreover, despite the poor performance of the economy during the Carter administration, only 10 percent of those interviewed made negative comments about the economic and welfare policies of the Democratic party. In sum, neither party now has a very firmly entrenched positive or negative public image on such issues compared with two or three decades ago.[6] The Republicans may have been in a relatively better position in 1980 than in the past, but they are still far from establishing the clear and enduring edge which the Democrats once held.

Similarly, images of the parties in the areas of foreign policy and management of the government are also not nearly as clearly defined as they once were. In both 1952 and 1980 the Republicans were perceived favorably on these dimensions, while the Democrats were viewed negatively due to dissatisfaction with the performances of Truman and

Carter, respectively. The key difference to note is that in 1980 one finds that such feelings were far less salient than in 1952. The fact that only 7 percent of those interviewed made positive comments about the Republicans on each of these dimensions in 1980 hardly constitutes a resounding statement of faith in Republican foreign policies or management capabilities. Nor is there any indication that Carter's failures in these areas are likely to have a long-term negative impact on the Democratic party, as the comparable negative figures in 1952 were nearly three times as high.

That the Democratic party largely escaped blame for the entire range of problems of the Carter administration, from the economy to Iran, might be interpreted as an incredible stroke of good fortune—*especially considering that such problems were quite salient in open-ended evaluations of Jimmy Carter in 1980.* However, such a pattern is more likely a symptom of the growing dissociation of public perceptions of candidates and presidents from the political parties which they nominally represent. With the rise of television, candidates no longer need the parties to convey their messages; voters are now able to see for themselves just what the candidates are like. As a result, a number of recent presidential campaigns—most notably that of Richard Nixon in 1972— have been able to consciously downplay partisan appeals.

In 1980, however, neither candidate really made any effort to avoid party associations. Reagan clearly attempted to be more of a Republican team man than any nominee in the party's recent history, while Carter stressed his Democratic affiliation to the utmost, given that his low approval ratings made it difficult to offer much else in the way of a positive appeal. Yet in spite of these strategies, table 2 shows that very few people evaluated the parties in 1980 on the basis of their standard-bearers. For example, only 1 percent of the sample stated that they liked the Republicans because of Ronald Reagan. Whether this figure will be much greater in the future if the Reagan program succeeds remains to be seen, but if so, it would mark a reversal of the historical trend since 1952. In this candidate-centered media age, people simply have become less accustomed to praising or blaming the parties for presidential performance. Therefore, even if the Reagan economic program works, it may have no effect on long-term partisan loyalties *unless* it becomes solidly incorporated into the public's image of the Republican party.

What other hope thus is left for the creation of a new alignment to replace the current state of volatility? One possible stimulus which has been discussed throughout the last decade is the range of new policy questions which can be broadly classified as "social issues." Such subjects as abortion, prayer in schools, pollution, equal rights for women, legalization of marijuana, environmental protection, nuclear power plants, homosexual rights, etc., were simply not matters of public debate two decades ago, and many commentators have argued that the party which best positions itself on them can benefit tremendously.

In the early 1970s much of this discussion centered on the issues of the New Left, which many thought would be capable of mobilizing a large segment of America's socially liberal youth. More recently, attention has turned to the New Right and the evangelical movement, whose aim is to reverse what their members perceive as a deterioration of traditional moral values in American life. Yet our data on party images indicate that neither party was much liked or disliked by the public in 1980 because of their stands on social issues. Furthermore, social issues were also rarely mentioned in open-ended evaluations of the candidates. Only 3 percent of those interviewed stated that they liked Reagan because of a social-issue stand, compared with 1 percent for Carter, while 6 percent disliked Reagan and 2 percent disliked Carter because of a social issue. In part, this may be due to a lack of clear and opposing stands on such issues by the parties and candidates. However, it is doubtful that even the most distinct differences could have a major effect on partisan loyalties as long as social issues continue to be overshadowed by questions of economic prosperity and national defense.

SUMMARY AND CONCLUSION

Party coalitions have thus undergone several processes of decay over the last three decades with surprisingly little effect on the relative long-term strength of the two parties nationwide. Nevertheless, processes of partisan change described in this chapter have increased the possibilities of both short-term and long-term change in the near future. With the weakening of the public's images of the parties, it is no wonder that volatility has become the new catchword of American politics. As the long-term forces which serve to anchor electoral behavior decline, the potential increases for large oscillations in the vote due to short-term issue and candidate factors. Furthermore, given that there is less for people to return to in terms of what V. O. Key called a "standing decision," there is also an increased potential for the translation of short-term forces into long-term ones. Such a process, however, will require that the issues and candidates responsible for the short-term changes become firmly linked with public images of the parties—which, as of the 1980 election, had not yet occurred. When—and if—it does, a new era of American electoral politics will have begun.

VI

*The Future of
American Politics*

15

JOHN B. ANDERSON

Developing a "Grand Coalition"

Reagan and blacks, labor, the New Right. Social groups and the tax cuts. Minorities. The "trickledown" theory. The Democrats and affirmative action. The youth vote. The South. The Midwest-Northeast Coalition. Environmental issues. Current foreign policy and defense spending. Political disaffection.

History does indeed teach us that nothing is permanent. A certain, and understandable, political hubris has led some observers of the current scene to suggest that the 1980 election was a watershed event which presages a critical realignment of the parties. They would compare it to elections of the

1850s, the 1890s, and the 1930s. Norman Podhoretz has spoken of a new American majority. Richard Wirthlin, the Reagan campaign pollster, predicts that Democratic defectors and Independents may remain with the Republican party for a long time. David Broder has written about a "rolling realignment" based on GOP gains among union families, middle-income groups, and high school and college graduates.

Only six months into the Reagan administration, despite the president's initial success with Congress in enacting his economic recovery program, it still seems premature to predict that his winning coalition in November 1980 will stand the test of time.

The object of this paper, however, is not to deal with realignment. Rather, I would like to undertake an examination of the question: Have we begun to see the emergence of new coalitions that will affect the political dynamics of the American electoral system? Unquestionably there were forces at work in 1980 which distinguished that national election from others in our history. But were they ephemeral blips on the political radar screen which will fade as we descend from the heights of a presidential campaign? Or are these forces likely to maintain the necessary cohesion that will make them a factor in elections yet to come?

In his campaign, Ronald Reagan frequently spoke of forming a coalition of shared values. He seemed to imply that these were values which transcended divisions along traditional socioeconomic lines. Tinged with a new patriotism which would make America once again a "shining city set upon a hill," it was a compound of emphases upon a new nationalism and a return to limited government. This was skillfully blended with appeals to restore the role of the home, the family, and individual responsibility for economic improvement as the basis for a more healthy society.

Although Mr. Reagan was fond of quoting such Rooseveltian rhetoric as "We have a rendezvous with destiny," he did very little to fashion the kind of coalition which led FDR to victory in four presidential campaigns. There was very little reaching out to the black vote. For example, he did not even address the annual convention of the oldest and most prestigious black group, the NAACP. The endorsement of a few peripheral black leaders like the Reverend Ralph Abernathy did little to disguise his disinterest in the black vote. When he did appear before the NAACP convention in June of 1981, the tepid nature of his reception indicated that very little had changed since the election. In short, blacks do not appear to be likely candidates for inclusion in the new coalition of shared values.

Although there were appeals to rank-and-file union members, outside of the Teamsters—and a few relatively small unions like that of the professional air traffic controllers—there were few overtures for the support of organized labor. Other minority groups and the disadvantaged generally were given little political sustenance.

He did actively court the support of religious fundamentalists. Witness his statement at a meeting of 15,000 held in Dallas during the campaign, where he said to his audience, composed largely of Protestant fundamentalist ministers, "Of course, you can't endorse me, but I endorse you." Their embrace of Ronald Reagan was largely based on the fact that they shared common ground on such emotional social issues as abortion, women's rights, and prayer in schools.

There are surveys which indicate that as many as two-fifths of all Americans could be categorized as evangelical or fundamentalist, and about one-third profess to be "born-again Christians." However, it is extremely difficult to believe that there is sufficient cohesiveness among the members of this group in either social or economic terms to constitute a viable political coalition. Once you get past the so-called "hot button" social issues, there is not a sufficient commonality of interests to survive the vicissitudes of a presidential term. This is not to say that the anti-

abortionists, the Eagle Forum of Phyllis Schlafly with its opposition to the Equal Rights Amendment, and other groups
fighting everything from pornography to other forms of per-
missiveness will not continue to exist. What I do challenge is
the assumption that they will maintain an alliance which
can be elevated to the status of a continuing political coalition. One of the most redoubtable figures in the Moral Majority is the Reverend Jerry Falwell of the electronic church.
Indeed, another leading light in this rather ill-defined grouping of conservative political-action committees and clergy-
men, Richard Viguerie, hailed Falwell as the most important
asset of the New Right. So disaffected was Reverend Falwell
with President Reagan's first nominee to the U.S. Supreme
Court that he said it might cause him to withhold his support
of the president's economic policies. Others have pointed out
that the evangelical, "born-again Christians" whom
Reverend Falwell claims to represent played a far
less significant role in President Reagan's election than
they assert.

One does not have to be an economic determinist to believe
that a "born-again Christian" who wants to retire at sixty-
two and finds his social security benefits have been reduced
will also find that an issue that overrides a candidate's position on abortion, ERA, or prayer in school.

At this writing, it seems likely that President Reagan's
proposals for draconian cuts in social programs may prevail.
The poor and disadvantaged will feel the impact most
sharply and will retain their traditional view of the GOP as
the party of the rich. If President Reagan continues to insist
on structuring his tax program along lines conferring larger
reductions on the well-to-do, it will be difficult to merge
lower-income groups into his "coalition of shared values." On
the other hand, if the Democrats continue to attempt to compete with the Republicans for the hearts and minds of Middle
America, an interesting shift could result. It should be noted
in this regard that this phrase, "Middle America," has

become the vogue in Democratic circles. In the House of Representatives, the Democratic chairman of the Ways and Means Committee has used the definition of an annual income of $20,000 to $50,000 as the parameters of Middle America. It is this group that House Democrats have sought to attract in fashioning their counterproposals to the president's tax package.

There are millions of Americans, black and white, who will feel ignored by both major parties. True, they are today poorly organized and poorly led. Nevertheless, I believe there is the potential that this socioeconomic group could desert its traditional moorings in the Democratic party if an alternative is found. Many members of this permanent underclass obviously would be composed of blacks and Hispanics, and the latter constitutes the fastest-growing ethnic minority in the nation. A program directed to the interests of these voters—or at least potential voters—might be combined with an appeal to those upper-middle and higher income groups who are socially conscious enough to see the dangers to society in continued benign neglect of groups which come to feel that they are no longer receiving the attention of either major political party. The president believes that the "trickle-down theory" will work to the extent that low-income groups will participate in the success of his economic recovery program.

Although the Democrats profess disdain for his economic theories, they show little sign of formulating the kind of program that would benefit those who are being bypassed by the president's plan. Indeed, their deafening silence on the issue of affirmative action will, I believe, confirm the suspicion of racial minorities that they have become not only the "truly needy" but the "truly forgotten." Poorly educated, untrained, unskilled—they simply will not be able to successfully compete in an increasingly sophisticated labor market. There will be increasing numbers in the more affluent sectors in our society who will perceive the connection between their frustration and despair and pandemic social disorders like violent crime and a loss of general civic peace. This will not be limited to a few "do-gooders." A growing number of the youth, although allegedly more conservative than a decade or two ago, will be recruited to this point of view. This could be the bridge that will bring together groups which otherwise seem so widely separated.

Much has been made already of an emerging Republican–Southern Democrat coalition emerging in the House of Representatives. This has been accompanied by the suggestion that the de facto coalition will become de jure when Southern Democrats formally switch their party allegiance. The election of a Democrat in a Mississippi district in a July by-election occasioned by the resignation of the Republican incumbent will probably serve to scotch those premature predictions. After all, what is sauce for the goose is sauce for the gander. If President Reagan can sweep to victory by attracting voters from both parties, why shouldn't Democratic congressmen continue to court Republicans by voting with the president while they continue to use the Democratic line to gain access to the ballot?

Another grouping of potentially greater significance, I believe, is made up of Midwestern and Northeastern congressmen from eighteen states who already number over 200, and who are formally organized and staffed as the Midwest-Northeast Coalition. They are concerned about federal tax policies that are accelerating the movement of investment capital away from the nation's economically distressed areas that they represent. They believe that defense procurement unfairly benefits the new and more rapidly growing areas of the South and West. They are resentful as well of the tax policies of these regions, where severance taxes and royalties from the production of oil, gas, and coal will bring an estimated $220 billion into the coffers of about nine states, again largely in the South and West. In votes on such items as the federal reimbursement formula for state expenditures under Medicaid, we have already seen a tilt along lines which pit the Frost Belt against the Sun Belt. This blurring of party loyalties in favor of a regional approach to policymaking decisions reflects the continued attenuation of the traditional partisan division along a Republican-Democratic axis.

An emerging coalition of opposition to the present administration may well come from a revival of environmental groups. Temporarily submerged by a tide of reaction to over-regulation of business, they are once again showing signs of new political activism. If Secretary of the Interior Watt persists in his avowed intentions to lease 200 million acres of offshore lands each year for the next five years, it is safe to predict that deeply held environmental concerns will eventually produce a bipartisan front of opposition which will not respond to pleas for party loyalty.

I have left until last an emerging coalition which could have a profound significance for future voting patterns. Under the impact of the huge military expenditures planned by the Reagan administration, coupled with its one-dimensional view of world problems as inspired by the Soviets and the Communist conspiracy, I predict a revival of a long-dormant peace movement. Resumption of the draft, which seems almost inevitable to man the kind of forces the present administration wants to create, would obviously accelerate the revival of this political force. However, even without reinstatement of the draft, there are gathering signs of a growing concern about the administration's foreign policy imperatives.

The new nationalism has yet to provoke the traditional testing of a new American president by the Soviets. It is difficult, despite growing signs of strains within the Soviet empire, to believe that this will not occur, for we are on a collision course. Current dissembling about willingness to negotiate a reduction of tensions cannot mask the administration's intention to pursue a hard-line policy. The explosive

ingredients are all there. A tactical retreat on El Salvador—
or seemingly a modulation of initial policy—is, to say the
least, inconclusive. The clear signs of rapprochement with
South Africa, although 40 percent of imported oil comes from
three African countries, Algeria, Libya, and Nigeria, are a
clearer indication that the Reagan administration looks out
at a bipolar world. Incipient criticism of a lack of clear and
pacific goals in foreign policy has already appeared. Some
has emanated from Democratic party circles, but increasingly it has demonstrated a reluctance to take sharp issue with
the president on our present paranoia. Witness the willingness of House Democrats to engage in one-upmanship in
defense spending during the battle on the spring budget
resolution.

I can foresee the emerging of a grand coalition of those left
behind in the administration's economic blueprint—youth,
more affluent upper-middle and higher income groups disturbed by growing signs of social pathology, and those concerned about our hawkish military and foreign policy. I do
not believe they will see one of the traditional parties as an
appropriate vehicle. The next campaign for the presidency
could be the forge on which they hammer out the synthesis
for an approach quite distinctive from that of either the Republican or the Democratic party. The constituent elements
of what I foresee as a "Grand Coalition" will initially develop
separately. But with the attenuation of party loyalties that
we have witnessed in recent years, it will eventually bring
together not only Independents, but will draw off many
nominal Republicans and Democrats as well. The process of
"party decomposition" of which Walter Dean Burnham
wrote many years ago has yet to run its course.

16

WALTER DEAN BURNHAM

Toward Confrontation?

The census, demographic and secular realignment, and the "democratic class struggle." Regional triage. Ideological coalitions. Reagan and the Republican Right. The new coalition. The "American dream." Political capitalism. Repealing the Great Society and the New Deal.

I

A number of analysts have begun to ask whether the 1980 election was one of those rare episodes in American political history, a critical election. There are some signs that it may have been (Clymer 1981, pp. 1, 62). In any case, this election was pretty clearly an important turning point in our modern political history. Whatever happens to the new Reagan coalition in the years ahead, American politics seems unlikely ever to return to its pre-1980 pattern.

Before discussing the political reasons for this judgment, we should pause to review another important domestic event of 1980: the census. In the aggregate, 17 congressional seats (and electoral votes) were transferred from the declining industrial Northeast and Midwest to the growing Sun Belt states of the South and West. Because of accelerated population movements out of central cities within states, the net political effect will be to transfer the lion's share of these seats from core-city, declining-sector liberal Democrats to suburban and small-town Republicans and conservative Democrats, with probably about a dozen falling to the Republicans in 1982.

The South and West are already areas of strong secular realignment toward the Republican party, at least in federal elections. The 1980 election demonstrated this realignment, and survey data show that it is still under way. One recent poll found a Republican gain in aggregate party identification from 1980 to 1981 of 11 percent in the South and West, compared with a national average of 8 percent.

The New Deal Democratic coalition, which lasted down through the 1960s, was based upon what Seymour Martin Lipset once called "the democratic class struggle" in highly concentrated metropolitan areas plus a solid South, reinforced by semiradical "colonial" support in much of the West. What the 1980 census ratifies is that the demographic conditions—and ultimately, the economic conditions—for this coalition have disappeared. The population is shifting away from its old industrial heartland, and the social and economic conditions which sustained the solid Democratic South have largely been abolished.

Obviously, as the problems of growth, inequality, and service delivery emerge in the newly favored regions, it can be expected that some form of "democratic class struggle" will develop there, overlain and crosscut by ethnic conflict. But it appears to be a sociologically defensible proposition that the present dispersal of the population tends to favor conservatism.

To this must be added the regional triage factor. Regional battles are likely to become major features of national political conflict, inside and outside Congress, irrespective of which president or party is in power. But under a conservative administration, the decline of the old industrial heartland will become more and more explicit. In particular, the vast increase in military consumption expenditures which is projected through mid-decade will considerably accelerate the transfer of wealth and power toward the South and West.

The major questions which the 1980 election presents turn upon the behavior of the American electorate, the peculiarities of each of the major parties, and the emergence of ideological politics as the politics not of the opposition, but of the coalition in power.

Survey evidence makes it abundantly clear that ideologically identifiable behavior at the mass level was little if any more widespread in 1980 than in earlier elections. Thirty-eight percent of Reagan supporters gave as their primary reason that "it is time for a change"; only 11 percent, that "he's a real conservative" (*New York Times* post-election survey, 9 November 1980, p. 28). To a large extent, the 1980 election was a retrospective judgment on the performance of the Carter administration. It is also worth remembering that both candidates were unpopular prior to the election, with Gallup reporting the lowest combined "very favorable" ratings since the beginning of the American Institute of Public Opinion's polls on this subject.

One would have thought that a largely nonideological and disaffected electorate would be unpromising material from which to construct an ideological coalition. Yet ideological politics is a keystone of the new coalition. Neither its dynamics nor its prospects can be comprehended if that fact is lost to view in the shadow of Ronald Reagan's charming, low-keyed personality. Ronald Reagan is not merely another conservative politician. He has long been a leading figure in the American Right. Some of the most conspicuous figures surrounding him in the executive, in Congress, and outside government are people who have had continuous and close links to what we used to call not so long ago the "Radical Right" (see Bell 1963; Lipset and Raab 1978). To be sure, the new power bloc contains many straightforward, old-style, economic conservatives and corporate plutocrats. It also, however, includes many "populists of the Right" who tend to represent small capital and the aggrieved middle class, and genuine Radical Right types like Interior Secretary Watt. Its dominant thrust is not old-conservative, or even Nixon-Ford conservative; it is Right-wing, and is deeply informed and guided by a comprehensive ideological program.

The Republican party is genuinely a party of the Right, and would be so understood in any comparative context. Even so, its domination by men with an ideological program cannot readily be explained within the usual incremen-talist/pluralist frames of reference so beloved of American political scientists. Nor would theorists of general party decline have prepared us for the remarkable consolidation around this Right-wing ideological pole which has occurred within the Republicans' ranks. *In power*, the new coalition represents something altogether new in the history of modern American politics. It is not incrementalist at all, even if it will no doubt have to make certain practical com-promises from time to time.

If the Republican party is clearly a party of the Right by any comparative standard, it has no Left counterpart in the American electoral market. Instead, there are the Demo-crats, the so-called "majority party." This party has never been even remotely a Left party in comparative terms. It is a patchwork aggregation of extremely diverse interests, ranging from some important sectors of big capital to ghetto blacks and industrial workers. This mix was reflected in the nature and policies of the Carter administration: conflicting, crosspressured, incoherent even below any ideological horizon, and ultimately offering little or nothing positive to the lower half of the American population. In defeat, this party and its intellectual proponents have shown an extraordinary demoralization verging on outright disintegration. This is one of the great questions posed by the 1980 election. What happened to this party and why? What kind of a "majority party" is it which falls apart at a single, if powerful, blow of adverse political fortune? How can the apparently invincible coalition of yesterday turn so swiftly into the paper tiger of today? If the chief question about the Republicans is their enthusiastic convergence behind a restorationist ideological program, the chief question about the Democrats is the converse—their manifest collapse into an incoherence restrained only by reaction to Reagan's dramatic policy challenges. The two questions are intimately connected.

II

This is a country which has been historically, and still is, dominated by one major tradition of political consciousness: individualist liberalism. The point has been made sufficiently often and persuasively to need no elaborate statement here. This belief system stands upon four pillars: property, liberty, democracy, and religion. The quest has been perennial for the realization of the "American dream" based upon these four pillars and upon the assumption of mass affluence.

For a generation after 1945 the United States seemed well on the way to realizing this "dream" in empirical fact—so much so that some analysts could perhaps be pardoned for assuming that the "end of ideology" had arrived. Unfortunately, this was based on an historical conjuncture which was as unprecedented as it proved temporary: American military and economic hegemony in the world, and the survival of cultural orthodoxies derived from an earlier era. In the 1970s the empire, the economy, and the culture were seen to be undermined, with unpleasant consequences for many Americans. What the average voter saw, increasingly, was a *loss of control.* Crime, violence, and indiscriminate hedonism appeared to dominate the cultural-social sphere. Runaway inflation, apparently lavish spending, and stagnant real incomes prevailed in the domestic economy. Completing the chain, Soviet expansionism, the rise of the Organization of Petroleum Exporting Countries, and humiliation at the hands of Iranian revolutionaries were leading facts of life on the international plane. This loss of control threatens—and more importantly, is widely seen to threaten—Americans' core values: the nuclear family, religious ideals, and ultimately the "American dream" itself. The swing to the right is an obvious response to such loss of control.

As a movement dedicated to restoring "the American dream" *despite everything,* the emerging coalition of the Right has three major ideological components—cultural preservationism, free-enterprise capitalism, and a militant if comparatively liberal imperialism linked with anti-Sovietism. To be brief, we shall confine the discussion below to some of the economic issues and their setting.

III

In any capitalist society, an enduring tension exists between profitable investment and mass consumption. Attempts by governments to maximize either of these desirables tend to put pressure on the other, and thus on the stability of the political economy as a whole. The lessons of 1929 suggest that unregulated market capitalism cannot successfully manage this tension and that, absent interventionist public policy, it is plagued by overwhelming problems of underconsumption and disequilibrium. The lessons of the 1970s suggest that the state's pursuit of mass consumption strategies to maintain a politically acceptable social balance—"political capitalism"—compromises the capacity of the economic system to accumulate capital. On this point there is now a remarkably broad consensus among economists who otherwise differ sharply in their analyses and policy prescriptions.

The strategies of political capitalism depended on the economic pie growing at least as rapidly as the demands on its resources. Central to all political capitalism, and especially to its American variant, was the denial of the fundamental contradiction between accumulation and consumption. More positively, the assumption was that social harmony could and would exist so long as the state compensated for the inadequacies of market capitalism without touching the core of capitalism itself. This was what most Americans wanted to hear. In our halcyon days of international ascendancy and rapid economic growth, political capitalism marched hand in hand with the status of the Democrats as the majority party. The 1970s were marked by the destruction of the assumptions on which political capitalism was based. With political capitalism thus discredited, the path was clear for a return to "basics" which had long been the Republicans' stock-in-trade. This party ratified its acceptance of Right-wing ideology by nominating Ronald Reagan. His election marked the bankruptcy of the old order. But it has also challenged him and his market-ideology allies to deliver on their promise to restore the "American dream."

IV

If this analysis is on the right track, it seems probable that the implementation of the policies specific to the ruling ideology will provoke a politics of confrontation. For, in order to realize its purposes, the Reagan coalition must not only repeal the Great Society and some parts of the New Deal. *It must necessarily and explicitly repeal the theory and practice of social harmony which underlay both.* There are many Americans who will not relish the practical consequences.

This conclusion may well be resisted. After all, Ronald Reagan has truly remarkable gifts in the field of symbolic collective bonding. Patriotism, the flag, the "American way of life," and capitalism are values as pervasive as they are profound. But in the end, they are unlikely to conceal the fact that the Reagan administration is making explicit choices promoting the well-being of some Americans at the expense of others. Indeed, it must do this if it is to be true to its ideological principles.

If supply-side economics is associated with a resumption of growth and widely desired social and imperial control, this new coalition may dominate American politics for a long time to come. If it is not, rhetoric about American values will not suffice to contain the political damage. The pressures on America to "rejoin world history," foretold a quarter-century ago by Louis Hartz, are now overwhelming. So are the resistances within our political culture. The Reagan administration is now, in its turn, the vortex of this clash between apparently irresistible forces and immovable objects. If it also fails, then *both* the Democrats' political capitalism and the Republicans' market capitalism will have achieved bankruptcy together. In all likelihood, this would at some point turn the contemporary vacuum of political leadership and popular support into an outright crisis of the regime itself.

17

MICHAEL HARRINGTON

The Prospects for
Reaganomics

**Economic failure and political success—Roosevelt and
Reagan.** *Laissez-faire dirigisme* **in the current adminis-
tration. Liberal concepts in a conservative program.
The tax cut. Carter, Kennedy, Nixon, Ford. The
Thatcher/Reagan comparison. Reagan ideology and its
opposition.**

The election of Ronald Reagan in 1980 brought to the United
States a political phenomenon it has never really known in
the twentieth century: a completely ideological government.

Reagan likes to compare himself to Franklin Roosevelt,
another president who came to power during a time of structural economic and social crisis. Leaving aside the obvious

dissonance in this comparison—that Roosevelt was a liberal and Reagan is a conservative—it is most instructive to regard the two men in terms of their attitude toward political programs. Roosevelt was, of course, elected after a campaign in which he did not mention anything remotely resembling either the first or the second New Deals. He did, however, attack Herbert Hoover from the Right, charging that the Depression was in some measure a consequence of excessive federal spending.

Once in office, the centerpiece of Roosevelt's first period was the National Industrial Recovery Act (NIRA) and the National Recovery Administration (NRA). That was, to be sure, based on a theory—produced by the *dirigiste* wing of American business—which saw unrestrained competition as the cause of the crash and regulated monopoly planning as the proper response. At the same time, Roosevelt set in motion a vast public employment program, but he did so primarily as a relief measure and not out of any commitment to a Keynesian analysis—not the least because Keynesianism remained *terra incognita* for him throughout his entire life.

When the Supreme Court declared the NIRA unconstitutional, Roosevelt was being challenged by radical-Rightist movements (Huey Long, Father Coughlin and, much more ambiguously, by the old-age organization led by Francis Townsend). He therefore pragmatically moved to the second New Deal—the Wagner Act, Social Security, and other welfare-state measures. However, neither he nor the Congress knew that they were creating a "welfare state." For instance, the Social Security bill assumed that the private economy would provide jobs for those under sixty-five; "relief" was a temporary expedient, and Aid for Dependent Children, an afterthought.

In 1936 Roosevelt campaigned on the basis of a pre-Keynesian promise to cut back on the deficit. Following that policy was one of the reasons for the extremely sharp downturn of late 1936 and 1937, a recession within the

Depression; as is well known, the end of mass unemployment did not come until Dr. Win-the-War had taken over from Dr. New Deal during World War II. The New Deal, then, was improvised, pragmatic, untheoretical—the work of a man who, Oliver Wendell Holmes once said, had a second-rate intellect and a first-rate temperament.

Ronald Reagan is almost the exact opposite case. Not only did he run on a radical, experimental, economic platform, in the first months of his administration he managed—with greater political skill than had been seen in Washington since the days of Lyndon Johnson—to pass much of it into law.

The fact that Reaganomics are contradictory does not change this judgment. For the fact is that Reagan has presented the warring elements in his program as interrelated parts of a coherent vision. That they are inconsistent will have much to do with the administration's failure, but it does not alter the ideological nature of the government which proposes them.

As president, Reagan adopted an extremely optimistic version of Kennedy Keynesianism in the form of a three-year, 25 percent across-the-board, personal income-tax cut and a series of concessions to corporations which move toward the abolition of the corporate income tax. He simultaneously embraced Milton Friedman monetarism, praising the Federal Reserve for pursuing a deflationary strategy which had yielded the highest interest rates in recent American history, and he sharply reduced social spending while proposing an arms build-up which, by some measures, is more rapid than that undertaken during the Vietnam War. He did so in the name of what may be called *laissez-faire dirigisme*.

Reagan is *dirigiste*, since neither he nor any conservative economist living in the real world wants a market determination of, say, capital funds. Rather, he uses federal power to rig capital markets so as to increase the monies available to the private sector. Since this strategy is private-sector oriented, it can claim to be *laissez faire*; but it achieves—or rather, proposes to achieve—those private-sector outcomes by means of *dirigiste* legislation. The price of capital is already an artificial construct depending very much upon depreciation allowances, tax policy, Federal Reserve actions, etc. Reagan has made no move to change that system, but he has radically reoriented it, putting liberal structures and concepts at the service of conservative ends.

The most radical innovation in this tactic is the tax cut. Although it is justified in the name of the success of the Kennedy-Johnson reduction of the 1960s, it is introduced under completely different circumstances—above all, in a time of chronic inflation, totally unlike the years of almost imperceptible price increases under Kennedy—and with an ideologically motivated emphasis upon giving more money to the rich than the liberal Democrats ever did (though it should be noted that the rich were the prime beneficiaries under Kennedy and Johnson, too). Thus, the economic policy of the greatest power in the world has been made to depend upon a series of extremely ideological assumptions which have never been put to any kind of a test: that the rich and the corporations will use the funds being made available to them for job-generating investments and not for speculation; that the nonrich will be spurred to work harder by the possibility of even higher after-tax incomes. In theory, this will produce a boom, led by capital investment and fueled by individual productivity.

The fate of this program will determine the political meaning of the 1980 elections—i.e., the numerical results of the vote are in and Reagan is president, but the meaning of his presidency, what happened in November 1980, will not be determined for at least a year. Before turning to the difficult question of how one will determine success or failure of Reagan's initiative, a word about the liberal Democratic opposition.

It is clear that 1980—or rather, the Carter presidency—

marked the exhaustion of traditional liberalism as it has been defined since Franklin Roosevelt. The underlying theory of liberal economic policy—that unemployment and inflation moved in opposite directions and therefore could be "traded off" against one another—ceased to operate in 1970 (the reasons for that development are detailed in my book, *Decade of Decision* [1980]). The only serious attempt to face up to this fact in the 1980 campaign—and it did not, in my opinion, go far enough—was Senator Edward Kennedy's advocacy of price and wage controls. That had the merit of recognizing that the nation faced a structural problem in stagflation, one that could not be resolved by some variant of the standard liberal policy. It was limited, however, in that it did not attack some of the basic causes of that shift (among them, corporate price-fixing power, the most expensive health system in the Western world, agricultural subsidies which put tax funds to work raising the costs of food).

Carter became the standard-bearer of the Democratic tradition, even though his identification with it was quite weak. And yet—and here an important paradox emerges—the conservatives, the most ideological political movement to reach the center of major-party politics in this century as well as the most radical innovators in economic policy, managed to convince a significant portion of the electorate that their liberal opponents were radical ideologists. Few noticed that the Carter presidency had been without any organizing theme in domestic questions, or that the Great Society had been applauded vigorously by *Fortune* magazine and other organs of the business press, not the least because it had been based upon the notion of a partnership between big business and the federal government.

So it was that the thesis launched by Richard Nixon right after the 1972 elections—that the 1960s failed because Washington "threw money at problems"—was approved by the majority of the voters in 1980. The fact that the largest deficits occurred under the Nixon-Ford administrations, and that they were the effect, rather than the cause, of the crisis, was overlooked. Indeed, the Democrats themselves were half-convinced that they had been wrong, which was one reason why their alternative tax bill in 1981 was 95 percent Reaganite and, in terms of some of its concessions to the corporate rich, 110 percent Reaganite. And that points to two liberal possibilities in the years ahead, both of them fraught with political consequences.

On the one hand, the Democratic liberals could adopt a tactic of waiting for Republican failure without developing any alternative to Reaganomics. This tactic would be based on the judgment that the Republicans' extremely ideological politics would end up by discrediting any ideology whatsoever. Or there could be a movement from within the Democratic party to frame a new alternative, a counterideology to Reagan's and a replacement for the Roosevelt-to-Johnson tradition. In the immediate aftermath of the 1980 elections, it was the first course that prevailed. Since I am convinced that the structural crisis of the system will not respond to either the Reagan approach or to a liberal pragmatism in the time of radical transformations, this is the variant which provides the worst of all worlds.

But is it guaranteed that Reagan will fail? That, it seems to me, is the crucial question for one trying to analyze the 1980 elections. If the new administration's contradictory mix of radically conservative policies actually functions to end, or to seriously ameliorate, the worst economic crisis in a generation, I have little doubt that the Republican party will become the majority party for the next generation. In that sense, all of the classic preconditions for a realignment are at hand—a major issue that cannot be resolved in the old way, a breakdown of traditional loyalties, the entrance of new political forces into the electorate, a new alternative—and if Reagan could prove to be the master of events, he would indeed be the functional equivalent of Franklin Roosevelt.

But note once more how ambiguous that analogy is.

Roosevelt did not end the Great Depression; in 1939, when the shift from New Deal to War Deal began, unemployment in the United States still ran at around 15 percent. To be sure, the New Deal had reduced the jobless rate by 40 percent, but that still left millions in the street. My point is that it is not objective economic performance which is decisive, but economic performance as it is perceived by the electorate. Working people, even those who were still out of a job, were willing to forgive Roosevelt his failures because they saw them as outweighed by his successes; they focused upon the 40 percent reduction in unemployment rather than the 60 percent persistence of it. The issue, then, is not whether Ronald Reagan will fail—of that, I have little doubt—but whether he will be seen to have failed.

The new administration fears, of course, any comparison of its future to Margaret Thatcher's past and present. And indeed, there are significant differences between the United Kingdom and the United States which make any facile equation of Reagan with Thatcher questionable. And yet, if I may hazard a prediction at a time when all such anticipations of the future have become quite problematic, I believe that the essential and underlying failure of the British conservatives will be repeated in the United States. Mrs. Thatcher has run aground on a combination of large deficits and tight money, a fact which has earned her criticisms from some of her monetarist gurus who believe that she has not been sufficiently mean in her social policy. And I am convinced that an American variant of the same phenomenon is in the making, that Mr. Reagan's tax cuts and military spending will increase the federal shortfall while his monetarism will paralyze the private sector.

That does not mean, however, that I predict that the 1980 elections will therefore be decided retrospectively against those who were its nominal victors. Political consequences do not, as I have noted, follow inevitably from economic trends. I would therefore define two major possible futures (and expect that reality would, in its sloppy way, mix them up). On the one hand, there could be Reaganite economic failure and political success, somewhat on the Roosevelt model, with liberal indecisiveness providing a critical element for the latter component—i.e., the president would look quite good by comparison with any serious alternatives. On the other hand, the failure of the Reagan economic program could force American liberalism and its chosen instrument, the Democratic party, to take a more radical course. In that case, the emergence of an extremely ideological presidency would have the effect of conjuring up a rather ideological opposition. That variant would mean the most significant shift in American politics since the Civil War.

In either case, however, there is a fundamental judgment which holds true. The 1980 elections were not a mandate for the new but a repudiation of the old liberalism as it came to be incarnated by Jimmy Carter. Whether that vote turns out to be an endorsement of the basic revisions in economic and social policy carried out by the most ideological president in this century depends upon events which are partly, but only partly, beyond his control. He will fail economically, of that I am sure; but whether that failure will be perceived politically by the electorate is another question. The 1980 polls are still open.

18

HOWARD PHILLIPS

More Independent Presidential Candidacies?

The 1984 election prospects—Democratic, Republican, Left-liberal, Independent. Influences on the electorate. Ronald Reagan. George Bush. Major-party and independent candidates—John Anderson, George Wallace, Eugene McCarthy. Conservative groups and their opportunities. Community-based activism. The challenge of redirecting U.S. politics.

In 1984 many American voters will ask themselves: "Am I better off than I was four years ago?"

If the answer is a decisive yes, the incumbent president, barring some significant personal disqualification, will be reelected, and the Republican party will enjoy continued gains in subpresidential elections.

In that case, the Democrats, their own Left-liberal inclinations at the national level somewhat moderated by (a) political reality and (b) the desire for reelection of their congressional incumbents, will probably have to contend with an electorally significant Left-liberal independent presidential candidacy.

So long as the electorate is hopeful about the future and reasonably satisfied with the present under the Republicans, the Democrats are threatened by a political realignment which would make theirs a minority "me too" party frequently confronted by disabling challenges from the Left, particularly in presidential campaigns.

Interestingly, in such pro-Republican circumstances, the possibilities for quadrennial assaults from the Left would be greater than those from the Right, despite the absence of majority support for basic Left-wing premises and policies (e.g., anti-American nationalism, the expansionary state, equality of result, separation of law from morality, class representation, and the politicization of intermediary institutions).

The reasons why such Left-based assaults on Democratic candidates in an era of Republican ascendance may succeed (in causing defeat) include (a) likely support within the media, the academy, and other Establishment elites with power to heavily influence the shaping of the national agenda, and (b) the organizational clout available because of continued federal funding (through VISTA [Volunteers in Service to America], the Legal Services Corporation, the Community Services Administration, the Department of Education, and many other federal agencies) of tens of thousands of full-time Leftist activists who would be emotionally sympathetic to such an assault.

But what if the electorate is not "hopeful about the future and reasonably satisfied with the present" in 1984?

What if uncontrolled inflation is eroding the dreams of a better life for those whose support is essential to Republican political strength? What if high interest rates have destroyed the life's work of millions of small and middle-sized farmers and businessmen? What if taxation, despite a reduction in its rate of growth, is more oppressive than ever?

And what if—despite Ronald Reagan's eloquent anti-Soviet rhetoric—continued reliance on arms control and detentist economic policies, combined with the failure to implement an effective strategy of military renewal, leads to an ever more obvious and dangerous weakening of our strategic position, not least of all in the Caribbean and the Gulf of Mexico?

In that case, if President Reagan is seeking reelection, while his personal popularity may remain sufficiently high to assure his personal success on voting day, the prospect of a moderate conservative majority—expressed through the Republican party—taking hold in the Congress will have been vastly, perhaps irretrievably, diminished.

Indeed, if George Bush were the GOP presidential nominee in 1984 and such dire circumstances prevailed, it would be not merely possible but likely that a conservative challenge to his election would be undertaken in order to distinguish the conservative cause from the policies of the incumbent Republican administration. Even without such a challenge, in the circumstances described, Mr. Bush would be vulnerable to defeat.

There are many conservatives who believe that, even (or, perhaps, especially) if a contest for the GOP nomination or an independent conservative presidential candidacy were likely to prove decisive in causing Mr. Bush's defeat, it should be supported in order to preserve the possibility of authentic conservative political dominance at some future point.

Given the present political situation, a conservative candidacy in opposition to Mr. Bush would be far more likely to be mounted through an independent presidential campaign than within the Republican party.

Certainly, if Bush is the incumbent president at the time of the 1984 GOP convention, it is hard to imagine that he would have an intraparty challenger as formidable as was Ronald Reagan when he opposed President Gerald Ford's nomination in 1976.

Even as merely a sitting vice-president, Bush would be quite difficult to successfully oppose inside the GOP, absent some now unforeseen issue or event. Bush's intraparty advantages, should he run for president in 1984, are considerable.

First of all, liberal Republicans—while not by any means a GOP majority—have significant residual strength in the Republican national nominating process. Indeed, when their candidate has a moderate and partisan reputation, they can often be in striking distance of victory (as Bush was against Reagan during much of the 1980 campaign).

But Bush has a lot more than that going for him in terms of clinching the 1984 GOP nomination: (a) a White House chief of staff (James Baker) who was Bush's campaign manager; (b) operational control of significant executive branch patronage resources; (c) a presidential organization prebuilt in 1980; (d) Ronald Reagan's seal of approval, conferred by his 1980 selection of Bush to run for vice-president; (e) President Reagan's muting of issues which tend to divide conservative and liberal Republicans; and (f) the tendency of Republican activists to subordinate ideology to partisanship in pursuit of electoral success, thus diminishing the prospect for a winning challenge primarily premised on distinctions of policy.

For all these reasons, a victorious intraparty challenge to a "Bush for President" bid in 1984 is unlikely. And the kind of political leader prepared to mount a campaign in pursuit of goals other than immediate victory is probably going to recognize that his or her opportunity for service may be greater outside the GOP than within it.

It is increasingly clear that one need not, in the future, be the candidate of a major political party to win the presidency. Political parties no longer have a monopoly on the two required elements of such success: ballot access and media recognition. Only in their continuing ability to confer "legitimacy" can parties make a unique contribution. And, in the right circumstances, legitimacy, too, can be acquired by an independent candidate.

In 1980 John Anderson won ballot access and media recognition to a degree unprecedented for a presidential candidate. However, as a candidate simultaneously lacking "charisma," a major popular constituency, a major issue, and a geographic base, there were limits to his potential. In recent years both George Wallace and Eugene McCarthy have been the real pioneers of presidential politicking outside the boundaries of the two established parties—Wallace combining personal appeal and issues with an electoral college base, and McCarthy adding his considerable charm and intellect to what was at least a retrospective national constituency.

What might have happened in 1976 if Ronald Reagan had written off the GOP nomination, gained ballot position in all fifty states, and divided the November vote with Gerald Ford and Jimmy Carter? With name recognition, a national constituency, and a Sun Belt electoral base, Governor Reagan would have been formidable. Only the lack of a legitimating mechanism or event (e.g., participation in pre-election debates), in my view, might have denied him the presidency in the circumstances of that year.

But even if Ronald Reagan had been elected as an independent in 1976, the long-term impact of his success would have been as uncertain as his short-term relationships with Republicans and Democrats in the Congress during the period of his tenure.

Conservatives in 1976 did not yet have the resources to successfully contend on the same field with the major parties, the national media, and the other hierarchical elements of an entrenched liberal Establishment.

In 1984, even without an independent presidential candidate as renowned and established as was the former governor of California in 1976, conservatives could wage a campaign organizationally far more potent than any of which we were capable even five years ago.

Furthermore, our grass-roots base, communications, and leadership network are now of an order sufficient to permit a conservative president, elected independently of party, to govern effectively, in terms of both congressional and popular support.

With the fall of Nixon, the idea that conservatives could best advance their cause by partisan loyalty and uncritical acceptance of incumbent decisions was easier to challenge. Fidelity to principle and policy objective made a lot more sense with the demythologization of the man who, since the 1950s, had been the instrument of many conservative hopes.

Single-issue concerns during the 1970s inspired the formation of many new conservative groups and the strengthening of many already on the scene. Led by activists unchained by either partisanship or careerism, conservatives felt free to challenge the "consensus, compromise, conciliation, and cooperation" liberalism of Gerald Ford, and to bring pressure on Republicans as well as Democrats when dissatisfied.

New Right leaders—declining to accept as a self-concept the liberal view of conservatives as representing nothing more than the Right wing of the Republican party, permitted by direct mail to communicate with the like-minded on their own terms and to gather resources adequate to sustain a steadily expanding professional corps—reached out to working Americans regardless of party, seeking to build a nonpartisan coalition which would tie together pro—free market, pro-defense, and pro-family elements. The New Right consciously sought to develop its own research institutions, leadership networks, public-interest law firms, political action committees, publications, and lobbies, paralleling the array of extra-party organizations existing on the Left.

Partly in response to the legal restrictions and imperatives of the Federal Election Law Amendments of 1974, such entities developed in greater number and variety than might otherwise have been the case.

The New Right recognized the strategic weakness of fighting on a national battlefield where the unorganized conservative "general interest" would likely continue to be politically overpowered by the federally subsidized, Establishment-reinforced, particular-interest groups of Great Society liberalism. It encouraged grass-roots organization and efforts to influence Congress through action at the state and congressional-district levels. Strategically, the goal was 435 local congressional-district political battlefields instead of a single national field of conflict.

Political outcomes are shaped by competing armies of activists more than by majorities of passive sympathizers. Liberalism's national institutional advantages could best be countered through the local mobilization of conservative, issue-oriented activists.

Even without national positions of strength in Big Media, Big Business, Big Law Firms, Big Labor, Big Education, Big Banks, or Big Bureaucracy, conservatives could succeed by asserting superior political energy at a critical point: the grass-roots electoral arena.

Conservative activists at the community level, assisted by new national support groups (such as the Heritage Foundation, the Conservative Caucus, the National Conservative Political Action Committee [NCPAC], and the Committee for the Survival of a Free Congress) could do what the liberals had done nationally for years: (a) set the agenda for debate, (b) recruit and train leaders, (c) lobby successfully on significant legislative issues, and (d) create a popular perspective on incumbent performance consistent with their own philosophical criteria.

The rise of the Moral Majority and similar groups, which have been able to recruit activists motivated by value-oriented concerns, contributed mightily to this strategy of community-based action. In the age of television, real community in America exists primarily in only three areas: the place of education, the place of work, and the place of worship. Of these three, only at the place of worship does there generally exist continuing community, with shared values.

In 1977 and 1978 conservatives demonstrated their ability to hinge the national political debate on one of their overriding concerns: the proposed surrender of the U.S. canal and zone at Panama. Although defeated in Washington, conservatives were victorious in the country. Three incumbent liberals—Clark, Haskell, and McIntyre—fell in 1978, in large part because of that issue (another contributing factor was the right-to-life issue, also raised by conservative activists). By 1981, 29 pro—Canal Treaty senators had returned to private life.

Again, in 1979 and 1980, the New Right generated the principal opposition to ratification of SALT II, helping make Jimmy Carter's national security policies a major issue, not just in the presidential contest, but in the increasingly visible (thanks to NCPAC) Senate races as well. The national media and liberal pressure groups no longer had a monopoly in deciding the referendum questions which help determine electoral outcomes.

The Reagan victory of 4 November 1981, combined with the 13-seat Senate turnover, make possible an historic redirection of American politics. But inadequate response to the challenge is also possible. The danger for conservatives is that their cause will be judged without having been tried.

Can U.S. strategic survivability be achieved so long as the Reagan administration continues the Carter policy of adhering to the expired provisions of SALT I and the unratified terms of SALT II? These treaties perpetuate a decisive Soviet strategic superiority as a result of which U.S. retaliatory forces and the American people are presently in grave jeopardy.

Can the economic future of the average American be viewed optimistically when, in fiscal year 1981, the federal deficit as of 30 May 1981 already totalled $64.44 billion, with four full months remaining in that twelve-month budget period? Is it not necessary to do more than reduce the increase in federal spending if we're serious about controlling inflation and reducing high interest rates (caused by federal credit demands to offset multibillion-dollar deficits)?

Can a conservative electoral mandate ever be converted to public policy, so long as the federal government continues to provide, each year, billions of dollars to Left-wing activist groups which are anti-family, anti-defense, and anti—free market?

The body politic is suffering from cancer (a liberal disease), and seems ready to take the advice of its new doctors — even if major surgery is prescribed. The danger is that the Reagan-Bush doctors, amid much self-congratulation for daring, may yet lack the nerve to do all that is necessary to cure the patient. If the cancer persists, having only been trimmed rather than removed, the still breathing but less comfortable patient will, after a certain time, put new doctors in charge.

To forestall acquiescence in a Leftist prescription, if the New Right believes the Reagan-Bush Republican remedy to be inadequate to the challenge, it will be necessary to offer dissent while the patient (the body politic) can still hear. In that way, hope will endure that the patient can yet be cured if he knows where to turn for assistance and is not yet in the clutches of medicine men from the Democratic Left. That is why an independent conservative presidential campaign in 1984 is very possible.

19

NORMAN PODHORETZ

The New
American Majority*

Comparing the elections of 1972 and 1980. Left and Right politicians. Carter/McGovern; Reagan/Nixon. The mandate: a realignment? Economics and foreign policy. Drawing the line. The Republican opportunity.

Reagan was bound to win the 1980 election, and to win by a very large margin. To understand why this was so, we have to go back to Nixon's overwhelming victory in 1972. He carried all but one of the fifty states, whereas Reagan only took forty-four, and Nixon's lead in the popular vote (20 points) was twice as large as Reagan's. But Nixon enjoyed all the ad-

*Condensed from an article published in *Commentary*.

vantages of an incumbent president. For a challenger, running as the candidate of the minority party and with a well-financed independent also in the race, to carry such opposition strongholds as New York and Massachusetts and to get 51 percent of the popular vote—10 percent more than the sitting president—represents an impressive landslide. And if we add to this the fact that Reagan's triumph was accompanied by the first Republican sweep of the Senate in twenty-five years, we can say that what the 1980 landslide lacked in numerical spread, it compensated for in depth.

The differences aside, the resemblance between 1972 and 1980 is striking. There has recently been much talk about the collapse of the old Roosevelt coalition and a consequent realignment, as though this were the news of the 1980 election. Yet Nixon's 1972 inroads into many of the major constituencies of the old Roosevelt coalition were so dramatic that the "new Republican majority" seemed indeed to have emerged in that election. The parallels with 1980 are obvious. Like Nixon, Reagan carried the Catholics and half of the blue-collar vote, and he did as well as Nixon with blacks and somewhat better with Jews.

Those who had been responsible for the Democratic debacle in 1972 were quick to blame it on McGovern's failings as a candidate. But the reality of 1972 was that the Democratic party had fallen into the hands of people whose ideas and attitudes were out of tune with a majority of the voters, including a very substantial proportion of traditional Democrats. The political perspective of these new "McGovernite" liberals represented a bowdlerized version of the ideas and attitudes of the radical movement of the 1960s. As such, it came into direct conflict with the traditional liberalism of the Democratic party. Indeed, it had been in opposition, not to conservatism or to the Republicans, but to the liberalism of the Democrats that the radical movement of the 1960s defined itself.

In foreign policy, liberal Democrats up until 1968 believed

in the use of U.S. power to contain the spread of Communism in general and Soviet expansionism in particular; in economic policy, they believed in growth as the means to general prosperity; and in social policy, they believed in eradicating discrimination against individuals as the best route to social justice.

In each of these areas, the radical movement repudiated the liberal position. In foreign policy, it attacked the use of American power to contain Communism as politically ill advised and morally wrong; in economic policy, it attacked growth as destructive of the quality of life of working people and of the quality of the physical environment; and in social policy, it attacked equality of opportunity as an instrument of "tokenism."

The result was that, by the end of the 1960s, the old-time liberals within the Democratic party were badly demoralized. Their leader, Lyndon Johnson, had been forced to resign from the presidency, and though they had managed to win the nomination for Hubert Humphrey in 1968, they had been unable to win the election; four years later, they were even unable to win the nomination. The Leftist insurgents had taken over the party. They also took over the title of "liberal"—not so long before, a term of derision on radical lips, but indispensable to success in mainstream American politics. Those who remained liberals in the older sense were now called "neoconservatives," and nothing they could say or do succeeded in shaking off the label.

Yet the Leftists' victory was a pyrrhic one. Having humiliated their centrist rivals within the Democratic party, they were themselves humiliated by Richard Nixon; they only managed to get 40 percent of the vote against a man who was not exactly popular.

In 1976 the party chose a candidate whose virtues were mainly negative; he belonged neither to the centrists nor to the Leftists. This advantage carried over into the general election. Carter ran not so much against Gerald Ford or the

Republican party as against "Washington." By this he meant, and was understood to mean, that he no more belonged to the Democrats with their taint of McGovernism than to the Republicans with their taint of Watergate. And so he was elected.

As it turned out, however, he did belong to the Democrats—specifically, to the McGovernite wing of the party. In exercising unilateral "restraint" in both the maintenance and the deployment of American power, Carter stuck with scarcely a single deviation to the McGovernite line in international affairs. And if the McGovernism was less visible in the domestic arena, it was there in the continued resort to quotas and in the administration's general tone. Carter and his apologists told us that we could do nothing about the relative decline of our military and economic power. They said it was inevitable, the result of vast historical forces, and that when we finally made peace with it we would wind up in a better and more secure position in the world.

Then came Iran. Carter's response to an incredible insult to the nation of which he was president looked—and was— weak enough in its own right to establish his administration's McGovernism. The seizure of the hostages confronted the nation with an image of its own impotence so concrete and so vivid that denial or obfuscation became impossible.

If Carter 1980 was an updated version of McGovern 1972, who was Ronald Reagan? Carter thought that Reagan was another Goldwater and therefore easy to beat. But actually, Reagan represented an updated version of Nixon 1972. As personalities, Reagan and Nixon could not be farther apart. As a political figure, however, Reagan was unmistakably offering himself as the legitimate heir to Nixon's usurped throne. And in winning the Republican nomination, he demonstrated that there was indeed a demand in the party to reconstitute the new majority that Nixon had coaxed into emerging but that he had never had a chance to consolidate.

Writing in support of McGovern shortly before the 1972

election, Arthur Schlesinger, Jr., had attributed "the disquietudes of the nation" to a widespread "disgust with the way things have recently been managed in this country." The truth, however, was that the disgust most Americans were indeed feeling in 1972 had nothing whatever to do with the way the Nixon administration had been managing things. It was almost entirely a disgust, as Elizabeth Hardwick (a supporter of McGovern, but unlike Schlesinger, capable of disinterested observation) described it at the time,

for show-off students, for runaways, for attacks on the family and the system, for obscenity, for pot, for prisoner-pity, for dropping out, for tuning in, for radical chic, for storefront lawyers, for folk singers, for muggings, for addicts, for well-to-do Wasps grogged on charity binges.

Matching this wave of cultural disgust, as I myself added in a postelection analysis,

was a wave of political disgust directed against the bureaucrats, the lawyers, and the judges who in the name of what they considered racial justice were taking it upon themselves to order the busing of children from one school to another, the building of public-housing projects in middle-class neighborhoods, and the institution of job quotas for accredited "minorities."

The new majority was made up of people, among them large numbers of Democrats, who shared in these sentiments of disgust and who felt that the Republican party agreed with them and the Democratic party did not.

Eight years later some of the items on these lists were period pieces, evoking nostalgia rather than passion. But the general picture, reinforced by the addition of several new elements like gay liberation and abortion, remained the same. And so did the disgust, which had, if anything, grown in proportion to the spread of the new culture to larger and larger areas of American society. As Nixon had before him, Ronald Reagan spoke for those disgusted.

With his nomination, the stage was so clearly set for a resumption of the trends interrupted by Watergate that the landslide which followed would have been absolutely predict-able if not for one question: whether, because of his age or because of his reputation as a simpleminded actor, Reagan the individual might be rejected, even by an electorate clamoring for "Reaganism." The age factor was disposed of during the primaries and was scarcely ever mentioned dur-ing the election itself. The issue of simplemindedness en-joyed a somewhat long life span. During the first two weeks or so of the campaign, the entire journalistic fraternity of the United States seemed to be engaged in a frantic hunt for "gaffes" in Reagan's speeches and statements. Then sud-denly—and quite mysteriously—the "gaffe" story died, and the journalistic fraternity began attacking Carter for the "meanness" of his campaign against Reagan.

Yet the Reagan victory cannot be understood in terms of Carter's unpopularity alone. There was a powerful positive message in the Reagan campaign to which the American people were very decidedly in a mood to respond. It was this: the decline of America, far from being inevitable, is a conse-quence of bad policies and can therefore be reversed by shift-ing to other policies. What we need is an economic policy that will unleash the productive energies of an artificially ham-pered people, a program of rearmament that will strengthen our defenses and provide us with the power to contain Soviet expansionism, and a legal structure that will encourage the revitalization of values of "family, work, and neighborhood." In electing Ronald Reagan, the American people announced that they were willing—nay, eager—to begin moving in this direction.

Although Reagan's vote amounted to only 26.7 percent of the eligible electorate, this was only 3.4 percent less than Franklin Roosevelt got in 1932. It was clearly not a mandate to press for every constitutional amendment proposed by the Moral Majority, or to enact a particular schedule of tax cuts, or to raise the defense budget by a certain figure. But it did reflect an intense yearning to make the country productive and powerful once more.

Many Democrats are trying to persuade themselves that 1980 will not mark a historic realignment. Within a year or two, they say, the voters will discover that Reagan can do nothing about inflation or unemployment or American vulnerabilities abroad, and they will then turn on him as they turned on Carter. Even some of Reagan's own supporters take this view. "We'll be a majority party," said Congressman Jack Kemp of New York, "when we implement the policies that will bring about the prosperity and the full employment without inflation we have promised. If we fail, this will not turn out to be a significant election."

With all due respect to this bipartisan consensus, I would say that it misreads the election. In the first place, the notion that the economic issue—inflation and unemployment— was the decisive factor seems to me mistaken. No doubt there is a great deal of anxiety over inflation, but the truth is that it has not yet begun to hurt enough people badly enough to fuel serious political passions. Unemployment is also a great anxiety, but it concerns many fewer people than inflation, and it no longer has as much political significance as it did in the 1930s. In my judgment, economic conditions contributed to the landslide as one more symptom of national decline, not on their own account. To an extent unprecedented in American electoral experience, economics and foreign policy were tied together—a fact reflected in the unprecedented levels of concern with foreign and defense policy that showed up in survey data.

My second objection follows from this view of how the American people perceived the economic issues. I would guess that so long as an impression is created of movement toward a resurgence of American power in the most general sense, the new majority will remain in place even if Reagan's economic policies are less than fully successful in the next two or three years. The main reason I believe this to be the case is that the atmosphere surrounding the Reagan victory has been amazingly benign. The relatively kind treatment

Reagan began to receive in the media during the later stages of the campaign has spilled over and swelled into a mood of titillated expectancy such as has not been felt since the election of John F. Kennedy, even among commentators whom one would expect to be hostile.

The one truly dark cloud in the otherwise sunny sky smiling over Ronald Reagan's election concerns the Moral Majority. On issues like abortion and homosexuality, even many people who voted for Reagan are genuinely worried about a wave of bigotry and repression. On these issues, moreover, many liberals seem to have been energized rather than demoralized, as witness the rash of postelection public statements by such groups as the American Civil Liberties Union, who see in the Moral Majority a threat "to every principle of liberty that underlies the American system of government."

Nevertheless, even here, one senses the presence of an opposing current—a feeling, almost, of relief at the thought that now, at least, a line will be drawn to keep things from going further than they already have gone. The liberal culture of recent years had been unable to draw any such line; it may not be altogether averse to having the dirty work done by others—while, of course, deploring and disclaiming any responsibility.

If, then, 1980 was, as the *Economist* nicely put it, "the election that Watergate postponed," and if it really did signify the artificially delayed emergence of a new Republican majority, what will become of the Democrats? One possibility is that they will move further to the Left. If they do, they are likely to remain in opposition for a very long time.

The other possibility is that they will try to move back to the center. If they do—and this is their only hope of ever regaining majority status—they will be in the comical position of having to say "me too" to an intellectual tradition that once belonged to them by right.

It is much easier to foresee an outcome of an election than to predict what any new administration will actually do once

it gets into power. But the landslide of 1980 has given the Republicans a new majority to build on as they try to reverse
the decline of American power. It is a truly historic
opportunity.

20

RICHARD M. SCAMMON

The Republican
Prospects

A dual standard of political behavior. Party labels and their appeal. Republicans facing the future; prospective party members, including the South. Congressional and presidential majorities. The problem of ousting. Party survivorship.

Any consideration of electoral and political coalitions in the 1980s must start with the different character of American presidential and congressional operations. To talk broadly of this coalition or that must give way to a consideration of the facts of life in American politics since the end of the Second World War, thirty-five years ago.

Beginning with 1946, we have had eighteen renewals—partial or total—of the two Houses of Congress. In that period, 18 new Houses of Representatives and 18 new Senates have been called to order. On the House side, the count has been 16 Democratic and 2 Republican; in the Senate, 15 Democratic and 3 Republican. Taken together, whatever people have said of their political loyalties and however they may have voted for president, the Congress count has been 31 under a Democratic gavel, 5 under a Republican. Even in the great Nixon presidential landslide of 1972, substantially larger than the Reagan victory in 1980, both sides of Congress contained a majority of Democrats.

In the same period, the nine presidential elections have run 5-to-4 Republican, with the overall presidential vote of these elections favoring the Republicans by a few millions of votes. At least in terms of November voting allegiances, there is a dual standard of political behavior.

But basic appeals of the two party labels have not varied greatly in the period since the last great realignment of political coalitions as shaped by Franklin D. Roosevelt in 1932/1934/1936. In a very general way, and subject to many ad hoc adjustments, Democrats have had more success with self-identified liberals, big-city voters, certain minorities (especially blacks, Jews, Hispanics, and Roman Catholics), the very young (especially students), the poor and unemployed, the less educated, trade unionists, and the South.

The broad appeal of Republicans—again, with many individual changes and adjustments in different states and years—has been to conservatives, whites, Protestants, those better off financially, the better educated, the managerial and professional class, those in the "Independent" group, and rural and small-town voters outside the South.

The changes observed in 1980 are what give some Republicans hope for broader adjustments in the clientele coalitions of the 1980s. Not adjustments as big as those in the

1972 Nixon-landslide presidential voting, but hopefully more permanent. After all, the huge 1972 Nixon victory was followed four years later by a return of Democrats to the White House, and the current Republican effort will be directed to trying to make the observed changes in 1980 a good deal more long range than those in 1972.

Specifically, Republican prospects are likely to be highest in the lower-middle-class, working-class group of white voters, especially with those who are Roman Catholic. Many voters in this group are the upwardly mobile men and women who are part of the postwar "bourgeois working class" of America. Republicans feel that many of these voters are now paying more in taxes than they are getting back, and that their view of politics—and their search for a party to represent them—has a better chance of turning to the GOP than ever before in the past half-century since the Great Depression and FDR.

Jewish electors will also be Republican targets, especially at the presidential level. Many Republicans feel that Jewish voters, traditionally liberal and humanist and Democratic in their views, might be appealed to on a specific basis of concern for the survival of Israel. While presidents, Republican or Democratic, might be expected to be basically pro-Israel, there is a hope among some Republicans that the pro-military, pro-defense Republican attitude will find strong support among Jewish voters, that Republican administrations might be seen as more ready to help in a crisis while a Democratic administration might wring its hands and "turn to the United Nations." Rightly or wrongly, those of this opinion would hold that a Republican in the White House would normally be a better guarantor of Israeli survival than a Democrat, pro-Israel though he might be, in whose party it is alleged the anti-military, pacifist wing would be more influential than in the Republican party.

Finally, the new Republican appeal to the South need not be labored. It is perhaps the greatest anomaly of American politics that the Southern quadrant, on most public issues the most conservative of all the four major areas of the United States, should have turned to the Democratic party as the instrument of its regional representation. The reasons for this choice are perfectly clear in U.S. history, but the Republicans hope that this will change within the next decade, change even more than it has already.

In the four Roosevelt administrations, every state of the Old Confederacy voted for Roosevelt every time—four elections, eleven states, forty-four states for FDR. More recently, the Democrats carried ten of the eleven Confederate states when they nominated a Deep South candidate in 1976; but in 1968 they carried only one (Texas), in 1972, none, and in 1980, only one (Georgia).

On the Senate side, the Republican takeover of 1980 was in part accomplished by party gains in the South, to the point that today the Democrats have only half the Southern members of the Senate—11 of 22—with Senator Byrd of Virginia an Independent. To find a similar point in history at which the Senate was only half-Democratic in its Southern membership, it would be necessary to go back into the early 1870s—over a century ago. From the late 1870s to this past January, Southern senators have been heavily Democratic.

In the House, the Southern representation is still Democratic, but each state in the area has at least one Republican. The state delegation of Virginia is 9-to-1 Republican, with the single Democratic member a very conservative member indeed. Naturally, the Republicans hope that an expanded coalition in the 1980s, with a special appeal to their potential clientele in the South, will produce party results comparable to those in the Senate.

But congressional majorities are not necessarily presidential majorities. While major lines of appeal and client support may produce *comparable* results, the tabulated results on election night often vary—as *vide* the Democratic Congress elected in 1972 as Republican president Nixon won a reelection landslide. The reasons are not complex: presidential races have a high personal context, and the selection process often seems to resemble picking a chief executive officer for a large company. Moreover, the presidential candidate has little leeway in his campaign. He cannot say one thing in Jackson, Michigan, today and have a completely opposite doctrine in Jackson, Mississippi, tomorrow.

This doesn't mean he can't shade a fact or two here and there, and he can certainly emphasize one subject here today and another there tomorrow. But he cannot plug for school busing on Monday and stand strong against it on Tuesday. He will simply be caught up in the media coverage and will end up worse off than had he stuck with one position or the other.

For Congress, an entirely different picture. A black Democrat from a northern inner city has little enough in common with a conservative "boll weevil" Southern Democrat. In fact, it is obvious that were the two candidates to exchange political views, both would lose—badly. Even if there is no real personal commitment by a member to the views of his constituents, most of those elected are survivors—they want to come back. And while Congress may not be as "responsible" as the idealist might wish, it certainly draws high marks as being "representative."

In building congressional coalitions, the Democratic members have been traditionally drawn from a broader base than have the Republican, which is not surprising—there have been more of them. In the 1980s there appears to be little reason to believe any real form of strong party leadership will emerge to force party cohesion along stronger lines than at present. Any moves to "coalesce" by punishing dissenters run into two major obstacles—the purgers may well lose control of the Congress and/or may themselves get purged on some other issue at a later time.

To take an example from the current work in the House, a move to oust minority Democrats because they support Re-

publican proposals on budget cuts could easily reverse the
majority status of the Democrats and turn the Democrats
into the minority—with many organizational problems, loss
of chairmanships, loss of staff, and all the rest. Moreover, if
the minority is to be ousted if it does not go along with the
majority, there is a real problem as to what happens to today's majority if it becomes a minority.

In June 1981 the majority of House Democrats voted
against funding Justice Department legal actions to enforce
school busing. If logic is to prevail, the minority on that vote,
including every black member in the House, would have to be
excluded from the caucus, denied committee assignments,
and "read out of the party." Of course, one might argue that
only small minorities should be booted out, while big
minorities would suffer just a wrist slap. But it would be hard
to maintain to the general public that big crime is exempt
while little crime is punished. The picture of the party in
Congress cast up by such a procedure would not be an edify-
ing one in building coalitions for the 1980s.

The bottom line seems to be that Republican and Democratic party discipline in Congress is likely to be tempered by
the practical considerations of survivorship, right through to
1990, and that electoral coalitions for congressional elections
will continue to be highly pragmatic. The dominant theme of
coalitions to and in Congress will be "representativeness"—
not of broad, national dogma, but of each senator's state and
of each representative's district.

VII

Conclusion

21

SEYMOUR MARTIN LIPSET

The American Party System: Concluding Observations

Party influence in congressional and parliamentary political systems. Multiparty government and the third-party effort. Electoral coalitions. Nomination by primary vote—popular choice. The spread of ideology. Strengthening party control. The independent voter. Factors influencing future change.

It is an accepted truism in political science that American political parties are weaker than comparable organizations elsewhere. Currently, they have little say about the nomination of candidates for public office, particularly at the national level. Unlike the situation in most other democratic countries, national legislators here are under little constraint to follow the policies advanced by a president or congressional leader of their party.

REASONS FOR PARTY WEAKNESS

The reasons for party weakness are inherent in the division of powers in the constitutional system. The Founding Fathers, who drew up the Constitution, did not anticipate or desire parties, while their experience with autocratic British power had taught them to fear strong executive authority. They deliberately designed a government in which political power would be fragmented between and within federal and state governments, among an executive not responsible to parliament, two legislative houses, and the judiciary, each of which would be motivated to restrain the others.

In parliamentary countries, the cabinet and prime minister are responsible to parliament, and the fact that the government falls or new elections are called when a majority votes against the incumbents encourages party discipline. Members of parliament almost invariably follow party policy. Candidates for parliament are usually chosen for their contribution to party activities. The electorate generally votes for a party, not for the particular individuals running in the constituencies. Cabinet members are chosen from parliament. Parties have strong national organizations, frequently own newspapers, and are represented to the media by officially designated spokespersons.

In the United States, on the other hand, party strength in Congress has no bearing on the choice of president, how long he holds office, or the composition of his cabinet. Members of the latter rarely come from congressional ranks. Even though the president and members of Congress are elected independently, the contests for all representatives and a rotating third of the senators are held at the same time as that for president. Still, many voters do not vote by party; they may split their tickets by supporting a Republican for president and a Democrat for the Senate and/or the House. In the six presidential years from 1956 to 1976, over 30 percent of the House districts were carried by a presidential nominee of one party and a House candidate of a different party (Bibby, Mann, and Ornstein 1980, p. 19). As a result, the president, though the official leader of his party, has no control—and sometimes not much influence—over the behavior of his party colleagues in Congress. Representatives and senators are more interested in the particular concerns of their constituents than in the proposals of their own party's president or their party leaders in Congress.

THE PARTY SYSTEM

The fact that the president is chosen in a national election rather than by parliament plays a special causal role in the nature of the party system (Schattschneider 1942). Since the executive power—the presidency—cannot be divided among parties, and the cabinet is appointed by the head of state and responsible only to him, elections for president have been forced into a two-candidate or two—major party race ever since the first election took place in 1796. In a parliamentary country, voters may support and elect representatives of small parties to parliament; these representatives, in turn, may influence the choice of prime minister or may even have cabinet members in a coalition, multiparty government.

Efforts to form stable third parties in the United States invariably fail because the effective constituency in national elections is basically the entire country (Lipset 1977,

pp. 126–30). The emphasis on presidential elections has prevented third parties from building up enduring local constituency strength in the way that labor, agrarian, religious, or
ethnic based parties have done in parliamentary, single-
member, district systems. American third parties thus have
gained their greatest strength in municipal—or occasionally, state—elections, and have invariably lost support
in subsequent presidential elections. They have also been
more successful in congressional races held in nonpresiden-
tial election years.

Significant third-party efforts have occurred invariably
under conditions in which particular factions or interest
groups have found themselves excluded from the coalition
with which they are normally involved because of presidential nominations or the adoption of policies that affront their
concerns. Thus, in 1924, both major parties nominated conservatives, a development that led to the candidacy of Robert
La Follette on the Progressive ticket. In 1948, and again in
1968, the Democratic presidential nominees were anathema
to Southern white racists, a fact which produced independent
candidacies by Southern Democratic politicians Strom
Thurmond and George Wallace. But support for these and
other third-party candidacies, such as John Anderson's in
1980, had always been vitiated by those factors that lead
people to see a third-party vote as "wasted." Hence, as opinion
polls taken during election years have shown, backing for
third-party candidates drops off sharply as Election Day approaches. But if a third-party candidate does reasonably
well, one or the other of the major parties will make overtures to his supporters and bring them back into the main
two-party system by the following election.

Recognizing the near impossibility of creating a new national party has led many American radicals, who would
have preferred a party of their own, to operate as factions
within one of the major parties. At different times since the
late 1910s, socialist or near socialist groups have either con-

trolled or greatly influenced a major party in a number of states. Currently, various socialist organizations—the Social Democrats, USA, led by Bayard Rustin, the Democratic Socialist Organizing Committee chaired by Michael Harrington, and the Campaign for Economic Democracy formed by Tom Hayden—are working within the Democratic party. And at the other end of the political spectrum, Richard Viguerie (1981, pp. 87–88), leader of the New Right movement, notes that conservatives like himself, who would like to "organize a brand new broadly based party, designed to replace the Republican Party," have been forced to recognize that "the two party system ... is probably too solidly entrenched for any such effort." Hence they, too, consciously accept the fact of coalition politics and seek "to nominate conservative candidates, promote conservative positions and create conservative majorities in both parties."

The United States is at least as heterogeneous in social structure as most other countries with numerous parties, but the diverse American classes, ethnic groups, religions, regions, value groups, which could form the base of separate parties, must coalesce into two very broad coalition parties if they want to influence the outcome of the presidential contest. In effect, the United States has a concealed multiparty system; its many factions take part in *pre-election coalitions,* called parties. In much of Europe, autonomous and relatively homogeneous parties join to form a *post-election coalition* government (Lipset 1979, pp. 286–317).

PARTIES AS COALITIONS

Given the diversity of membership, American parties have always been loose coalitions of dissimilar elements. The Democratic party, the oldest continuously operating party in the world, included Southern slaveholders and Northern

Jacksonian populists and labor-union advocates before the Civil War. Its opponents, then known as "the Whigs," combined within one national party Southern plantation owners, Northern business interests, and middle-class evangelical Protestants, many of the latter strongly abolitionist.

The Republicans, from the Civil War on, tended to represent the dominant cultural and economic groups of the country—largely urban and rural, Northern evangelical, Protestant whites of British and Northern European descent, and industrialists—plus the blacks, who kept voting for the party of Lincoln. Democratic supporters were drawn from highly diverse "out" groups—recent immigrants, non-pietistic Protestant sects, non-Protestant elements, trade unionists, and Southern white Protestants—who, for historic and regional economic and cultural reasons, opposed the Republicans (see chapter 5 by Paul Kleppner).

In the first third of this century, the Republicans included some of the most Left-wing politicians in the country, some near socialists from Midwest radical agrarian areas, *and* spokespeople for big business from Eastern states, plus the impoverished blacks. The Democratic coalition assembled by Franklin Roosevelt in the 1930s incorporated Southern racists, blacks, evangelical whites—who had backed the anti-Catholic and anti-Semitic Ku Klux Klan and favored prohibition of liquor—and most Catholics, Jews, and trade unionists.

It should be obvious, from this listing of the various elements in both electoral coalitions, that they could not have cooperated in the same "party" if there had been any real party discipline—i.e., if in the 1920s North Dakota and other Midwestern Republican radicals who favored government ownership of major industries had to support the program of those primarily concerned with the welfare of business, or if during the 1930s Democratic representatives of black or trade-union districts were obliged to vote for the policies of Southern racists. What brought these groups together was the need to nominate and support a presidential candidate; but the condition for their membership in a national party was total absence of party discipline at the legislative level.

The glue that helped preserve what there was of a national party structure, and that sustained relatively strong local organizations, was patronage. Many federal jobs, such as postmasters, did not come under civil service merit rules and were awarded to loyal members of the president's party, usually on recommendation of local party leaders. State and city or county organizations were much stronger than the national, in part because of their extensive local patronage, but also because such parties were less heterogeneous in social composition and thus less factionalized than the national organization.

The national parties basically have only existed to select a presidential nominee at a national convention every four years. Until recently, the convention brought together party leaders from all the states to decide on the party's choice. Given the diversity within each party, nominees—almost invariably—had to be nonideological individuals chosen because they were least likely to antagonize the various elements in the party and electorate, and because their past record suggested political or administrative competency.

CHANGES IN THE PARTIES

This system gradually has broken down since the 1930s. As Everett Ladd points out in chapter 7, the Roosevelt New Deal helped to realign the base of the parties as class and ideology came to differentiate the two coalitions more dramatically than before. Reacting to the Great Depression, the Democratic party took on a social-democratic cast. It included the growing number of economic Leftists, even most avowed socialists and communists, the rapidly increasing trade-union movement, many of the previously Republican Midwestern, agrarian radicals, and the blacks, while it retained the support of the Southern, largely rural and impoverished, whites.

The Roosevelt coalition advocated a strongly interventionist welfare and planning state that supported trade unions and higher, guaranteed, farm prices. While the Republicans gained some support from previously Democratic business people, they did not make up for the massive party losses, and the GOP became the minority party in Congress and in presidential elections.

From the New Deal era on, economic and social ideology divided the two coalitions. The Democrats added social liberalism, particularly support of black civil rights, to their economic liberalism. The Republicans remained anti-statist, opposed—in principle if not in practice—to government intervention, whether for economic, welfare, or social (civil rights) concerns. During the post–World War II period, white Southerners began to leave their Democratic national home, at times for regional, racist, third parties but, together with other less-privileged social conservatives, more permanently for the Republican ranks. And as noted by Ladd and by Schneider (chapters 7 and 9), the Democrats gained among sectors of the socially liberal, college-educated, and professional population.

The more coherent ideological and interest differences between the two major coalitions logically should have produced more unified and more disciplined parties. Such was not to be, however, because of the decline in patronage and the enlargement of the system of nominating candidates through publicly held party primary elections. Reform elements, including most intellectuals, had long sought to weaken party organizations and leadership, which they labeled scornfully as "machines" and "bosses," by placing government employment under the merit civil service, and by changing the nomination process from one controlled by delegates selected by lower-level party organizations to one in which candidates and/or convention delegates are selected in primary elections, open to participation by any voter who declared or registered him or herself as a party supporter.

Both of these proposed reforms were gradually carried out at the national and local levels. The elimination of patronage reduced the number of nonideological party activists who worked hard before elections to mobilize support for all party nominees and who were uncritically loyal to the leaders of the organizations. The spread of the primaries limited the ability of professional party leaders to choose those who ran for office. Whoever could mobilize money and other forms of support could run in the primaries, regardless of his or her past relations with the party organization or leaders.

The presidential nomination process, however, remained under control of party leaders until the 1960s (Shafer 1981, pp. 96–100). But the protest movements of that decade engendered a strong wave of support for the greater democratization of society, which included extending the system of primaries. New Politics reformers in the Democratic party took the lead in changes which by 1980 meant that, for most of the states, Democrats designated their delegates for presidential nomination conventions in primary elections while the Republicans were reluctantly forced to follow suit. Since three-quarters of the delegates in both parties were chosen in primaries or bound by their results, this meant that primary voters chose the nominee.

The breakdown of organization and the extension of popular choice in nominations gave increased influence to better educated, more ideologically committed persons. Such people are more likely to vote in primaries, which tend to be low turnout contests, and more willing to work actively for primary candidates. As a result, Right-wing Republicans and Left-wing Democrats have become influential within their parties to a far greater extent than their numbers in the electorate or among party adherents suggest.

As this process developed, ideology penetrated into party leadership itself. Those who serve on national and state committees increasingly reflect the views of their opinionated activists rather than those of typical party supporters who take a more moderate or centrist position.

The differences between those most active in the parties and party supporters are pointed up in the results of two midyear 1981 surveys—conducted by CBS News and the *Los Angeles Times*—which dealt with the views of those in the leadership of their parties as well as of their rank and file. Some findings of the CBS News polls are presented in table 1.

As is evident from table 1, the national Democratic leaders are much more liberal than those who identify with the party, while among Republicans, party supporters are less conservative than those on the national committee. A similar pattern of variations between the opinions of party activists (members of the state committees) and the rank and file was revealed in polls taken in mid-July among Californians by the *Los Angeles Times*. Richard Bergholz (1981, pp. 1, 18) reported for the poll:

Democratic Party activists view themselves as more liberal than rank-and-file Democrats, while Republican activists see themselves as more conservative than the GOP members. . . .

A clear majority—65%—of the Democratic activists said they were liberals, while only 26% of the Democratic rank and file said they were liberal. . . .

On the Republican side, ideological differences showed up, though to a lesser degree. A whopping 81% of the activists . . . said they were conservatives, while 60% of the GOP voters put themselves in that category.

Most Democratic voters take conservative positions on such issues as voluntary prayers in schools, the death penalty and Proposition 13, the property tax–cutting initiative passed in 1978, whereas the Democratic Party activists take the liberal view.

Most Republican voters line up in support of the equal rights amendment while the party officials are overwhelmingly against it.

Table 1

Views of Members of the Democratic and Republican National Committees and Party Supporters, 1981

	Democratic		Republican	
	Com- mittee	Rank and File	Com- mittee	Rank and File
Political philosophy				
Liberal	36%	24%	1%	11%
Moderate	51%	42%	31%	33%
Conservative	4%	29%	63%	51%
Military/defense spending				
Increase	22%	48%	89%	60%
Decrease	18%	13%	1%	5%
Keep same level	51%	36%	7%	31%
Equal rights amendment				
Favor	92%	61%	29%	46%
Oppose	4%	29%	58%	44%
Too much government regulation of business				
Agree	35%	59%	98%	72%
Disagree	49%	30%	1%	22%

Source: CBS News Election and Survey Unit (5 June, 12 June 1981).

EFFECT ON NOMINATIONS

New Politics, Left-wing, candidate George McGovern was
able to defeat Hubert Humphrey for the Democratic nomination in 1972 by winning in the primaries. The support of most
party and trade-union leaders for his opponent Hubert
Humphrey was not enough to bring the bulk of the less educated, pro-Humphrey, Democratic electorate to vote in the
primaries. In 1976 an unknown Jimmy Carter, who started
off actively campaigning for the presidency in 1974, presented himself at the end of the Watergate era as an anti-
Washington, anti-Establishment, populist spokesman of the
common people and was able to win the nomination against
much better known opponents, who had backing from party
and trade-union leaders. In 1980, though, an elected incumbent, Carter, in turn, had a difficult contest for renomination
against New Politics Senator Edward Kennedy. The president was saved from a humiliating defeat in the primaries by
foreign events, the Iranian hostage situation and the Rus-
sian invasion of Afghanistan, and by the damage to the Kennedy candidacy that resulted from the reemergence of the
Chappaquiddick issue—his role in the death of a woman in
an automobile accident.

The Republicans, as the smaller party with only 25 percent
of the electorate identifying with them, were influenced even
earlier than the Democrats by strong ideologues—in their
case, ardent antistatist, *laissez-faire*, conservatives. Barry
Goldwater, as leader of the party's rightist faction, captured
the GOP nomination in 1964 by beating the candidate of the
moderate wing, Nelson Rockefeller, in key primaries. In 1976
Ronald Reagan, identified as a spokesman for the Right
wing, came very close to defeating an incumbent, centrist,
Republican president—Gerald Ford—in the primaries. And
in 1980 he swept through these contests and received the

nomination, although many party leaders and outside observers believed that, from an electoral-appeal point of view,
a more moderate Republican such as George Bush or Howard
Baker would do better in the general election. As events
turned out, of course, Reagan went on to win overwhelmingly
against Jimmy Carter. This victory, however, does not
necessarily prove that Reagan was a strong candidate in his
own right, since Carter—according to the opinion polls—
was regarded as the least-competent president since polling
began in the 1930s and was held responsible by most voters
for extremely adverse economic conditions.

The opposition to strong party organization among the
more populistically inclined reformers also has affected the
operation of Congress. Although, as noted, there has been
much less party discipline here than in European parlia-
ments, some party leadership structure and power has existed in the form of the influence over the legislative agenda
and process by committee chairpeople. These limited powers
were reduced in the mid-1970s by reforms linked to attitudes
influenced by the Watergate affair.

THE 1980s

The United States enters the 1980s with her national party
structure, as reflected in the power and influence of the
presidential and congressional party leadership, in weaker
condition than in any period since the Civil War. But the
situation may be about to change. Given the disastrous conclusions to the last four administrations—Johnson,
Nixon, Ford, Carter—and the seeming inability of the executive to cope with the domestic economy and foreign policy,
there is an increasing tendency among opinion molders, political scientists, journalists, and politicians, to put some of
the responsibility for these outcomes on the political and

electoral systems. Many criticize the elements which make it difficult to mobilize the presidency and Congress behind common policy. For the first time in close to three decades, discussions of reforming the system do not refer to proposals to weaken the power of officials and extend that of the electorate. Reformers are looking now for ways to enhance the authority of presidential and congressional leadership, and to revise the nomination process in ways designed to increase the influence of party leaders, e.g., by designating various elected officials and party officers *ex officio* voting delegates to party conventions.

As the "out" party, the Republicans began a process of strengthening party organization and control following their defeat in 1976. As noted by David Broder in chapter 1, the party's national committee under the leadership of its chairman, Bill Brock, undertook an extensive program of recruiting, counseling, and financing legislative and congressional candidates, and of trying to define congressional elections in national partisan rather than in local terms. Following the GOP's gains in the 1980 elections, its representatives in the Senate and the House exhibited more party discipline in support of their president's legislative program in the 1981 session than occurred at any time since the early 1930s.

The Democrats, in turn, responding to the tighter organization of their opponents and their electoral losses, have also shown a disposition to close ranks and to give congressional party leaders more power. Although a number of conservatives, largely Southerners, opposed the party's leadership and supported the Reagan spending-and-taxation program, the Democratic defectors to the bipartisan conservative coalition were, in fact, considerably fewer in number in 1981 than in the congressional sessions of the 1960s and 1970s (Bibby, Mann, and Ornstein 1980, pp. 104–6). As reported by Richard Cattani (1981, p. 3), the 43 Democrats in the House who voted for the Reagan tax package in July and had previously served in Congress had a strongly conservative voting record. "Their liberal-conservative ratings for 1980, according to the Americans for Democratic Action scores on key votes, averaged 23.9 percent. This was remarkably close to the conservative 21.4 percent of all Republican congressmen in 1980."

The Democratic party is also about to change the procedures of selecting national convention delegates. The 1982 Democratic miniconvention will be held under new rules which give party leaders considerable representation. It is probable that party officials and elected officeholders will have increased influence at the 1984 nominating convention, at the expense of reducing somewhat the number of delegates chosen in primaries. The party's new national chairman, Charles Manatt, has appointed a commission to propose revisions in procedures for choosing delegates to national conventions. At the first meeting of the Commission on Presidential Nominations in August 1981, Donald Fraser, cochairman with George McGovern of the 1970 party organization commission which produced the sharp increase in primaries, set the tone for the 1980s, stating "presidential primaries denigrate a party's responsibility for selecting its own candidate." He proposed that no state party be allowed to choose more than half its delegation through a primary. The 1981 commission was divided between two major factions—labor union representatives and supporters of Walter Mondale who favored cutting back on the primaries, and New Politics backers of Edward Kennedy and minority group members who wanted to preserve the predominance of the primaries (Broder 1981, p. 8).

It is much too early, however, to predict that party organization will be greatly strengthened. The growing concern to do so on the part of many in the political elite is countered by the declining commitment to party and to voting participation by the electorate. The proportion who identify themselves as "independents" rather than as Democrats or Republicans, who do not vote for the same party regularly, who do not vote at all, or who express cynicism about the political process and the role of government, has grown greatly since the mid-1960s. While majorities of those interviewed in opinion polls indicate that they still support government policies designed to protect people against misfortunes flowing from economic or health reverses or to enhance opportunity for the deprived, they have increasingly lost faith in the competency of their leaders and even of the institutions themselves. Hence, they would still prefer to further reduce rather than increase the power of officials.

The traditional American disdain for politicians—the word itself is invidious—and for parties and politics in general, has grown. Although the differences between a libertarian, antistatist, business-linked, socially conservative Republican party and a much more interventionist, statist, trade-union linked, socially permissive Democratic party are great, the proportion of the public who feel that it makes little or no difference who is elected has increased steadily. In any case, these variations in the dominant outlook of both parties, while real, should not be exaggerated. Among the Republicans, the growing number of advocates of supply-side economics emphasize tax reductions, while actually opposing many spending cuts that are favored by *laissez-faire* enthusiasts. The Democrats, on the other hand, have responded to the growing sentiment that government intervention has hampered economic development and encouraged inflation. Their congressional leadership is emphasizing the need to encourage investment to foster growth through reducing taxes on business, liberalizing depreciation allowances, and modifying regulatory policies.

THE FUTURE

What may be anticipated, given this background? At most, there will be some minor adjustments in the nominating process to give leaders more influence. But the basic structural features, dictated by the division of powers in the Constitution, will continue to produce weak parties and tensions between Congress and the presidency, even when the same party controls both institutions. American presidents will still find it difficult to commit the country to an effective foreign policy.

The two major parties will continue, more or less as they have been—as Nelson Polsby notes in chapter 8—to function as mechanisms through which highly diverse groups and strata compete to nominate and elect candidates and to influence public policy. Ideologically motivated tendencies and pressure groups, such as those supported by feminists, religious fundamentalists, environmentalists, opponents of abortion, will play a major role in this process. The Democrats will continue to fight among themselves in the "five parties" that Tip O'Neill says they would break into in a parliamentary system—socialists, who include a few congressmen and the heads of some major trade unions, a New Politics Left led by Edward Kennedy, a New Deal center identified with Walter Mondale, a neoconservative (or, as they prefer to call themselves, neoliberal) faction linked to Henry Jackson and Daniel Patrick Moynihan, and on the Right the conservative "boll weevils," led by Philip Gramm of Texas, who support Reagan's economic program. The GOP is divided into three tendencies: a small liberal Left which, however, involves a number of senators—Percy, Mathias, Weicker, Cohen, Spector, Packwood, and Heinz—a center supportive of Vice-President Bush and Senate majority leader Baker, and the New Right, led in Congress by Jesse Helms. Ronald Reagan bridges the center and Right, but as the emphasis in policy debate shifts from the economic issues to the social ones, it is probable, as I noted in chapter 2, that the president will be positioned in the center. Roughly 20 percent of the Democratic House members are "boll weevils," while about 10 percent of the Republicans are classified as liberal "gypsy moths."

The direction in which the parties and the country move from one election to another will continue to depend on larger, often uncontrollable events, the state of the business cycle, international developments, as well as on the competency of the president and other leaders. Democrats and Republicans will govern the United States, but whether they can deal with the major problems of contemporary society effectively, given a government consciously designed by its eighteenth-century founders to be weak, is questionable. But it is the only political system we have, and providence or luck has given us great men, such as Lincoln and Roosevelt, as leaders during periods in which effective leadership was necessary.

NOTES

4. Richard Jensen: "Party Coalitions and the Search for Modern Values: 1820–1970"

1. Third parties (Anti-Masons in the 1830s, Know-Nothings in the 1850s, Populists in the 1890s, Progressives in the 1910s, Farmer Labor in the 1930s) occasionally lasted for two to ten years, only to vanish or merge with a major party.

2. Inversions of the pattern did exist; for example, plantation eastern North Carolina voted Democratic, while the Mountain West voted Whig.

3. Data from Lipset (1970, pp. 338–40). More detailed analyses of voting trends appear in Nie, Verba, and Petrocik (1976), and in Ladd with Hadley (1978).

5. Paul Kleppner: "Coalitional and Party Transformations in the 1890s"

1. See Grover Cleveland's statement, "To the Democratic Voters," 16 June 1896, and his letter to Edward M. Shepard, 7 February 1900; both in Nevins (1933, pp. 440–41, 525). The contrast between what Cleveland regarded as the traditional principles of the party and what he termed the Bryanite "heresy" is a common theme in his political correspondence from 1896 through 1902.

2. For the detailed data supporting these observations concerning the third-party system, see Burnham (1975b, pp. 295–98), and Kleppner (1978, chapters ii, vi).

3. Burnham (1975b, p. 300) reports the gubernatorial data. The data on Republican control at the national level are in U.S. Bureau of the Census (1975, part 2, p. 1083). The partisan division among elected state representatives has been calculated from data provided by the Inter-university Consortium for Political and Social Research, University of Michigan.

4. For the current controversy over whether the post-1896 turnout decline was due principally to changes in election rules (especially the adoption of personal-registration requirements) or to behavioral influences, see Converse (1972), Burnham (1974a, 1974b), Converse and Rusk (1974). For the purposes intended for the data in table 2, it is not necessary to partition the effects between the two categories of potential causes. However, it is useful to observe that while the cities were covered by personal-registration requirements, most of the rural counties used were not.

5. The phrase is from Haber (1964, p. x): "Efficiency meant social harmony and the leadership of the 'competent.' Progressives often called this social efficiency."

6. For detail on the matters discussed in this and the following paragraphs, see Formisano (1971), Jensen (1971), Kleppner (1970, chapter v; idem 1978, chapter viii).

7. For the West, see Wright (1974).

8. For the impact of the depression and analyses of the changes in the tactics and characters of both parties in 1896, see Jensen (1971, pp. 296–308), Kleppner (1970, pp. 269–368), and McSeveney (1972, pp. 32–221). For a discussion of the leadership displacement, see Hollingsworth (1963, pp. 52–83, 156–71).

9. My understanding of the systemic implications of electoral change as expressed throughout this chapter has been greatly influenced by the brilliantly insightful work of Walter Dean Burnham and has drawn freely from it (see Burnham 1970, 1974c, 1975b).

10. For longitudinal data showing the decline of party as a determinant of legislative voting behavior, see Burnham (1975a), and Clubb and Traugott (1977).

6. Jerome M. Clubb: "Party Coalitions in the Early Twentieth Century"

1. This general view of American electoral eras is developed in Clubb, Flanigan, and Zingale (1980).

2. Basic studies of the period are those by Jensen (1971), Kleppner (1970, 1978), and Marcus (1971).

3. Tables 1 and 2 are based upon U.S. Bureau of the Census (1975) and upon data provided by the Inter-university Consortium for Political and Social Research. The consortium bears no responsibility for the interpretations presented here.

4. Estimates of voter participation are from U.S. Bureau of the Census (1975), pp. 171–72. The estimates of voter participation in congressional contests are from Burnham (1975b, p. 301).

5. Explanations for declining turnout rates are discussed and debated in Burnham (1965, 1970), Converse (1972), and in an exchange between Burnham, Converse, and Rusk (1974, pp. 1002–57).

6. The discussion of the political events of the 1920s in this and the following paragraphs draws heavily upon Burner (1967) and Sundquist (1973). The interpretation of those events presented here sometimes differs from those of Burner and Sundquist.

7. Everett Carll Ladd: "The Shifting Party Coalitions—from the 1930s to the 1970s"

1. The distributions in party identification by the self-described ideology of respondents are shown in the following table. These data are from seven separate Yankelovich surveys covering the January-October 1976 span. The total number of cases in the combined seven-study data set is 7,977.

2. Carter gained 45 percent of the vote among Southern white Protestants, compared to 50 percent among all voters. This estimate is based upon analysis of data from the American Institute of Public Opinion studies no. 959, 960, 961, 962 (1976); from the *New York Times*/CBS News Election Day Poll (1976); from Yankelovich surveys no. 8540, 8550, 8560 (1976); and it draws as well from an examination of aggregate vote

data. The author wishes to acknowledge the assistance of the Joint Center for Policy Studies, Washington, D.C., in the aggregate vote analysis.

3. Middle-class and lower-class blacks may differ fully as much as middle-class and lower-class whites in expectations, life-styles, social and cultural values, etc.; but in their general orientations to the two major parties, blacks—whatever their socioeconomic position—have been responding to a common stimulus. The sociology and politics of race—specifically, the pattern of discrimination that has affected virtually all black Americans—have resulted in a set of electoral commitments that is singularly untouched by income, occupation, education, or other such status components.

9.   William Schneider: "Democrats and Republicans, Liberals and Conservatives"

1. The best of these studies is Converse (1976).

2. Technically, the Pearson product-moment correlation is equal to the average cross product of two variables in standardized form.

3. Stokes (1966, pp. 170–71): "Let us call '*position* issues' those that involve advocacy of government actions from a set of alternatives over which a distribution of voter preferences is defined. And . . . let us call '*valence* issues' those that merely involve the linking of the parties with some condition that is positively or negatively valued by the electorate."

4. This "two-dimensional" hypothesis is consistent with many of the findings and interpretations in the recent research literature on American voting behavior. Nie, Verba, and Petrocik (1976, see pp. 194–209, 291–302) make use of a liberal/conservative issue continuum throughout their study of *The Changing American Voter*, and they apply an explicitly two-dimensional paradigm—"issues" and "party"—at several points in their analysis. Rusk and Weisberg (1976, pp. 370–88) find that a two-dimensional space—partisanship and a "new issue factor"—accounts for the perceptions of politician candidates and groups by survey respondents in 1968 and 1970. Some researchers have used a variation of the two-dimensional theme—namely, two alternative behavior patterns, "issue voting" as contrasted with "party voting." See, for instance, the symposium in *The American Political Science Review* (66 [June 1972] :415–70), with articles by Pomper, Boyd, Brody and Page, and Kessel. See also Niemi and Weisberg (1976, pp. 161–75), and Nie, Verba, and Petrocik (1976, pp. 319–44). Miller and Levitin (1976, pp. 21–62) discuss the use of the "normal vote" concept to operationalize the distinction between party voting and issue voting. The usual implication is that "partisan" behavior is inertial and responsive to "old" cleavages, while "issue-oriented" behavior is more responsive to current political conflicts and is even, perhaps, more "rational." The hypothesis of a dual alignment is consistent with most of the evidence presented in these studies; moreover, it has the advantage of being a more straightforward and parsimonious interpretation.

5. Throughout most of the twentieth century, the voting behavior of Southern states was quite "extreme" relative to the rest of the country (virtually unanimous for the Democrats in most elections). These large deviations from the national norm had a distorting influence on the correlation coefficients. In order to obtain interpretable factors, the eleven Southern states were weighted lower than the non-Southern states.

The final factor solution was a weighted Varimax-rotated factor matrix using states as units and percentaged presidential and congressional votes as variables. A detailed discussion of the factor analysis procedure, including weights and alternative rotations, can be found in the appendix to the earlier version of this paper (Schneider 1978, pp. 255–67). Table A–2 in that appendix presents the complete factor solution for the period 1896–1976. A similar factor-analysis procedure was used for a somewhat different purpose (to identify "critical elections") by MacRae and Meldrum (1969, pp. 487–506). Other researchers who have factor-analyzed aggregate voting statistics include Rogin (1967, pp. 120–31, 286–90) and McHale and Shaber (1976, pp. 291–306). The data used in this study were obtained from two sources: (1) Petersen (1963) and (2) the archival holdings of the Inter-university Consortium for Political and Social Research, Ann Arbor, Michigan. Two data sets were obtained from the consortium; see Burnham, Clubb, and Flanigan (1977a, 1977b). Neither the original collectors of these data nor the consortium bear any responsibility for the analysis or interpretation presented here.

6. In 1968 both Nixon and Humphrey won 46 percent of the vote outside the South. Both did significantly worse in the eleven Southern states, where Nixon won 35 percent and Humphrey, 30 percent. (Figures are computed from *Congressional Quarterly* [1975]).

7. Data from Lipset and Raab (1978) show that among 1968 residents of the South, the Wallace vote was 10 percent among those who grew up outside the South and 30 percent among those who grew up within the South. Among 1968 non-Southern residents, the Wallace vote doubled from 7 percent among those who grew up outside the South to 14 percent among those who grew up within the South.

8. "The extensive modern literature on social class and political behavior has shown persistently that individuals of higher status (subjectively or objectively) tend to give 'conservative' responses on questions of economic policy and tend as well to vote Republican; individuals of lower status tend to respond more 'radically' and vote Democratic" (Campbell et al. 1964, p. 191).

9. "The poorer strata everywhere are more liberal or leftist on economic issues; they favor more welfare state measures, higher wages, graduated income taxes, support of trade unions, and so forth. But when liberalism is defined in non-economic terms—as support of civil liberties, internationalism, etc.—the correlation is reversed. The more well-to-do are more liberal, the poorer are more intolerant" (Lipset 1981, p. 92).

10. See also Lipset's discussion (1981, pp. 318–22) of "Tory radicalism" in the Republican party.

11. The Liberal party does not normally endorse New Left candidates. In the 1973 New York City mayoral election, the Liberal party did not endorse Herman Badillo, the most radical candidate, or Abraham Beame, a Democratic party regular; the official Liberal candidate, Albert Blumenthal, more nearly fit the mold of a traditional reformer. The Conservative party has been noticeably uncomfortable with "unrefined" backlash candidates like Mario Procaccino and Mario Biaggi, preferring instead a more traditional and dignified brand of conservatism exemplified by such candidates as James Buckley and John Marchi.

12. In the 1972 Center for Political Studies' National Election Survey (N = 2,123), 21 percent of the sample was over sixty years of age, but 29 percent of "strong Demo-

crats" and 37 percent of "strong Republicans" were over sixty. Among college-educated respondents under thirty (N = 295), 70 percent identified as either a liberal or a conservative, compared with 45 percent of the sample as a whole. But in this same group, only 53 percent identified with a political party, compared with 65 percent of the sample as a whole.

13. Writing in the late 1950s, Seymour Martin Lipset (1968, p. 325) stated that "Such factors as occupational status, income, and the class character of the district in which people live probably distinguish the support of the two major parties more clearly now than at any other period in American history since the Civil War."

14. A separate factor analysis was performed using data from non-Southern states only. In this case, the three Democratic presidential votes between 1964 and 1972 displayed a clearer trend: declining salience of partisanship (Johnson .72, Humphrey .68, McGovern .52) and increasing salience of ideology (Johnson −.47, Humphrey −.59, McGovern −.64). Inclusion of the South makes the three contests look very much alike—i.e., predominantly ideological. Outside the South, the ideological effect accumulated more gradually.

15. The proper ideological classification of nineteenth-century Populism has been widely debated among historians. One of the leading interpreters of the movement, Norman Pollack (1962, p. 11), has argued that "Populism regarded itself as a class movement, reasoning that farmers and workers were assuming the same material position in society." But a farmer-labor coalition failed to emerge, an outcome which Pollack (1962, p. 61) blames on the "conservative, retarding influence" of labor. One must distinguish here between the rhetoric of Populism, which often had a socialistic tone of "class conflict" and, indeed, incorporated many socialist ideas and programs, and the actual nature of the movement. Populism remained resolutely agrarian in its social base, a sectoral and not a class movement. In terms of our two-dimensional scheme, Populism epitomizes extreme economic radicalism coupled with deep cultural conservatism.

16. Lubell (1956, p. 151) noted that the Progressive parties in the Farm Belt "served as halfway stations for two distinct streams of insurgents—those who were leaving the Republican party in protest against big-business domination, and those who had forsaken the Democratic party in vengeful memory of 'Wilson's War.' Wrenching these two voting streams apart, Hitler's war moved the economic liberals into the Democratic party and the isolationists into the Republican party."

17. See Lipset (1970, chapter 9, especially pp. 303−24, 342−48), who notes that high-status Protestant denominations tend to promote a liberal social and political outlook, while lower-status, more fundamentalist Protestant denominations are more conservative doctrinally and politically. These differences tend to affect the political beliefs and behavior of *active adherents* of the different denominations.

18. "To structure an ethnic and religious model of the Farm Belt, Kansas and Nebraska are the strongly Anglo-Saxon Protestant states, while Wisconsin, Minnesota, and North Dakota are predominantly Catholic-Lutheran and German-Scandinavian. Iowa and South Dakota fall in between in both geography and demography" (Phillips 1970, p. 361n).

19. Counting in terms of 1968 electoral votes, Phillips (1970, p. 473) found 189 of the 270 electoral votes needed to form a new majority in his "projected bastions" and "con-

tingent bastions." Thus, an additional 81 electoral votes would have to be won in the "battleground" states; that number was one-third of the 243 electoral votes available in those states in 1968.

11. Patrick H. Caddell: "The Democratic Strategy and Its Electoral Consequences"

1. This voting calculus is based on multivariate regression analysis, a statistical device which links other independent variables to a fixed variable—in this case, presidential preference. We were then able to rank order the other variables by their relative impact on the voter's candidate preference.

2. *New York Times*/CBS News Election Day Survey. These results also suggest the adverse impact of the economy. Blue-collar voters who said their real income had declined over the past year favored Reagan 2 to 1, while other blue-collar workers supported Carter by a similar margin.

3. Although Carter was accused of running a "mean" campaign, California voters, when we asked in October which candidate was conducting a "mean" campaign, picked Reagan 28 percent to 7 percent Carter, with most—65 percent—saying "neither" or "both."

4. Undecideds rated Carter 55–35 percent *favorable*, and Reagan 30–54 percent *unfavorable*.

5. There has been great controversy over the apparent failure of the polls to detect a Reagan landslide. Most public, national, and state polls concluded their interviews by early Saturday to meet Sunday deadlines. Those surveys were therefore conducted in the heat of the debate reaction. Anticipating a possible "bounceback," we began to conduct daily self-contained full national surveys to monitor possible swings. For Saturday, Sunday, and Monday we were able to record movements on those individual days. Ours was apparently the only polling program to conduct single-day surveys that last weekend.

6. The polls, while all indicated a narrowed partisan gap, have not been consistent. Indeed, polls conducted by telephone tended to find much greater Republican margin gains than those surveys conducted in person. While unexplained, these differences are nonetheless intriguing.

7. They allocated many partisan "leaning" independents to both parties.

8. Only 33 percent of those who voted in 1980 were in the 18–35 age group (source: U.S. Census Bureau).

12. E. J. Dionne, Jr.: "Catholics and the Democrats: Estrangement but Not Desertion"

1. Kathleen A. Frankovic is a superb source of information on Catholic voting behavior, as is her study of the subject (Frankovic 1974). She was also helpful with advice on how to use the *New York Times*/CBS computer system. I am grateful for her insights.

2. For a summary of the 1976 CBS Poll results and the 1980 *New York Times*/CBS results, see Pomper (1981, pp. 71–72).

3. The data presented apply to the whole country save New York and California. In those states, voters were asked their preferences in senatorial contests.

13. Alan M. Fisher: "Jewish Political Shift? Erosion, Yes; Conversion, No"

1. American Institute of Public Opinion (AIPO) 148–51, 153–57, 159 (29 January–8 July 1980).

2. AIPO 155 (13 May 1980).

3. AIPO 160 (29 July 1980).

4. *Los Angeles Times* poll, *Los Angeles Times* (19 March 1980), p. 13.

5. AIPO 155, 162 (13 May, 9 September 1980).

6. NBC: July National Poll (24 July 1981), p. 10.

7. AIPO 151, 155, 161–62 (24 March–9 September 1980).

8. AIPO 151, 157, 159, 162–64 (24 March–4 November 1980).

14. Martin P. Wattenberg and Arthur H. Miller: "Decay in Regional Party Coalitions: 1952–1980"

1. This growth in the independent categories on the party identification scale has actually been more due to an increase in the proportion of respondents who say that they have "no preference" than to an increase in self-identified independents. See Miller and Wattenberg, (1981) for a detailed analysis of various types of independents across time.

2. Such a conclusion is also supported by data obtained after the election when election-study respondents were again asked the standard party identification question. Our estimate of the normal vote from these postelection interviews is exactly 54 percent Democratic.

3. See any SRC/CPS Election Study codebook for details on how each region is defined.

4. In each year up to five likes and dislikes have been coded for each open-ended question. Thus both indices of net affect can theoretically range from −5 to +5.

5. In 1952 the mean number of responses to the party likes/dislikes questions was 4.7; by 1980 this had dropped to 2.7.

6. Similarly, when asked which party would do a better job in handling inflation, only 42 percent of those interviewed in 1980 thought one party would do a better job than the other, and regarding unemployment, the comparable figure was just 39 percent.

REFERENCES

Allen, Howard W., and Allen, Kay Warren. In press. "Vote Fraud and Data Validity." In *Analyzing Electoral History: A Guide to the Study of American Voting Behavior*, ed. Jerome M. Clubb, William H. Flanigan, and Nancy H. Zingale. Beverly Hills, CA: Sage Publications.

Andersen, Kristi. 1979. *The Creation of a Democratic Majority, 1928–1936.* Chicago, IL: University of Chicago Press.

Bell, Daniel. 1973. *The Coming of Post-Industrial Society.* New York: Basic Books.

————, ed. 1963. *The Radical Right.* New York: Doubleday.

Bergholz, Richard. 1981. "The Times Poll. Voters and Party Leaders Far Apart on the Issues." *Los Angeles Times* (2 August).

Bialer, Seweryn, and Sluzar, Sophia. 1977. *Sources of Contemporary Radicalism.* Boulder, CO: Westview Press.

Bibby, John F.; Mann, Thomas E.; Ornstein, Norman J. 1980. *Vital Statistics on Congress, 1980.* Washington, D.C.: American Enterprise Institute for Public Policy Research.

Bonomi, Patricia; Burns, James MacGregor; Ranney, Austin, eds. 1981. *The American Constitutional System under Strong and Weak Parties.* New York: Praeger Publishers.

Broder, David S. 1981. "Demos Again Wrestling with Delegate Reforms." *San Francisco Chronicle* (22 August).

Bruce-Briggs, Barry, ed. 1979. *The New Class?* New Brunswick, NJ: Transaction Books.

Burner, David. 1967. *The Politics of Provincialism: The Democratic Party in Transition, 1918–1932.* New York: Alfred E. Knopf.

Burnham, Walter Dean. 1965. "The Changing Shape of the American Political Universe." *American Political Science Review* 43 (March).

————. 1970. *Critical Elections and the Mainsprings of American Politics.* New York: W. W. Norton and Company.

————. 1975a. "Insulation and Responsiveness in Congressional Elections." *Political Science Quarterly* 90 (Fall).

————. 1975b. "Party Systems and the Political Process." In *The American Party Systems: Stages of Political Development*, ed. William Nisbet

Chambers and Walter Dean Burnham. 2d ed. New York: Oxford University Press.

———. 1974*a*. "Rejoinder." *American Political Science Review* 68 (September).

———. 1974*b*. "Theory and Voting Research: Some Reflections on Converse's 'Change in the American Electorate.'" *American Political Science Review* 68 (September).

———. 1974*c*. "The United States: The Politics of Heterogeneity." In *Electoral Behavior: A Comparative Handbook*, ed. Richard Rose. New York: The Free Press.

———; Clubb, Jerome M.; Flanigan, William H. 1977*a*. "State-Level Congressional, Gubernatorial, and Senatorial Election Data for the United States, 1824–1972." ICPSR 75. In *Guide to Resources and Services, 1977–1978*. Ann Arbor, MI: Inter-university Consortium for Political and Social Research.

———; Clubb, Jerome M.; Flanigan, William H. 1977*b*. "State-Level Presidential Election Data for the United States, 1824–1972." ICPSR 19. In *Guide to Resources and Services, 1977–1978*. Ann Arbor, MI: Inter-university Consortium for Political and Social Research.

———; Converse, Philip E.; Rusk, Jerrold G. 1974. [Exchange.] *American Political Science Review* 68 (September).

Campbell, Angus, and Converse, Philip E., eds. 1972. *The Human Meaning of Social Change*. New York: Russell Sage Foundation.

———; Miller, Warren E.; Stokes, Donald E. 1960. *The American Voter*. New York: Wiley and Sons.

———; Miller, Warren E.; Stokes, Donald E. 1964. *The American Voter: An Abridgement*. New York: Wiley and Sons.

———; Miller, Warren E.; Stokes, Donald E., eds. 1966. *Elections and the Political Order*. New York: John Wiley.

Cattani, Richard J. 1981. "Analyzing President's Tax Triumph." *Christian Science Monitor* (3 August).

CBS News Election and Survey Unit. 1981*a*. "CBS News Democratic National Committee Survey" (5 June).

———. 1981*b*. "CBS News Republican National Committee Survey" (12 June).

Chambers, William Nisbet, and Burnham, Walter Dean, eds. 1975. *The American Party Systems: Stages of Political Development*. 2d ed. New York: Oxford University Press.

Clubb, Jerome M.; Flanigan, William H.; Zingale, Nancy H., eds. In press. *Analyzing Electoral History: A Guide to the Study of American Voting Behavior*. Beverly Hills, CA: Sage Publications.

———. 1980. *Partisan Realignment: Voters, Parties, and Government in American History*. Beverly Hills, CA: Sage Publications.

Clubb, Jerome M., and Traugott, Santa. 1977. "Partisan Cleavage and Cohesion in the House of Representatives, 1861–1974." *Journal of Interdisciplinary History* 7 (Winter).

Clymer, Adam. 1981. "Poll Finds Nation Is Becoming Increasingly Republican." *New York Times* (3 May).

————, and Frankovic, Kathleen A. 1981. "The Realities of Realignment." *Public Opinion* 4 (June/July).

Conte, Christopher. 1981. "Tax Cuts Ought Not to Be Delayed Despite a Record Budget Gap, Reagan Aide Says." *Wall Street Journal* (9 January).

Converse, Philip E. 1972. "Change in the American Electorate." In *The Human Meaning of Social Change*, ed. Angus Campbell and Philip E. Converse. New York: Russell Sage Foundation.

————. 1966a. "The Concept of a Normal Vote." In *Elections and the Political Order*, ed. Angus Campbell, Philip E. Converse, Warren E. Miller, and Donald E. Stokes. New York: John Wiley.

————. 1976. *The Dynamics of Party Support: Cohort-Analyzing Party Identification.* Beverly Hills, CA: Sage Publishing Company.

————. 1966b. "On the Possibility of Major Political Realignment in the South." In *Elections and the Political Order*, ed. Angus Campbell, Philip E. Converse, Warren E. Miller, and Donald E. Stokes. New York: John Wiley.

————, and Rusk, Jerrold G. 1974. "Comments." *American Political Science Review* 68 (September).

Crosland, Anthony. 1974. *Socialism Now.* London: Jonathan Cape.

Dionne, E. J., Jr. 1980. "Even Carter's Successes May Be Helping Reagan." *New York Times* (29 June).

Dogan, Mattei, and Rokkan, Stein, eds. 1969. *Quantitative Ecological Analysis in the Social Sciences.* Cambridge, MA: MIT Press.

Evans, Roland, and Novak, Robert. 1972. "Nixon Woos Jewish Voters." *Washington Post* (21 June).

Fair, Ray C. 1978. "The Effect of Economic Events on Votes for President." *Review of Economics and Statistics* 60 (May).

Fisher, Alan M. 1979. "Realignment of the Jewish Vote?" *Political Science Quarterly* (Spring).

Formisano, Ronald P. 1971. *The Birth of Mass Political Parties: Michigan, 1827–1861.* Princeton, NJ: Princeton University Press.

Frankovic, Kathleen A. 1974. "The Effect of Religion on Political Attitudes." Doctoral dissertation, Rutgers University.

————. 1981. "Public Opinion Trends." In *The Election of 1980: Reports and Interpretations*, ed. Gerald M. Pomper. Chatham, NJ: Chatham House Publishers.

Furgurson, Ernest B. 1981. "GOP Chairman Blames Congress for President's Drop in Polls." *Baltimore Sun* (24 June).

Glaser, Vera. 1981. "Tough Issues Await Congress." *S.F. Examiner and Chronicle* (9 August).

Glazer, Nathan, and Moynihan, Daniel P. 1970. *Beyond the Melting Pot.* Cambridge, MA: MIT Press.

Goodwyn, Lawrence. 1976. *Democratic Promise: The Populist Movement in America*. New York: Oxford Press.

Greeley, Andrew M. 1978. "Catholics and Coalition: Where Should They Go?" In *Emerging Coalitions in American Politics*, ed. Seymour Martin Lipset. San Francisco, CA: Institute for Contemporary Studies.

———. 1974. *Ethnicity in the United States: A Preliminary Reconnaissance*. New York: Wiley Interscience.

Greer, Scott. 1961. "Catholic Voters and the Democratic Party." *Public Opinion Quarterly* 25 (Fall).

Haber, Samuel. 1964. *Efficiency and Uplift: Scientific Management in the Progressive Era, 1890–1920*. Chicago, IL: University of Chicago Press.

Hibbs, Douglas A., Jr., and Fassbender, Heino, eds. 1981. *Contemporary Political Economy*. Amsterdam: North-Holland Publishing Company.

Himmelfarb, Milton. 1981. "Are Jews Becoming Republican?" *Commentary* 71 (August).

———. 1973. *The Jews of Modernity*. New York: Basic Books.

Hollingsworth, J. Rogers. 1963. *The Whirligig of Politics: The Democracy of Cleveland and Bryan*. Chicago, IL: University of Chicago Press.

Horowitz, Irving Louis. 1972. "The Jewish Vote." *Commonweal* 99 (13 October).

Hunt, Albert R. 1981. "A Conversation with Barry Goldwater." *Wall Street Journal* (3 August).

Inglehart, Ronald. 1977. *The Silent Revolution: Changing Values and Political Styles Among Western Publics*. Princeton, NJ: Princeton University Press.

Inter-university Consortium for Political and Social Research. 1977. *Guide to Resources and Services, 1977–1978*. Ann Arbor, MI: Inter-university Consortium for Political and Social Research.

Jensen, Richard J. 1978. "Party Coalitions and the Search for Modern Values: 1820–1970." In *Emerging Coalitions in American Politics*, ed. Seymour Martin Lipset. San Francisco, CA: Institute for Contemporary Studies.

———. 1971. *The Winning of the Midwest: Social and Political Conflict, 1888–1896*. Chicago, IL: University of Chicago Press.

Johnson, Willard R. 1973. "Should the Poor Buy No Growth?" *Daedalus* 102 (Fall).

Keller, Bill. 1981. "Democrats and Republicans Try to Outbid Each Other in Cutting Taxes for Business." *Congressional Quarterly Weekly Report* 39 (27 June).

Kelman, Steven. 1981. *Regulating America, Regulating Sweden: A Comparative Study of Occupational Safety and Health Policy*. Cambridge, MA: MIT Press.

Kimball, Larry J. 1981. "Economic Forecast." *Top Priority* 4 (Winter).

Kirkpatrick, Jeane. 1979*a*. "Politics and the New Class." In *The New Class?*, ed. Barry Bruce-Briggs. New Brunswick, NJ: Transaction Books.

———. 1979*b*. "Why We Don't Become Republicans." *Commonsense* 2 (Fall).

Kleppner, Paul. 1970. *The Cross of Culture: A Social Analysis of Midwestern Politics, 1850–1900.* New York: The Free Press.

———. 1978. *The Third-Electoral Era, 1853–1892: Parties, Voters, and Political Cultures.* Chapel Hill, NC: University of North Carolina Press.

Kousser, J. Morgan. 1974. *The Shaping of Southern Politics: Suffrage Restriction and the Establishment of the One-Party South, 1880–1910.* New Haven, CT: Yale University Press.

Kuklinski, James H., and West, Darrell M. 1981. "Economic Expectations and Voting Behavior in United States House and Senate Elections." *American Political Science Review* 75 (June).

Ladd, Everett Carll. 1979. "The American Party System Today." In *The Third Century*, ed. Seymour Martin Lipset. Chicago, IL: University of Chicago Press.

———. 1970. *American Political Parties: Social Change and Political Response.* New York: W. W. Norton.

———. 1981*a*. "The Brittle Mandate: Electoral Dealignment and the 1980 Presidential Election." *Political Science Quarterly* 95 (Spring).

———. 1977*a*. "The Democrats Have Their Own Two-Party System." *Fortune* 96 (October).

———. 1977*b*. "Liberalism Upside Down: The Inversion of the New Deal Order." *Political Science Quarterly* 91 (Winter).

———. 1981*b*. "The 1980 Presidential Election: In Search of Its Meaning." *Public Affairs Review.*

———. 1981*c*. "Party 'Reform' Since 1968: A Case Study in Intellectual Failure." In *The American Constitutional System under Strong and Weak Parties*, ed. Patricia Bonomi, James MacGregor Burns, Austin Ranney. New York: Praeger Publishers.

———. 1980. "Realignment? No. Dealignment? Yes." *Public Opinion* 3 (October/November).

———. 1978. "The Shifting Party Coalitions—1932–1976." In *Emerging Coalitions in American Politics*, ed. Seymour Martin Lipset. San Francisco, CA: Institute for Contemporary Studies.

———. 1977*c*. "The Unmaking of the Republican Party." *Fortune* (September).

———, with Hadley, Charles D. 1978. *Transformations of the American Party System: Political Coalitions from the New Deal to the 1970s.* 2d ed. rev. New York: W. W. Norton.

———; Hadley, Charles D.; King, L. R. 1971. "A New Political Realignment?" *The Public Interest* (Spring).

Lipset, Seymour Martin, ed. 1978. *Emerging Coalitions in American Politics.* San Francisco, CA: Institute for Contemporary Studies.

————. 1979. *The First New Nation: The United States in Historical and Comparative Perspective.* New York: W. W. Norton and Company.

————. 1981. *Political Man: The Social Bases of Politics.* Expanded ed. Baltimore, MD: Johns Hopkins University Press.

————. 1976. *Rebellion in the University.* Chicago, IL: University of Chicago Press (Phoenix Edition).

————. 1970. *Revolution and Counterrevolution.* Rev. ed. Garden City, NY: Anchor.

————, ed. 1979. *The Third Century.* Chicago, IL: University of Chicago Press.

————. 1977. "Why No Socialism in the United States?" In *Sources of Contemporary Radicalism,* ed. Seweryn Bialer and Sophia Sluzar. Boulder, CO: Westview Press.

————, and Raab, Earl. 1981. "The Election and the Evangelicals." *Commentary* 71 (March).

————, and Raab, Earl. 1978. *The Politics of Unreason: Right-Wing Extremism in America, 1790–1977.* Expanded ed. Chicago, IL: University of Chicago Press.

————, and Schneider, William. 1981. "Lower Taxes and More Welfare: A Reply to Arthur Seldon." *Journal of Contemporary Studies* 4 (Spring).

Lubell, Samuel. 1956. *The Future of American Politics.* 2d ed. rev. Garden City, NY: Doubleday-Anchor, Inc.

————. 1971. *The Hidden Crisis in American Politics.* New York: W. W. Norton.

McHale, Vincent E., and Shaber, Sandra. 1976. "From Aggressive to Defensive Gaullism: The Electoral Dynamics of a 'Catch-All' Party." *Comparative Politics* 8 (January).

MacRae, Duncan, Jr., and Meldrum, James A. 1969. "Factor Analysis of Aggregate Voting Statistics." In *Quantitative Ecological Analysis in the Social Sciences,* ed. Mattei Dogan and Stein Rokkan. Cambridge, MA: MIT Press.

McSeveney, Samuel T. 1972. *The Politics of Depression: Political Behavior in the Northeast, 1893–1896.* New York: Oxford University Press.

Mann, Thomas. 1981. "Elections and Change in Congress." In *The New Congress,* ed. Thomas E. Mann and Norman J. Ornstein. Washington, D.C.: American Enterprise Institute for Public Policy Research.

————, and Ornstein, Norman J., eds. 1981*a. The New Congress.* Washington, D.C.: American Enterprise Institute for Public Policy Research.

————, and Ornstein, Norman J. 1981*b.* "The 1982 Election: What Will It Mean?" *Public Opinion* 4 (June/July).

Marcus, Robert D. 1971. *Grand Old Party: Political Structure in the Gilded Age.* New York: Oxford University Press.

Miller, Arthur H. 1981. "What Mandate? What Realignment?" *Washington Post* (28 June).

————, and Wattenberg, Martin P. 1981. "The New Style Apolitical." Unpublished manuscript.

Miller, Warren E., and Levitin, Teresa E. 1976. *Leadership and Change: The New Politics and the American Electorate.* Cambridge, MA: Winthrop Publishers, Inc.

Moller, Herbert. 1968. "Youth as a Force in the Modern World." *Contemporary Studies in Society and History* 10 (April).

Moore, Thomas G. 1981*a*. "Domestic vs. Republican Administrations: A Quizzical Note." Typescript. Hoover Institution, Stanford University (February).

———. 1981*b*. "Re-Regulation by Reagan." Typescript. Hoover Institution, Stanford University (June).

Nevins, Allan, ed. 1933. *Letters of Grover Cleveland.* Boston, MA: Houghton.

Nie, Norman H.; Verba, Sidney; and Petrocik, John R. 1976. *The Changing American Voter.* Cambridge, MA: Harvard University Press.

Niemi, Richard G., and Weisberg, Herbert F., eds. 1976. *Controversies in American Voting Behavior.* San Francisco, CA: W. H. Freeman and Company.

Orren, Gary R. 1978. "Candidate Style and Voter Alignment in 1976." In *Emerging Coalitions in American Politics*, ed. Seymour Martin Lipset. San Francisco, CA: Institute for Contemporary Studies.

———, and Dionne, E. J., Jr. 1981. "The Next New Deal." *Working Papers for a New Society* 8 (May/June).

Parker, Glenn R., and Davidson, Roger H. 1979. "Why Do Americans Love Their Congressmen So Much More Than Their Congress?" *Legislative Studies Quarterly* 4 (February).

Petersen, Svend. 1963. *A Statistical History of the American Presidential Elections.* New York: Frederick Ungar Publishing Company.

Phillips, Kevin P. 1970. *The Emerging Republican Majority.* New York: Anchor Books.

Pollack, Norman. 1962. *The Populist Response to Industrial America.* Cambridge, MA: Harvard University Press.

Pomper, Gerald M., ed. 1981*a*. *The Election of 1980: Reports and Interpretations.* Chatham, NJ: Chatham House Publishers.

———. 1981*b*. "The Presidential Election." In *The Election of 1980*, ed. Gerald Pomper. Chatham, NJ: Chatham House.

———. 1975. *Voters' Choice.* New York: W. W. Norton.

Rabushka, Alvin. 1981. "The Attractions of a Flat-Rate Tax System." *Wall Street Journal* (25 March).

Raines, Howell. 1981. "Reagan Reversing Many U.S. Policies." *New York Times* (3 July).

Ranney, Austin, ed. 1981. *The American Elections of 1980.* Washington, D.C.: American Enterprise Institute for Public Policy Research.

Reagan, Ronald. 1981. "Government and Business in the '80s." *Wall Street Journal* (9 January).

Reeves, Richard. 1981. "Rough Going." *San Francisco Chronicle* (23 July).

Rogin, Michael Paul. 1967. *The Intellectuals and McCarthy: The Radical Specter.* Cambridge, MA: MIT Press.

Rose, Richard, ed. 1974. *Electoral Behavior: A Comparative Handbook.* New York: Free Press.

Rosenbaum, Aaron. 1981. "Woo and Woe on the Campaign Trail." *Moment* 6 (January).

Rusk, Jerrold G., and Weisberg, Herbert F. 1976. "Perceptions of Presidential Candidates: Implications for Electoral Change." In *Controversies in American Voting Behavior,* ed. Richard G. Niemi and Herbert F. Weisberg. San Francisco, CA: W. H. Freeman and Company.

Schattschneider, E. E. 1942. *Party Government.* New York: Rinehart and Company.

———. 1960. *The Semi-Sovereign People.* New York: Holt, Rinehart, and Winston.

Schneider, William. 1978. "Democrats and Republicans, Liberals and Conservatives." In *Emerging Coalitions in American Politics,* ed. Seymour Martin Lipset. San Francisco, CA: Institute for Contemporary Studies.

———. 1981. "The November 4th Vote for President: What Did It Mean?" In *The American Elections of 1980,* ed. Austin Ranney. Washington, D.C.: American Enterprise Institute for Public Policy Research.

Schwartz, Michael. 1976. *Radical Protest and Social Structure: The Southern Farmers' Alliance and Cotton Tenancy, 1880–1890.* New York: Academic Press.

Shafer, Byron E. 1981. "Anti-Party Politics." *The Public Interest* (Spring).

Shortridge, Ray M. In press. "Estimating Voter Participation." In *Analyzing Electoral History: A Guide to the Study of American Voting Behavior.* Beverly Hills, CA: Sage Publications.

Stockman, David. 1981. "National Urban League Speech." Office of Management and Budget (20 July).

Stokes, Donald E. 1966. "Spatial Models of Party Competition." In *Elections and the Political Order,* ed. Angus Campbell, Philip E. Converse, Warren E. Miller, and Donald E. Stokes. New York: John Wiley.

Sundquist, James L. 1973. *Dynamics of the Party System: Alignment and Realignment of Political Parties in the United States.* Washington, D.C.: The Brookings Institution.

Touraine, Alain. 1971. *The Post-Industrial Society.* New York: Random House.

Tufte, Edward. 1978. *Political Control of the Economy.* Princeton, NJ: Princeton University Press.

U.S. Bureau of the Census. 1975. *Historical Statistics of the United States: Colonial Times to 1970.* Washington, D.C.: Government Printing Office.

Viguerie, Richgard A. 1981. *The New Right: We're Ready to Lead.* Falls Church, VA: The Viguerie Company.

Wall Street Journal. 1981. "Reagan's Regulation" (editorial, 13 August).

Wicker, Tom. 1981. "The Going Gets Rough." *The New York Times* (18 August).

Wilson, James Q. 1981. "Foreword." In *Regulating America, Regulating Sweden: A Comparative Study of Occupational Safety and Health Policy,* by Steven Kelman. Cambridge, MA: MIT Press.

———. 1980. "Reagan and the Republican Revival." *Commentary* 70 (October).

Wright, James Edward. 1974. *The Strange Career of Jim Crow.* New Haven, CT: Yale University Press.

ABOUT THE AUTHORS

JOHN B. ANDERSON served as Republican congressman from Illinois for ten consecutive terms before running for the presidency as an independent candidate. In the spring quarter of 1981 he was guest professor in political science at Stanford University, his courses entitled "The Legislative Process: Congress in Transition," and "Political Parties in Transition."

DAVID S. BRODER, a political correspondent and associate editor of the *Washington Post*, is a syndicated political columnist. He was awarded the 1973 Pulitzer Prize for distinguished commentary. He is the author of *The Party's Over: The Failure of Politics in America* (1972), he coauthored with Stephen Hess *The Republican Establishment* (1967), and he wrote the introduction to the institute's 1978 publication, *Emerging Coalitions in American Politics*. His most recent book is *The Changing of the Guard: Power and Leadership in America* (1980).

WALTER DEAN BURNHAM is professor of political science at the Massachusetts Institute of Technology. Coeditor with Martha Wagner Weinberg of *American Politics and Public Policy* (1978), the books he has written and edited will include the forthcoming *Dynamics of American Electoral Politics*. His many articles on party politics and the American voter include "The 1980 Earthquake: Realignment, Reaction or What?" in *The Hidden Election* (1981), edited by Thomas Ferguson and Joel Rogers, and "The Constitution and American Capitalism" in *How Capitalistic Is the Constitution?* (1981), edited by Robert Goldwin and William A. Schambra.

PATRICK H. CADDELL heads Cambridge Survey Research, which conducted polling for three presidential campaigns—those of George McGovern and Jimmy Carter—and for many gubernatorial and congressional races. He also founded Cambridge Reports, Inc., in 1974 to conduct in-depth trend surveys in the United States for private corporations as well as federal and state government units, and he recently established Caddell Associates, an international consulting and business survey firm.

JEROME M. CLUBB is executive director of the Inter-university Consortium for Political and Social Research, a research scientist in the Center for Political Studies of the Institute for Social Research, and professor of history, University of Michigan. He has written a number of articles on American political development and social history, and is the author or editor of several books, including, most recently, *Partisan Realignment: Voters, Parties, and Government in American History* (1980) with William H. Flanigan and Nancy H. Zingale, with whom he is also working on the forthcoming *Analyzing Electoral History: A Guide to the Study of American Voting Behavior.* His chapter is based on the one he wrote for the institute's 1978 publication, *Emerging Coalitions in American Politics.*

E. J. DIONNE, JR., a political reporter for the *New York Times,* covered the polls and public opinion during the 1980 presidential election. He has analyzed political surveys for Market Opinion Research International (London), and his articles have appeared in *Commonweal, Public Opinion, The New Republic,* and other publications.

ALAN M. FISHER, assistant professor of political science at California State University, Dominguez Hills, has written several articles on Jewish voters in the elections. His forthcoming publications include *Political and Social Perspectives of American Jews, Demography of American Jewry,* and *Anonymity and Survey Research.*

MICHAEL HARRINGTON, national chair of the Democratic Socialist Organizing Committee, is professor of political science at Queens College, New York. His most recent book is *Decade of Decision: The Crisis of the American System* (1980), and his other books include *The Vast Majority: A Journey to the World's Poor* (1977), and *The Twilight of Capitalism* (1976). He is also coeditor of *The Seventies: Problems and Proposals* (1972).

S. I. HAYAKAWA, U.S. senator (R—California), is a member of the Senate Republican Policy Committee and of the National Republican Senatorial Committee. A well-known semanticist and president emeritus of San Francisco State University, he is the author of several books, including *Symbol, Status and Personality* (1963), which was translated into four languages.

RICHARD JENSEN is professor of history at the University of Illinois, Chicago, and director of the Family and Community History Center of the Newberry Library. His publications deal with U.S. political, social, and intellectual history over the last century, and with quantitative methods in history. He wrote *The Winning of the Midwest: Social and Political Conflict, 1888–1896* (1971), *Historian's Guide to Statistics* (1974), *Illinois: A Bicentennial History* (1978), and the forthcoming *Grass Roots Politics*.

PAUL KLEPPNER, editor of the *Historical Methods Newsletter*, is professor of history and political science at Northern Illinois University, De Kalb. He is the author of *The Cross of Culture: A Social Analysis of Midwestern Politics, 1850–1900* (1970), *The Third-Electoral Era: Parties, Voters, and Political Cultures* (1978), and of other books and articles. His current research, sponsored by the National Endowment for the Humanities and the National Science Foundation, is concerned with "Social Predictors of Partisanship and Participation: The Fourth-Party System, 1893–1933." In the institute's 1978 publication, *Emerging Coalitions in American Politics,* his chapter was entitled "From Ethnoreligious Conflict to 'Social Harmony.' "

EVERETT CARLL LADD, professor of political science, is executive director of the Roper Center for Public Opinion Research and director of the Institute for Social Inquiry, University of Connecticut. He is a member of the editorial boards of *Public Opinion, Political Behavior,* and *Politics and Behavior.* His many publications include *Where Have All the Voters Gone? The Fracturing of America's Political Parties* (rev. ed. 1981) and, with C. D. Hadley, *Transformations of the American Party System: Political Coalitions from the New Deal to the 1970's* (rev. ed. 1978). In addition to his chapter in the 1978 institute publication, *Emerging Coalitions in American Politics,* he wrote on "Political Parties and Governance in the 1980s" in *Politics and the Oval Office* (1981).

SEYMOUR MARTIN LIPSET is Caroline S. G. Munro Professor at Stanford University and a senior fellow at Hoover Institution on War, Revolution and Peace at the same university. He is coeditor of *Public Opinion* magazine. President of the American Political Science Association and past president of the International Society of Political Psychology, he is forthcoming president of the Sociological Research Association. His books include *Politi-*

cal Man: The Social Bases of Politics (expanded edition 1981), *The Politics of Unreason: Right-Wing Extremism in the U.S. 1790–1977* (expanded edition 1978), written with Earl Raab and awarded the Gunnar Myrdal Prize, the *The First New Nation* (1979). In addition to editing the institute's 1978 publication, *Emerging Coalitions in American Politics,* Dr. Lipset wrote the chapter on "Equity and Equality in Government Wage Policy" in *Public Employee Unions* (1976), and in 1978, "Racial and Ethnic Tensions in the Third World" in *The Third World: Premises of U.S. Policy.*

ARTHUR H. MILLER, associate professor of political science at the University of Michigan, is senior study director of the university's Center for Political Studies. He has written numerous articles on voting behavior, political alienation, and the impact of mass media on public opinion. His most recent book, coauthored with Warren E. Miller and Edward Schneider, is *American Political Trends: The National Election Studies Sourcebook 1952–1978* (1980).

HOWARD PHILLIPS is national director of The Conservative Caucus, Inc., in Vienna, Virginia. He is chairman of the Conservative National Committee and president of The Conservative Caucus Research, Analysis, and Education Foundation. A former deputy director and acting executive director of the President's Council on Youth Opportunity, he was also acting director of the U.S. Office of Economic Opportunity.

NORMAN PODHORETZ, editor of *Commentary,* is a member of the board of the Committee on the Present Danger and a founder of the Coalition for Democratic Majority. His better-known books include *Making It* (1968), *Breaking Ranks: A Political Memoir* (1979), and *The Present Danger* (1980). He is also the author of the forthcoming *Why We Were in Vietnam,* to be released in the spring of 1982.

NELSON W. POLSBY, professor of political science at the University of California, Berkeley, was managing editor of the *American Political Science Review* from 1971 to 1977. Editor of *The Modern Presidency* (1973) and the eight-volume *Handbook of Political Science* (1975), among other publications, his books include *Congress and the Presidency* (revised 1976), *Political Promises* (1974), *Presidential Elections,* coauthored with Aaron Wildavsky (5th ed. 1980), and the most recent, with Geoffrey Smith, *British Government and Its Discontents* (1980). His current chapter is based on one written for the institute's 1978 book, *Emerging Coalitions in American Politics.*

RICHARD M. SCAMMON has been director of the Elections Research Center in Washington, D.C., since 1955 and editor of the biennial *America Votes* series since 1956. A former division chief in the U.S. State Department and director of the census under President Kennedy, in 1973 he was a member of the U.S. delegation to the United Nations. He is elections consultant to NBC News.

WILLIAM SCHNEIDER is a senior research fellow at the Hoover Institution on War, Revolution and Peace at Stanford University. He is also senior editor of *Opinion Outlook*, a Washington-based newsletter, and political consultant to the *Los Angeles Times*. Coauthor with Seymour Martin Lipset of *The Confidence Gap: Business, Government, and Labor in the Public Mind* (forthcoming), his articles on public opinion and voting behavior in the United States and Western Europe have been widely published in newspapers and journals. Dr. Schneider taught political science at Harvard University, and in 1980 was awarded an international affairs fellowship by the Council on Foreign Relations.

MARTIN P. WATTENBERG is a Ph.D. candidate in political science at the University of Michigan whose research is in voting behavior and political parties in the United States and Western Europe. His articles on these subjects have been published in the *American Political Science Review, Public Opinion Quarterly,* and *Comparative Politics.*

RICHARD B. WIRTHLIN, an economist, is president of Decima Research and of Decision/Making/Information. Past director of the Survey Research Center at Brigham Young University, he has supervised several hundred survey research projects, both national and regional in scope, for a variety of private, university, and government clients. He was director of planning and strategy during the Reagan/Bush presidential campaign.

INDEX

465

PUBLICATIONS LIST*

THE INSTITUTE FOR CONTEMPORARY STUDIES

260 California Street, San Francisco, California 94111

Catalog available upon request

BUREAUCRATS AND BRAINPOWER: GOVERNMENT
REGULATION OF UNIVERSITIES
$6.95. 170 pages. Publication date: June 1979
ISBN 0−917616−35−9
Library of Congress No. 79−51328
Contributors: Nathan Glazer, Robert S. Hatfield, Richard W. Lyman, Paul
Seabury, Robert L. Sproull, Miro M. Todorovich, Caspar W.
Weinberger

THE CALIFORNIA COASTAL PLAN: A CRITIQUE
$5.95. 199 pages. Publication date: March 1976
ISBN 0−917616−04−9
Library of Congress No. 76−7715
Contributors: Eugene Bardach, Daniel K. Benjamin, Thomas E.
Borcherding, Ross D. Eckert, H. Edward Frech III, M. Bruce Johnson,
Ronald N. Lafferty, Walter J. Mead, Daniel Orr, Donald M. Pach,
Michael R. Peevey

THE CRISIS IN SOCIAL SECURITY: PROBLEMS AND PROSPECTS
$6.95. 222 pages. Publication date: April 1977; 2d ed. rev., 1978, 1979
ISBN 0−917616−16−2/1977; 0−917616−25−1/1978
Library of Congress No. 77−72542
Contributors: Michael J. Boskin, George F. Break, Rita Ricardo Campbell,
Edward Cowan, Martin S. Feldstein, Milton Friedman, Douglas R.
Munro, Donald O. Parsons, Carl V. Patton, Joseph A. Pechman,
Sherwin Rosen, W. Kip Viscusi, Richard J. Zeckhauser

*Prices subject to change.

THE ECONOMY IN THE 1980s: A PROGRAM FOR
GROWTH AND STABILITY
>$7.95 (paper), 462 pages. Publication date: June 1980
>ISBN 0–917616–39–1
>Library of Congress No. 80–80647
>$17.95 (cloth). 462 pages. Publication date: August 1980.
>ISBN 0–87855–399–1. Available through Transaction Books,
>Rutgers–The State University, New Brunswick, NJ 08903

Contributors: Michael J. Boskin, George F. Break, John T. Cuddington, Patricia Drury, Alain Enthoven, Laurence J. Kotlikoff, Ronald I. McKinnon, John H. Pencavel, Henry S. Rowen, John L. Scadding, John B. Shoven, James L. Sweeney, David J. Teece

EMERGING COALITIONS IN AMERICAN POLITICS
>$6.95. 524 pages. Publication date: June 1978
>ISBN 0–917616–22–7
>Library of Congress No. 78–53414

Contributors: Jack Bass, David S. Broder, Jerome M. Clubb, Edward H. Crane III, Walter De Vries, Andrew M. Greeley, S. I. Hayakawa, Tom Hayden, Milton Himmelfarb, Richard Jensen, Paul Kleppner, Everett Carll Ladd, Jr., Seymour Martin Lipset, Robert A. Nisbet, Michael Novak, Gary R. Orren, Nelson W. Polsby, Joseph L. Rauh, Jr., Stanley Rothman, William A. Rusher, William Schneider, Jesse M. Unruh, Ben J. Wattenberg

THE FAIRMONT PAPERS: BLACK ALTERNATIVES CONFERENCE,
SAN FRANCISCO, DECEMBER 1980
>$5.95. 174 pages. Publication date: March 1981
>ISBN 0–917616–42–1
>Library of Congress No. 81–80735

Contributors: Bernard E. Anderson, Thomas L. Berkley, Michael J. Boskin, Randolph W. Bromery, Tony Brown, Milton Friedman, Wendell Wilkie Gunn, Charles V. Hamilton, Robert B. Hawkins, Jr., Maria Lucia Johnson, Martin L. Kilson, James Lorenz, Henry Lucas, Jr., Edwin Meese III, Clarence M. Pendleton, Jr., Dan J. Smith, Thomas Sowell, Chuck Stone, Percy E. Sutton, Clarence Thomas, Gloria E. A. Toote, Walter E. Williams, Oscar Wright

FEDERAL TAX REFORM: MYTHS AND REALITIES
>$5.95. 270 pages. Publication date: September 1978
>ISBN 0–917616–32–4
>Library of Congress No. 78–61661

Contributors: Robert J. Barro, Michael J. Boskin, George F. Break, Jerry R. Green, Laurence J. Kotlikoff, Mordecai Kurz, Peter Mieszkowski, John B. Shoven, Paul J. Taubman, John Whalley

GOVERNMENT CREDIT ALLOCATION: WHERE DO WE GO
FROM HERE?

$4.95. 208 pages. Publication date: November 1975
ISBN 0–917616–02–2
Library of Congress No. 75–32951

Contributors: George J. Benston, Karl Brunner, Dwight M. Jaffe, Omotunde
E. G. Johnson, Edward J. Kane, Thomas Mayer, Allan H. Meltzer

NATIONAL SECURITY IN THE 1980s: FROM
WEAKNESS TO STRENGTH

$8.95 (paper). 524 pages. Publication date: May 1980
ISBN 0–917616–38–3
Library of Congress No. 80–80648
$19.95 (cloth). 524 pages. Publication date: August 1980
ISBN 0–87855–412–2. Available through Transaction Books,
Rutgers–The State University, New Brunswick, NJ 08903

Contributors: Kenneth L. Adelman, Richard R. Burt, Miles M. Costick,
Robert F. Ellsworth, Fred Charles Ikl´e, Geoffrey T. H. Kemp, Edward
N. Luttwak, Charles Burton Marshall, Paul H. Nitze, Sam Nunn,
Henry S. Rowen, Leonard Sullivan, Jr., W. Scott Thompson, William
R. Van Cleave, Francis J. West, Jr., Albert Wohlstetter, Elmo R.
Zumwalt, Jr.

NEW DIRECTIONS IN PUBLIC HEALTH CARE: A PRESCRIPTION
FOR THE 1980s

$6.95 (paper). 279 pages. Publication date: May 1976;
3d ed. rev., 1980
ISBN 0–917616–37–5
Library of Congress No. 79–92868
$16.95 (cloth). 290 pages. Publication date: April 1980
ISBN 0–87855–394–0. Available through Transaction Books,
Rutgers–The State University, New Brunswick, NJ 08903

Contributors: Alain Enthoven, W. Philip Gramm, Leon R. Kass, Keith B.
Leffler, Cotton M. Lindsay, Jack A. Meyer, Charles E. Phelps,
Thomas C. Schelling, Harry Schwartz, Arthur Seldon, David A.
Stockman, Lewis Thomas

OPTIONS FOR U.S. ENERGY POLICY

$6.95. 317 pages. Publication date: September 1977
ISBN 0–917616–20–0
Library of Congress No. 77–89094

Contributors: Albert Carnesale, Stanley M. Greenfield, Fred S. Hoffman,
Edward J. Mitchell, William R. Moffat, Richard Nehring, Robert S.
Pindyck, Norman C. Rasmussen, David J. Rose, Henry S. Rowen,
James L. Sweeney, Arthur W. Wright

PARENTS, TEACHERS, AND CHILDREN: PROSPECTS FOR CHOICE
IN AMERICAN EDUCATION

> $5.95. 336 pages. Publication date: June 1977
> ISBN 0−917616−18−9
> Library of Congress No. 77−79164

Contributors: James S. Coleman, John E. Coons, William H. Cornog, Denis
P. Doyle, E. Babette Edwards, Nathan Glazer, Andrew M. Greeley,
R. Kent Greenawalt, Marvin Lazerson, William C. McCready,
Michael Novak, John P. O'Dwyer, Robert Singleton, Thomas Sowell,
Stephen D. Sugarman, Richard E. Wagner

PARTY COALITIONS IN THE 1980s

> $8.95 (paper). 480 pages. Publication date: November 1981
> ISBN 0−917616−43−X
> Library of Congress No. 81−83095
> $19.95 (cloth). 480 pages. Publication date: November 1981
> ISBN 0−917616−45−6.

Contributors: John B. Anderson, David S. Broder, Walter Dean Burnham,
Patrick Caddell, Jerome M. Clubb, E. J. Dionne, Jr., Alan M. Fisher,
Michael Harrington, S. I. Hayakawa, Richard Jensen, Paul Kleppner,
Everett Carll Ladd, Seymour Martin Lipset, Arthur D. Miller, Howard
Phillips, Norman Podhoretz, Nelson W. Polsby, Richard M. Scammon,
William Schneider, Martin P. Wattenberg, Richard B. Wirthlin

POLITICS AND THE OVAL OFFICE: TOWARDS
PRESIDENTIAL GOVERNANCE

> $7.95 (paper). 332 pages. Publication date: February 1981
> ISBN 0−917616−40−5
> Library of Congress No. 80−69617
> $18.95 (cloth). 300 pages. Publication date: April 1981
> ISBN 0−87855−428−9. Available through Transaction Books,
> Rutgers−The State University, New Brunswick, NJ 08903

Contributors: Richard K. Betts, Jack Citrin, Eric L. Davis, Robert M.
Entman, Robert E. Hall, Hugh Heclo, Everett Carll Ladd, Jr., Arnold
J. Meltsner, Charles Peters, Robert S. Pindyck, Francis E. Rourke,
Martin M. Shapiro, Peter L. Szanton

THE POLITICS OF PLANNING: A REVIEW AND CRITIQUE OF
CENTRALIZED ECONOMIC PLANNING

> $5.95. 367 pages. Publication date: March 1976
> ISBN 0−917616−05−7
> Library of Congress No. 76−7714

Contributors: B. Bruce-Briggs, James Buchanan, A. Lawrence Chickering,
Ralph Harris, Robert B. Hawkins, Jr., George W. Hilton, Richard
Mancke, Richard Muth, Vincent Ostrom, Svetozar Pejovich, Myron
Sharpe, John Sheahan, Herbert Stein, Gordon Tullock, Ernest van
den Haag, Paul H. Weaver, Murray L. Weidenbaum, Hans
Willgerodt, Peter P. Witonski

PUBLIC EMPLOYEE UNIONS: A STUDY OF THE CRISIS IN
PUBLIC SECTOR LABOR RELATIONS

$6.95. 251 pages. Publication date: June 1976; 2d ed. rev., 1977
ISBN 0−917616−24−3
Library of Congress No. 76−18409

Contributors: A. Lawrence Chickering, Jack D. Douglas, Raymond D.
Horton, Theodore W. Kheel, David Lewin, Seymour Martin Lipset,
Harvey C. Mansfield, Jr., George Meany, Robert A. Nisbet, Daniel
Orr, A. H. Raskin, Wes Uhlman, Harry H. Wellington, Charles B.
Wheeler, Jr., Ralph K. Winter, Jr., Jerry Wurf

REGULATING BUSINESS: THE SEARCH FOR AN OPTIMUM

$6.95. 261 pages. Publication date: April 1978
ISBN 0−917616−27−8
Library of Congress No. 78−50678

Contributors: Chris Argyris, A. Lawrence Chickering, Penny Hollander
Feldman, Richard H. Holton, Donald P. Jacobs, Alfred E. Kahn, Paul
W. MacAvoy, Almarin Phillips, V. Kerry Smith, Paul H. Weaver,
Richard J. Zeckhauser

TARIFFS, QUOTAS, AND TRADE: THE POLITICS
OF PROTECTIONISM

$7.95. 332 pages. Publication date: February 1979
ISBN 0−917616−34−0
Library of Congress No. 78−66267

Contributors: Walter Adams, Ryan C. Amacher, Sven W. Arndt, Malcolm D.
Bale, John T. Cuddington, Alan V. Deardorff, Joel B. Dirlam, Roger
D. Hansen, H. Robert Heller, D. Gale Johnson, Robert O. Keohane,
Michael W. Keran, Rachel McCulloch, Ronald I. McKinnon, Gordon
W. Smith, Robert M. Stern, Richard James Sweeney, Robert D.
Tollison, Thomas D. Willett

THE THIRD WORLD: PREMISES OF U.S. POLICY

$7.95. 334 pages. Publication date: November 1978
ISBN 0−917616−30−8
Library of Congress No. 78−67593

Contributors: Dennis Austin, Peter T. Bauer, Max Beloff, Richard E. Bissell,
Daniel J. Elazar, S. E. Finer, Allan E. Goodman, Nathaniel H. Leff,
Seymour Martin Lipset, Edward N. Luttwak, Daniel Pipes, Wilson E.
Schmidt, Anthony Smith, W. Scott Thompson, Basil S. Yamey

UNION CONTROL OF PENSION FUNDS: WILL THE NORTH
RISE AGAIN?

$2.00. 41 pages. Publication date: July 1979
ISBN 0−917616−36−7
Library of Congress No. 78−66581

Author: George J. Borjas

480

WATER BANKING: HOW TO STOP WASTING
AGRICULTURAL WATER
$2.00. 56 pages. Publication date: January 1978
ISBN 0—917616—26—X
Library of Congress No. 78—50766
Authors: Sotirios Angelides, Eugene Bardach

WHAT'S NEWS: THE MEDIA IN AMERICAN SOCIETY
$7.95 (paper). 296 pages. Publication date: June 1981
ISBN 0—917616—41—3
Library of Congress No. 81—81414
$18.95 (cloth). 300 pages. Publication date: August 1981
ISBN 0—87855—448—3. Available through Transaction Books,
Rutgers—The State University, New Brunswick, NJ 08903
Contributors: Elie Abel, Robert L. Bartley, George Comstock, Edward Jay
Epstein, William A. Henry III, John L. Hulteng, Theodore Peterson,
Ithiel de Sola Pool, William E. Porter, Michael Jay Robinson, James
N. Rosse, Benno C. Schmidt, Jr.

JOURNAL OF CONTEMPORARY STUDIES
$15/one year, $25/two years, $4/single issue. For delivery outside the
United States, add $2/year surface mail, $10/year airmail
A quarterly journal that is a forum for lively and readable studies on foreign
and domestic public policy issues. Directed toward general readers as
well as policymakers and academics, emphasizing debate and
controversy, it publishes the highest quality articles without regard
to political or ideological bent.

8833